Chinese Energy Companies in Africa

Over the last decade, Chinese energy companies have engaged in the acquisition of oil and gas in Africa. This book investigates the activities of Chinese energy companies throughout a number of African countries, including Nigeria, Angola, Sudan and Tunisia.

Based on seven years of empirical research and hundreds of interviews with Chinese government and company representatives, *Chinese Energy Companies in Africa* breaks original ground in understanding the emergence of domestic interest groups in foreign policy. It examines the impact of non-state actors on Chinese foreign policy, and in particular the increasing role played by national oil companies (NOCs). Supported by extensive data, this is also the first publication of its kind to focus on the foreign policy behaviour of an authoritarian state and the role herein played by non-state actors. In addition to the main cases put forward, a chapter of comparative mini-cases is included.

This book creates important implications for both policymakers and scholars; it will serve as a valuable resource for those involved in the fields of foreign policy, international security and international relations.

T. Kasandra Behrndt-Eriksen is Adjunct Lecturer at the Department of Political Science at the University of Copenhagen. She researches and teaches on China's foreign policy.

Routledge Contemporary China Series
Edited by Victor Teo and Sungwon Yoon

Youth Economy, Crisis, and Reinvention in Twenty-First-Century China
Morning Sun in the Tiny Times
Hui Faye Xiao

The Chinese Economy and its Challenges
Transformation of a Rising Economic Power
Charles C.L. Kwong

Keywords in Queer Sinophone Studies
Edited by Howard Chiang and Alvin K. Wong

Macau 20 Years after the Handover
Changes and Challenges under "One Country, Two Systems"
Edited by Meng U Ieong

Doing Labor Activism in South China
The Complicity of Uncertainty
Darcy Pan

Chinese Energy Companies in Africa
Implications for the Foreign Policy of an Authoritarian State
T. Kasandra Behrndt-Eriksen

China's International Socialization of Political Elites in the Belt and Road Initiative
Theodor Tudoroiu

Regional Inequality in Transitional China
Haifeng Felix Liao, Yehua Dennis Wei and Li Huang

For more information about this series, please visit: www.routledge.com/Routledge-Contemporary-China-Series/book-series/SE0768

Chinese Energy Companies in Africa

Implications for the Foreign Policy of an Authoritarian State

T. Kasandra Behrndt-Eriksen

Routledge
Taylor & Francis Group
LONDON AND NEW YORK

First published 2021
by Routledge
2 Park Square, Milton Park, Abingdon, Oxon OX14 4RN

and by Routledge
605 Third Avenue, New York, NY 10017

First issued in paperback 2022

Routledge is an imprint of the Taylor & Francis Group, an informa business

Publisher's Note
The publisher has gone to great lengths to ensure the quality of this reprint but points out that some imperfections in the original copies may be apparent.

British Library Cataloguing-in-Publication Data
A catalogue record for this book is available from the British Library

Library of Congress Cataloging-in-Publication Data
A catalog record for this book has been requested

ISBN 13: 978-0-367-54234-4 (pbk)
ISBN 13: 978-1-138-39000-3 (hbk)
ISBN 13: 978-0-429-42357-4 (ebk)

DOI: 10.4324/9780429423574

Typeset in Times New Roman
by Apex CoVantage, LLC

Contents

List of figures vi
List of tables viii
List of abbreviations x
Preface xiv

1 Chinese energy companies' acquisitions abroad 1

2 The foreign policy of an authoritarian state 11

3 The Chinese energy sector 43

4 Nigeria: from "Angola Model" to "Addax Model" 59

5 Angola: independent NOCs impacting foreign policy 87

6 Sudan: a change of foreign policy 118

7 Tunisia: Chinese companies involved for profit 153

8 Mini-cases 175

9 Conclusion 236

Appendices 257
Index 267

Figures

1.1	Explanatory mode	6
3.1	Share price performance of major oil firms, 2002–14	51
4.1	Map of Nigeria	60
4.2	Infrastructure: Nigeria	64
4.3	Sino-Nigerian trade, 2002–12	65
4.4	Ratio of economic interests to state interests/domestic stability	67
4.5	Ratio of economic interests to state interests	68
4.6	Ratio of economic interests to domestic stability	68
4.7	Ratio of state interests to domestic stability	69
4.8	Incidents of pipeline vandalism in Nigeria, 2002–11	77
5.1	Map of Angola	88
5.2	Angola, infrastructure	92
5.3	Sino-Angolan bilateral trade, 2002–12	93
5.4	Ratio of economic interests to state interests/domestic stability	95
5.5	Ratio of economic interests to state interests	95
5.6	Ratio of economic interests to domestic stability	96
5.7	Ratio of state interests to domestic stability	96
6.1	Map of Sudan	119
6.2	Sudan oil concession map	121
6.3	Infrastructure: Sudan	123
6.4	Sino-Sudanese bilateral trade, 2002–12	124
6.5	Ratio of economic interests to state interests/domestic stability	126
6.6	Ratio of economic interests to state interests	127
6.7	Ratio of economic interests to domestic stability	128
6.8	Ratio of state interests to domestic stability	128
7.1	Map of Tunisia	154
7.2	Sino-Tunisian bilateral trade, 2002–12	157
7.3	Ratio of economic interests to state interests/domestic stability	159
7.4	Ratio of economic interests to state interests	159
7.5	Ratio of economic interests to domestic stability	160
7.6	Ratio of state interests to domestic stability	160
8.1.1	Map of Kazakhstan	176
8.1.2	Ratio of economic interests to state interests/domestic stability	179

8.1.3	Ratio of economic interests to state interests	179
8.1.4	Ratio of economic interests to domestic stability	180
8.1.5	Ratio of state interests to domestic stability	180
8.2.1	Map of Canada	186
8.2.2	Ratio of economic interests to state interests/domestic stability	189
8.2.3	Ratio of economic interests to state interests	189
8.2.4	Ratio of economic interests to domestic stability	190
8.2.5	Ratio of state interests to domestic stability	190
8.3.1	Map of Uzbekistan	199
8.3.2	Ratio of economic interests to state interests/domestic stability	201
8.3.3	Ratio of economic interests to state interests	202
8.3.4	Ratio of economic interests to domestic stability	202
8.3.5	Ratio of state interests to domestic stability	203
8.3.6	China–Central Asia Pipeline	207
8.4.1	Map of Denmark	209
8.4.2	Map of Greenland	210
8.4.2a	Map of Faroe Islands	211
8.4.3	Ratio of economic interests to state interests	214
8.4.4	Ratio of economic interest to domestic stability	214
8.4.5	Ratio of state interests to domestic stability	215
9.1	Results from the quantitative analyses for the eight case countries	243

Tables

2.1	Possible outcomes	24
2.2	Indicators of strategic importance	28
2.3	Level of strategic importance	29
2.4	Outcome on the African continent	31
2.5	Outcome for the whole universe of countries	32
3.1	Comparisons of major oil firms	52
3.2	Comparisons of major oil firms	53
4.1	Level of strategic importance: Nigeria	65
4.2	Acquisition of Addax	74
4.3	Abductions of Chinese workers in Nigeria, since 2002	78
5.1	Level of strategic importance: Angola	93
5.2	Sinopec's acquisition of a stake in Block 18	99
5.3	The Sonaref Refinery	102
5.4	The failed acquisition of Block 32	106
6.1	Level of strategic importance: Sudan	125
6.2	Abductions of Chinese workers (2004–13)	136
7.1	Level of strategic importance: Tunisia	157
7.2	Acquisition of Atlantis	162
8.1.1	Level of strategic importance: Kazakhstan	177
8.1.2	CNOOC and Sinopec's failed acquisition	181
8.1.3	CNPC acquires PetroKazakhstan	183
8.2.1	Level of strategic importance: Canada	187
8.2.2	CNPC's acquisition of AOSC	191
8.2.3	CNPC's failed acquisition of Encana	194
8.2.4	CNOOC acquires Nexen	197
8.3.1	Level of strategic importance: Uzbekistan	200
8.4.1	Level of strategic importance: Denmark	212
9.1	Results for the eight case countries	241
9.2	Results from mini-cases versus main cases	242
A.1	The three large NOCs in China	261
A.2	Nigeria's level of strategic importance	261
A.3	Angola's level of strategic importance	262
A.4	Sudan's level of strategic importance	263

A.5 Tunisia's level of strategic importance 263
A.6 Kazakhstan's level of strategic importance 264
A.7 Canada's level of strategic importance 265
A.8 Uzbekistan's level of strategic importance 265
A.9 Denmark's level of strategic importance 266

Abbreviations

AC	Arctic Council
AFRICOM	Africa Command
AGIP	Azienda Generale Italiana Petroli
AOSC	Athabasca Oil Sands Corporation
AP	Associated Press
AQIM	al-Qaeda in the Islamic Maghreb
AU	African Union
BP	British Petroleum plc.
bpd	barrels per day
CAD	Canadian dollars
CADF	Chain Africa Development Fund
CAGR	compound annual growth rate
CASS	Chinese Academy of Social Sciences
CBM	coal bed methane
CCECC	China Civil Engineering Construction Corporation
CCP	Chinese Communist Party
CDB	China Development Bank
CGC	China Geo-Engineering Corporation
CIF	China International Fund
CMC	Central Military Commission
CNOOC	China National Offshore Oil Corporation
CNPC	China National Petroleum Corporation
CNPCI	China National Petroleum Corporation International Ltd.
CPA	comprehensive peace agreement
CPPCC	Chinese People's Political Consultative Conference
CSS	cyclic steam stimulation
DAC	Development Assistance Committee
ENI	Ente Nazionale Idrocarburi S.P.A.
ETAP	The Entreprise Tunisienne d'Activites Petrolieres
ETIM	East Turkestan Independence Movement
EU	European Union
Eximbank	Export-Import Bank of China

FDI	foreign direct investment
FIE	foreign-owned enterprises
FNLA	National Liberation Front of Angola
FOCAC	Forum on Chinese-Africa Cooperation
FPSO	floating production, storage and offloading unit
GNPOC	Greater Nile Petroleum Operating Company
HRW	Human Rights Watch
ICC	International Criminal Court
IEA	International Energy Agency
IMF	International Monetary Fund
IMO	International Maritime Organization
IMU	the Islamic Movement of Uzbekistan
IOC	international oil company
JDZ	Joint Development Zone
JEM	Justice and Equality Movement
JV	joint venture
KMG	KazMunaiGas National Company
KNOC	South Korean National Oil Corporation
KUFPEC	Kuwait Foreign Petroleum Exploration Company
kW	kilowatts
LNG	liquefied natural gas
M&A	mergers and acquisitions
MENA	Middle East–North Africa
MEND	Movement for the Emancipation of the Niger Delta
MFA	Ministry of Foreign Affairs
MINFIN	Ministry of Finance
MOF	Ministry of Finance
MOFCOM	Ministry of Commerce
MOSOP	Movement for the Survival of the Ogoni People
MoU	memorandum of understanding
MPI	Ministry of Petroleum Industry
MPLA	Popular Movement for the Liberation of Angola
NCP	National Congress Party
NDRC	National Development and Reform Commission
NEA	National Energy Administration
NEC	National Energy Commission
NK	North Kairouan Block
NNPC	Nigerian National Petroleum Corporation
NOC	national oil company
NPC	National Petroleum Commission
NSR	Northern Sea Route
NYSE	New York Stock Exchange
ODA	official development assistance
OECD	Organization for Economic Cooperation and Development

OML	oil mining license
ONGC	Oil and Natural Gas Corporation
OPEC	the Organization of the Petroleum Exporting Countries
OPL	oil processing/prospecting license
Petrobras	Petroleo Brasileiro SA
Petronas	Petroliam Nasional Bhd
PLA	People's Liberation Army
PLAN	People's Liberation Army Navy
PRC	People's Republic of China
PRIC	Polar Research Institute of China
PSA	Production Sharing Agreement
Res.	resolution
RFR	right of first refusal
RMB	renminbi
RSS	Republic of South Sudan
SAF	Sudan Armed Forces
SAGD	steam-assisted gravity drainage
SASAC	State-owned Assets Supervision and Administration Commission
SCO	Shanghai Cooperation Organization
SDPC	State Development Planning Commission
SEO	the State Energy Office
SETC	the State Economic and Trade Commission
Shell	Royal Dutch Shell Company Limited
Sinopec Corp. Ltd	China Petroleum and Chemical Corporation
Sinopec Gr.	China Petrochemical Corporation
SIPC	Sinopec International Petroleum Exploration and Prod. Corp.
SLA	Sudan Liberation Army
SLK	Sidi El Kilani
SOE	state-owned enterprise
Sonangol	Sociedade Nacional de Combustiveis de Angola
SPLA	the Sudan People's Liberation Army
SPLA/M	the Southern People's Liberation Army/Movement
SPLM	Sudan People's Liberation Movement
SPLM/A	Sudan People's Liberation Movement/Army
SPR	strategic petroleum reserve
SRF	Sudan Revolutionary Front
SSA	Sub-Saharan Africa
SSI	Sonangol Sinopec International
Sudapet	Sudan National Petroleum Corporation
Total	Total S.A.
UAE	United Arab Emirates
UN	United Nations
UNAMID	African Union-United Nations Hybrid Mission in Darfur
UNCLOS	UN Convention on the Law of the Sea

UNITA	National Union for the Total Independence of Angola
UNSC	United Nations Security Council
USGS	United States Geological Survey
WB	World Bank
WTO	World Trade Organization

Preface

Writing this book has been an epic journey. Early on, it took me to the United States, where, at Harvard University, I became part of an extremely stimulating and rewarding research environment working with Chinese politics. This led to an intensive two-and-a-half-year period studying Chinese in both Boston and Beijing. My ability to read and speak fluent Chinese, including subsequent periods of study in Boston and Beijing, came to shape the project.

I wish to thank the people and institutions without whom this project would never have come to life. First, I thank Iain Johnston for his support. I also wish to thank professors and colleagues at Harvard University, including Tony Saich, Julian Chang, Arthur Spirling, Noel Maurer, Will Norris, and my Chinese teachers at Harvard University, including Emily Huang, Yan Lei, and Li Yun. I wish to thank the participants in the comparative politics and the Chinese politics workshop in the government department at Harvard University as well as the participants in the Chinese politics workshop at the Ash Center at the Harvard Kennedy School. In Beijing, my thanks go to Chu Shulong, Zhu Feng, Wang Suolao, Yu Tiejun, Li Anshan, Liu Haifang, Edward Steinfeld, and numerous others. I also wish to thank my colleagues and fellow students at Tsinghua University and Beijing University.

I wish to thank scholars in Copenhagen who offered feedback on earlier drafts of parts of the book, including Jens Bartelson and Rune Saugman Andersen.

Institutions devoted to the study of Chinese politics have supported me along the way, both intellectually and/or by hosting me. Thank you to the Ash Center at the Harvard Kennedy School, the School of Public Policy at Tsinghua University, and the School of International Studies at Beijing University for hosting me. I am also grateful to the Inter-University Program at Tsinghua University and all of the teachers there.

I would like to thank my friends in Cambridge/Boston, Beijing, and Copenhagen for their support and friendship.

I am indebted to financial support from the Eliteforsk Travel Stipend provided by the Danish Ministry of Science in 2011, Augustinus Fonden, S.C. Van Fonden, Oticon Fonden, Krista and Viggo Petersens Fond, Laurits Andersens Fond, Sasakawa Fonden, and ØK's Almennyttige Fond. Also a special thanks to Ørslev Kloster.

Last but not least, I wish to thank my entire family for their emotional support. In particular, my heartfelt thanks to my parents, Helle and Ditlev, and to my brother, Mads, for always greeting me with a smile, and a very special tribute to my grandmother Birthe, who, like me, has spent part of her life in China.

My father, Ditlev, is no longer here, but he would have been the one to be the happiest to see this book in print. I dedicate it to him with love and gratitude.

1 Chinese energy companies' acquisitions abroad

China's overall power has grown rapidly over the last decade. In all areas of power, not least economically and militarily, the capabilities of the country have increased, both in absolute and relative terms. In the debate on the "rise" of China, it is argued that as China's capabilities grow relative to other powers, China is rising. However, while there seems to be consensus on China rising, there are different perspectives on how this "rise" is to be understood. According to most realist theory, as the capabilities of a state grow relative to other states, the foreign policy of that state is expected to become more expansionist,[1] and according to some, it should grow similar to that of fascist Japan or Wilhelmine Germany.[2] According to other strains of realist theory, however, China's foreign policy is expected to be peaceful regardless of its growing capabilities; that is, it will act as a status quo power.[3] The view that China will behave differently is also reflected in Chinese official rhetoric. Here, the view is that China's rise will be peaceful and that China's foreign policy in the years to come, despite the state's increasing capabilities, will seek to maintain the status quo.[4]

In contrast to many power transitions in the past, China's current economic growth has occurred largely while accepting the norms of the international system. Still, the question of how China will make use of the military power that its increasing wealth is rendering possible remains unsettled. While these tensions are yet to be resolved, given the country's economic growth, China will clearly come to require increasing imports of resources in the future.

China has displayed a need for increased energy supplies in recent years in order to maintain its economic growth. Its growing economy, which has boasted average annual growth rates of 10 percent since 1990, has been accompanied by an increasing need for resources domestically.[5] At the same time, China's economic growth has been accompanied by increasing domestic energy consumption. In 2010, China replaced the United States as the world's largest national energy consumer. While the country was largely self-sufficient in natural resources when the People's Republic of China (PRC) was established in 1949, demand has outgrown supply in recent years, and China went from being an oil exporter to an oil importer in 1993. The Chinese leadership expects Chinese energy imports to increase, coming to account for 60–80 percent of China's oil consumption by

2020. China's growing trade surplus and massive foreign currency reserves allow the country to finance the import of resources.

To ensure sufficient supplies of energy resources to fuel the growing economy, the Chinese government launched its "Going Out" policy (走出去/*zouchuqu*) in 2001. Consequently, over the last decade, Chinese energy companies have become engaged in regions as diverse as Africa, Latin America, and Central Asia. In 2009, Chinese companies spent $18.2 billion[6] on merger and acquisition deals, which equates to 13 percent of the total global oil and gas acquisitions in this period (61 percent of all acquisitions by national oil companies). In 2010, Chinese companies spent $29.39 billion on merger and acquisition deals, and Chinese oil companies are now operating in 31 countries, with oil and gas production in 30 of them.[7]

As a number of studies note, the growing need for oil imports renders the role of national oil companies in securing sufficient energy increasingly important. In other words, with the growing need for imports, the role of the Chinese national oil companies (NOCs) in securing the resources necessary for the regime to survive has become more important.[8]

Following the increase in activities abroad, evidence has emerged in the last ten years that state-owned enterprises (SOEs) have become stronger and more profitable. Chinese SOEs have been listed on international stock exchanges and are among the world's largest companies in terms of revenue. Moreover, a tendency has been observed according to which SOEs have acquired an increasing influence on economic decision-making in China. There have even been instances in which SOEs have had an impact on foreign policy.

Here, the proposition is that the empirical variation found in the relationship between the government policies and the activities of the NOCs, a subgroup of the SOEs, provides a window for understanding China's energy policy in recent years. To illuminate the relationship between the NOCs and the Chinese government, this book thus explores the research question: to what extent do the activities of the Chinese energy companies in a number of countries and regions reflect state interests, economic interests, or a concern with domestic stability (*weiwen*)?

The claim here is that the rise of the SOEs has been accompanied by a key change among the actors in foreign policy and in the "Going Out"/走出去 policy launched by the Chinese government in 2001. The SOEs now have attained an increasing influence on foreign policy. However, while there would appear to be evidence indicating that the SOEs have become increasingly strong, this claim has not previously been tested.

This book offers such a test: it presents cases in which one would expect the SOEs to have an impact on foreign policy, such as that of Sudan. In the period up to the 2008 Olympic Games in Beijing, Chinese foreign policy *vis-à-vis* Sudan had been characterized by principles of non-interference and a respect for domestic politics. In this instance, however, faced with an international campaign to boycott the Beijing Olympics, the Chinese leadership placed pressure on Sudan's President Omar Al Bashir to accept UN forces within Sudanese territory.[9] The argument was that as Chinese companies were involved in Sudan, the Chinese leadership was responsible for the genocide in Sudan. But the evidence indicates that when the Chinese leadership intervened, Chinese companies operating in Sudan suffered financial losses. Pressure from the international community led Beijing to change its foreign policy stance *vis-à-vis* Sudan. In other words, this is an instance in which the activities and interests of Chinese companies had an impact on Chinese foreign policy. Moreover, it is argued here that the physical risks that Chinese oil workers have been subjected to in recent years as a result of their activities in countries such as Sudan speak to the intricate linkages between the activities of the companies abroad and the concern of the Chinese Communist Party (CCP) with ensuring domestic stability. The argument rests on the assumption that the ability to maintain domestic stability is, in turn, a prerequisite for the CCP to remain in power. The argument is that, faced with increasing domestic discontent arising from the deaths of Chinese workers abroad, particularly in Sudan in 2008, the Chinese leadership became involved in the issue, which led to a shift in foreign policy. This instance provides evidence of how the activities of Chinese SOEs abroad affect foreign policy. Whereas the driver was external in the case of the pressure placed on the Sudanese leader in the period up to 2008, the driving force in terms of the killed Chinese workers abroad is domestic: it is about securing domestic stability. These two instances also provide evidence of how the activities of Chinese SOEs have bearing on foreign policy. This book will thoroughly examine whether, and how, the SOE activities have an impact on foreign policy. As the SOEs can be seen as an interest group, by implication, this book presents a rigorous test of the importance of interest groups in foreign policy.

The rise of SOEs

The explanation here of China's behavior is rooted in three theories that can explain the activities of the Chinese energy companies (as detailed in Chapter 2).

First, the activities of the Chinese NOCs can be seen as evidence of state interest. Here, the sheer dimension of the acquisitions of energy resources by the NOCs abroad in terms of size as well as the pattern of the acquisitions point to state interests. Moreover, the manner in which acquisitions are accompanied by loans, aid, and a long range of diplomatic visits from the Chinese government to the recipient countries, together with the building of transnational oil and gas pipelines, indicates that the acquisitions made by the NOCs are part of a highly coordinated Chinese government strategy.

Second, it has been suggested that the behavior of the companies on the ground in different countries and regions reflects the economic interests of the companies proper. In other words, according to this view, companies are led by profit motives, and their activities occasionally conflict with state interests. Building on liberalism, a hypothesis is presented here that can explain this. The idea is that one characteristic of the (Chinese) authoritarian state is that authority is fractured: the weaker the state capacity, the more likely that large economic interests, including non-state actors, will influence economic decision-making. In turn, this explains why and how these economic interests can capture decision-making and have an influence on foreign policy in the authoritarian state. It is worth noting that some of the large SOEs, including the NOCs, can be seen as non-state actors.

Third, it has been noted that the activities of the companies abroad reflect a domestic need for resources that are necessary in order to maintain *domestic stability* (维稳/*weiwen*) and, thus, to sustain CCP (not state) rule. The proposition is that the state and the CCP are intricately linked, as the stability of the CCP is seen as a prerequisite for the state to maintain stability.[10] Thus, the activities of the companies abroad can be seen as a reflection of the CCP's need to sustain regime stability, which again is a prerequisite for the state to sustain domestic stability.

These three literatures build a framework that will help us analyze the activities of the Chinese energy companies.

Foreign policy of the authoritarian state

The framework is presented in such a way as to illuminate the role of NOCs for Chinese foreign policy. Here, we present a theoretical framework capable of explaining the role played by NOCs in foreign policy, offering streams from three different literatures: the international relations literature, the literature on political economy, and the literature on Chinese politics. The argument here is that this theoretical framework can explain the foreign policy of an authoritarian state and that presenting these three different literatures can help inform us about its foreign policy and help develop such a theory.

Heavily inspired by liberalism, the overall hypothesis guiding this study is that, in the authoritarian state, interest groups (non-state actors) can gain influence on foreign policy because of the fragmented character of the state. Here, I focus on one authoritarian state: China. The study argues that the ability of non-state actors to influence foreign policy is a particular characteristic of the foreign policy of the authoritarian state. While the framework presented to analyze the foreign policy of the authoritarian state is particularly suited for the case of China, it might be applicable to other authoritarian states as well.

Thus, the objective of this study is, firstly, to explain the role played by non-state actors in foreign policy. Specifically, the study examines one important type of non-state actor: NOCs. Secondly, the study takes a first step toward a theory of the foreign policy of the authoritarian state and the role of non-state actors in such a state. It provides a test of the role of non-state actors in foreign policy, applying hypotheses from the three literatures noted earlier across a number of cases. It argues that the ability of NOCs to influence decision-making is a particular characteristic of the foreign policy of the authoritarian state. As with the framework as a whole, this first step toward a theory of the foreign policy of an authoritarian state presented here is particularly suited to the case of China, but it might be applicable to other authoritarian states as well.

It is worth noting that in the bodies of literature on international relations and Chinese politics, there are very few contributions focusing on the foreign policy of the authoritarian state and the role of non-state actors therein (see Chapter 2 for more detail). In fact, there are no existing theories capable of capturing the foreign policy of the authoritarian state. Thus, even if what is presented here is merely a first step toward the foreign policy of the authoritarian state, it is still a valuable contribution to the discussion.

How is the study then executed? The general idea in this book is that relations between the government and companies in particular countries or regions are related to the amount of oil and level of strategic importance of the country or region in question to China. Thus, the independent variable consists of two parts: the level of oil and the level of strategic importance of the various countries or regions. See the following diagram (Figure 1.1) for an overview of the theory and the hypotheses utilized.

I develop a framework according to which, depending on different values for the independent variable, that is, the level of oil and level of strategic importance of a given country, the SOEs in some countries have an impact on foreign policy while the SOEs in other countries do not, as seen in Figure 1.1.

Three hypotheses are presented: one speaks to the dominance of state interests, another to the dominance of SOE interests, and the last to the concern with domestic stability dominating. The hypothesis concerning *state interests* follows from the structural realist assumption about the relationship between companies and the state. In this scenario, the companies are seen as an extension of the state. The hypothesis is that even when SOE interests are very strong, security interests dominate foreign policy. The hypothesis about *economic interests* is based on an understanding of companies as rational, profit-maximizing entities that, according to a means-ends calculus, pursue action. Companies are seen as a profit-driven, independent interest group. The hypothesis is that, even when security interests are strong, economic interests will dominate. The hypothesis that the concern with *domestic stability* (维稳/*weiwen*) dominates is based on the perspective that, in the country in question, activities are related to the CCP's concern with maintaining power. In other words, the more the leadership is concerned with domestic legitimacy, the more it requires economic growth and, subsequently, the more it needs energy. It is therefore important to consider *the salience of the concern with legitimacy for the Chinese leadership*.

The project combines qualitative and quantitative analyses for empirical leverage in order to test the portability of the explanations. The variation between the African countries provides a rich empirical context for examining the impact of SOEs on foreign policy and the possible change in key actors over the last ten years.

The chapters that follow draw on a large set of materials written in Chinese, including CCP documents, news reports, academic articles, and business articles. These sources shed light on the motives driving Chinese foreign policy, together with those driving the Chinese NOCs and their acquisitions abroad.

Perspectives

My findings and the framework I have developed for explaining them are important for empirical and theoretical reasons. *Empirically*, I find that, over a ten-year

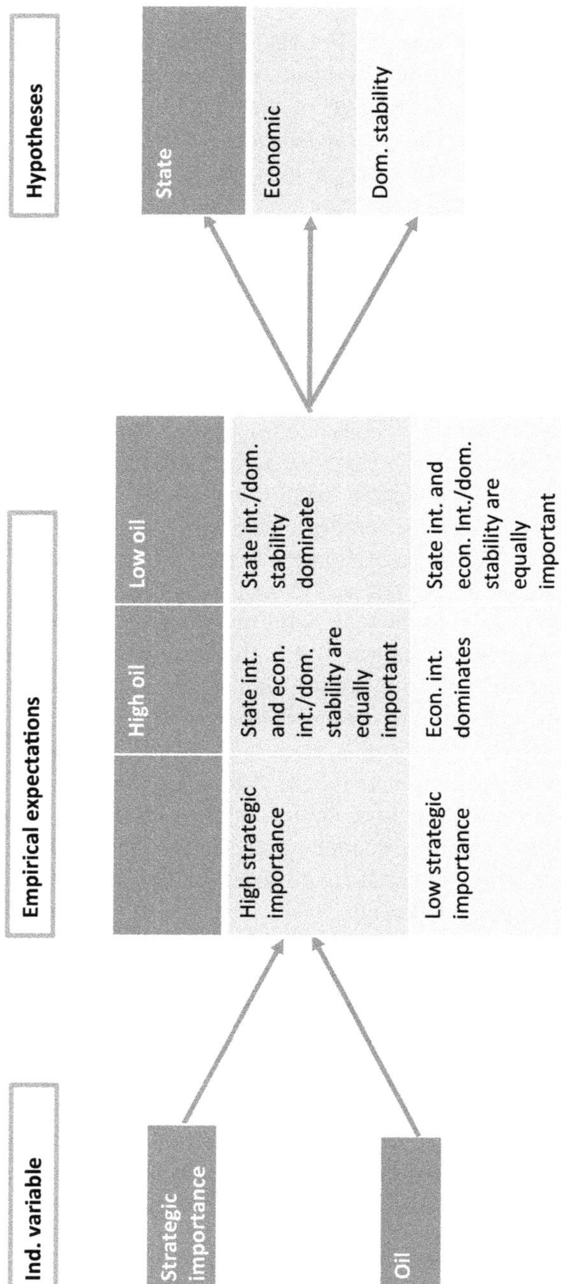

Figure 1.1 Explanatory model

period stretching from 2002–12, the NOCs were driven by economic interests. The argument here is that when economic interests dominate, that would be consistent with a greater role being played by NOCs. The book illuminates particular instances in which the NOCs have an impact on and play a role in foreign policy as well as instances in which the NOCs have not played any role. Moreover, the study shows that, over this ten-year period, state interests and concerns with domestic stability have increased. The book demonstrates how companies are now facing increased constraints in their business activities from the Chinese leadership.

Theoretically, the book contributes with a framework that can illuminate the increasing role of NOCs in foreign policy. It tells us how, theoretically, the rise of SOEs affects foreign policy and what motivates Chinese foreign policy. The book thus adds to the theory concerning the role of non-state actors in relation to the foreign policy of the state, which is an underexplored topic. It presents a model that can illuminate the particularities of the authoritarian state and explain the role that NOCs have in the foreign policy of such a state.

The study also contributes with insights regarding the importance of domestic stability to Chinese foreign policy and how this motive relates to the NOC activities in a number of countries. More generally, this study adds to a larger body of literature on the impact of first-level variables as related to structural variables. It shows how important insights can be gained from including first-level variables in analyses that are not captured when considering structural variables alone. In addition, it contributes with insights concerning the role of natural resources in the foreign policy of the state and with an explication of the role played by NOCs in this regard. Finally, in addition to these more specific goals, the book offers insights regarding the rise of China. It illuminates whether China can be thought of as rising as a revisionist or a status quo state and how concerns with energy matter in this regard.

The argument presented here is that China is motivated by economic interest. This is tested in a larger number of cases than what has been done before.

Overview of the book

The study consists of nine chapters. The first summarizes the questions motivating the study, the most significant findings, and their implications for our understanding of Chinese foreign policy.

Chapter 2 reviews the literature on the foreign policy of the authoritarian state, assesses three broad literatures to this end, and develops a theoretical model of the foreign policy of an authoritarian state. It then develops a strategy for measuring the dependent variables in this study – state interests, economic interests, and concern with domestic stability (维稳/*weiwen*) – and presents the indicators reflecting these three. It offers an index of strategic importance and presents the case selection of this study as well as the methods applied to analyze the cases.

Chapter 3 is a background chapter that illustrates why and how companies can be thought of as separate entities from the political system in China. The chapter tells the story of the (flawed) reform process and the respective levers of control available to the companies and government.

Chapters 4–7 comprise the empirical section of the study. The first four are African cases: Sudan, Angola, Nigeria, and Tunisia, which provide results within one region. The results suggest that the respective empirical expectations regarding expected behavior are supported to some extent. The specific empirical expectations find support in the cases of Nigeria (Chapter 4) and Tunisia (Chapter 7), whereas they are only partly supported in the cases of Angola (Chapter 5) and Sudan (Chapter 6).

Chapter 8 includes the four mini-cases of Kazakhstan, Canada, Uzbekistan, and Denmark in order to examine how far the conclusions that I find for the African cases can be generalized across regions. The results from the mini-cases suggest that the data generally support the empirical expectations presented. These expectations find support in the cases of Kazakhstan, Canada, and Denmark, whereas they are only partially supported in the case of Uzbekistan. The mini-case results thus indicate that the results from the main cases are in fact generalizable.

Finally, Chapter 9 presents and restates the findings of this study and discusses their implications for international relations theory.

Notes

1 E.g., John J. Mearsheimer, *The Tragedy of Great Power Politics* (New York, NY: Norton, 2001); David Shambaugh, "Containment or Engagement of China? Calculating Beijing's Responses," *International Security* 21 (2) (Fall 1996): 180–209; Randall L. Schweller, "Bandwagoning for Profit: Bringing the Revisionist State Back In," *International Security* 19 (1) (Summer 1994); Hans J. Morgenthau, *Politics Among Nations: The Struggle for Power and Peace*, 5th ed (New York, NY: Alfred A. Knopf, 1978).

2 See Robert Kagan, "What China Knows That We Don't: The Case for a New Strategy of Containment," *Weekly Standard*, January 20, 1997; Paul Wolfowitz, "Bridging Centuries – Fin de Siecle All Over Again," *National Interest* (Spring 1997): 3–8.

3 E.g., Kenneth Waltz, *Theory of International Politics* (Reading, MA: Addison-Wesley, 1979).

4 Information Office of the State Council of the People's Republic of China, "China's Peaceful Development Road," White Paper, December 12, 2005, accessed December 15, 2015, www.china.org.cn/english/features/book/152684.html. See also Zheng Bijian, "China's 'Peaceful Rise' to Great-Power Status," *Foreign Affairs* 84 (5) (September–October, 2005): 18; Zhang Xiaoming [张小明]. 中国的崛起与国际规范的变迁 ["China's Rise and Changes of International Norms"], *外交评论 [Foreign Affairs Review*] 1 (2011). This is to some extent a cultural argument (based on the idea that Chinese behavior is different from what it would be following assumptions inherent in "traditional" realist theories).

5 Information Office of the State Council of the People's Republic of China, "China's Energy Conditions and Policies," White Paper on Energy, December 2007, accessed December 15, 2015, www.ccchina.gov.cn/WebSite/CCChina/UpFile/File229.pdf; Information Office of the State Council of the People's Republic of China, "China's Energy Conditions and Policies," *China's Energy Policy 2012*, White Paper, October 2012, accessed December 15, 2015, www.gov.cn/english/official/2012-10/24/

content_2250497.html; British Petroleum (BP), "BP Statistical Review of World Energy," June 2014, accessed December 15, 2015, www.bp.com/statisticalreview.

6 Unless otherwise indicated, monetary amounts are in U.S. dollars.

7 Julie Jiang and Jonathan Sinton, *Overseas Investments by China's National Oil Companies: Assessing the Drivers and Impacts* (Paris, France: Organization for Economic Cooperation and Development/ International Energy Agency, Paris, February 2011), 10.

8 Erica S. Downs, *China's Quest for Energy Security* (Santa Monica, CA: RAND, 2000); Phillip C. Saunders, "China's Global Activism: Strategy, Drivers, and Tools," Institute for National Strategic Studies, Occasional Paper No. 4 (Washington, DC: National Defense University Press, 2006); David Zweig and Bi Jianhai, "China's Global Hunt for Energy," *Foreign Affairs* 84 (25) (September–October 2005): 25–38; Thomas J. Christensen, Alastair I. Johnston and Robert Ross, "Conclusions and Future Directions," in *New Directions in the Study of China's Foreign Policy*, eds. Alastair I. Johnston and Robert Ross (Stanford, CA: Stanford University Press, 2006), 379–420, 408.

9 Zhai, Jun (翟隽), "中国 积极推动解决达尔富尔问题," ["China Actively Pushed the Resolving of the Darfur problem"], 求是杂志 (*Qiushi Zazhi*) 11 (2007): 61–3.

10 See Frederick Starr, ed., *Xinjiang: China's Muslim Borderland* (New York, NY: M.E. Sharpe, 2004). However, what is at stake is not the state as such but the CCP's rule. China is a one-party state where the survival of the state is tied to the survival of the party. Thus, we focus on the role of CCP, not the state.

References

British Petroleum (BP), "BP Statistical Review of World Energy." June 2014. Accessed 12/15/2015. www.bp.com/statisticalreview.

Christensen, Thomas J., Alastair I. Johnston and Robert Ross. "Conclusions and Future Directions." In *New Directions in the Study of China's Foreign Policy*, edited by Alastair I. Johnston and Robert Ross, 379–420. Stanford, CA: Stanford University Press, 2006.

Downs, Erica S. *China's Quest for Energy Security*. Santa Monica, CA: RAND, 2000.

Information Office of the State Council of the People's Republic of China. "China's Peaceful Development Road." White Paper, December 12, 2005. Accessed 12/15/2015. www.china.org.cn/english/features/book/152684.html.

Information Office of the State Council of the People's Republic of China. "China's Energy Conditions and Policies." White Paper on Energy, December 2007. Accessed 12/15/2015. www.ccchina.gov.cn/WebSite/CCChina/UpFile/File229.pdf.

Information Office of the State Council of the People's Republic of China. "China's Energy Conditions and Policies." White Paper, October 2012, China's Energy Policy 2012. Accessed 12/15/2015. www.gov.cn/english/official/2012-10/24/content_2250497.html.

Jiang, Julie and Jonathan Sinton. *Overseas Investments by China's National Oil Companies: Assessing the Drivers and Impacts*. Paris: Organization of European Community Development/International Energy Agency (IEA), February 2011.

Kagan, Robert. "What China Knows That We Don't: The Case for a New Strategy of Containment." *Weekly Standard*, January 20, 1997.

Mearsheimer, John. J. *The Tragedy of Great Power Politics*. New York, NY: Norton, 2001.

Morgenthau, Hans J. *Politics Among Nations*, New York, NY: Alfred Knopf, 1948.

Saunders, Phillip C. "China's Global Activism: Strategy, Drivers, and Tools." Institute for National Strategic Studies, Occasional Paper No. 4. Washington, DC: National Defense University Press, 2006.

Schweller, Randall L. "Bandwagoning for Profit: Bringing the Revisionist State Back." *International Security* 19 (1) (Summer 1994): 72–107.

Shambaugh, David. "Containment or Engagement of China? Calculating Beijing's Responses." *International Security* 21 (2) (Fall 1996): 180–209.

Starr, Frederick, ed. *Xinjiang: China's Muslim Borderland*. New York, NY: M.E. Sharpe, 2004.

Wolfowitz, Paul. "Bridging Centuries – Fin de Siecle All Over Again." *National Interest* (Spring 1997).

Waltz, Kenneth. *Theory of International Politics*. Reading, MA: Addison-Wesley, 1979.

Zhai, Jun (翟隽). "中国 积极推动解决达尔富尔问题", ["China actively pushed the resolving of the Darfur problem"]. 求是杂志 (*Qiushi Zazhi*) 11 (2007): 61–3.

Zhang, Xiaoming. [张小明], 中国的崛起与国际规范的变迁 ["China's Rise and Changes of International Norms"]. *外交评论* [*Foreign Affairs Review*] 1 (2011): 34–47.

Zheng Bijian. "China's 'Peaceful Rise' to Great-Power Status." *Foreign Affairs* 84 (5) (September–October 2005): 18–24.

Zweig, David and Bi Jianhai. "China's Global Hunt for Energy." *Foreign Affairs* 84 (25) (September–October 2005): 25–38.

2 The foreign policy of an authoritarian state

Following the Chinese government's Going Out policy (走出去/*zouchuqu*), Chinese state-owned enterprises (SOEs) have grown stronger and more profitable over the last decade. The Chinese SOEs are now among the largest and most profitable companies in the world. In fact, a rise of the SOEs has taken place, and they now have increasing influence on foreign policy. The claim here is that the rise of SOEs over the last ten years has led to a shift in the key foreign policy actors, such that the SOEs now play an independent role in foreign policy. Moreover, this rise of SOEs and their influence on foreign policy is a particular characteristic of the foreign policy of the authoritarian state. This chapter seeks to unpack the foreign policy of the authoritarian state and present its characteristics.

The question of how the foreign policy of the authoritarian state can be characterized remains unresolved. How can the foreign policy of an authoritarian state be characterized? How should we conceive of the foreign policy of the authoritarian state in order to derive and test hypotheses about its effect on behavior? This chapter presents a framework for analyzing the foreign policy of the authoritarian state.

How do we think about authoritarian foreign policy? The limited existing contributions to this literature focus on the "audience costs" of authoritarian states and carry the logic that there are audience costs to defecting, making foreign policy more foreseeable. Audience costs, or the domestic punishment that leaders would incur for backing down from public threats, are thought to increase the ability of leaders to convey their preferences credibly during military crises.[1] The assumption is that, because democracies have higher audience costs, they are less likely to bluff than non-democracies.[2]

Jessica Weeks finds this not necessarily to be so.[3] She argues that authoritarian regimes may exhibit predictable variation in their ability to generate audience costs – and elections are not the only way for domestic groups to hold leaders accountable.[4] Weeks develops a logic of autocratic audience costs that takes into account how most authoritarian leaders require the support of domestic elites who act as audiences, playing a similar role to voting publics in democracies. Weeks's contribution is that she unpacks authoritarian states, analyzes the differences in audience costs between different regime types, and finds variations in the types of authoritarianism.[5] Here, the purpose is not to look at audience costs, that is, not to address how domestic actors or outsiders view stepping down from office. Rather, Weeks is one of the first to talk about the foreign policy of an authoritarian state.

The literature on the foreign policy of the authoritarian state is, thus, not very developed: the only work being the audience cost work. There is, then, a hole in the literature that I can fill. My work adds to this limited body of literature by examining how other state actors possibly matter.

This study extends this examination of the foreign policy of the authoritarian state and seeks to unpack the foreign policy of such a state. I argue that one of the characteristics of the foreign policy of the authoritarian state is the rise of state-owned enterprises (SOEs) and their impact on foreign policy. It is as such an inductive claim that emerges from the discussion of the case of China.

This chapter provides a thorough presentation of the characteristics of the foreign policy of an authoritarian state.

The literature on authoritarian foreign policy

Other scholarly attempts assess variations in authoritarianisms – that is, they focus on the institutions within the state that matter in different types of regimes, for example, one where the military plays a role and one where it does not, and how this relates to foreign policy. For example, Barbara Geddes has identified one dimension for understanding the internal logic of authoritarian regimes, namely, whether the regime is led by civilians or the military and the degree of personal power of the dictator, which again is related to the variation in constraints and preferences across dictatorships.[6] I am not interested here in variation in the use of force across different authoritarian regimes but rather in understanding the workings of a single authoritarian regime.

In contrast to the institutional argument, a series of studies carried out by Mark Peceny et al. concludes that personalist dictatorships in which the leader only depends on a small number of supporters are more likely to initiate conflicts than both democracies and other authoritarian regime types.[7] I will not go into this here, as my purpose is not to assess the variation in authoritarian regimes and their impact on foreign policy. Moreover, as China is a one-party state rather than a personalist regime, this issue is not relevant here.

Within the international relations literature, attempts to understand the foreign policy of an authoritarian state are limited. Some work has been done that looks at the differences in audience costs across regime types as well as the variations in the types of authoritarianisms.[8] However, the literature has not adequately assessed what the character of the regime means for the foreign policy of the state and whether the foreign policy of an authoritarian state differs from that of a democratic one, and if so, how. Within the strain of international relations theory referred to as *structural realism*, domestic factors, including regime type, are not included in the analysis, and the state is generally treated as a "black box." Within *classical realism*, as within *neo-classical realism*, attempts have been made to see how domestic factors, such as regime type or state strength, in addition to a structural factor, influence foreign policy.[9] For example, Randall Schweller argues that, in addition to structural factors, a second-level hypothesis specifying regime type, whether democratic or non-democratic, and the type of leader and challenger should be included in analyses in order to provide more determinate predictions of the outcomes of power shifts.[10] The problem is, however, that adding unit-level variables to a structural theory causes methodological inconsistencies.

Some realist scholars have studied the regime type and its impact on foreign policy. Robert Ross, for example, emphasizes the characteristics of domestic politics in China, in particular the character of the authoritarian state.[11] However, Ross does not venture into a systematic analysis of what the "authoritarian-ness" is and how these characteristics influence foreign policy.

There is a body of literature on the foreign policy of developing nations, some of which are authoritarian states. Several scholars, including Mohammed Ayoob, Edward Azar, and Brian Job, have noted that domestic security concerns dominate in developing countries.[12] However, these works have not sufficiently specified how domestic security influences the foreign policy of a developing country. Secondly, they also do not fully explore how the foreign policy of the developing country is related to whether the country is authoritarian or not, that is, the regime type.

Within the liberal school of international relations theory, attempts have been made to examine the role of regime type with respect to foreign policy outcomes. This school bases its explanations of the international behavior of states on the basis of their internal characteristics.[13] Democratic peace theory presents the assumption that democracies are less likely to engage in armed conflict with other democracies and that, internationally, democracies produce peace more than war for the same reasons that they resolve domestic conflicts better than dictatorships.[14] In the background of this assumption, the foreign policy of authoritarian states would be expected to be non-peaceful.[15] However, these liberal theories do not systematically examine the mechanisms of the foreign policy of the authoritarian state, other than to recognize a general notion of non-peacefulness. Nor do these theories address whether the role of non-state actors in influencing foreign policy is a particular characteristic of the authoritarian state. Thus, to understand the workings of an authoritarian state and how variations in authoritarianism affect foreign policy, neither realist nor liberal theories are helpful.

Existing attempts to explain the foreign policy of the authoritarian state thus rest on uncertain theoretical foundations. The existing measures of understanding how the foreign policy of the authoritarian state functions are imperfect, because they do not explicitly deal with the impact of "the authoritarian" character of the state on its foreign policy. Consequently, we still have much to learn about the foreign policy of the authoritarian state. I attempt to fill this gap by building a theoretical framework that explains the workings of the foreign policy of the authoritarian state. Three hypotheses are tested here as potential explanations of the foreign policy of the authoritarian state, drawing on insights crucial to understanding the foreign policy of such a state. The general claim here is that there has been a change in the key actors in Chinese foreign policy over the last decade and interest groups now have an increasingly important role in foreign policy.[16] Moreover, and importantly, the claim is that this shift is a characteristic of the foreign policy of the authoritarian state.

Theoretical framework

Within the international relations literature, attempts to understand the foreign policy of an authoritarian state – and in particular the role of SOEs and their impact on the foreign policy of the state – are limited.

This study examines and unpacks the foreign policy of an authoritarian state. It argues that one characteristic of the foreign policy of the authoritarian state is the rise of interest groups, specifically non-state actors, and their impact on foreign policy. To examine and test this proposition, three theoretical perspectives are presented.

First, I present a theory that stresses structural factors. I argue that the collapse of the Soviet Union has led to a growth in the recent China–US rivalry, a rivalry aimed at being the strongest state in the international system. The question here becomes whether the only or primary explanation for the behavior of states – that is, their strategic interest – is a structural one, as there could be other drivers, even if the result is the same. The logic is that China will be worried because of the rivalry about influence with the United States. In this rivalry for influence, sufficient, stable energy supplies are necessary for economic growth. Here, the national oil companies play an important role, as they are responsible for ensuring the energy supplies upon which the state depends for survival. Along the lines of this argument, the companies can be seen as an extension of the state.

Second, I present a theory that captures the functioning of the foreign policy of an authoritarian state. Building on insights from the Chinese politics literature, a hypothesis can be established according to which the political and administrative systems have been fragmented, which in turn has led to the pluralization of the policy process and reduced state capacity. In turn, the pluralization of the policy process and weakened leadership have enabled SOEs to influence economic decision-making. The argument is that an authoritarian state can be characterized by the ease with which economic interests can influence economic decision-making – that following the rise of SOEs, economic interests influence economic decision-making, ultimately having an impact on foreign policy.

Third, I present a theory emphasizing how the foreign policy of an authoritarian state is related to concerns with domestic legitimacy. The hypothesis is that concerns with maintaining domestic stability (维稳/*weiwen*) dominate and that activities of the companies in the recipient country are related to the CCP's concern with maintaining power. The logic is that the more the leadership is concerned with domestic legitimacy, the more it needs economic growth. As economic growth requires sufficient energy supplies, the role of the Chinese companies in this regard has become important. Specifically, it can be noted here that the ability of the CCP to maintain power relates to whether it has legitimacy, which in turn depends on economic growth. Thus, the activities of the companies abroad can be seen as a reflection of the need for the CCP to sustain regime and domestic stability. In other words, this hypothesis can be understood as a proxy for the state's concern with legitimacy.

The three hypotheses are used instrumentally in this study's analysis. The theoretical underpinnings of each hypothesis are examined in turn.

Structural factors

For an account of how structural factors might explain the foreign policy of the state, the dominant theory in international relations theory is structural realism. Following structural realism, as Kenneth Waltz presents it, state behavior can be deduced from the distribution of power in the international system.[17] The state is treated as a "black box", and the regime type is excluded from analysis. Following structural realism, the assumption is that rising states will balance the current hegemon. Under bipolarity, the system's two dominant powers possess relatively corresponding amounts of power, offsetting each other and maintaining the balance of power in the international system. According to Waltzian structural realism, such a unipolar world order is unstable, and it is a matter of time before the system will again tend towards bi- or multipolarity.

Since the collapse of the Soviet Union, the international system has been characterized by (near) unipolarity. In the last decade, China's power relative to the United States has grown. In a (nearly) unipolar world, according to structural realists, candidate poles such as China are expected to try to balance against the United States.[18] Thus, the collapse of the Soviet Union would explain the recent China–US rivalry. It has been suggested that under certain conditions, the likelihood of China using force against the United States is not insubstantial.[19]

The assumption here is that companies are acting in keeping with state interests and are used as tools of the state to pursue goals. As the rivalry with the United States becomes more intense, increasing amounts of energy are required. We can implicitly deduce from the theory that as economic growth and thus energy grow increasingly important for the state, it becomes increasingly important to control company activities. The China-specific story is, thus, that the companies are granted no independence since the collapse of Soviet Union and that they have been used as foreign policy tools.

While we can deduce from the theory that energy would be considered implicitly important for the foreign policy of the state, at the same time, structural realism has been criticized for a lacking explication of the role of energy for the foreign policy of the state, as well as its ability to function as a theory of the foreign policy of the state.[20] Despite the assumption of the different dimensions of power as being fungible, the theory does not sufficiently account for the relationship between the different components of power and how they can be combined into an aggregate score, such as the role of economic versus military capabilities. Moreover, the theory subsumes energy to the other dimensions of power.[21] Thus, structural realism generally fails in its attempt to explain the role of energy and how it affects foreign policy.

In order to better understand the need for energy as an influence on foreign policy, a mechanism for understanding the role of energy in foreign policy must be identified, including how energy companies are used as tools of the state to pursue goals. Such a mechanism could contribute to our understanding of how companies are controlled and how they are used to pursue state goals. Realist theories can help guide the identification of such a mechanism. For example, quoting David Zweig and Bi Jianhai, Thomas Christensen et al. note that being an energy-hungry state is a "new characteristic that drives much of China's current foreign policy behavior."[22] In the realist tradition, however, the role of energy in the foreign policy of states is understudied. Attempts have been made to address the role of energy in foreign policy through the lens of the relationship between energy security and foreign policy,[23] the analysis of resources as important for state power as in power transition theory,[24] the role of resource endowment for the foreign policy of the state,[25] and the importance of raw materials and resources to the economy and thus for the state.[26] However, all of these accounts suffer from a lack of clarification of the role of energy in the foreign policy of the state and, in general, share the assumption that, in guiding foreign policy, resources are considered less important than other dimensions, such as the military. Hendrik Spruyt has focused on grand strategy and the use of statecraft, defined as instruments used by policy-makers in their attempts to exercise power.[27] Similarly, David Baldwin has focused on the efficacy of economic techniques of statecraft.[28] Here, one might argue that the energy companies are used as part of an "economic technique" for achieving foreign policy goals. However, the link between the economic techniques and foreign policy is not very explicit.

In other words, the literature lacks sufficient clarity regarding *how* the state would be able to *use* the companies to pursue foreign policy objectives. There is a need for analysis of how to conceptualize the role of energy in the foreign policy of a state and how sufficient energy supplies can yield power to the state.

Thus, in the last decade, China's power relative to the United States has grown. In a (nearly) unipolar world, according to structural realists, candidate poles such as China are expected to try to balance against the strongest state in the system, the United States. In doing so, sufficient energy supplies are important for continued economic growth and thus for augmenting the relative power of the state. Thus, when we consider a rising China, the role of energy in that country's domestic *and* foreign policies is fundamental. In other words, when we consider a structural realist explanation, the assumption is that state interests dominate and that the increasing role of energy in Chinese foreign policy could be explained by the collapse of the Soviet Union. According to this theory, one would therefore expect to see a change in the foreign policy behavior of China around 1991, shortly after the fall of the Soviet Union. The hypothesis concerning state interest should be seen in the context of the emergence of the United States as the main security concern.

Foreign policy of the authoritarian state

Here, we will establish a hypothesis about the characteristics of the foreign policy of the authoritarian state.[29] The hypothesis presented here speaks to how SOEs might influence foreign policy. The logic is that following the reform processes in China and the liberalization of the market, the SOEs have become strong while the political system has become increasingly fragmented and policy decision-making has become increasingly pluralized. The weakened leadership has led to a weakened state capacity; as a result, it has become easier for other non-state actors to influence decision-making. Together, these three aspects can illuminate how SOEs as interest groups can influence foreign policy and the role played by companies in the foreign policy of the state.

First, SOEs have grown strong.[30] It is generally acknowledged that, as a result of the reform process, China has experienced rapid economic growth.[31] The subsidiaries of the SOEs are listed on foreign stock exchanges. The profits of the shareholding companies of the large national oil companies (NOCs) have increased in recent years. In the period from 1998–2006, the combined net income of the three large Chinese NOCs, China National Petroleum Corporation (CNPC), China Petrochemical Corporation (Sinopec), and China National Offshore Oil Corporation (CNOOC), increased from 16.5 to 228 billion RMB.[32] In the period from 2007 to 2014, their combined net income was 234 billion RMB in 2007 and 214 billion RMB in 2014.[33] In 2009, the SOEs provided the government with one-sixth of its total revenue in the form of taxes.[34] Increased profits have thus meant increased government revenue.

At the same time, the NOCs employ hundreds of thousands of people. The SOEs employ large numbers of people compared to the small number in the energy administration in the Chinese government. Moreover, in recent years, the senior management in the large NOCs has been "internationalized." As a result of the need for increasing oil imports, the NOCs have come to play an important role in obtaining foreign assets instead of relying on the international market. In turn, this enables them to fill oil reserves and make profits. One might postulate that this financial growth and the expertise that they possess (which is in high demand), together with their importance in securing oil stakes, have rendered the government more responsive to NOC interests and increased their ability to influence government decisions. Sheer numbers as well as the complexity of issues related to the energy field render the assumption of government control difficult. All in all, a process in which the SOEs have grown more powerful has taken place.

Second, the fragmentation of both the political and administrative systems in China has been observed by several scholars.[35] This fragmentation has led to several things. A larger number of actors are now involved in Chinese policy decision-making than in the Maoist era and a larger number of voices are trying to influence policy, including groups, organizations, and individuals.[36] Processes of decentralization have taken place in the course of reform. Authority has been delegated to lower-level actors, such as provinces, and their toleration of increased initiative has given rise to the growing number of actors influencing Chinese foreign policy.[37] Authority over foreign policy has become fractured. Within the Chinese bureaucracy, the Ministry of Foreign Affairs is now only one actor in the foreign policy realm. There are many others, each with its own set of motives. A characteristic of the fragmented bureaucracy is the lack of reform of the energy sector and the lack of a Ministry of Energy to oversee important decisions. Within the government, different agencies have divergent agendas. Moreover, the energy administration in the Chinese government is very small, whereas the energy companies employ a large number of people. Interestingly, this weakened energy bureaucracy contributes to the increasing independence of the NOCs. In this manner, the fragmented bureaucratic system, together with decentralization processes, has opened up a larger role for SOEs. Consequently, SOEs will be more likely to influence policy.

Third, over the course of the last decades, elite politics in China have changed. The leadership has become weaker, and the leadership style and decision-making processes have also changed. In the literature on Chinese foreign policy decision-making, scholars have focused on how different leaders affect processes and outcomes.[38] Here, the assumption is that the variation of leadership types – from rule by Maoist charisma to a system where the party leadership is more equal than others to a more institutionalized consensus, where politics is less dangerous – is related to and has an effect on foreign policy. Over the last five decades, there has been a shift in leadership from the charismatic leadership of Mao to Deng Xiaoping's "strong man" leadership to the "informal" leadership of Jiang Zemin and finally to Hu Jintao as a weak consensus-builder. This signifies a change in the decision-making process from one characterized by strong men to another characterized by weak consensus-making. The Chinese leadership has become increasingly weaker, and in the Jiang-Hu era, it has become easier for SOEs and other non-state actors to influence decision-making.[39]

During this period, the leadership has also become more focused on securing economic growth to ensure its survival. One way to do this is the development of the large SOEs. Consequently, the increasingly large and profitable SOEs have been able to exert greater influence on policy-making. Here, I see SOEs as an interest group with well-defined economic interests in terms of profit-maximization. I operate here with an interest group defined as a group that "seeks to maximize well-defined economic or ideational interests and usually outlasts the leadership of any particular individual."[40]

The literature is relatively limited in terms of *how* SOEs can influence policy-making. At the same time, based on the literature and my own material, I here suggest some of the ways SOEs can influence policy-making. The organization of the Chinese central government bureaucracy gives certain sectors more clout than others. For example, Susan Shirk notes that industry has more clout than agriculture and that, within industry, heavy industry has more clout than light industry.[41] In the absence of a Ministry of Energy, the SOEs can have closer contact to the relevant government agencies, such as the NDRC and the Politburo.[42] SOEs can also influence policy-making via the formulation of China's energy security policy. Here, SOEs can exert a limited influence on foreign policy, because the SOE leaders are members of official decision-making bodies.[43] A third way SOEs can influence policy is through the close ties between the political leadership and these companies. The top leaders often "travel" between positions in the companies and the government: for example, former member of the 17th Politburo

Standing Committee Zhou Yongkang was previously the head of CNPC, and Su Shulin, former head of Sinopec, is now the governor of Fujian Province.[44] Thus, the NOCs are thought to have close ties with the top leadership and might be able to make their interests heard at the top because of shared interests and backgrounds. Finally, the increasing overseas activities of Chinese firms inadvertently affect the background for the elites' foreign policy agenda and the pressures to which the central foreign policy must respond. For example, the SOE activities in Sudan impact foreign policy (as seen in Chapter 6). The companies' activities create new interests that the state defends.

In summary, a hypothesis has been established about the characteristics of the foreign policy of the authoritarian state in which the rise of SOEs in Chinese foreign policy is a significant part. The fragmentation of the political and administrative systems, pluralization of the policy process, and weakened leadership have enabled SOEs to influence economic decision-making. This, in turn, might have an impact on foreign policy. The hypothesis is that SOE interests will dominate, thus having an impact on foreign policy.

*Domestic legitimacy: concerns with domestic stability (*weiwen*)*

The hypothesis is that concerns with domestic stability (*weiwen*) have an impact on the foreign policy of the authoritarian state.

In recent years, Chinese leaders have grown progressively more concerned with "social stability" (社会管理, 维持稳定/*shehui guanli, weichi wending*).[45] Since reforms started in 1978, and particularly since Tiananmen in 1989, there have been an increasing number of "mass incidents."[46] The regime is increasingly worried about these "mass incidents," which are seen as posing a threat to the regime. This concern has been reflected in the increasing degree to which the Chinese regime talks about stability. The assumption here is that the degree to which the regime talks about social stability is a proxy for the state's concern with legitimacy – as well as the CCP's concern with survival and the legitimacy of the regime. The argument, then, is that concern with social stability (维持稳定/*weichi wending*, or in short: 维稳/*weiwen*) influences foreign policy.

The Chinese regime is marked by a high level of domestic insecurity. Shirk notes that "China may be an emerging superpower, but it is a fragile one."[47] Chinese leaders are concerned with their own political survival, a mass protest movement, lack of support from the military, a protest fueled by nationalism as well as ethnic unrest, and concerns with "color revolutions" – the revolutions that brought down authoritarian regimes in countries like Serbia (2000), Georgia (2003), Ukraine (2004), and Kyrgyzstan (2005).[48]

Regardless of whether they are toward the Democratic People's Republic of Korea (DPRK), Taiwan, or the Syrian civil war, policies *vis-à-vis* these countries are always linked to concerns with and their implications for domestic stability. Examining the concern with domestic stability is therefore important. Crucially, a link can be presented between the SOEs and the role of social stability, as the oil companies have the important task of ensuring the critical supply of resources for the economy to continue to grow, which is seen as a vital factor in the Chinese regime's survival. Here, the mechanism is that the more the Chinese regime is concerned about domestic legitimacy, the more it needs economic growth, and the more it needs economic growth, the less independent the companies will be.

How do concerns with domestic legitimacy in the shape of, for example, large-scale socioeconomic unrest relate to foreign policy? This is a question that remains unexplored, as remarked by Christensen et al.[49] The general logic in the literature, as presented by Shirk, is that when understanding Chinese foreign policy, domestic influences trump international factors.[50] In the face of violent protest, domestic concerns will always be the top priority. Only in the event of a crisis involving Japan, Taiwan, or the United States will international considerations trump domestic concerns. In these instances, due to the "fragile" character of the state, popular nationalist sentiment can spin out of control and will increasingly force the Chinese government to adopt more aggressive foreign and military policies.[51]

At the same time, and importantly, while this literature sheds light on how concerns with domestic legitimacy impact foreign policy, the exact mechanism under which concerns with domestic legitimacy are translated into the foreign policy of the authoritarian state remains unclear.

Still, the general logic in the literature is that nationalism explains the link between concerns with legitimacy and foreign policy.[52] In order to shore up legitimacy, authoritarian leaders will resort to nationalism or be challenged by threats from nationalist movements, which, in turn, will lead to a conflictual foreign policy.

The question of how the concern with domestic legitimacy impacts the role of the SOEs in Chinese foreign policy is underexplored. The literature offers little with regard to this link. One exception is Shirk, who argues, "Economic growth prevents unrest – and . . . in this process Chinese businesses and local governments have a stake in keeping foreign trade and investment flowing. This in turn influences Chinese foreign policy."[53] Shirk thus sheds light on a notable relationship, namely that not only does concern with economic growth relate to domestic legitimacy but rather the energy companies also help ensure the economic growth important for social stability. As ensuring sufficient resources is a requirement for domestic stability, as well as social stability, which, in turn, is a prerequisite for a stable foreign policy, the activities of the energy companies influence foreign policy in this manner. Here, I provide a further hypothesis, namely that given the importance of economic growth, the energy companies have an important role to play. The more important economic growth is, the less independent the companies are assumed to be. For the purpose of this discussion, if I see an increase in the frequency of the mentioning of concerns with social stability (维稳/*weiwen*), I assume that the companies are less independent.

The Chinese government is concerned with the safety of Chinese workers because the issue touches on the concern with social stability and domestic legitimacy and is therefore also of significance to questions of national security. The Chinese oil worker holds a central position in Chinese society and in its relations with other countries. This also explains why the killing of Chinese workers in foreign countries has implications not just on the ground in the respective country but more importantly for domestic stability in China and for the legitimacy of the CCP. This component illustrates how the pursuit of economic interests affects Chinese national interests, as it has an impact on regime stability through the risk it poses to CCP survival in the event of the death of Chinese workers abroad.

In summary, a link between domestic legitimacy and how it influences the foreign policy of the authoritarian state has been established. The hypothesis is that the more the regime is concerned with social stability, the less independent the energy companies will be.

Even when it looks as though SOEs and foreign policy interests are strong, the activities of the NOCs in various countries are explained by the CCP's interest in regime survival.[54] In this manner, a link is established between authoritarian foreign policy and concerns with domestic legitimacy among the Chinese leadership. This hypothesis relates to the capacity of the Chinese regime to maintain domestic stability.

Hypotheses

Based on the three theoretical perspectives, three hypotheses are derived.

The *first* hypothesis is that state interests dominate relative to SOE interests and domestic stability. This hypothesis follows from the structural realist assumption concerning the relationship between companies and the state according to which the companies are seen as an extension of the state. The hypothesis is that even when SOE interests are very strong, security interests will dominate foreign policy.

The *second* hypothesis is that economic interests dominate relative to state interests and domestic stability. Along the lines of this perspective, companies are seen as rational, profit-maximizing entities acting according to a means-ends calculus. Moreover, they are seen as independent interest groups. The hypothesis is that even when security interests are strong, economic interests will dominate. Even when state interests are at stake, the companies will pursue their independent economic interests. The interests of the SOEs will dominate, thus affecting foreign policy. This will hold particularly true in instances where companies deem that a large profit can be made, irrespective of whether the state supports their actions. This hypothesis is particularly suited to account for the (Chinese) authoritarian state, where the fragmentation of the political and administrative systems and weakened leadership explain how SOEs can influence economic decision-making, thus having a possible effect on foreign policy.

The *third* hypothesis is that domestic stability dominates relative to state and economic interests. The hypothesis that the concern with maintaining domestic stability (*weiwen*) dominates is based on the idea that in the recipient country, activities are related to the CCP's concern with maintaining power. The more the leadership is concerned with domestic legitimacy, the more it needs economic growth, which, in turn, increases the need for energy. Here, the NOCs play an important role in terms of obtaining the resources necessary to maintain domestic stability.

It should be noted that this book builds on the *premise* that the companies are profit-maximizing.

By evaluating these three hypotheses, this book sheds light on the characteristics of the foreign policy of the authoritarian state. The argument is that, herein, the rise of SOEs in Chinese foreign policy is a significant part of the foreign policy of the authoritarian state. Furthermore, depending on which hypothesis provides explanatory power, this study contributes to the debate on whether structural factors, characteristics of the Chinese authoritarian state, or concerns with social stability and legitimacy can explain the change we see in key actors in foreign policy over the last decade.

Alternative explanation

Challenges to the preceding hypotheses can be presented: first, there is a more China-specific explanation, according to which, given the particular factors pertaining to the relationship between SOEs and the government, it is not helpful to operate with a distinction between economic and state interests. In China, 114 of the large companies (央企/*yangqi*) have been managed by the State-owned Assets Supervision and Administration Commission (SASAC) since 2003. Moreover, 53 of the largest companies, including the three large oil companies – CNPC, Sinopec, and CNOOC – are managed by the Central Organization of the CCP. As Chinese companies are integrated into the political system, it might be premature to operate with the assumption that they are independent and run simply on profit-maximizing terms.[55] It would be premature to stipulate that the companies run their own operations in addition to conducting their own foreign policy.[56]

Second, there is a China-specific body of literature challenging the fruitfulness of seeing the companies as profit-maximizing entities. For example, Edward Steinfeld notes that

> a system, where authority is separated from accountability and control over assets is frequently detached from responsibility for liabilities, develops a logic of its own for all the players involved . . . managers can choose any number of systemic reasons why their poorly performing firm is entitled to investment; so long as information remains sketchy, all of these reasons appear to be plausible.[57]

This perspective speaks to how the companies are following a “garbage can model,” whereby authority is separated from accountability and control over assets.[58] Every entity can pass on the blame – but the public ultimately pays. This is a more complicated model of distorted impulses. It explains why companies cannot be expected to act according to the logic of profit maximization. Similarly, scholars point out that there are specific characteristics pertaining to the Chinese state – that is, social responsibility and rules for how many people the companies must employ, which means that they are not able to act according to the dictum of profit maximization.[59]

Third, following Raymond Vernon's work, an alternative hypothesis might be that the company-government relationship is explained by other factors altogether.[60] Vernon argues that there has been a change in the relationship between governments and companies over the last decades in Western countries. Whereas governments were hostile to multinational companies in the 1980s, Western governments (e.g., the United Kingdom and the United States) had closer ties with corporate interests in the 1990s. Thus, a tendency toward the convergence of international oil companies (IOCs) and the government has been observed. While one might expect more congruence between corporations and governments in the single-party state,[61] Vernon's contribution is that corporations and governments also have close ties in Western countries. Thus, even in democracies, the assumption of the independence of the company is unrealistic, for which reason the distinction between economic and state interests also appears unrealistic in democracies.

Fourth, an alternative hypothesis might be that the reason for the variation found relates to the particularities of the society in the recipient country. It might therefore be important to consider the nature of the regime as it is related to how China can pursue its interests. The assumption here is that in a more pluralistic society, it becomes more difficult for China, including Chinese companies, to pursue its interests. However, this hypothesis has the recipient country as the explanatory factor, which is inconsistent with the research design presented here.

Fifth, J. Katzer et al. note that China's ever-deepening integration into the global economy is even blurring the distinction between foreign and domestic.[62] While the Chinese government owns a controlling interest in all of the Chinese energy companies, they are also listed on overseas stock exchanges, have foreigners on their boards of directors, and receive financing and guidance from international investment banks. Along the lines of the international political economy, the argument here is that the state is losing ground to non-state actors, including international institutions and practices. Similarly, Steinfeld argues that Chinese companies are involved in a learning process and that the Chinese state is becoming more like Western states via the emulation of Western practices and its participation in the international economy (as through the activities of its energy companies when they "go out").[63] However, this perspective overestimates the degree to which China is losing its "state-ness," as well as the degree to which China is becoming like the rest.

Sixth, another way to go about analyzing China's energy policy is to consider the behavior of the companies as the result of international effects. For example, Philip Andrews-Speed notes how energy rarely rises to the top of the list of priorities for the highest levels of government but that rising prices affect energy policy in all countries.[64] He argues that China's WTO membership has meant that the country has become more integrated into the world energy system, which, in turn, puts pressure on China to make short-term adjustments, including reducing tariffs on energy imports and removing non-tariff barriers; adjustments to its energy sector; and longer-term reforms, including pressure for the further liberalization of the energy sector.[65] In other words, along the lines of this argument, international factors (institutions) have a bearing on a country's (energy) policy. However, this hypothesis has international factors as the explanatory factor, whereas the research design here focuses on elements pertaining to China as the explanatory factor.

Despite the validity of these alternative hypotheses, this study applies the framework of the three hypotheses described earlier pertaining to state interests, economic interests, and concerns with domestic stability (*weiwen*) and then examines the extent to which China operates according to liberal or nationalist economic theory or according to concerns with domestic stability. While these hypotheses might be simplistic, at the same time, it is argued here that they will help shed light on which motives are considered most important and key aspects concerning the motives behind the activities of the Chinese energy companies. Thus, even if there are important indications that the companies are integrated into the state, for matters of simplicity, I operate here with the simpler terms of state interests, economic interests, and concerns with domestic stability (*weiwen*) as clearly separate.

Research methodology: case study

To test the validity of the three hypotheses presented earlier, I set up a framework in which, depending on different values for the independent variable, one would expect that in some countries, the SOEs have an impact on foreign policy and in some, they do not.

When considering the relationship between the government and companies, there are two general lines of explanation for the variation found. On the one hand, it is argued that the role of energy security for the state interests alone can explain matters. On the other hand, it is argued that the economic interests of companies singularly explain matters. Here, it is argued that neither of these alone can account for the characteristics of the relationship or the variation found, as in addition to oil, the strategic importance of the particular country to China must also be considered. For that reason, this study presents a theory about what the amount of oil and the strategic importance of a country to the Chinese leadership mean for government-business relations. My general theory is that the relations between the government and companies in particular countries or regions are explained by the amount of oil in the country and its strategic importance to China. Thus, there are two key independent variables: the level of oil and the level of strategic importance that various countries or regions hold for the Chinese leadership.

Based on this logic, as shown in table 2.1, there are four possible outcomes:

Table 2.1 Possible outcomes

	High oil	*Low oil*
High strategic importance	1. Econ. int. and state int./dom. stability are equally important	3. State int./dom. stability dominate
Low strategic importance	2. Econ. int. dominates	4. Econ. int. and state int./dom. stability are equally important

Conceptualizing the variations in government-company coordination in the manner presented here provides a view of the role of security and (geo-)political factors in the country's energy policy and the capacity of the Chinese state in directing the engagement in the various countries and regions. An alternative to my theory is that the amount of oil alone is sufficient to explain the variation in government-company relationships. However, I do not deem this argument to be convincing.[66]

From these hypotheses, four specific empirical expectations are derived and guide this study:

First, for a country that is of high strategic importance to China and has a high level of oil: in this case, the companies have an incentive to be involved because of the large quantities of oil in order to maximize profits. At the same time, the government attributes strategic importance to the country or region. The assumption is that here both economic and state interests/domestic stability (*weiwen*) will dominate. Thus, in terms of specific empirical expectations, economic and state interests/domestic stability (*weiwen*) are expected to be equally important.

Second, for a country that is of limited strategic importance to China but has significant oil reserves (high level of oil): in this case, the companies have an incentive to become involved because of the large quantities of oil, but as the government attributes little strategic importance to the country, the state will not seek to pursue its interests there. Thus, in terms of specific empirical expectations, economic interests are expected to dominate.

Third, for a country that is of high strategic importance to China but has limited oil reserves: in this case, the companies have little incentive to become involved because of the limited availability of oil. The government attributes high strategic value to the country and pursues its state interests. Here, state interests will dominate. Thus, in terms of specific empirical expectations, state interests and domestic stability (*weiwen*) are expected to dominate.

Fourth, for a country that is of limited strategic importance to China and has limited oil reserves: in this case, the companies have little incentive to become involved in the country because of the limited availability of oil. Similarly, the government attributes limited strategic importance to the country or region. With that background, economic and state interests/domestic stability (*weiwen*) will dominate equally. Thus, in terms of specific empirical expectations, economic and state interests/domestic stability (*weiwen*) are expected to be of equally little importance.

Based on the three hypotheses and the logic presented here, the decisive empirical expectations are as follows: *Hypothesis 1* about "state interests" predicts that when both state interests *and* SOE interests are strong, strategic security interests will dominate. *Hypothesis 2* about "economic interests" predicts that when both energy resources are abundant *and* strategic interests are *high*, SOE interests will dominate. *Hypothesis 3* about "concerns with domestic stability" predicts that when SOE interests and strategic interests are both strong, behind the scenes, CCP interests will dominate policy.

Depending on which hypothesis provides explanatory power, this research contributes to the debate on whether structural factors, characteristics of the Chinese authoritarian state, or concerns with legitimacy can explain the change we see in key actors in foreign policy over the ten-year period under study here. Moreover, by evaluating these hypotheses, the project sheds light on the characteristics of the foreign policy of the authoritarian state. The argument here is that for the foreign policy of the authoritarian state, the influence of large economic interests is a significant characteristic. The argument presented in this study is that SOEs have become increasingly important for foreign policy. At the same time, this study shows that the independence of the companies has varied over this ten-year period and that they are now facing more constraints than they have in the past.

While the framework presented here might be able to work across states and find variation in types of authoritarianisms, this study only considers the case of China as an example of the argument. It uses the Chinese case as a plausibility probe of the argument. As I focus only on one state, this analysis therefore does not allow for cross-national variation. At the same time, as this framework is something few people have considered, I deem that this problem is counterbalanced by the novelty of the approach.

The dependent variable

The dependent variable in this study is defined as the degree to which state interests, economic interests, or concerns with domestic stability (*weiwen*) dominate and is defined as the ratio of these three. For the quantitative analysis, the object of analysis will be texts, that is, words, that reflect underlying motives rather than more objective measurements of, for example, physical activities or the level of government control, because it enables a stronger analysis.[67]

For the qualitative analysis, we consider the following indicators. Indicators for the hypothesis concerning *state interests* include official statements made by the Chinese leadership, such as White Papers and visits made by senior leaders to the country or a visit from the country in question to China. Another indicator is aid flows, not as the actual figure but in terms of the importance attributed to the aid given. Yet another indicator is other statements, including statements by political leaders.

Indicators for the hypothesis concerning *economic interests* include evidence that a certain acquisition was profitable,[68] including whether the rationale was to acquire a certain technology or whether it was to gain access to important reserves or assets. It also encompasses the following more specific indicators: the level of the premium paid by the acquirer for the acquisition target relative to the target's share price, how the share price of the acquisition target develops in the period close to the acquisition, and how the share price of the Chinese company involved develops around the time of the acquisition.

In terms of the indicators for the hypothesis regarding *the concern with domestic stability (weiwen)*, I consider evidence that Chinese nationals, including oil workers and construction workers, are killed in the recipient country and evidence of the attention such incidents receive domestically, including the attention given to such incidents on social media, such as *Weibo* (微博), a Chinese microblogging website. We consider evidence on social media that netizens are concerned and that the Chinese leadership takes action to mediate in the situation, such as the Ministry of Foreign Affairs (MFA) putting pressure on the country in question. Finally, we see statements from the state leaders reflecting this. The hypothesis is that if and when Chinese netizens voice criticism of such incidents on social media, this pressures the Chinese leadership to act, which will ultimately have an effect on foreign policy.[69]

Thus, overall, the indicators of the dependent variable are more indirect and impressionistic.

The argument here is that whether the state or economic interests dominate in the actual case is the best proxy for how to see whether there is consistency between the company activities and government policy. The preceding indicators for the three hypotheses are observed in the analysis of the cases that make up the study.

The independent variable

The independent variable has two parts: the *level of oil* and the *level of the strategic importance* of the various countries or regions to China.

For some analysts, the level of oil or energy supplies should be included as an indicator of strategic importance given the centrality of energy concerns for the CCP. In a number of government documents, it is clear that energy is a central concern of the Chinese leadership and regarded as part of that which the leadership considers to be in its strategic interests. Here, however, I argue that countries are important for the Chinese leadership for reasons other than oil. Thus, a country can be important to the Chinese leadership from a non-energy perspective in terms of political and military concerns having to do with territorial disputes, threats to domestic unity, and factors that contribute to destabilizing the country, such as terrorism and ethnic separatists. When considering the relationship between the government and the company in the actual case, this political and military component is as important as oil. The two can therefore be thought of as separate and can be measured independently of one another.[70]

Strategic importance signifies the strategic value of the country to the Chinese leadership. Its measurement entails a comprehensive analysis of all countries with five indicators (with weighted component parts) reflecting that which makes a country strategically important to China (see the Appendix for details).[71] The level of strategic importance is conceptualized by accounting for the following political factors (the level of political relations and its role in CCP regime stability), geographic factors (salience of territory), military/security factors (role to be played by the other great power), and economic factors (bilateral trade), as shown in table 2.2.

Table 2.2 Indicators of strategic importance

1. Level of political relations
2. Role for CCP regime stability
3. Salience of territory
4. Role for other great power
5. Share of economy

1 *Level of political relations*. The Chinese government attributes strategic importance to a country, first, in terms of the level of partnership, that is, whether diplomatic relations, a strategic partnership, or a comprehensive strategic partnership have been established, and, second, in terms of the frequency of state visits of senior leaders to the country and from the country to China,[72] including 1) visits from any Politburo members, 2) other country visits by the prime minister and president (*not* the foreign minister), and 3) military exchanges from both sides. Visits can help the Chinese NOCs overcome political opposition overseas or factors that advance Beijing's political interests.

2 *Role for CCP regime stability*. The hypothesis is that the level of regime stability relates to the threat to Chinese domestic stability and the CCP's ability to maintain power. Indicators are, first, whether an extremist group has established a branch in the recipient country with links to al-Qaeda – as the assumption is that the existence of an extremist group with links to al-Qaeda in the recipient country has implications for Chinese regime security, because it can damage Chinese economic, political, and security interests, and, second, the level of fatalities to Chinese nationals by militant activities by these (i.e., whether militant activities have been conducted against Chinese nationals and on Chinese territory) – that is, the level of fatalities involving Chinese nationals abroad. This component works both in the border regions as well as farther abroad, as in Sudan in recent years. In terms of whether extremist groups have established a branch in the country in recent years, al-Qaeda has managed to set up branches in most North African countries, including in the Sahel-belt and the Horn of Africa (e.g., Nigeria, Algeria, Egypt, Syria, and Sudan).[73] While the aim of the al-Qaeda branches in Africa – the establishment of a Muslim government in the country in question – is unrelated to China, if any terrorist or extremist movement succeeds in establishing an al-Qaeda branch, then by implication, that would be seen as a threat to China because of the possible threat that extremist movements worldwide represent to the stability of the Chinese state. Thus, the assumption is that the existence of an extremist group with links to al-Qaeda in the recipient country has implications for Chinese regime security, because it can damage Chinese economic, political, and security interests. The third indicator is relations with Taiwan: it is measured by evaluating the relations of the other country with Taiwan. Given that Chinese foreign policy has often been focused on efforts to suppress Taiwan's international presence and bilateral relationships – at least until the Ma Yingjiu administration – the Chinese leadership may calculate the importance of another country in terms of its position on the Taiwan issue.

3 *Salience of territory*. This component can be thought of as a proxy for geographic attributes.[74] Indicators for salience of territory include whether there are ethnic ties to China and the strategic location. In terms of the former component, ethnic ties to China make the country more important to the Chinese leadership. In terms of strategic location, geographic proximity to China, whether the particular country is in proximity to the sea, and its level of infrastructure are important factors for trade and export. This component also considers whether there are military bases in the country.

4 *Role for other great powers*. This geo-political component is a proxy for the importance of territory for any great power or the sphere of influence of another great power. Indicators include whether the country has a military alliance with the United States, in which case there is likely to be a US military base, the assumption being that the presence of US military bases would increase the strategic importance of the country to China. A second indicator is whether there are (or have been) United Nations' sanctions against the country, which would make the country hold greater strategic importance for China.

5 *Bilateral trade*. Even if the value of the bilateral trade in some cases correlates with the country's oil reserves, it is included here, because it is relevant when estimating the importance attributed to the country. South Africa is the best possible example of a country with high strategic importance despite having limited oil reserves.

The level of strategic importance thus has five indicators.[75] In order to measure the level of strategic importance, the components are added. Table 2.3 illustrates the level of strategic importance for each of the cases measured along the five components.

One could critique this definition of strategic importance in the preceding figure in the following way: it could be argued that the definition is unnecessarily broad. For example, factor 5, bilateral trade, is strongly correlated with "high oil," and there is a certain overlap between resource endowment and bilateral trade.

Table 2.3 Level of strategic importance[1]

Country	*1. Level of political relations*	*a. Level of partnership*	*b. Number of state visits of senior leaders to country* *– from China* *– to China*
Nigeria	1	1	1
Angola	1	1	1
Sudan	0	0	0
Tunisia	0	0	0
Kazakhstan	2	2	2
Canada	0	1	0
Uzbekistan	1	1	1
Denmark	1	2	1

[1] In the following table, the level of strategic importance of each country is assigned a numerical value for each judgment: 2 for high, 1 for medium, 0 for low.

(Continued)

Table 2.3 (Continued)

	2. Role for CCP regime stability	*a. Whether an extremist group has established a branch*	*b. Level of fatalities from militant activities (on Chinese nationals)*	*c. Relations with Taiwan*	*3. Salience of territory*	*a. Ethnic ties*	*b. Strategic location*
Nigeria	2	+	2	–	1	–	1
Angola	0	–	0	–	1	–	1
Sudan	2	+	2	–	2	–	2
Tunisia	1	+	–	–	0	–	0
Kazakhstan	2	+	0	–	2	+	2
Canada	0	–	0	–	0	–	1
Uzbekistan	2	+	0	–	2	+	2
Denmark	0	+	0	–	0	–	1

Table 2.3 (Continued)

	4. Role for other great power	*a. U.S. alliance partner*	*b. UN sanctions*	*5. Bilateral trade*	*Total*
Nigeria	2	–	–	2	2
Angola	1	–	–	2	1
Sudan	2	–	+	1	2
Tunisia	1	–	–	0	0
Kazakhstan	1	–	–	2	2
Canada	1	+	–	2	0
Uzbekistan	2	–	–	0	2
Denmark	1	+	–	0	0

One could argue that "bilateral trade" should be taken out in order to avoid overlap between strategic importance and resource endowment. However, I keep it here, because South Africa is the best possible example of a country with high strategic importance despite having limited oil reserves.

I treat the five indicators equally. Also, the default would be to treat them equally, as the starting point would be to assume that they are of equal value. Furthermore, it would be hard to find out how the Chinese leadership estimates the country (another reason why it makes sense to treat them equally).

Case selection and variation

Based on the collection of data for the preceding components of the independent variable, a case selection is made in order to ensure maximum variation. This study includes the whole universe of countries and regions. A quantitative survey, that is, a coding, of all countries in terms of their amount of oil, production of oil and oil reserves, and level of strategic importance is carried out, allowing for maximum variation on the dependent variable. Based on this assessment, four cases are selected that vary maximally in terms of the two key independent variables. This allows for high external validity and for the results to be generalized across the universe of countries. Including regions allows for the results to be checked for the significance of geography.

In order to control for confounders – that is, variables other than oil and strategic importance that influence the dependent variable – I narrow the universe of cases down and focus on only one region rather than including all of them. As the region with the most countries is Africa, I choose cases within Africa in order to allow for the greatest variation on the independent variable. Based on a coding of all of the countries in Africa in terms of the two components of the independent variable, I select four countries that vary maximally in terms of the two independent variables. The four cases selected are thus the country with the highest level of strategic importance and highest level of oil; the country with the highest level of strategic importance and lowest level of oil; the country with the lowest strategic importance and highest level of oil; and the country with the lowest strategic importance and lowest level of oil, respectively.[76] Based on the compilation of data on the countries and the case selection, four African countries were selected: Nigeria (high strategic importance/high oil), Angola (low strategic importance/ high oil), Sudan (high strategic importance/low oil), and Tunisia (low strategic importance/low oil), as illustrated in table 2.4. These comparisons are justifiable and promising for several reasons. These four ensure maximum variation. Moreover, many activities have taken place in these countries in recent years, with the exception of Tunisia, which should allow for many data entries.

The "low strategic importance/high oil" category is empty, as there is no country with abundant oil that is not of at least medium strategic importance to China. Angola would come closest to this category. While this might be a problem, it confirms the adage that what is analytically possible is not always to be found in reality.

As the African continent will not allow for the full variation on the independent variable and as I argue that it is important to control for the effect of regions, in addition to having four main cases from Africa, I include a chapter with mini-cases selected based on the full universe of countries – that is, from across regions. The mini-cases selected are Kazakhstan (high strategic importance/high oil), Canada (low strategic importance/high oil), Uzbekistan (high strategic importance/low oil), and Denmark (low strategic importance/low oil), as illustrated in table 2.5. The analysis of these mini-cases will reveal the full possible variation of the independent

Table 2.4 Outcome on the African continent

	High oil	*Low oil*
High strategic importance	Nigeria (Africa)	Sudan (Africa)
Low strategic importance	Angola (Africa)	Tunisia (Africa)

Table 2.5 Outcome for the whole universe of countries

	High oil	*Low oil*
High strategic importance	Kazakhstan (Central Asia)	Uzbekistan (Central Asia)
Low strategic importance	Canada (North America)	Denmark (Europe)

variable and examine the extent to which the conclusions I find for Africa can be generalized across regions. Given that the countries here allow for the full variation on the independent variable, the results will be able to examine the full effect of these on the cases and generate a more comprehensive analysis of the evidence of the three hypotheses presented in this study. In this way, including regions makes it possible to control the results for the role of geography. At the same time, the mini-cases chapter is intended as a supplement and will be less extensive than the main cases. They will also be of shorter length than the main cases.

Research methodology: quantitative and qualitative methods

This study applies two measurement strategies: one qualitative, the other quantitative. In terms of quantitative methods, I rely on the large-n study. In terms of the qualitative methods, I rely on the ideographic method doing case studies and interviews. Utilizing both quantitative and qualitative methods, each case study will evaluate which of the hypotheses has the preponderance of evidence, that is, whether the first, second, or third hypothesis is correct.[77] The quantitative part of the study enables a first cut at whether the hypothesis presented is supported. The qualitative part then enriches and provides further investigation for the reasons and validity of the results of the quantitative part.

The methodology of the quantitative part utilizes quantitative content analysis, that is, text analysis. Robert Philip Weber defines content analysis as "a research methodology that utilizes a set of procedures to make valid inferences from text."[78] The procedure for the content analysis is the following: materials written in Chinese are sampled from the China Academic Journals Full-text (CNKI) database (中国知网). This is the largest Chinese language database and includes different types of literature, such as CCP texts, newspaper articles, academic texts, and PhD dissertations, and can be seen as representing the discourse in the Chinese state media. The quantitative content analysis is based on sampled articles from the database. For each country, 100 articles are selected by random sampling out of a large population of articles. The sampled articles can therefore be seen as representative of the whole database. The quantitative analysis is carried out using the computer program *Yoshikoder*. Computer-aided text analysis is useful in order to analyze a large number of articles.[79] A coding scheme is developed based on the extensive qualitative reading of texts. After developing the coding scheme for the three hypotheses, I analyze each text for the term frequencies of the three terms.[80]

The qualitative part entails the thick qualitative analysis of the selected countries to allow for maximum variation in the shape of structured, focused comparisons.[81] This work involves the theory-guided process tracing of the coordination between government and company in the countries and cross-case comparison of the main hypotheses and their indicators outlined earlier. The qualitative analysis will focus on a number of key decisions that are relevant in order to illustrate whether state interests, economic interests, or a concern with domestic stability (*weiwen*) dominates in the concrete case. The qualitative part of the analysis builds on materials such as my own interviews with companies and government representatives, various "yearbooks" (年鉴/*nianjian*) published by the Chinese government, newspaper articles, and academic articles.

Finally, the project seeks to demonstrate the extent to which the measurements and conclusions from the qualitative and quantitative parts are corroborated.

Notes

1 James D. Fearon, "Domestic Political Audiences and the Escalation of International Disputes," *American Political Science Review* 88 (3) (September 1994): 577–92.
2 Fearon, "Domestic Political Audiences."
3 Jessica L. Weeks, "Audience Costs: Regime Type and Signaling Resolve," *International Organization* 62 (1) (Winter 2008): 35–64.
4 Weeks's argument builds on rational choice and game theory models; see Robert Pahre and Paul Papayoanou, "Using Game Theory to Link Domestic and International Politics," *The Journal of Conflict Resolution* 41 (1) (February 1997): 4–11; Robert Pahre, "Endogenous Domestic Institutions in Two-Level Games and Parliamentary Oversight in the European Union," *The Journal of Conflict Resolution* 41 (1) (1997): 147–74.
5 Barbara Geddes, *Paradigms and Sandcastles: Theory Building and Research Design in Comparative Politics* (Ann Arbor, MI: University of Michigan Press, 2003), 48–50; Barbara Geddes, "Authoritarian Breakdown," Paper, University of California Los Angeles (January 2004), 26, accessed January 20, 2013, www.international.ucla.edu/cms/files/authn_breakdown.pdf.
6 Geddes, "Authoritarian Breakdown."
7 Mark Peceny and Caroline C. Beer, "Dictatorial Peace?" *American Political Science Review* 96 (1) (March 2002): 15–26; Mark Peceny and Christopher K. Butler, "The Conflict Behavior of Authoritarian Regimes," *International Politics* 41 (4) (2004): 565–81; Bruce Bueno de Mesquita, Alastair Smith, Randolph M. Siverson and James D. Morrow, *The Logic of Political Survival* (Cambridge, MA: MIT Press, 2003).
8 Weeks, "Audience Costs," 35–64.
9 Gideon Rose, "Neoclassical Realism and Theories of Foreign Policy," *World Politics* 51 (1) (October 1998): 144–72.
10 Randall Schweller, "Domestic Structure and Preventive War: Are Democracies More Pacific?" *World Politics* 44 (2) (January 1992): 235–69, 248–9.
11 Robert Ross, *Chinese Security Policy: Structure, Power and Politics* (London, UK: Routledge, 2009), 3.
12 Mohammed Ayoob, *The Third World Security Predicament: State Making, Regional Conflict, and the International System* (Boulder, CO: Lynne Rienner, 1995); Edward Azar, *The Management of Protracted Social Conflict: Theory and Cases* (Hampshire, UK: Aldershot, 1990); Brian Job, ed., *The Insecurity Dilemma: National Security of Third World States* (Boulder, CO: Lynne Rienner, 1992); Brian Job, "Track 2 Diplomacy: Ideational Contribution to the Evolving Asia Pacific Security Order," in *Asian*

Security Order: Instrumental and Normative Features, ed. Mutiah Alagappa (Stanford: Stanford University Press, 2003).

13 For a review of these different approaches, see Andrew Moravcsik, "Taking Preferences Seriously: A Liberal Theory of International Politics," *International Organization* 51 (4) (Autumn 1997): 513–53.

14 For the liberal argument on the democratic peace theory, see Bruce Russett and John Oneal, *Triangulating Peace: Democracy, Interdependence and International Organizations* (New York, NY: Norton, 2001).

15 Edward D. Mansfield and Jack Snyder, "Democratization and the Danger of War," *International Security* 20 (1) (Summer 1995): 5–38; Alastair I. Johnston, "China Middle Class Attitudes Towards International Affairs: Nascent Liberalization?" *The China Quarterly* 179 (September 2004): 605.

16 The specific ten-year period from 2003–12 is examined here.

17 Kenneth Waltz, *Theory of International Politics* (Reading, MA: Addison-Wesley, 1979).

18 Christopher Layne, "The Unipolar Illusion: Why New Great Powers Will Rise," *International Security* 17 (4) (Spring 1993): 5–51; Kenneth Waltz, "Evaluating Theories," *American Political Science Review* 91 (4) (December 1997): 913–17; David Shambaugh, "Containment or Engagement of China? Calculating Beijing's Responses," *International Security* 21 (2) (Fall 1996): 180–209; John J. Mearsheimer, *The Tragedy of Great Power Politics* (New York, NY: Norton, 2001).

19 Thomas J. Christensen, "Chinese Realpolitik," *Foreign Affairs* 75 (5) (September–October 1996); Alastair Iain Johnston, *Cultural Realism: Strategic Culture and Grand Strategy in Chinese History* (Princeton, NJ: Princeton University Press, 1995).

20 Kasandra Behrndt-Eriksen, "China's Engagement in Africa: A Strategy to Secure Survival," Paper presented at the 3rd China Goes Global Conference, Harvard University, October 2, 2009.

21 Stefano Guzzini, "The Concept of Power: A Constructivist Analysis," *Millennium: Journal of International Studies* 33 (3) (June 2005): 537–8; Stephen G. Brooks, "Dueling Realisms," *International Organization* 51 (3) (Summer 1997): 445–77, 453.

22 Thomas J. Christensen, Alastair I. Johnston and Robert Ross, "Conclusions and Future Directions," in *New Directions in the Study of China's Foreign Policy*, eds. Alastair I. Johnston and Robert Ross (Stanford, CA: Stanford University Press, 2006), 379–420, 408; David Zweig and Bi Jianhai, "China's Global Hunt for Energy," *Foreign Affairs* 84 (25) (September–October 2005): 25–38.

23 Robert Ross, "China's Naval Nationalism: Sources, Prospects and the U.S. Response," *International Security* 34 (2) (Fall 2009): 46–81.

24 Abramor F.K. Organski, *World Politics* (New York, NY: Alfred A. Knopf, 1965); Abramo F.K. Organski and Jack Kugler, *The War Ledger* (Chicago: University of Chicago Press, 1980).

25 Hans J. Morgenthau, *Politics Among Nations* (New York, NY: Alfred Knopf, 1948).

26 Stephen Krasner, *Defending the National Interest: Raw Materials, Investment and U.S. Foreign Policy* (Princeton, NJ: Princeton University Press, 1978), 38.

27 David A. Baldwin, *Economic Statecraft* (Princeton: Princeton University Press, 1985).

28 Baldwin, *Economic Statecraft.*

29 The hypothesis presented pertains to the characteristics of the Chinese authoritarian state and, thus, might not be able to be generalized across authoritarian states *per se*.

30 The political economy literature and its focus on the developmental state and the liberal model can contribute with perspectives concerning the state's capacity to steer the economy. See, for example Peter Evans, *Embedded Autonomy: States and Industrial Transformation* (Princeton, NJ: Princeton University Press, 1995); Alexander Gerschenkron, *Economic Development in Historical Perspective* (Cambridge, MA: Belknap, 1962); Chalmers Johnson, "Political Institutions and Economic Performance:

The Government – Business Relationship in Japan, South Korea and Taiwan," in *The Political Economy of the New Asian Industrialism*, ed. Frederic C. Deyo (Ithaca, NY: Cornell University Press, 1987); Nicholas R. Lardy, *China's Unfinished Economic Revolution* (Washington, DC: Brookings Institution, 1998), 4, 6, 52–6.

31 Barry Naughton, *Growing Out of the Plan: Chinese Economic Reform, 1978–1993* (Cambridge, UK: Cambridge University Press, 1995); Yasheng Huang, *Capitalism with Chinese Characteristics: Entrepreneurship and the State* (New York, NY: Cambridge University Press, 2008).

32 PetroChina, Sinopec Corp. and CNOOC Ltd. Annual Reports for 1998–06.

33 PetroChina, Sinopec Corp. and CNOOC Ltd. Annual Reports for 2007–14.

34 L. Fei, "SOEs' Taxes Higher Than Private Firms," *Global Times,* August 25, 2010.

35 See, for example, Kenneth Lieberthal and Michel Oksenberg, *Policy Making in China: Leaders, Structures and Processes* (Princeton, NJ: Princeton University Press, 1988), 22; David M. Lampton, "China's Foreign and National Security Policy-Making Process: Is It Changing and Does It Matter?" in *The Making of Chinese Foreign and Security Policy in the Era of Reform, 1978–2000*, ed. David M. Lampton (Stanford, CA: Stanford University Press, 2001), 11; Andrew Mertha, "'Fragmented Authoritarianism 2.0': Political Pluralization in the Chinese Policy Process," *The China Quarterly* 200 (December 2009): 995–1012.

36 Joseph Fewsmith and Stanley Rosen: "The Domestic Context of Chinese Foreign Policy: Does Public Opinion Matter?" in *The Making of Chinese Foreign and Security Policy in the Era of Reform, 1978–2000*, ed. David M. Lampton (Stanford: Stanford University Press, 2001), 152; Andrew Mertha, *China's Water Warriors: Citizen Action and Policy Change* (Ithaca, NY: Cornell University Press, 2008), 39; Lampton, "China's Foreign and National Security Policy-Making Process," 17, 27; Linda Jakobson and Dean Knox, "New Foreign Policy Actors in China," SIPRI Policy Paper 26 (September 2010): vi, 48.

37 Lu Ning, "The Central Leadership, Supraministry Coordinating Bodies, State Council Ministries, and Party Departments," in *The Making of Chinese Foreign and Security Policy in the Era of Reform, 1978–2000*, ed. David M. Lampton (Stanford, CA: Stanford University Press, 2001), 39–60, 58.

38 A. Doak Barnett, *The Making of Foreign Policy in China: Structure and Process* (Boulder, CO: Westview Press, 1985); Alastair Iain Johnston, "Learning Versus Adaptation: Explaining Change in Chinese Arms Control Policy in the 1980s and 1990s," *The China Journal* 35 (January 1996): 34; Lampton, "China's Foreign and National Security Policy-Making Process," 32; Joseph Fewsmith, *China since Tiananmen: The Politics of Transition* (Cambridge, UK: Cambridge University Press, 2001), 6; Tang Tsou, "Chinese Politics and the Top: Factionalism or Informal Politics? Balance-of-Power Politics or a Game to Win All?" *China Journal* 34 (July 1995): 95–156; Bruce Gilley, *Tiger on the Brink: Jiang Zemin and China's New Elite* (Berkeley, CA: University of California Press), 1998.

39 Fewsmith, *China Since Tiananmen*, 6.

40 Yasheng Huang, *Inflation and Investment Controls in China: The Political Economy of Central – Local Relations during the Reform Era* (Cambridge, UK: Cambridge University Press, 1996), 58.

41 Susan L. Shirk, *The Political Logic of Economic Reform in China* (Berkeley, CA: University of California Press, 1993), 115, 338.

42 Interviews with Chinese informants, 2012.

43 Bo Kong, *China's International Petroleum Policy* (Santa Barbara, CA: Praeger), 2010.

44 *Xinhua News Agency*, "Sinopec Chairman Su Shulin Resigns," April 21, 2011.

45 Peter Hays Gries and Stanley Rosen, "Introduction: Popular Protest and State Legitimation in 21st Century China," in *State and Society in 21st Century China: Crisis, Contention and Legitimation*, eds. Peter H. Gries and Stanley Rosen (New York, NY:

Routledge, 2004), 2; Susan L. Shirk, *Fragile Superpower: How China's Internal Politics Could Derail Its Peaceful Rise* (Oxford, UK: Oxford University Press, 2007).

46 These are also called "mass disturbances." China's Ministry of Public Security (MPS) reports numbers on "mass disturbances" involving fifteen or more people. These mass incidents include rural riots, violent urban demonstrations, organized religious protests, and demands to end one-party rule. The sources of the mass incidents are primarily local single-issue protests in the shape of conflict over fired workers and poorly compensated farmland and protests over pollution. The State Security Bureau has released figures of 58,000 protests in 2003; 74,000 in 2004; and 87,000 in 2005. See Albert Keidel, "China's Social Unrest: The Story Behind the Stories," *Carnegie Endowment Policy Brief* 48 (September 2006): 2–8.

47 Shirk, *Fragile Superpower*, 6.

48 E.g., during 2005, Hu Jintao told universities and think-tanks to update the political lessons of Tiananmen by analyzing the "color revolutions" that brought down authoritarian regimes in countries like Serbia (2000), Georgia (2003), Ukraine (2004), and Kyrgyzstan (2005) (Shirk, *Fragile Superpower*, 8–11, 54).

49 Christensen, Johnston, and Ross, "Conclusions and Future Directions," 408.

50 Shirk, *Fragile Superpower*.

51 In the context of China, nationalism is based on the idea of the "century of humiliation," which can only end when Japan apologises, in the event of the reunification of Taiwan, or if the United States treats China as an equal (Peter Hays Gries, *China's New Nationalism: Pride, Politics, and Diplomacy* [Berkeley, CA: University of California Berkeley Press, 2004]; Peter Hays Gries, "Popular Nationalism and State Legitimation in China," in *State and Society in 21st Century China: Crisis, Contention and Legitimation*, eds. Peter H. Gries and Stanley Rosen [New York, NY: Routledge, 2004], 181).

52 Peter J. Katzenstein, "International Relations and Domestic Structures: Foreign Economic Policies of Advanced Industrial States," *International Organization* 30 (Winter 1976): 1–45; Douglas C. Foyle, "Public Opinion and Foreign Policy: Elite Beliefs as Mediating Variable," *International Studies Quarterly* 41 (1) (1997): 141–69; James Reilly, *Strong Society, Smart State: The Rise of Public Opinion in China's Japan Policy* (New York, NY: Columbia University Press, 2012), 1, 3, 7, 24, 52–3.

53 Shirk, *Fragile Superpower*, 11.

54 It is worth noting that what is at stake is CCP rule, not the state.

55 For an article from the authoritative "求是杂志" (Qiushi Zazhi) that demonstrates the control of CCP, see *求是杂志 (Qiushi Zazhi) (求是杂志)*, 两论起家传统与大庆的科学发展 ("Two Views on Scientific Development as Related to the Daqing Tradition") 11 (2008): 40–1.

56 E.g., Victor Shih, *Factions and Finance in China: Elite Conflict and Inflation* (Cambridge, UK: Cambridge University Press, 2010), 7–8.

57 Edward Steinfeld, *Forging Reform in China: The Fate of State-Owned Industry* (Cambridge, UK: Cambridge University Press, 1998), 74.

58 Steinfeld, *Forging Reform in China*, 74, 45–6.

59 Interview with Chinese informant, 2012. For studies comparing the performance of privatized and state firms, see, for example, Roman Frydman, Cheryl W. Gray, Marek Hessel, and Andrzej Rapaczynski, "When Does Privatization Work? The Impact of Private Ownership on Corporate Performance in The Transition Economies," *Quarterly Journal of Economics* 114 (4) (1999): 1153–91; Peter Hartley and Kenneth B. Medlock, "A Model of the Operation of A National Oil Company," *Energy Economics* (Rice University: James Baker III Institute for Public Policy, 2007); Kasandra Behrndt-Eriksen, "Profitability of NOCs: A Case Study," paper presented at the Chinese Politics Seminar, J.F. Kennedy School of Government, Harvard University, May 2011.

60 Raymond Vernon, *In the Hurricane's Eye: The Troubled Prospects of Multinational Enterprises* (Cambridge, MA: Harvard University Press, 1998).

61 I thank Professor Tony Saich for this point.

62 J. Katzer et al., *The Future of Coal: Options for a Carbon-Constrained World* (Cambridge, MA: Massachusetts Institute of Technology, 2007), accessed December 15, 2015, http://web.mit.edu/coal/The_Future_of_Coal.pdf.

63 Edward Steinfeld, *Playing Our Game: Why China's Rise Doesn't Threaten the West* (Oxford, UK: Oxford University Press, 2010).

64 Philip Andrews-Speed, *Energy Policy and Regulation in the People's Republic of China* (The Hague: Kluver Law International, 2004).

65 Andrews-Speed, *Energy Policy and Regulation in the People's Republic of China*, 358.

66 In the preceding matrix, "domestic stability" refers to the "*concern* with domestic stability." Moreover, state interests and *weiwen* are combined here (denoted as "state interests / *weiwen*"), as is also done in the quantitative analysis. This is because when state interests are expected to dominate, so is the concern with domestic stability (*weiwen*), as the two have the same driver. For example, much of the concern with worker safety directly bears on national security and therefore has direct security implications. Thus, what might be seen as evidence of state interests might in turn be evidence of the concern with domestic stability. Still, conceptually, they are treated here as separate.

67 See Steinfeld, *Forging Reform in China*, 74; John D. Huber and Charles R. Shipan, "Politics, Delegation, and Bureaucracy," in *The Oxford Handbook of Political Economy*, eds. Barry R. Weingast and Donald A. Wittman (New York, NY: Oxford University Press, 2006), 256–72.

68 The term "profitable" is used in the sense of being "accretive," defined as "accretive acquisitions of assets or businesses will add more value than the cost of the acquisition, either immediately or over time."

69 E.g., the Ministry of Foreign Affairs (MFA) has a *Weibo* account where netizens can participate in the debate (微博外交部/Weibo waijiaobu). Some companies, such as CNPC, also have their own *Weibo* site (Interview with Chinese informant, 2014).

70 The "level of oil" refers to the figures for production and total reserves. Here, both oil and gas are considered as part of the "oil" category, and they are added as 1 + 1, because, analytically speaking, they can be thought of as equally important sources of imports to China that cannot be substituted.

71 For the most part, the measures are drawn from a ten-year period (2002–12) covering most of the outward activities of the Chinese energy companies following the Going Out (走出去) policy.

72 For a detailed list of travels by the leadership, see Behrndt-Eriksen, *Chinese Energy Companies' Acquisitions Abroad*, 360–75.

73 Richard A. Lobban, *Global Security Watch – Sudan* (Santa Barbara, CA: Praeger, 2010), 75.

74 Inspired by Mitchel and Hensel, I here introduce a number of indicators of the salience of territory that can be used as a proxy for the strategic importance of the country to China. Sara M. Mitchell and Paul R. Hensel, "International Institutions and Compliance with Agreements," *American Journal of Political Science* 51 (4) (2007): 721–37. According to Mitchell and Hensel, territorial claim salience is based on six indicators: homeland territory, prior exercised sovereignty, contiguity, presence of valuable resources, strategic location, and ethnic ties. At the same time, note that Mitchel and Hensel's study is only applicable to states that share a land border with China.

75 This measurement is inspired by Mitchel and Hensel's measurement of importance, e.g., Mitchell and Hensel in their account of "salience of territory" use six factors (Sara M. Mitchell and Paul R. Hensel, "International Institutions and Compliance with Agreements," *American Journal of Political Science* 51 (4) (2007): 721–37). Other scholars build on this model, e.g., Taylor Fravel, who in his account of the salience

of disputed territory uses the same six factors (Taylor Fravel, *Strong Borders, Secure Nation: Cooperation and Conflict in China's Territorial Disputes* (Princeton, NJ: Princeton University Press, 2008).

76 According to BP 2012, proven reserves: oil= 0 billion barrels, gas= 0 trillion m^3.

77 Ole. R. Holsti, *Content Analysis for the Social Sciences and Humanities* (Reading, MA: Addison-Wesley, 1969), 17.

78 Robert Philip Weber, *Basic Content Analysis* (London, UK: Sage, 1985), 9. 12–21; Kimberly A. Neuendorf, *The Content Analysis Guidebook* (Thousand Oaks, CA: Sage, 2002), 10–13.

79 Kimberly A. Neuendorf, *The Content Analysis Guidebook* (Thousand Oaks, CA: Sage, 2002); Yu-Wen Chen, "Quantitative Content Analysis of Chinese Texts? A Methodological Note," *Journal of Chinese Political Science* 16 (December 2011): 431–43, 442.

80 Richard Craggs and Mary M. Wood, "Evaluating Discourse and Dialogue Coding Schemes," *Computational Linguistics* 31 (3) (September 2005): 289–96; 294; Holsti, *Content Analysis for the Social Sciences and Humanities*, 95.

81 My approach here builds on the comparative case-study methodology developed by Alexander George (Alexander L. George and Andrew Bennett, *Case Studies and Theory Development in the Social Sciences* (Cambridge, MA: MIT Press, 2005), 67–72).

References

Andrews-Speed, Philip. *Energy Policy and Regulation in the People's Republic of China*. The Hague: Kluwer Law International, 2004.

Ayoob, Mohammed. *The Third World Security Predicament: State Making, Regional Conflict, and the International System*. Boulder, CO: Lynne Rienner, 1995.

Azar, Edward. *The Management of Protracted Social Conflict: Theory and Cases*. Hampshire, UK: Aldershot, 1990.

Baldwin, David A. *Economic Statecraft*. Princeton, NJ: Princeton University Press, 1985.

Barnett, A. Doak. *The Making of Foreign Policy in China: Structure and Process*. Boulder, CO: Westview, 1985.

Behrndt-Eriksen, T. Kasandra. "China's Engagement in Africa. A Strategy to Secure Survival." Paper presented at the 3rd China Goes Global Conference, Harvard University, October 2, 2009.

Behrndt-Eriksen, T. Kasandra, "Chinese Energy Companies' Acquisitions Abroad. Implications for the Foreign Policy of an Authoritarian State." PhD diss., University of Copenhagen, 2016.

Behrndt-Eriksen, T. Kasandra. "Profitability of NOCs: A Case Study." Paper presented at the Chinese Politics Seminar, J.F. Kennedy School of Government, Harvard University, May 2011.

Brooks, Stephen G. "Dueling Realisms." *International Organization* 51 (3) (Summer 1997): 445–77.

Bueno de Mesquita, Bruce, Alastair Smith, Randolph M. Siverson and James D. Morrow. *The Logic of Political Survival*. Cambridge, MA: MIT Press, 2003.

Chen, Yu-Wen. "Quantitative Content Analysis of Chinese Texts? A Methodological Note." *Journal of Chinese Political Science* 16 (December 2011): 431–43.

Christensen, Thomas J. "Chinese Realpolitik." *Foreign Affairs* 75 (5) (September–October 1996): 37–52.

Christensen, Thomas J., Alastair I. Johnston and Robert Ross. "Conclusions and Future Directions." In *New Directions in the Study of China's Foreign Policy*, edited by Alastair I. Johnston and Robert Ross, 379–420. Stanford, CA: Stanford University Press, 2006.

Craggs, Richard and Mary M. Wood. "Evaluating Discourse and Dialogue Coding Schemes." *Computational Linguistics* 31 (3) (September 2005): 289–96.

Evans, Peter. *Embedded Autonomy: States and Industrial Transformation*. Princeton, NJ: Princeton University Press, 1995.

Fearon, James D. "Domestic Political Audiences and the Escalation of International Disputes." *American Political Science Review* 88 (3) (September 1994): 577–92.

Fei, L. "SOEs' Taxes Higher Than Private Firms." *Global Times*, August 25, 2010.

Fewsmith, Joseph. *China Since Tiananmen: The Politics of Transition*. Cambridge, UK: Cambridge University Press, 2001.

Fewsmith, Joseph and Stanley Rosen. "The Domestic Context of Chinese Foreign Policy: Does Public Opinion Matter?" In *The Making of Chinese Foreign and Security Policy in the Era of Reform, 1978–2000*, edited by David M. Lampton. Stanford, CA: Stanford University Press.

Foyle, Douglas C. "Public Opinion and Foreign Policy: Elite Beliefs as Mediating Variable." *International Studies Quarterly* 41 (1) (1997): 141–69.

Fravel, Taylor. *Strong Borders, Secure Nation: Cooperation and Conflict in China's Territorial Disputes*. Princeton, NJ: Princeton University Press, 2008.

Frydman, Roman, Cheryl W. Gray, Marek Hessel and Andrzej Rapaczynski. "When Does Privatization Work? The Impact of Private Ownership on Corporate Performance in The Transition Economies." *Quarterly Journal of Economics* 114 (4) (1999): 1153–91.

Geddes, Barbara. "Authoritarian Breakdown." University of California Los Angeles, January 2004. Accessed January 20, 2013. www.international.ucla.edu/cms/files/authn_breakdown.pdf.

Geddes, Barbara. *Paradigms and Sandcastles: Theory Building and Research Design in Comparative Politics*. Ann Arbor, MI: University of Michigan Press, 2003.

George, Alexander L. and Andrew Bennett. *Case Studies and Theory Development in the Social Sciences*. Cambridge, MA: MIT Press, 2005.

Gerschenkron, Alexander. *Economic Development in Historical Perspective*. Cambridge, MA: Belknap, 1962.

Gilley, Bruce. *Tiger on the Brink: Jiang Zemin and China's New Elite*. Berkeley, CA: University of California Press, 1998.

Gries, Peter Hays. *China's New Nationalism: Pride, Politics, and Diplomacy*. Berkeley, CA: University of California Berkeley Press, 2004.

Gries, Peter Hays. "Popular Nationalism and State Legitimation in China." In *State and Society in 21st century China: Crisis, Contention and Legitimation*, edited by Peter H. Gries and Stanley Rosen, 180–94. New York, NY: Routledge, 2004.

Gries, Peter Hays and Stanley Rosen. "Introduction: Popular Protest and State Legitimation in 21st Century China." In *State and Society in 21st Century China: Crisis, Contention and Legitimation*, edited by Peter H. Gries and Stanley Rosen, 1–23. New York, NY: Routledge, 2004.

Guzzini, Stefano. "The Concept of Power: A Constructivist Analysis." *Millennium: Journal of International Studies* 33 (3) (June 2005): 537–8.

Hartley, Peter and Kenneth B. Medlock. "A Model of the Operation of A National Oil Company." Energy Economics, Rice University: James Baker III Institute for Public Policy, 2007.

Holsti, Ole R. *Content Analysis for the Social Sciences and Humanities*. Reading, MA: Addison-Wesley, 1969.

Huang, Yasheng. *Capitalism with Chinese Characteristics: Entrepreneurship and the State*. New York, NY: Cambridge University Press, 2008.

Huang, Yasheng. *Inflation and Investment Controls in China: The Political Economy of Central – Local Relations during the Reform Era*. Cambridge, UK: Cambridge University Press, 1996.

Huber, John D. and Charles R. Shipan. "Politics, Delegation, and Bureaucracy." In *The Oxford Handbook of Political Economy*, edited by Barry R. Weingast and Donald A. Wittman, 250–72. New York, NY: Oxford University Press, 2006.

Jakobson, Linda and Dean Knox. "New Foreign Policy Actors in China." SIPRI Policy Paper No. 26, Stockholm: Stockholm International Peace Research Institute (September 2010).

Job, Brian, ed. *The Insecurity Dilemma: National Security of Third World States*. Boulder, CO: Lynne Rienner, 1992.

Job, Brian. "Track 2 Diplomacy: Ideational Contribution to the Evolving Asia Pacific Security Order." In *Asian Security Order: Instrumental and Normative Features*, edited by Mutiah Alagappa, 241–79. Stanford: Stanford University Press, 2003.

Johnson, Chalmers. "Political Institutions and Economic Performance: The Government – Business Relationship in Japan, South Korea and Taiwan." In *The Political Economy of the New Asian Industrialism*, edited by Frederic D. Deyo, 136–64. Ithaca, NY: Cornell University Press, 1987.

Johnston, Alastair I. "China Middle Class Attitudes Towards International Affairs: Nascent Liberalization?" *The China Quarterly* 179 (September 2004): 603–28.

Johnston, Alastair I. *Cultural Realism: Strategic Culture and Grand Strategy in Chinese History*. Princeton, NJ: Princeton University Press, 1995.

Johnston, Alastair I. "Learning Versus Adaptation: Explaining Change in Chinese Arms Control Policy in the 1980s and 1990s." *The China Journal* 35 (January 1996): 27–61.

Katzenstein, Peter J. "International Relations and Domestic Structures: Foreign Economic Policies of Advanced Industrial States." *International Organization* 30 (Winter 1976): 1–45.

Katzer, J. et al. *The Future of Coal: Options for a Carbon-Constrained World*. MIT Press, 2007. Accessed 12/15/2015. http://web.mit.edu/coal/The_Future_of_Coal.pdf.

Keidel, Albert. "China's Social Unrest: The Story Behind the Stories." *Carnegie Endowment Policy Brief*, 48 (September 2006): 2–8.

Kong, Bo. *China's International Petroleum Strategy*. Santa Barbara, CA: Praeger, 2010.

Krasner, Stephen. *Defending the National Interest: Raw Materials, Investment and U.S. Foreign Policy*. Princeton, NJ: Princeton University Press, 1978.

Lampton, David M. "China's Foreign and National Security Policy-Making Process: Is It Changing and Does It Matter?" In *The Making of Chinese Foreign and Security Policy in the Era of Reform, 1978–2000*, edited by David M. Lampton, 1–38. Stanford, CA: Stanford University Press, 2001.

Lardy, Nicholas R. *China's Unfinished Economic Revolution*. Washington, DC: Brookings Institution, 1998.

Layne, Christopher. "The Unipolar Illusion: Why New Great Powers Will Rise." *International Security* 17 (4) (Spring 1993): 5–51.

Li Tianxing [李天星]. 友谊长存, 携手发展" – 写在中国石油苏丹项目投产 10 周年之际 [Friendship forever, joining hands in Development – written at the 10 year anniversary of the operation of CNPC's Sudan project], *中国石油企业* (Chinese Oil Companies), November 15, 2009.

Li Zhongfa [李忠发]. 中苏合作给苏丹带来石油与和平 ["Sino – Sudan Cooperation Brings Oil and Peace to Sudan"]. *新华每日电讯 (Xinhua Daily Telegraph)*, November 19, 2009.

Lieberthal, Kenneth and Michel Oksenberg. *Policy Making in China: Leaders, Structures and Processes*. Princeton, NJ: Princeton University Press, 1988.

Lobban, Robert A. *Global Security Watch: Sudan*. Santa Barbara, CA: Praeger, 2010.

Lu Ning. "The Central Leadership, Supraministry Coordinating Bodies, State Council Ministries, and Party Departments." In *The Making of Chinese Foreign and Security Policy in the Era of Reform, 1978–2000*, edited by David M. Lampton, 39–60. Stanford, CA: Stanford University Press, 2001.

Mansfield, Edward D. and Jack Snyder. "Democratization and the Danger of War." *International Security* 20 (1) (Summer 1995): 5–38.

Mearsheimer, John J. *The Tragedy of Great Power Politics*. New York, NY: Norton, 2001.

Mertha, Andrew. *China's Water Warriors: Citizen Action and Policy Change*. Ithaca, NY: Cornell University Press, 2008.

Mertha, Andrew. " 'Fragmented Authoritarianism 2.0': Political Pluralization in the Chinese Policy Process." *The China Quarterly* 200 (December 2009): 995–1012.

Mitchell, Sara M. and Paul R. Hensel. "International Institutions and Compliance with Agreements." *American Journal of Political Science* 51 (4) (2007): 721–37.

Moravcsik, Andrew. "Taking Preferences Seriously: A Liberal Theory of International Politics." *International Organization* 51 (4) (Autumn 1997): 513–53.

Morgenthau, Hans J. *Politics Among Nations*. New York, NY: Alfred Knopf, 1948.

Naughton, Barry. *Growing Out of the Plan: Chinese Economic Reform, 1978–1993*. Cambridge, UK: Cambridge University Press, 1995.

Neuendorf, Kimberly A. *The Content Analysis Guidebook*. Thousand Oaks, CA: Sage, 2002.

Oil Lands Research. [石油政工研究]. 传承铁人精神 建设钢铁队伍 ("Passing on the Ironman Spirit, Building Steel Troops"), March 30, 2009.

Organski, Abramo F.K. *World Politics*. New York, NY: Alfred A. Knopf, 1965.

Organski, Abramo F.K. and J. Kugler. *The War Ledger*. Chicago, IL: University of Chicago Press, 1980.

Pahre, Robert. "Endogenous Domestic Institutions in Two-Level Games and Parliamentary Oversight in the European Union." *The Journal of Conflict Resolution* 41 (1) (1997): 147–74.

Pahre, Robert and Paul Papayoanou. "Using Game Theory to Link Domestic and International Politics." *The Journal of Conflict Resolution* 41 (1) (February 1997): 4–11.

Peceny, Mark and Caroline C. Beer. "Dictatorial Peace?" *American Political Science Review* 96 (1) (March 2002): 15–26.

Peceny, Mark and Christopher K. Butler. "The Conflict Behavior of Authoritarian Regimes." *International Politics* 41 (4) (2004): 565–81.

Qiushi Zazhi. (*求是杂志*), 两论起家传统与大庆的科学发展 ("Two Views on Scientific Development as related to the Daqing Tradition") 11 (2008): 40–1.

Reilly, James. *Strong Society, Smart State: The Rise of Public Opinion in China's Japan Policy*. New York, NY: Columbia University Press, 2012.

Rose, Gideon. "Neoclassical Realism and Theories of Foreign Policy." *World Politics* 51 (1) (October 1998): 144–72.

Ross, Robert. "China's Naval Nationalism. Sources, Prospects and the U.S. Response." *International Security* 34 (2) (Fall 2009): 46–81.

Ross, Robert. *Chinese Security Policy: Structure, Power and Politics*. London, UK: Routledge, 2009.

Russett, Bruce and John Oneal. *Triangulating Peace: Democracy, Interdependence and International Organizations*. New York, NY: Norton, 2001.

Schweller, Randall. "Domestic Structure and Preventive War: Are Democracies More Pacific?" *World Politics* 44 (2) (January 1992): 235–69.

Shambaugh, David. "Containment or Engagement of China? Calculating Beijing's Responses." *International Security* 21 (2) (Fall 1996): 180–209.

Shih, Victor. *Factions and Finance in China: Elite Conflict and Inflation*. Cambridge, UK: Cambridge University Press, 2010.

Shirk, Susan L. *Fragile Superpower: How China's Internal Politics Could Derail Its Peaceful Rise*. Oxford, UK: Oxford University Press, 2007.

Shirk, Susan L. *The Political Logic of Economic Reform in China*. Berkeley, CA: University of California Press, 1993.

Steinfeld, Edward. *Forging Reform in China: The Fate of State-Owned Industry*. Cambridge, UK: Cambridge University Press, 1998.

Steinfeld, Edward. *Playing Our Game: Why China's Rise Doesn't Threaten the West*. Oxford, UK: Oxford University Press, 2010.

Tsou, Tang. "Chinese Politics and the Top: Factionalism or Informal Politics? Balance-of-Power Politics or a Game to Win All?" *The China Journal* 34 (July 1995): 95–156.

Vernon, Raymond. *In the Hurricane's Eye: The Troubled Prospects of Multinational Enterprises*. Cambridge, MA: Harvard University Press, 1998.

Waltz, Kenneth. "Evaluating Theories." *American Political Science Review* 91 (4) (December 1997): 913–17.

Waltz, Kenneth. *Theory of International Politics*. Reading, MA: Addison-Wesley, 1979.

Wang Dongmei [王冬梅] and Li Zhanbin [李占彬]. 中国石油 ：用真诚奉献在异国创造和谐 ["CNPC: Creating Harmony Abroad through Sincere Devotion"], *工人日报* (*Workers' Daily*), January 16, 2008.

Weber, Robert P. *Basic Content Analysis*. London, UK: Sage, 1985.

Weeks, Jessica L. "Audience Costs: Regime Type and Signaling Resolve." *International Organization* 62 (1 (Winter 2008): 35–64.

Wu Fugui [吴富贵]. 中国石油健儿建功苏丹 ("CNPC's Heroes' Achievements in Sudan"). *国际人才交流* (*International Talent*) May 6, 2003.

Xinhua News Agency. "Sinopec Chairman Su Shulin Resigns." April 21, 2011.

Zweig, David and Bi Jianhai. "China's Global Hunt for Energy." *Foreign Affairs* 84 (25) (September–October 2005): 25–38.

3 The Chinese energy sector

This chapter provides a background for understanding the role of Chinese energy companies *vis-à-vis* the Chinese government. It provides context for understanding how Chinese companies operate domestically, as well as the relationship between the companies and the government. While the research question that ties this book together addresses the decisions made in individual countries, a closer focus on the Chinese energy administration and the relationship between the government and Chinese NOCs illustrates why it makes sense to operate with a distinction between economic and state interests, in the case of China as well. The economic-state interests distinction hinges on the assumption that the companies have an individual interest that is distinct from government interests and that they can be thought of as profit-maximizing.

The chapter briefly presents the Chinese energy administration, the different institutions within the government involved in energy decision-making, the history of the Chinese energy companies, and a history of the reform of the energy sector. Based on that background, the chapter examines the respective levers of control available to the government and companies. While analysis of decisions by the Chinese leadership as relates to government output is difficult to illuminate given the lack of transparency that characterizes the Chinese state, this chapter includes insights into this process to the extent possible.

The structure of the Chinese energy administration

This section presents the energy administration in China and the different government institutions involved in regulating the energy sector. The focus here is primarily on the supply side of Chinese energy governance.[1] The history of the three large energy companies – China National Petroleum Corporation (CNPC), China Petrochemical Corp. (Sinopec), and China National Offshore Oil Corporation (CNOOC) – can be traced back to October 1, 1949, when the Chinese government formed a Fuel Industry Ministry dedicated to the management of fuel. In July 1955, it was replaced by the Ministry of Petroleum Industry (MPI), which was to manage the petroleum industry. At this time, there was no distinction between the government and the petroleum industry, because the latter was simply part of the former. In 1988, the Ministry of Energy was established. At this time, the companies were established from the Ministries of Petroleum Industry, Coal Industry, and Nuclear Industry, while their administrative functions were transferred along with the power sector of the Ministry of Water Resources and Electric Power to the newly formed Ministry of Energy.[2]

Thus, the government created the CNPC after disbanding the Ministry of Petroleum Industry in 1988. This company was to be responsible for all upstream activities in China. Earlier, in 1983, Sinopec was established, and the downstream (refining and marketing) assets of the MPI and the Ministry of Chemical Industry were transferred to this new company. In 1982, CNOOC was established as a corporation under the Ministry of Petroleum Industry and was granted the exclusive right and responsibility to exploit offshore oil and gas resources in joint ventures with overseas partners. CNOOC is China's largest offshore oil and gas producer. In fact, after China's reform and opening up, the Chinese offshore oil industry was the first sector in China to start operations abroad and to invite foreign companies to China. Whereas Sinopec and CNOOC are both ministry-level companies, CNOOC has the lower status of a general bureau. The three large state-owned energy companies, CNOOC, CNPC, and Sinopec, hold a virtual monopoly on the Chinese energy industry.

Until 2004, there was a clear division of labor between the three companies: CNPC was in charge of domestic and external production of oil and gas; Sinopec was in charge of the downstream sector, including the refining business; and CNOOC conducted domestic and external exploration in joint ventures. Until then, CNPC and Sinopec (together with Sinochem and Zhuhai Zhenrong) had a monopoly on the import of crude oil, but in April 2004, CNOOC was also granted the right to import oil. While smaller domestic competitors have since emerged, they have not been able to challenge the current monopoly of the three large NOCs. Moreover, CNPC and Sinopec have since been granted approval to conduct offshore exploration, thereby breaking the CNOOC monopoly on these activities.

The three large NOCs have all created subsidiaries that have become listed on both the Hong Kong and New York stock exchanges. The parent company is the majority shareholder of the listed companies. CNPC owns 88 percent of its subsidiary, PetroChina; Sinopec owns 76 percent of its subsidiary, Sinopec Corporation; and CNOOC owns 66 percent of its subsidiary, CNOOC Ltd.[3]

The reform process

The energy sector in China has been characterized by numerous reforms in recent years. In particular, major government and industry reorganizations took place in 1993, 1998, 2003, and 2008.[4] I focus here on the most important of these reforms.

The Ministry of Energy, which had been created when the MPI was dissolved in 1988, was disbanded in 1993. From then until 2003, the State Development Planning Commission (SDPC) and State Economic and Trade Commission (SETC) were tasked with the responsibility for the energy sector. In 1998, another reform of the energy industry took place. In this process, 15 ministries were abolished, including the Ministries for Coal and Electrical Power, and the structure of many industrial sectors was changed in order to separate government and enterprise management. In this process of decentralization, many tasks previously undertaken by the Ministry of Petroleum and then the Ministry of Energy were to be undertaken by various actors, including the newly created companies. Furthermore, in preparation for China's entry into the World Trade Organization (WTO), a process took place in which core assets of the NOCs were listed on both domestic and foreign stock markets.

In 2003, the SETC was dissolved, and in its place, the National Development and Reform Commission (NDRC) Energy Bureau under the NDRC was established. The Energy Bureau was granted responsibility for coordinating various government energy plans and policies. Then, in 2005, the 13-member National Energy Leading Small Group (NELG), headed by the Chinese premier (then Wen Jiabao), and its secretariat, the State Energy Office (SEO), were established and tasked with coordinating the different horizontal ministries with petroleum portfolios. However, this agency was largely seen as failing in this endeavor.

As a result, in 2008, the government made an attempt to recentralize some of its power over energy policy. That year, the National Energy Administration (NEA) and the National Energy Commission (NEC) were established, both under the NDRC. NEA was to be responsible for managing the energy industry, drafting energy plans and policies, and approving foreign energy investments. NEC replaced the National Energy Leading Group; it is primarily a discussion body intended to strengthen energy decision-making and coordination.[5] These steps were taken in response to problems that the country had experienced, including power outages, and concerns with the growing demand for energy imports.

Even so, despite attempts to recentralize some of the decision-making in the Chinese energy sector in recent years, it is generally acknowledged that the Chinese energy sector is marked by a range of different problems. Given the lack of a ministry to oversee important decisions, the authority over the energy sector at the national level is fractured among many government agencies, the most important of which is the NDRC; others include the NEA, NEC, Ministry of Land and Resources, Ministry of Commerce, Ministry of Finance, and Ministry of Foreign Affairs. This means that decisions at the central level must be reached by consensus through bargaining, which involves many actors. Consequently, Chinese energy decision-making can be characterized as rather messy and occasionally the result of fighting among different actors, at both central and local levels. Given the lack of government authority in the energy sector,[6] one might speculate whether reduced state capacity is the result.

While the question of whether to re-create a Ministry for Energy has been debated in recent years, when both the former government (2008–13) and current government (2013–18) were formed, the proposal has been dismissed thus far.

The relationship between the NOCs and the central government

This section casts light on the relationship between the energy companies (NOCs) and the central government – that is, the levers of control available to the government *vis-à-vis* the companies. In fact, most of the literature on Chinese energy governance deals to some extent with the question of the ability of the government to control the NOCs.

Most of the analysis of China's energy governance has placed the central government in the driver's seat. Here, the companies are viewed as an extension of the state that can utilize state resources, including access to state financing and diplomacy. Here, of course, the problem becomes determining what is evidence of control.

Another part of the literature assumes that the companies are independent: they make autonomous decisions on their purchases and are profit-driven. This perspective rests on the idea that through the economic reforms initiated in the early 1980s, the Chinese economy and the Chinese energy sector have been increasingly liberalized and decentralized.[7] Following developmental state theory, the energy sector is seen as a strategic sector of the economy that is expected to remain more within the control of the central government than other sectors.[8] Thus, in terms of the hypothesis about Chinese liberalization, the energy sector can be seen as a "hard case." Still, along the lines of the argument about the liberalization of the Chinese energy sector, economic liberalization has even spread to the Chinese energy sector. This gradual spread of market elements in the economy has reduced the capacity of the government to exert control.

Part of this second perspective draws on the principal-agent literature when analyzing the relationship between the Chinese government and the energy companies.[9] Along these lines, the Chinese government delegates authority to the NOCs to implement government policies, after which it is up to the NOCs to decide where and how policies are implemented.[10] Referring to the principal-agent distinction, Trevor Houser, for example, focuses on the domestic price dynamic, arguing that while Beijing actively encouraged overseas investment in the past, the companies are now taking the lead and shaping policy to suit economic interests.[11] A few scholars are somewhere between these two perspectives, arguing that there is evidence of both and that, in the words of Bo Kong, "In the post-reform era, the Chinese petroleum economy is now governed by both the Chinese government and the NOCs."[12] The general problem with this body of literature is that it becomes tautological as, on the one hand, it argues that there is a strategy from the government and that the government is in control of the companies. At the same time, however, it assumes that the companies are in the driver's seat.

Alternative theory: local actors

Yet another perspective on the NOCs and the government is that in fact when considering the Chinese energy policy-making process, one has to consider the local level as between central and local governments, a large number of actors are involved and seek to influence decision-making.[13] The multiplicity of actors involved in the process and the fragmented character of the Chinese energy administration make the assumption of government control with the NOCs difficult. J. Katzer et al. observe that given the rapid growth of energy consumption in China, "actors at the grass roots level are making key decisions about China's physical and technological infrastructure – decisions with profound consequences for its long-term energy development."[14] Given the particular path of economic reform in China, actors at the local level, including local governments, local power producers, and so on can play a role in energy decision-making. As a result, the boundaries between state and non-state, public and private, commercial and non-commercial, and central and local have become blurred.

One could argue, in fact, that a three-layered energy decision-making system in China has developed with actors at both the central, "mid," and local levels all vying for influence.[15] Along these lines, China's energy policy-making process can be seen as a domain for negotiations among strong actors at both the central and local levels with conflicting interests, including companies, ministries, and individuals.

Here, however, we simply focus on the relationship between the companies and the government and the tools available to the government to control the companies.

Government control with the companies

The party-state has certain elements of power *vis-à-vis* the energy companies – that is, ways to influence the activities of energy actors, including through the ownership structure, the Nomenklatura system, the government investment approval system, the government's role as creditor and regulator, and finally government policy.

In terms of *ownership structure*, the Chinese NOCs are majority-owned by the government; roughly 70 percent of the shares are owned by the government. Thus, one avenue of control is that of the state as the majority shareholder. As one government official explained, "maybe the companies have shareholders and have made IPOs but the majority of these shares are held by the government (控股/konggu). So, yes, the CCP is in control."[16] However, while the Chinese government formally owns the companies, ownership does not always equate to control. The institution tasked to exercise formal authority over China's largest SOEs, including the NOCs, is the State Asset Supervision and Administration Commission (SASAC). SASAC performs the rights and obligations of shareholder on behalf of the government.

However, as the SASAC does not collect their profits (the NOCs and other large SOEs are only required to pay taxes, not dividends of their profits); nor does it appoint their top leaders (although it does choose their high-level managers). It is rather passive.[17]

A more important avenue of government control is through the *Nomenklatura system*, the system of appointing personnel of the large SOEs (for more detail, see Chapter 2).[18] The top leaders of the NOCs, including the company chairman and president, are directly appointed by the Organization Department of the CCP. The chairman then appoints the board. The executives of the listed subsidiaries of CNPC, Sinopec, and CNOOC are also appointed by the Organization Department. Importantly, the decisions by the Organization Department are subject to endorsement by the Politburo Standing Committee. There is often an overlap between NOC managers and senior government leaders, as CCP leaders and NOC leaders often "travel across" positions in the respective entities.[19] Importantly, this overlap can serve as a tool for the Chinese state to put SOE managers under the management of the CCP. In other words, the CCP appointment system can function as a way to control the NOC leaders and demonstrate the CCP's power.

The *government investment approval system* is another avenue through which the government can exercise control over the NOCs. All investments by the NOCs, both domestic and international, are subject to approval by the NDRC and the State Council. Specifically, all investments by the NOCs overseas larger than $30 million require approval from the NDRC. This was up from $1 million prior to 2004.[20] In turn, investments by the NOCs abroad that are worth more than $300 million require State Council approval.

Another avenue of government control is achieved through the government's role as *creditor*. The NOCs are provided access to loans from Eximbank and CDB, sometimes at below-market rates or even without interest, and other forms of financial assistance from the Chinese government. Loans are sometimes provided with the security of a supply of energy imports. Moreover, the acquisitions by the NOCs are occasionally backed up by the provision of infrastructure investment. Finally, aid has been provided by the Chinese government to the governments of oil-producing states. Such aid can help advance the interests of the Chinese government in the recipient country and pave the way for NOC investments. All of these avenues of financing can serve as a way to control the companies, as the NOCs have an incentive to become involved in the countries where the Chinese government is willing to offer loans or other credit to support acquisitions. It also demonstrates the impact of Chinese capital on the ability of Chinese NOCs to make acquisitions abroad.

Another avenue of government control is through its role as a *regulator*. The Chinese government can assert control over companies by implementing laws and regulations. For example, NEA's current plan to increase gas use to 8.3 percent of the total energy mix by 2015 has influenced the NOC business strategy to develop more gas business both at home and abroad.[21]

Finally, an avenue of government control is through the government's ability to determine *government policy*. Importantly, several policies have been presented in recent years related to the energy sector. In 2001, when China joined the WTO, a "going out" (走出去/*zouchuqu*) strategy to secure the resource supply was presented by then Premier Zhu Rongji and Hu Jintao, who was the general secretary of the CCP at the time. This strategy particularly encourages Chinese companies to invest overseas.[22] While no single publicly available policy document in China specifically delineates the country's energy policy/petroleum strategy, since 2000, a number of government documents have surfaced that together provide some parameters of government policy, including an official government strategy concerning its resource endowment situation, as well as numerous other documents, including government reports, government White Papers, speeches, and communiqués.[23]

All of the preceding represent avenues through which the Chinese government can exercise control over the NOCs.

Independent companies

Other parts of the literature assume that a process has taken place according to which the companies have grown stronger in their role *vis-à-vis* the government.[24] Here, we explore the tools the companies hold in relation to the government, including their quasi-governmental status, their ability to take initiative, the fact that they have internationally listed subsidiaries, the size of the companies, the fact that they have become professionalized in recent years, as well as the fact that they are profitable.

The NOCs hold a *quasi-governmental status*. Both CNPC and Sinopec originate as government ministries. Both are ministry-level corporations, and their general managers hold full or vice-ministerial rank. The key executives of the NOCs are usually members of the CCP Central Committee, which consists of the most politically powerful individuals in China. These positions give the NOCs influence over the policy-making process. Given their high rank, it is argued that they are able to bypass lower-ranking government departments, possibly even the Energy Bureau, and instead communicate and present their interests directly with the Chinese leadership.[25]

Another avenue through which the NOCs can have influence *vis-à-vis* the government is their ability to take *initiative*. For example, in some of the major energy projects, such as the West-East Gas Pipeline, initiatives are first taken by the NOCs and only later adopted by the government.[26] Moreover, the energy companies have been able to affect the government at certain points, as when Sinopec lobbied the government after the 2003–04 energy crisis to revise the oil pricing system because of Sinopec's losses.

Another avenue through which the NOCs can acquire influence is their *internationally listed subsidiaries*. As noted earlier, the subsidiaries of the three large Chinese NOCs – CNPC, Sinopec, and CNOOC – have been listed on domestic and international stock exchanges. This can function as a way to protect the companies from state intervention. At the same time, through the listing on overseas stock exchanges, a learning process is taking place. SOE managers learn the standard practices of the world economy and adapt to the global norms of corporate governance.[27]

Another avenue through which the NOCs can have influence *vis-à-vis* the government is the *size of the companies*. The NOCs are bigger than the government agencies tasked with the job to oversee them.[28] CNPC, Sinopec, and CNOOC employ 1.7 million, 1.02 million, and approximately 100,000 people, respectively. In contrast, NDRC only employs 750 people, and NEA, which formally is tasked with managing the NOCs, only has 112 personnel. Given the technical and complex character of the foreign acquisitions process and the understaffed government agencies, the government relies at times on expertise from the companies.[29] Sinopec employees, for example, have been involved in drafting the country's strategic oil reserve law as a result of their expertise.[30] In turn, this gives the energy companies a certain measure of influence over the government.

Another avenue through which the NOCs can have influence *vis-à-vis* the government is the fact that the NOCs have become increasingly professionalized: the NOCs have a top-down structure and have centralized their power in their headquarters. Lastly, because the Chinese energy companies listed on overseas stock exchanges have foreigners among their corporate directors and receive financing and guidance from international investment banks, the NOCs are learning and adopting Western management practices.

Another avenue through which the NOCs can have influence *vis-à-vis* the government is the fact that they have become very profitable. The three major NOCs – CNPC, Sinopec, and CNOOC – are very profitable companies. In 2005, the subsidiaries of the three large NOCs, PetroChina, Sinopec Ltd., and CNOOC Ltd., accounted for about 22 percent of the total profits earned by all of the state-owned enterprises in China. In the period from 1998 to 2006, the profit margins on earnings before taxes (EBT) increased from less than 1 percent to between 4 and 7 percent for China's energy industries.[31] In the period from 2002 to 2006, the value of NOC shares increased by 531 percent, whereas IOC share prices only increased by 113 percent in the same period. This can be seen as a reflection of the financial market's valuation of the profit potential of the two groups.[32] As the average size of new discoveries of the IOCs decline, their reserves are shrinking, and current fields are being depleted, the continued role of the IOCs is questioned. In contrast, the NOCs control larger and larger reserves.

Despite being listed on foreign stock exchanges and partly owned by investors outside China, the Chinese NOCs have been assumed *not* to be profit-maximizing or operating according to profit motives. The willingness to accept lower rates of return has been seen as indicative of the government's preference for acquiring actual oil over income and, thus, that security motives prevail over actual profit motives. Hartley et al. present a model of the NOCs[33] that can explain how, whereas IOC shareholders are expected to generate a return on equity of roughly 15 percent, the majority shareholder of China's NOCs – the Chinese government – occasionally settles for a lower rate of return, especially from the parent companies.

In the view of Peter Hartley and Kenneth Medlock, political influence, defined as the desire to maximize social welfare, including energy, should be included as a factor in addition to concerns with profit maximization.[34] Thus, an alternative view might be that the energy sector is a strategic sector requiring state control. Similarly, Vernon argues that the government can use energy companies to control other economies, thereby pursuing state objectives.[35] Along these lines, even Western profit-maximizing companies ultimately serve another purpose, which is to control another state. This would point out that in terms of energy companies, classical profitability measures make little sense.

Here, we compare IOCs and the NOCs and explore whether both groups can be considered profit-maximizing companies. The performance of NOCs and IOCs can be compared along the following indicators of profitability: 1) share price performance, 2) revenue,[36] 3) return on assets (ROA), and 4) enterprise value relative to revenue (EV/R). This comparison allows for a consideration of the extent to which NOCs are profit-maximizing companies. In the following, we include the three large Chinese NOCs – CNPC, Sinopec, and CNOOC – as well as the major IOCs.

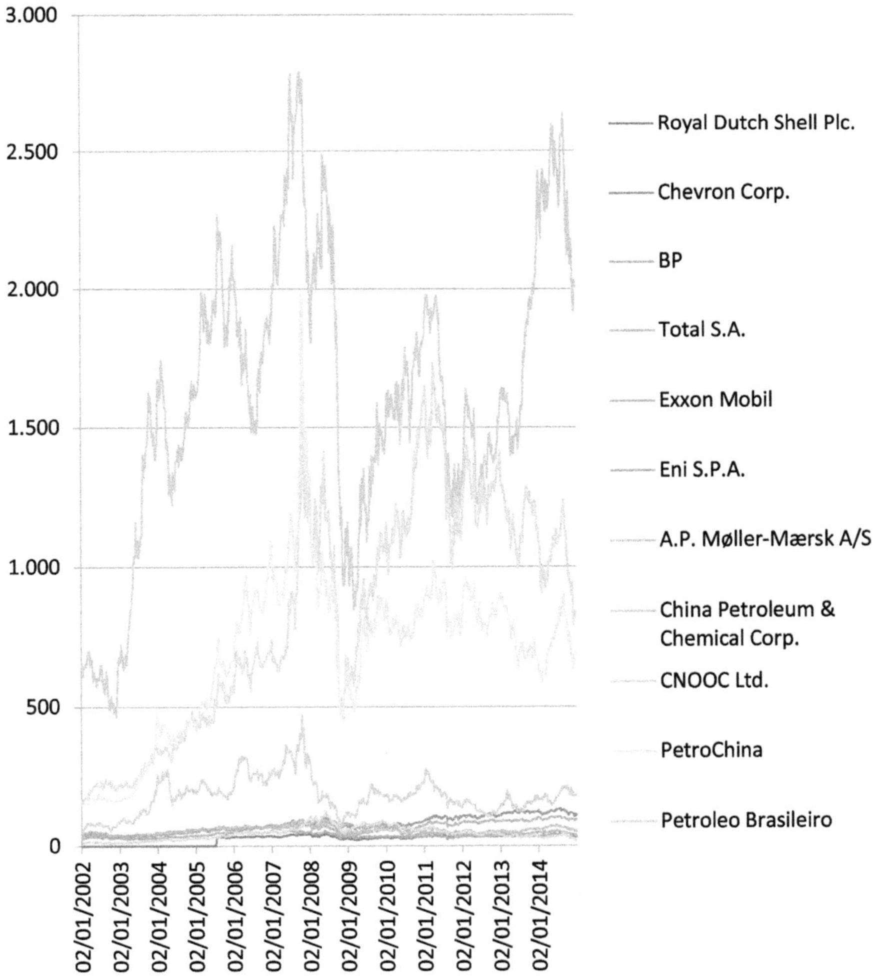

Figure 3.1 Share price performance of major oil firms, 2002–14[37]

The preceding graph, figure 3.1, illustrating the share price performance of the companies in the period from 2002 to 2014 reveals that the share prices of the NOCs move more or less in the same manner as the IOC shares. The results show that both IOCs and NOCs experienced a shock in 2007–08, since which time PetroChina and CNOOC have had relatively higher increases than the IOCs.[38] This indicates that NOCs are not less profitable companies.

But how do the IOCs and NOCs compare based on the other profitability measures mentioned earlier, namely revenue, return on assets, oil and gas reserves, and enterprise value to revenue?

As table 3.2 illustrates, the data for the year 2012 reveal that the NOCs are in line with or above the IOCs on the selected profitability measures. The return on assets of the three Chinese NOCs were around the average for the 12 companies (7.2 percent) or higher – CNOOC with 12.7 percent, PetroChina with 5.4 percent, and Sinopec with 5.1 percent. The revenue (compound annual growth rate [CAGR]) for the five-year period for each of the three companies was higher than the average for the 12 companies (5.4 percent) with 14 percent, 14 percent, and 15 percent,

Table 3.1 Comparisons of major oil firms

31 December 2010	*Revenue CAGR (5 year)*	*Return on assets (%)*	*Reserve oil (MMbbls)*	*Reserve gas (Bcf)*	*Enterprise value / revenue*	*Enterprise value / EBIT*
Royal Dutch Shell plc (NL)	3%	5.6%	6,146	47,135	0.49x	6.48x
Chevron Corporation (US)	–1%	9.1%	6,503	24,251	0.95x	7.11x
BP plc (GB)	2%	–3.4%	10,709	42,700	0.35x	–7.45x
TOTAL S.A. (FR)	1%	9.2%	5,987	25,788	0.72x	5.08x
Exxon Mobil Corporation (US)	0%	9.9%	11,673	78,815	1.11x	8.94x
Eni SpA (IT)	2%	7.9%	3,623	17,882	0.91x	5.62x
A.P. Møller – Mærsk A/S (DK)	4%	10.3%	–	–	1.05x	5.58x
China Petroleum & Chemical Corp. (CN)	13%	7.7%	2,889	6,447	0.56x	9.11x
CNOOC Ltd. (HK)	15%	15.7%	1,916	6,472	4.46x	11.41x
PetroChina Co. Ltd. (CN)	16%	7.6%	11,278	65,503	1.79x	13.60x
Petróleo Brasileiro S.A. – Petrobras (BR)	24%	6.4%	–	–	2.08x	9.87x
Public Joint Stock Company Gazprom (RU)	11%	8.0%	–	–	1.59x	5.08x
Average	7.5%	7.8%	5,060.3	26,249.4	1.34x	6.70x
Median	3.4%	7.9%	4,805.0	21,066.5	1.00x	6.79x

Table 3.2 Comparisons of major oil firms

31 December 2012	*Revenue CAGR (5 year)*	*Return on assets (%)*	*Reserve oil (MMbbls)*	*Reserve gas (Bcf)*	*Enterprise value / revenue*	*Enterprise value / EBIT*
Royal Dutch Shell plc (NL)	0%	6.9%	6,196	42,792	0.39x	4.78x
Chevron Corporation (US)	–3%	9.9%	6,481	29,195	0.92x	5.82x
BP plc (GB)	1%	2.5%	9,356	40,305	0.27x	8.59x
TOTAL S.A. (FR)	8%	8.7%	5,685	30,877	0.45x	3.47x
Exxon Mobil Corporation (US)	0%	11.0%	11,311	74,091	0.93x	6.86x
Eni SpA (IT)	3%	8.0%	3,350	20,957	0.72x	5.05x
A.P. Møller – Mærsk A/S (DK)	–2%	6.1%	–	–	1.00x	7.18x
China Petroleum & Chemical Corp. (CN)	14%	5.1%	2,843	6,730	0.40x	11.37x
CNOOC Ltd. (HK)	14%	12.7%	2,383	6,519	2.78x	8.03x
PetroChina Co. Ltd. (CN)	15%	5.4%	11,018	67,581	1.17x	14.64x
Petróleo Brasileiro S.A. – Petrobras (BR)	6%	3.4%	10,961	11,603	1.39x	11.30x
Public Joint Stock Company Gazprom (RU)	7%	7.1%	–	–	0.98x	3.53x
Average	5.4%	7.2%	5,798.7	27,554.1	0.95x	7.55x
Median	4.4%	7.0%	5,940.5	25,076.0	0.92x	7.02x

respectively. The enterprise value relative to revenue for CNOOC and PetroChina was higher than the average of 1.0x, while Sinopec was slightly lower. Still, when comparing the companies based on key measures of profitability, these tables (table 3.1 and table 3.2) reveal how it is reasonable to consider the three Chinese NOCs to be as profitable as the IOCs.[29]

It is worth noting that the strong performance in terms of the revenue and return on assets of the Chinese NOCs relative to the IOCs only proves that they are very profitable. It does not prove the notion that they are profit-maximizing; rather, it confirms that they are doing good business and are well-managed. These results support that the NOCs are profit-driven in their foreign investments. They consider their shareholders, are listed on stock exchanges overseas, and are focused on their financial performance.

While it is difficult to determine the extent to which this financial growth translates into political influence, it seems that the companies' contributions to the government revenue have resulted in an ability to shape government decisions. As the leadership is under mounting pressure to spend more money on social projects, such as education and health care, and the NOCs are helping to provide the necessary additional revenue, this has made the government more responsive to NOC interests.

Conclusion: why the companies are big and strong

In conclusion, then, a number of aspects point to government control over the NOCs, including the government's investment approval system, the fact that the companies are majority-owned by the Chinese government, the government's role in making strategic decisions, and the fact that the leaders of the NOCs are appointed by the CCP. As a result of the flawed reform processes, including numerous restructurings of the Chinese energy sector, China's energy-related government bureaucracy is fragmented and suffers from a lack of coordination. Energy policy-making in China has become decentralized and progressively pluralized. There is a lack of a Ministry of Energy to oversee important decisions and the government lacks funding and has a limited staff to regulate the energy sector. At the same time, over the course of the past decades, the economic power of the three large oil companies – CNPC, Sinopec, and CNOOC – has increased. They are listed on stock exchanges and increasingly involved in joint ventures abroad. Not only is there evidence of profit-maximizing behavior among the Chinese energy companies, but they have actually been just as or even more profitable than their Western counterparts in recent years. The companies have grown extremely large, whereas the government agencies responsible for managing them are much smaller in terms of manpower. As a result, the companies have grown strong *vis-à-vis* the government, and decision-making has shifted from the central government to the NOCs.

Thus, even if there are important avenues of government control over the NOCs, as pointed out earlier, there are also indications of the NOCs as operating relatively autonomously. It therefore makes sense to operate with a distinction between economic interests, understood as the commercial interests of Chinese companies, and state interests. The subsequent case studies to which we now turn will, on the basis of detailed and granular studies of specific key decisions involving Chinese decision-makers, illuminate the extent to which these companies can be viewed as independent.

Notes

1 When analyzing Chinese energy governance, one can distinguish between the supply-side and the demand side. Tools on the *supply side* include building a strategic petroleum reserve (SPR), building a refining base, building energy infrastructure, and acquisitions of energy abroad by the state-owned companies. This can be contrasted with steps on the *demand side*, which include energy conservation through both administrative and market incentives as well as control over energy prices (Bo Kong, "An Anatomy of China's Energy Insecurity and Its Strategies," Pacific Northwest National Laboratory Report, Prepared for the U.S. Department of Energy. Oak Ridge/U.S. Department of Energy, October 30–31, 2005).

2 As the focus of this book is on the activities of Chinese energy companies with regard to oil and gas, I focus mainly on the three large Chinese oil companies, CNPC, Sinopec, and CNOOC, as well as the regulations and processes pertaining to oil companies. Thus, Chinese energy companies that are primarily focused on coal or wind are not included in this analysis.

3 For data on the three large NOCs in China, see the Appendix.

4 For more on the reform processes in China in recent years, see Anthony Saich, *Governance and Politics of China*, 3rd ed. (Basingstoke: Palgrave Macmillan, 2001). For a detailed study of China's energy policy-making process, see Kenneth Lieberthal and Michel Oksenberg, *Policy Making in China: Leaders, Structures and Processes* (Princeton, NJ: Princeton University Press, 1988*)*. For a more recent contribution, see Phillip Andrews-Speed, *Energy Policy and Regulation in the People's Republic of China* (The Hague: Kluver Law International, 2004).

5 Bo Kong, *China's International Petroleum Strategy* (Santa Barbara, CA: Praeger, 2010), 18; Erica Downs, "China's 'New' Energy Administration: China's National Energy Administration Will Struggle to Manage the Energy Sector Effectively," *China Business Review* (November–December 2008): 1–4.

6 As is generally the case in the literature on the Chinese bureaucratic system, authority is understood here as "the ability to implement decisions." For more on how authority can be understood in the context of the Chinese bureaucratic system, see Lieberthal and Oksenberg, *Policy Making in China.*

7 Erica S. Downs, "Business Interest Groups in Chinese Politics: The Case of the Oil Companies," in *China's Changing Political Landscape: Prospects for Democracy*, ed. Cheng Li (Washington, DC: Brookings Institution, 2008), 121–41; Andrews-Speed, *Energy Policy and Regulation in the People's Republic of China*, 170; Edward Cunningham, "A Portfolio Approach to Energy Governance: State Management of China's Coal and Electric Power Supply Industries" (Ph. D. diss., Massachusetts Institute of Technology, 2009).

8 Cunningham, "A Portfolio Approach to Energy Governance," 11.

9 For more on the literature on the principal-agent relationship, see John D. Huber and Charles R. Shipan, "Politics, Delegation, and Bureaucracy," in *The Oxford Handbook of Political Economy*, eds. Barry R. Weingast and Donald A. Wittman (New York, NY: Oxford University Press, 2006): 256–72.

10 For one who utilizes the principal-agent framework when analyzing the Chinese energy administration, see Xiaojie Xu, "Chinese NOC's Overseas Strategies: Background, Comparison and Remarks," James Baker Institute for Public Policy, Rice University, March 2007).

11 Trevor Houser, "The Roots of Chinese Oil Investment Abroad," *Asia Policy* 5 (January 2008): 141–66.

12 Kong, *China's International Petroleum Policy*, 27.

13 Kong, *China's International Petroleum Policy*; J. Katzer et al., *The Future of Coal: Options for a Carbon-Constrained World*, MIT, 2007, accessed December 15, 2015, http://web.mit.edu/coal/The_Future_of_Coal.pdf; Cunningham, "A Portfolio Approach to Energy Governance;" Daniel Rosen and Trevor Houser, *China Energy: A Guide for the Perplexed* (Washington, DC: Peterson Institute for International Economics, 2007).

14 Katzer et al., *The Future of Coal*; Rosen and Houser, *China Energy*.

15 Kong, "An Anatomy of China's Energy Insecurity and Its Strategies," 21–2.

16 Interview with Chinese informant, 2012.

17 Barry Naughton, "Claiming Profit for the State: SASAC and the Capital Management Budget," *China Leadership Monitor* 18 (Spring 2006): 3. In May 2007, the Chinese government decided to have state-owned enterprises begin paying dividends. See Barry Naughton, "Strengthening the Center and Premier Wen Jiabao," *China*

Leadership Monitor 21 (Summer 2007): 1–3; Downs, "Business Interest Groups in Chinese Politics."

18 See, also John P. Burns, "Strengthening Central CCP Control of Leadership Selection: The 1990 Nomenklatura," *China Quarterly* 138 (June 1994): 458–91.

19 For example, in 2002, Li Yizhong, general manager of Sinopec, was made a full member of the CCP central committee. But Ma Fucai, general manager of CNPC, was only appointed as an alternate, because in the eyes of the Chinese leadership, Li did a better job than Ma at handling the protests of oil workers laid off by their respective companies. In contrast, the top leadership's selection of Wei Liucheng, chairman of both CNOOC Ltd., as an alternate member of the CCP central committee in 2002 and his subsequent appointment as governor of Hainan Province were rewards for his success at the helm of CNOOC Ltd. (Erica S. Downs, *China*, The Brookings Foreign Policy Studies Energy Security Series (Washington, DC: The Brookings Institution, December 2006), fn. 101).

20 National Development and Reform Commission of the People's Republic of China, 国家发展改革委关于做好境外投资项目下放核准权限工作的通知 ["Notice by National Development and Reform Commission on Investments Overseas and on the Approval Process in this regard"], 发改外资 [National Development and Reform Commission], 2011, No. 235, accessed December 15, 2015, www.ndrc.gov.cn/wzly/zcfg/wzzcjwtz/t20110318_399952.html.

21 OECD Reviews of Regulatory Reform, "China. Defining the Boundary Between the Market and the State," 2009, accessed December 15, 2015, www.oecd.org/china/42390089.pdf.

22 In fact, Chinese FDI rose from $3 billion in 1991 to $35 billion in 2003 to $92 billion in 2007 and to $88 billion in 2012 (National Bureau of Statistics of the People's Republic of China, *China Statistical Yearbook* 2013).

23 Information Office of the State Council of the People's Republic of China, *China's Energy Conditions and Policies*, December 2007; National Development and Reform Commission of the People's Republic of China, "China's National Climate Change Programme," June 2007, accessed December 15, 2015, http://en.ndrc.gov.cn/newsrelease/200706/P020070604561191006823.pdf.

24 E.g., Cunningham, "A Portfolio Approach to Energy Governance."

25 Downs, "Business Interest Groups in Chinese Politics."

26 Philip Andrews-Speed, Xuanli Liao and Roland Dannreuther, "The Strategic Implications of China's Energy Needs," Adelphi Paper No. 346 (London, UK: Oxford University Press, 20003, 57; Downs, China's "New" Energy Administration; Kong, *China's International Petroleum Policy*, 134.

27 Edward Steinfeld, *Playing Our Game: Why China's Rise Doesn't Threaten the West* (Oxford, UK: Oxford University Press, 2010.

28 Erica S. Downs, "Who's Afraid of China's National Oil Companies?" in *Energy Security: Economics, Politics, Strategies and Implications*, eds. Carlos Pascual and Jonathan Elkind (Washington, DC: Brookings Institution Press, 2010).

29 Interview with Chinese informant, 2014.

30 Downs, "Business Interest Groups in Chinese Politics," 129.

31 David Dollar and Shang-Jin Wei, "Das (Wasted) Kapital: Firm Ownership and Investment Efficiency in China," IMF Working Paper No. 07/9 (2007) (Washington, DC: International Monetary Fund, 2007); Rosen and Houser, *China Energy*, 12.

32 Amy M. Jaffe and Ronald Soligo, "The International Oil Companies," James A. Baker III Institute for Public Policy (Houston, TX: Rice University, November 2007), 37.

33 According to Hartley and Medlock, in addition to concerns for profit maximization, NOCs also receive political influence (Peter Hartley and Kenneth B. Medlock. "A Model of the Operation of a National Oil Company," *Energy Economics* [Houston, TX: Rice University, James Baker III Institute for Public Policy, 2007]).

34 Hartley and Medlock, “A Model of the Operation of a National Oil Company.”
35 Raymond Vernon, *Sovereignty at Bay: The Multinational Spread of U.S. Enterprises* (New York, NY: Basic Books, 1971).
36 Understood as the five-year historical “compound annual growth rate” (CAGR).
37 The graph shows the share price performance of major oil firms in the period from January 1, 2002–December 31, 2014.
38 Arguably, one cannot deduce from this that the companies are “profit maximizing.” One cannot “deduce rationality” 1:1. The companies are “profitable”/“achieve profit.”
39 I acknowledge that the management and performance of China’s NOCs is complicated, but for the purpose of the argument here, I don’t have to make it more complicated.

References

Andrews-Speed, Philip. *Energy Policy and Regulation in the People’s Republic of China*. The Hague: Kluver Law International, 2004.

Burns, John P. “Strengthening Central CCP Control of Leadership Selection: The 1990 Nomenklatura.” *China Quarterly* 138 (June 1994): 458–91.

Cunningham, Edward. “A Portfolio Approach to Energy Governance: State Management of China’s Coal and Electric Power Supply Industries.” PhD diss., Massachusetts Institute of Technology, 2009.

Dollar, David and Shang-Jin Wei. “Das (Wasted) Kapital: Firm Ownership and Investment Efficiency in China.” IMF Working Paper No. 07/9 (2007). Washington, DC: International Monetary Fund.

Downs, Erica S. “Business Interest Groups in Chinese Politics: The Case of the Oil Companies.” In *China’s Changing Political Landscape: Prospects for Democracy*, edited by Cheng Li, 121–41. Washington, DC: Brookings Institution, 2008.

Downs, Erica S. *China*. The Brookings Foreign Policy Studies Energy Security Series. Washington, DC: The Brookings Institution, December 2006.

Downs, Erica S. “China’s ‘New’ Energy Administration. China’s National Energy Administration Will Struggle to Manage the Energy Sector Effectively.” *China Business Review* (November–December 2008): 1–4.

Downs, Erica S. “Who’s Afraid of China’s National Oil Companies?” In *Energy Security: Economics, Politics, Strategies and Implications*, edited by Carlos Pascual and Jonathan Elkind, 73–104. Washington, DC: Brookings Institution Press, 2010.

Hartley, Peter and Kenneth B. Medlock. “A Model of the Operation of A National Oil Company.” Energy Economics. Report, James Baker III Institute for Public Policy, 2007. Houston, TX: Rice University.

Houser, Trevor. “The Roots of Chinese Oil Investment Abroad.” *Asia Policy* 5 (January 2008): 141–66.

Huber, John D. and Charles R. Shipan. “Politics, Delegation, and Bureaucracy.” In *The Oxford Handbook of Political Economy*, edited by Barry R. Weingast and Donald A. Wittman, 256–72. New York, NY: Oxford University Press.

Information Office of the State Council of the People’s Republic of China. “China’s Energy Conditions and Policies.” White Paper on Energy, December 2007. Accessed 12/15/2015. www.ccchina.gov.cn/WebSite/CCChina/UpFile/File229.pdf.

Jaffe, Amy M. and Ronald Soligo. “The International Oil Companies.” James A. Baker III Institute for Public Policy, Rice University, November 2007.

Katzer, J. et al. *The Future of Coal: Options for a Carbon-Constrained World*. MIT Press, 2007. Accessed 12/15/2015. http://web.mit.edu/coal/The_Future_of_Coal.pdf.

Kong, Bo. "An Anatomy of China's Energy Insecurity and Its Strategies." Pacific Northwest National Laboratory Report, Prepared for the U.S. Department of Energy, October 2005.

Kong, Bo. *China's International Petroleum Strategy*. Santa Barbara, CA: Praeger, 2010.

Lieberthal, Kenneth and Michel Oksenberg. *Policy Making in China: Leaders, Structures and Processes*. Princeton, NJ: Princeton University Press, 1988.

National Bureau of Statistics of the People's Republic of China. *China Statistical Yearbook 2013*. Beijing: National Bureau of Statistics, 2013.

National Development and Reform Commission of the People's Republic of China. "China's National Climate Change Programme." June 2007. Accessed 12/15/2015. http://en.ndrc.gov.cn/newsrelease/200706/P020070604561191006823.pdf.

National Development and Reform Commission of the People's Republic of China 国家发展改革委关于做好境外投资项目.下放核准权限工作的通知 ["Notice by National Development and Reform Commission on Investments Overseas and on the approval process in this regard"]. 发改外资 [National Development and Reform Commission] 235 (2011). Accessed 12/15/2015. www.ndrc.gov.cn/wzly/zcfg/wzzcjwtz/t20110318_399952.html.

Naughton, Barry. "Claiming Profit for the State: SASAC and the Capital Management Budget." *China Leadership Monitor* 18 (Spring 2006): 1–9.

Naughton, Barry. "Strengthening the Center and Premier Wen Jiabao." *China Leadership Monitor* 21 (Summer 2007): 1–3.

OECD Reviews of Regulatory Reform. "China. Defining the Boundary Between the Market and the State." 2009. Accessed 12/15/2015. www.oecd.org/china/42390089.pdf.

Philip Andrews-Speed, Xuanli Liao and Roland Dannreuther. "The Strategic Implications of China's Energy Needs, Strategic Implications of China's Energy Needs." Adelphi Paper no. 346. London, UK: Oxford University Press, 2000.

Rosen, Daniel and Trevor Houser. *China Energy: A Guide for the Perplexed*. Washington, DC: Peterson Institute for International Economics, 2007.

Saich, Anthony. *Governance and Politics of China*, 3rd ed. Basingstoke, UK: Palgrave Macmillan, 2001.

Steinfeld, Edward. *Playing Our Game: Why China's Rise Doesn't Threaten the West*. Oxford, UK: Oxford University Press, 2010.

Vernon, Raymond. *Sovereignty at Bay: The Multinational Spread of U.S. Enterprises*. New York, NY: Basic Books, 1971.

Xu, Xiaojie. "Chinese NOC's Overseas Strategies: Background, Comparison and Remarks." James Baker Institute for Public Policy. Houston, TX: Rice University, March 2007.

4 Nigeria

From "Angola Model" to "Addax Model"

Background

The state of China and Nigeria relations

Four periods can be distinguished in Sino-Nigerian relations. First, after Nigeria gained independence in 1960, the Nigerian government adopted a broadly pro-Western stance, and even if not supporting Taiwan actively, it did not seek relations with China.[1] Diplomatic relations were established in February 1971 but were very "slow" in the subsequent period, as visits and trade were limited.

The second phase is from 1999 with the "return" of democratic rule in Nigeria under the rule of President Obasanjo. Under the Obasanjo presidency, in the period from 1999 to 2007, economic relations developed rapidly. Obasanjo sought partners to buy oil concessions in return for infrastructure investments, as the country was in need of infrastructure. While Western oil companies had declined investments in infrastructure, some Asian governments, including the Chinese government, displayed interest. During Obasanjo's presidency, several leadership visits took place, as both President Jiang Zemin and President Hu Jintao visited Nigeria and President Obasanjo made several visits to Beijing. Importantly, in 2005, the two countries established a strategic partnership.

The third phase began in 2007 with Obasanjo's election loss and the rise to power of the Muslim Yar'Adua. Under Yar'Adua, relations became more difficult, and many of the existing agreements were cancelled. President Yar'Adua died in May 2010; since then, under the presidency of Jonathan (post-2011), relations between China and Nigeria have rebounded.

Thus, a possible *fourth phase* can be distinguished under Jonathan (post-2011) with indications of a rebounding relationship. In this way, a general process is visible from intensive engagement in the early 2000s to a cooling-off under Yar'Adua to a possible revival under Jonathan.

Literature on Nigeria

There are primarily three perspectives on the activities of Chinese energy companies in Nigeria: a liberal/political economy perspective, a realist/foreign policy

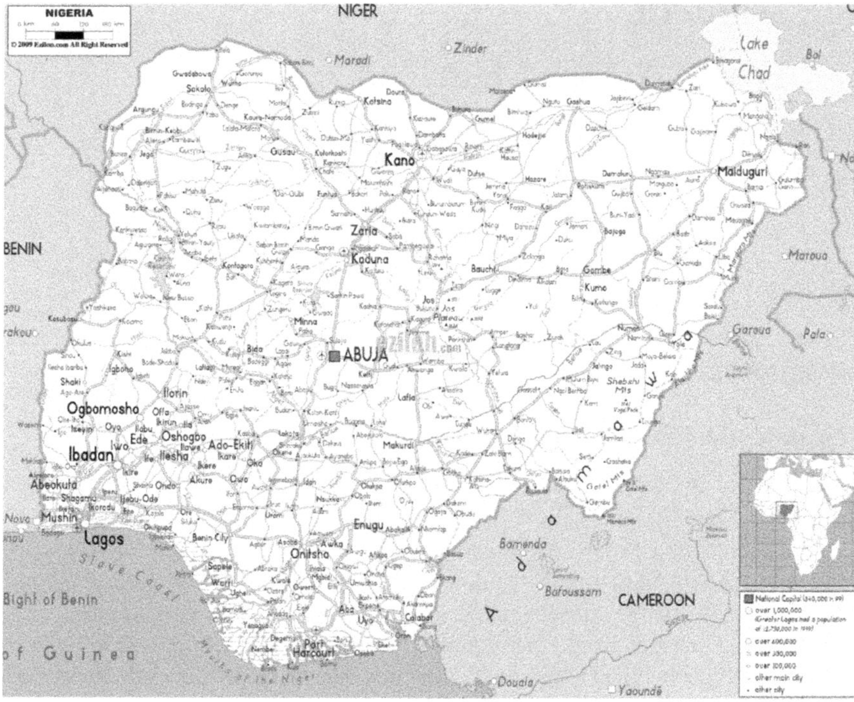

Figure 4.1 Map of Nigeria

perspective, or a focus on the developmental impact of the companies' activities in Nigeria.

From a *political economy perspective*, the general take in the literature on the oil industry in Nigeria and the political economy of oil in Nigeria is that they are characterized by dependence on foreign oil companies, particularly in the upstream sector, and that while oil is the backbone of Nigeria's economy, the oil sector is marred by mismanagement.[2] The literature stresses that through links to the elites in Nigeria, the Chinese NOCs are able to gain access to important energy reserves.[3]

From a *foreign policy* perspective, the view is that the Chinese companies in Nigeria are only after the oil and that their activities are part of an expansionist strategy being pursued by the Chinese state. In short, it is a strategy to "lock up oil." In this view, China can be thought of as a monolith and Chinese companies as an extension of the state (i.e., a foreign policy tool). Through its provision of access to liquidity and loans, the Chinese government can help its companies to win oil exploration contracts (long-term procurement contracts).[4] In this way, the government can gain access to important oil reserves and a guarantee that these resources are imported to China. This, in turn, offers China a way to expand its influence in Nigeria.

In contrast, some scholars who focus on the activities of Chinese NOCs in Nigeria downplay that the companies can be seen as an extension of the state and question the link established between the state leaders and companies. These scholars examine the oil cooperation between the two countries through detailed studies of particular acquisitions.[5] Theodore Moran argues that Chinese acquisitions actually have positive consequences for the global energy supply system, as they help expand and diversify the existing natural resources.[6]

Another standard take on this topic focuses on the impact of the activities of Chinese companies in Nigeria on *development* in Nigeria, the general idea being that investments by the Chinese government, aid donations, and the NOCs have positive developmental consequences for Nigeria.[7] The oil-for-infrastructure agreements were seen as attractive, as Nigeria required improvements to its infrastructure that were crucial for the economic development of the country.[8] These agreements were perceived as the embodiment of the South-South cooperation through which developing countries would help each other, and the activities of Chinese oil companies in Nigeria are therefore seen as having positive developmental consequences.[9]

Still, from the Nigerian side, there are also critical accounts addressing the effect of the Chinese activities in the country, as the concessional loans linked to the infrastructure agreements usually have a built-in conditionality regarding the use of Chinese labor, which, in turn, reduces the employment opportunities available to Nigerian workers.[10] Moreover, opening up the local market to Chinese products, such as cheap textiles, is seen as threatening the existence of local companies.[11]

Finally, some Western scholars and policy-makers question the impact of the activities of Chinese companies on development, as the access to loans, aid, and other forms of financing from the Chinese side removes the incentives for good governance, including transparency and accountability, and has a negative impact on development in Nigeria.[12] A so-called Chinese development model has become visible, as the Chinese government has provided access to aid and finance irrespective of the recipient country's adherence to norms of good governance.[13]

Thus, as seen earlier, the standard take on this topic is that Chinese companies are only involved in Nigeria in order to obtain preferential access to oil and that their activities are part of an expansionist strategy being pursued by the Chinese state. There is also a small body of literature closely studying the operations of the oil companies in Nigeria and the consequences for IOCs and world markets – hereby providing more nuanced accounts of the activities in Nigeria. Another standard take on this topic focuses on the developmental consequences of the Chinese activities in Nigeria, largely arguing that the activities of the Chinese NOCs might have a negative impact on development in Nigeria.

There are several limitations to the preceding literature. First, these contributions are limited to English-language materials, whereas this account also includes materials written in Chinese. Second, whereas most of the preceding literature assumes that the Chinese state and/or companies engaged in Nigeria are motivated by state interests, the analysis here opens up the question as to the extent to which this is actually the case. Thus, the assessment here will examine whether, and the extent to which, state interests, economic interests, and concerns with domestic stability dominate the activities of the Chinese companies in Nigeria. I therefore proceed in a different manner.

History of Chinese oil companies in Nigeria

The Nigerian oil sector has been largely dominated by the large IOCs. Shell and BP acquired the first concessions from the English colonial government in 1938. Oil was first discovered in 1956 in the Niger Delta by Shell–BP.[14] Today, the Nigerian oil industry is still dominated by the large IOCs, including Shell, Eni (Agip), ExxonMobil, Chevron, Philips, Total, and Texaco. Shell is the largest producer of oil in Nigeria and accounts for 50 percent of Nigeria's total oil production.[15]

Chinese companies first displayed interest in Nigeria in the early 2000s. Subsequently, a number of Chinese companies acquired oil stakes in Nigeria, including CNPC, Sinopec, and CNOOC.[16] Overall, Chinese companies have stakes in 20 blocks, four of which have the company as the sole owner. Sinopec has 14 stakes, CNPC four stakes, and CNOOC two stakes, Sinopec being the Chinese oil company with the largest oil reserves in Nigeria. Nevertheless, the total production by Chinese NOCs in Nigeria is limited compared to the IOCs.

China imports a limited share of Nigeria's oil. The largest export destination for Nigerian oil until 2012 was the United States, which dropped to the 10th position in 2014.[17] In the period from 2004–12, Nigeria's share of Chinese oil imports was less than 1.2 percent,[18] China still being a relative newcomer to the Nigerian oil sector. Moreover, although Asian refineries are said to be importing increasing amounts of crude oil, it is more difficult to ship crude oil from Nigeria to Asia/China than to the United States because of the greater distances. For example, Shell's Bonny Export terminal is 19,589 km away from Tianjin, China, compared to 9,410 km to New York.

Nigeria's strategic importance

Nigeria holds high strategic importance for China for the following reasons. First, in terms of the *level of political relations*, Nigeria and the PRC established formal diplomatic relations on February 10, 1971. In April 2005, Nigeria became the first African country to sign a strategic partnership with China. The visits between the two nations have been many and frequent.[19] Nigeria has supported China since 1960, as when it voted in favor of China's admission to the United Nations (UN) in the UN General Assembly in 1960 (which was also Nigeria's debut at the UN).[20] In return, Nigeria has received support from China for its bid for one (of possibly two) of the proposed permanent seats for Africa on the UN Security Council when enlargement takes place.

Second, in terms of the role for *CCP regime stability*, in recent years, Boko Haram, an ethnic fundamentalist group with links to al-Qaeda, has set up a branch in Nigeria called "Loro."[21] This group was behind the killing of four Chinese nationals in 2012 and three Chinese nationals in 2013 (for more, see Key Decision 3 later in this chapter). While the aim of the al-Qaeda branches in countries such as Nigeria is to establish a Muslim government in the country, and thus not related to China, at the same time, if any terrorist or extremist movement succeeds in setting up a branch, that would by implication be viewed as a threat to China because of the possible threat constituted by extremist movements worldwide to the stability of the Chinese state. In other words, the existence of a fundamentalist group in Nigeria has implications for Chinese regime security (for more detail, see Chapter 3). Moreover, in terms of Taiwan, Nigeria adheres to the so-called one-China policy.

Third, in terms of salience of territory, there are no ethnic ties to China in Nigeria, which generally holds true for all of the African countries. In terms of *strategic location*, Nigeria is located on the west coast of Africa, in the Gulf of Guinea, and has important access to the ocean. It is located in the Sahel Belt, a swath of countries connecting northern and western Africa. The region has strategic importance because of its role as a bridge between the Arab Maghreb and black, sub-Saharan Africa.[22] In terms of infrastructure, Nigeria has more than a dozen domestic crude oil pipelines that transport oil to the country's six export terminals. Nigeria has four refineries, Port Harcourt I and II, Warri, and Kaduna, with a combined capacity of 445,000 barrels per day (bpd), which as of 2013 were operating at less than 30 percent of capacity. Because of the poor state of the refineries, despite its rich oil reserves, Nigeria relies on imports of petroleum products. Despite the inadequate infrastructure in the country, Nigeria's proximity to the sea renders it of some strategic importance to China.

Fourth, in terms of the role of the *other great power*, the United States is not an alliance partner of Nigeria and has no military bases in Nigerian territory (nor does China). In 2009, the United States added Nigeria to its list of terror-prone states, classifying Nigeria as a "state sponsor of terrorism."[23] Finally, no UN sanctions have ever been issued against Nigeria.

Fifth, in terms of bilateral trade, Nigeria was China's third-biggest trading partner in Africa (US$10.57 billion) in 2012, behind South Africa and Angola ($59.9 billion and $37.5 billion, respectively).[24] Bilateral trade has increased in

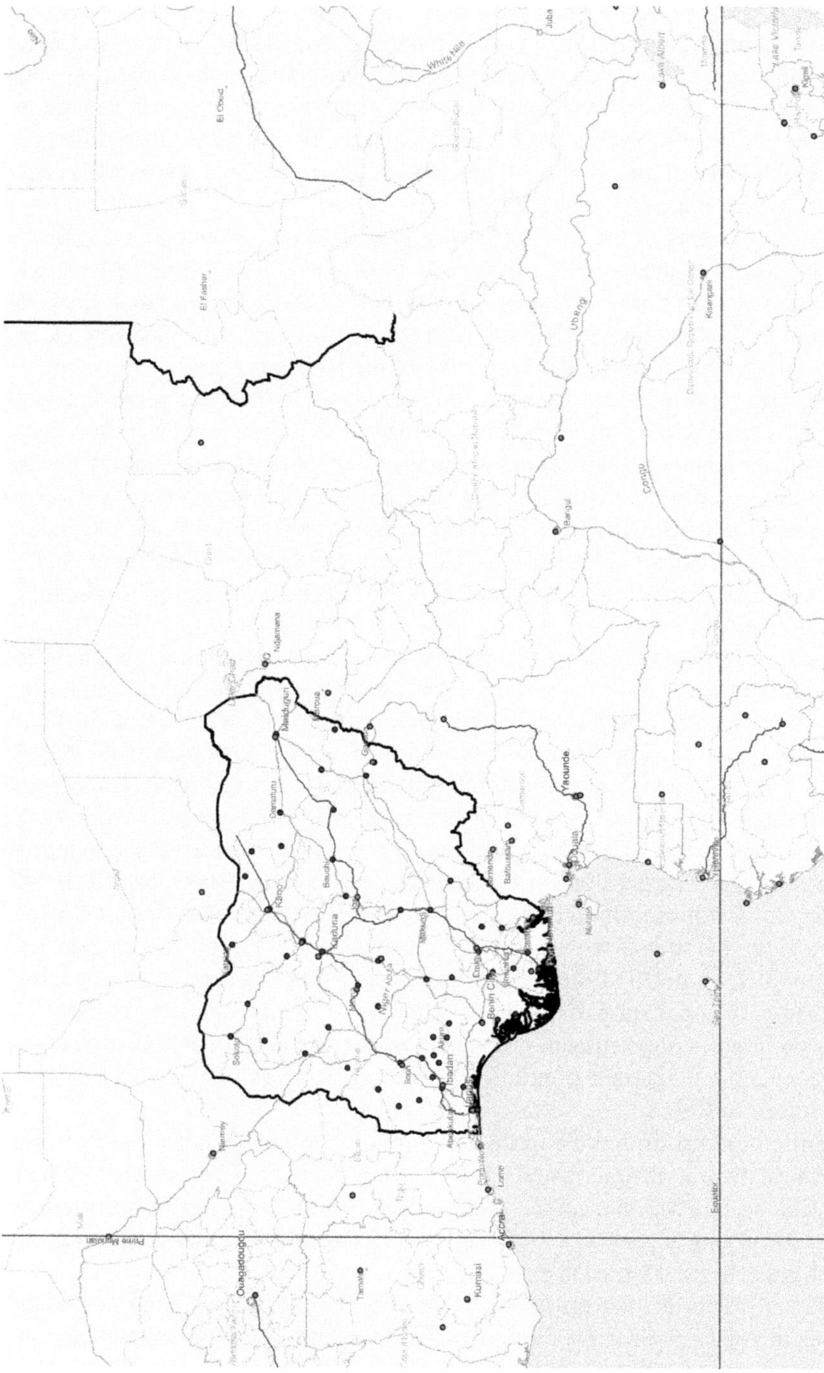

Figure 4.2 Infrastructure: Nigeria

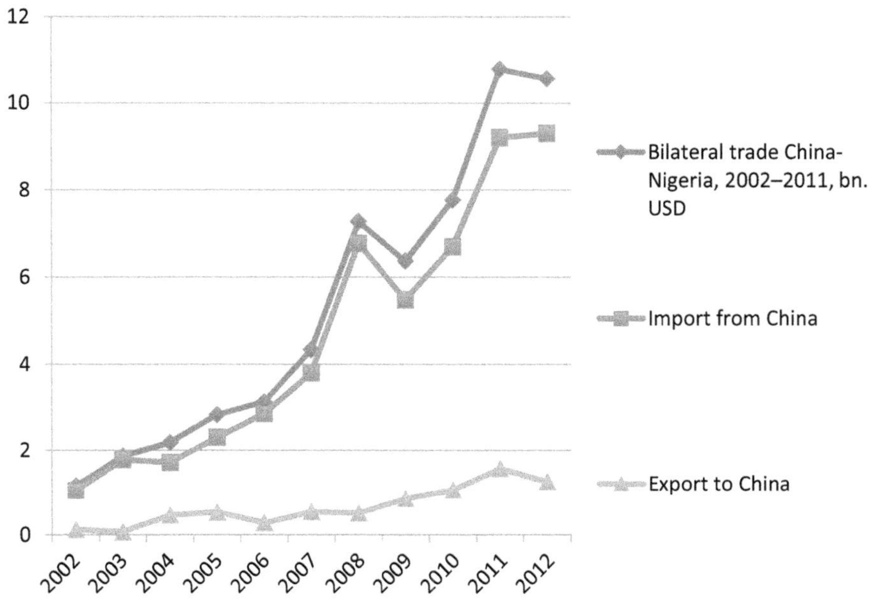

Figure 4.3 Sino-Nigerian trade, 2002–12

recent years, from $1.2 billion in 2002 to $10.57 billion in 2012, as illustrated in figure 4.3.

China accounted for 18.2 percent of Nigerian imports in 2012 and is now the largest single source of Nigerian imports.[25] In contrast, in terms of Nigerian exports, China accounts for a very limited share (less than 8.5 percent).[26] In fact, the Nigerian trade deficit with China amounted to more than $8 billion in 2012. Chinese foreign direct investment (FDI) in Nigeria increased from $24.4 million in 2003 to $390.35 million in 2007, after which it fell to $184.9 million in 2010.[27]

Thus, as presented earlier, Nigeria is of great strategic importance to China. This is reflected in the large number of visits between the two countries and their strategic partnership. Moreover, the existence of an extremist group linked to al-Qaeda in the country and the fact that Chinese nationals have been killed in Nigeria in recent years mean that the country plays an important role for

Table 4.1 Level of strategic importance: Nigeria (for more detail, see Appendix)

Country	*1. Level of political relations*	*2. Role for CCP regime stability*	*3. Salience of territory*	*4. Role of other great power*	*5. Bilateral trade*	*Total*
Nigeria	1	2	1	2	2	2

Chinese regime stability. Nigeria also has a strategic location with good ports, and, finally, bilateral trade is high. Bilateral trade has increased in recent years, from $1.2 billion in 2002 to $10.57 billion in 2012, as illustrated in figure 4.3.

Level of oil and gas

Nigeria has very rich oil and gas reserves and high production. In terms of oil, as of 2014, Nigeria possessed the 11th largest proven petroleum reserves in the world, amounting to 37.2 billion barrels.[28] It is the 12th largest oil producer in the world, producing 2.52 million bpd in 2013.[29] However, the violence in the Niger Delta has reduced Nigerian output in recent years.[30]

In terms of gas, as of 2014, Nigeria's gas reserves totaled 5.15 trillion m^3, mainly from onshore fields and the Niger Delta, amounting to the world's ninth largest natural gas deposits[31] and the largest natural gas reserves in Africa. Gas production was 31.36 billion m^3 in 2012 (25th in the world). Despite the massive reserves, because of its limited infrastructure in place to develop the sector, 75 percent of the associated gas is flared and 12 percent re-injected.[32]

Thus, as is evident from the preceding, Nigeria has very rich oil and gas reserves and high production.

The empirical expectation

As the preceding data illustrate, Nigeria is a country of high strategic importance to China with a high level of oil. Based on these characteristics and the history of the case, the hypothesis is that both economic and state interests will dominate in Nigeria. Thus, the empirical expectation is that in Nigeria, *the Chinese companies have an incentive to become involved because of the large quantities of oil in order to maximize profits. At the same time, the government attributes strategic importance to the country. For this reason, the hypothesis is that we will expect to find evidence of both state and economic interests.*

Quantitative content analysis

For Nigeria, as presented earlier, the hypothesis is that both state and economic interests will dominate. The quantitative analysis of the Chinese state media shows that 72 percent of the media content reveals a preponderance of economic interests over the ten-year period under investigation.[33] Thus, the activities are driven by commercial interests and the previous hypothesis is not supported. Still, the coding results for Nigeria show that, over the course of this period, the level of evidence of economic interests found in the articles changes. As illustrated in figure 4.4, in 2005, the ratio of economic interests to state interests/domestic stability (*weiwen*) peaked (ratio of 10.1:1). Economic interests also dominated relative to state interests and concerns with domestic stability in other years in the course of the ten-year period, with ratios of 1.5:1–2.5:1 in 2003–04,

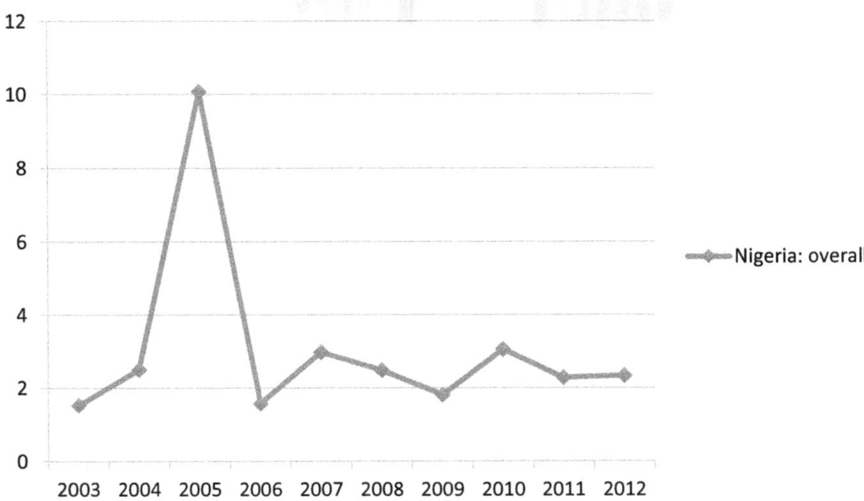

Figure 4.4 Ratio of economic interests to state interests/domestic stability

and 1.6:1–3.1:1 in 2006–12. Thus, while the ratio of economic interests to state interests/domestic stability dominated the entire period, there were variations in the degree, as seen in the following.

Zooming in and scrutinizing particular ratios, such as that of economic to state interests, we see that the dominance of economic interests peaks in 2005 (ratio of 24.9:1), as figure 4.5 shows. Economic interests were also strong relative to state interests in the years 2007 (ratio of 7.9:1) and 2010 (ratio of 7.7:1). In contrast, state interests were relatively more important in 2003 (ratio of 2.8:1), 2006 (ratio of 4.12:1), 2009 (ratio of 4.4:1), and 2012 (ratio of 3.6:1). Economic interests peaking relative to state interests in 2005 is somewhat surprising, as the strategic partnership between the two countries was formed in 2005. In turn, the fact that state interests were relatively more important in 2006 would follow from Hu Jintao's state visit to Nigeria that year.

Studying the relationship between economic interests and concerns with domestic stability (*weiwen*), we see that, overall, economic interests dominated relative to concern with domestic stability, particularly in the years 2005 (ratio of 54.8:1), 2007 (ratio of 46.29:1), 2010 (ratio of 36.45:1), and 2012 (ratio of 35.7:1), as figure 4.6 shows. Still, we see that the concerns with domestic stability were relatively stronger compared to economic interests in 2003 (ratio of 6.5:1), 2006 (ratio of 18:1), 2009 (ratio of 12.4:1), and 2011 (ratio of 20.4:1). This is surprising, as Chinese workers were targeted – attacked and/or killed – in 2007, 2008, 2012, 2013, and 2014 but not in any of those four years. In fact, in 2012, the year when most Chinese workers were targeted (and killed), the data does not reflect this.

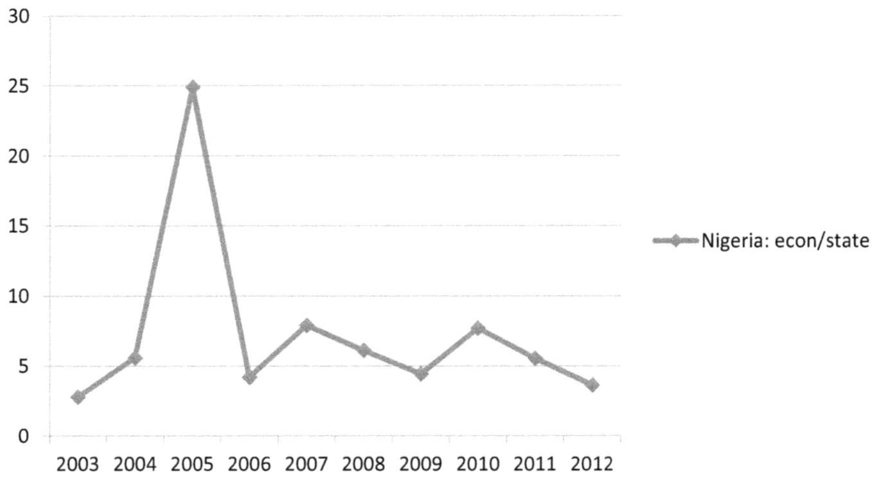

Figure 4.5 Ratio of economic interests to state interests

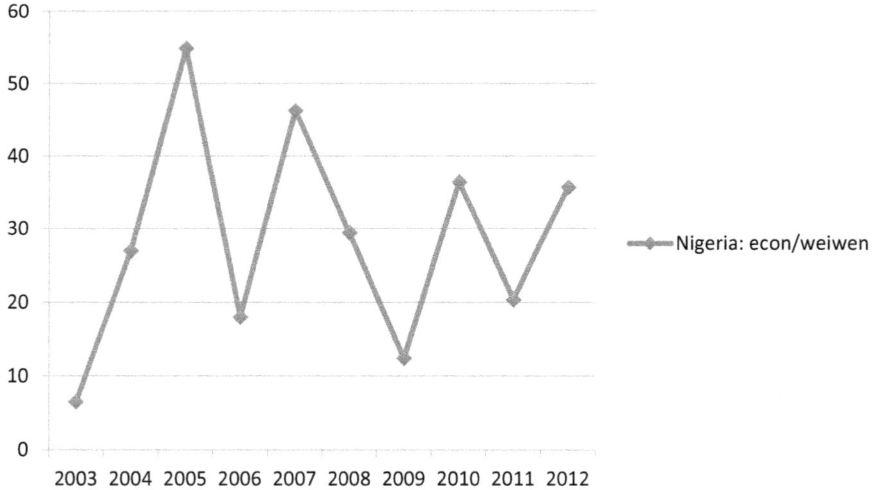

Figure 4.6 Ratio of economic interests to domestic stability

Finally, considering the ratio of state interests to concerns with domestic stability (*weiwen*), as illustrated in figure 4.7, we see that state interests dominate the whole period (ratios of 2.2:1–5.9:1) but that state interests are particularly strong in 2012 (ratio of 9.8:1). This is surprising as, given the killing of numerous Chinese workers in 2012, we would have expected the dominance of the concerns with domestic stability (*weiwen*) to be greatest that year.

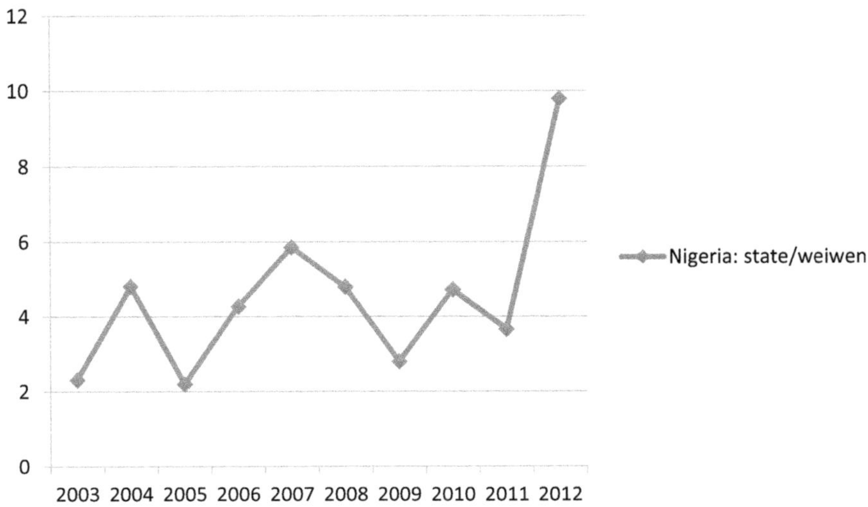

Figure 4.7 Ratio of state interests to domestic stability

Overall, the preceding results are surprising. Whereas economic interests and state interests were expected to dominate equally according to the hypothesis presented earlier, the results here show that economic interests dominate. The remainder of this chapter considers why this is the case.

Qualitative analysis: 3 key decisions

We now turn to three key decisions, the idea being that a focus on certain key decisions will illuminate important aspects of the activities of Chinese companies in Nigeria. We focus on three cases that allow for analysis of variation over time. First, we focus on the construction of a major deal following Hu Jintao's 2006 visit, which resulted in both the awarding of four oil stakes in 2006 to CNPC in return for infrastructure and loans and the promise to CNOOC of winning four oil stakes in the upcoming licensing round. Second, we focus on Sinopec's acquisition of Addax in 2009. Third, we focus on the case of the Chinese workers who were killed in Nigeria in 2012. While one could have focused exclusively on CNOOC's acquisition of oil blocks in 2006 as a key decision, this acquisition is included here as part of the large oil-for-infrastructure agreement in 2006–07. The argument is that these three decisions presented here are the most significant and representative in terms of the activities of Chinese companies in Nigeria over the last decade. Analysis of these activities will thus help us understand if Chinese foreign policy toward Nigeria is dominated by state interests, economic interests, or concerns with domestic stability (*weiwen*).

Key Decision 1: oil for infrastructure, 2006–07

We focus here on the agreement giving CNPC the right to explore four oil blocks in return for the construction of a refinery, a deal which was signed during Hu Jintao's visit in 2006 and accompanied by an Eximbank loan. If state interests dominate, the donation of credit would influence the Nigerian government to favor China to win the oil blocks and build the refinery. The building of infrastructure (refineries), aid, visits, and so forth would be combined in order to win resource deals, and we would see clear statements from the political leadership in favor of such investments. If economic interests dominate, we would see that the acquisition and construction of the refineries were aimed at obtaining assets and technology and profitable growth. Should concerns with domestic stability (*weiwen*) dominate, we would see evidence of workers killed in Nigeria, statements made by state leaders, and comments on Chinese social media reflecting concerns with Chinese worker safety in Nigeria.

State interests – oil block in return for refinery

On April 26, 2006, President Hu Jintao visited Nigeria, meeting with President Olusegun Obasanjo and signing several unspecified cooperation agreements, including a four-point plan to improve bilateral relations. A seven-point memorandum of understanding (MoU) was also signed that gives the CNPC preferential rights to bid on four oil extraction blocks at an oil-licensing round in May 2006, which in return would commit Chinese companies to play a role in the construction of Nigerian infrastructure. At the MoU signing ceremony in 2006, a strategic partnership between the two parties was signed – the first of its kind in Africa.[34]

The Obasanjo government held four licensing rounds, in 2000, 2005, 2006, and 2007, the latter three of which were part of the oil-for-infrastructure scheme. The idea behind the oil-for-infrastructure loans was that the Nigerian government would guarantee oil blocks at discounted rates with right of first refusal (RFR) in return for investment in downstream and infrastructure projects.[35] Thus, the awarding of oil licenses was tied to construction of infrastructure.

CNPC did not bid in the first licensing round in 2005, supposedly because of a communication failure.[36] Then, in May 2006, the Nigerian government held a mini-round designed specifically for "serious downstream investors only."[37] During this round, on May 19, 2006, CNPC was awarded right of first refusal (RFR) on pre-assigned blocks to bid in the licensing round. This came, interestingly, one month after a visit paid by Hu Jintao. In this licensing round, CNPC bought four blocks for $4 billion using RFR; namely, the oil production licenses (OPL) 298, 471, 721, and 732.[38] These four oil blocks were the aforementioned that the CNPC could have bid for in the 2005 round. As part of the agreement, CNPC would purchase a controlling stake in the Kaduna Refinery for $2 billion.[39] The two countries also granted Abuja export credit worth $500 million in return for a daily supply of 70,000 bpd of crude oil from Nigeria.[40]

The agreement made during Hu Jintao's April 2006 visit also consisted of an agreement on an Eximbank loan of $2.5 billion earmarked for infrastructure projects.[41] The loan was preconditioned on CNOOC being awarded four oil blocks, one of which had to be producing, in the upcoming 2007 licensing round.[42]

The Eximbank loan consisted of two facilities: a $500 million facility and a $2 billion facility. Of the latter, $1.3 billion was to fund the first phase of the Lagos-Kano Railway.[43] It would help upgrade and modernize the 1,315 km railway, which had been damaged during the civil war (1967–70). The Eximbank loan would also fund the construction of a 2,600 mw hydroelectric power (HEP) station at Mambilla in Taraba State, which, when completed, will be the largest single power project in Nigeria.[44]

The motive behind the oil-for-infrastructure agreements was that whereas the Chinese companies formerly gained access to Nigerian oil primarily via purchases on the spot market, the Chinese government now sought increased ownership of Nigerian oil reserves, the purpose of which was to meet the increasing Chinese demand for oil.[45] One Chinese oil industry magazine article reflects the importance of Chinese companies gaining access to equity oil in Africa that China can ship back to China, as the cost of equity oil is lower than oil on the international market.[46]

Visits were conducted to back up the agreement. In April 2006, for example, Hu Jintao visited Nigeria, after which the Eximbank loan was finalized. And in April 2005, Obasanjo visited Beijing, during which a strategic partnership was settled. In the course of the visit, President Olusegun Obasanjo stated that the "African people will never forget China's support in their struggle against colonialism and racial segregation" and that the countries "join hands to maintain the interests of developing countries, boost south-south cooperation and promote the establishment of a fair and reasonable new international political and economic order."[47] This points to the mechanism being that the Eximbank loan is a means by which China can demonstrate its friendship with Africa – the South-South agenda – which might ultimately contribute to a domestic agenda regarding domestic stability. Nigerian leaders emphasizing the close ties between China and Africa offer evidence of the appreciation of the recipient.

Overall, the construction of this extensive agreement, including both CNPC being awarded stakes and a large Eximbank loan, reflect state interests.

Economic interests

Obasanjo did not win the 2007 election; instead, his handpicked successor, a Muslim from northern Nigeria, Yar'Adua, took over. In Nigeria, the electoral cycle typically alternates between the northern Muslim and southern Christian elites.[48] When inaugurated on May 29, 2007, President Yar'Adua cancelled most of Obasanjo's oil-for-infrastructure contracts, including the railway project, the Mambilla hydropower electric plant, and the refinery, as President Obasanjo had not signed the MoU required to confirm the terms of the $2.5 billion loan before leaving office, for which reason the mobilization fee for the projects was never appropriated.[49] Consequently, the Eximbank loan was never granted. Similarly, even if CNOOC had been granted an RFR to bid as part of the Eximbank loan, CNOOC ended up not bidding in the 2007 licensing round.[50] Moreover, CNPC had acquired several oil blocks in 2006 (OPLs 471, 721, and 732), but the oil blocks were cancelled as the new government disapproved of the way in which OML 65 had been given away outside of normal procedures.[51] The cancellation of these agreements provides evidence of the high level of risk for Chinese companies when involved in Nigeria, a setting in which agreements risk being cancelled after the next election.[52] Still, even if the agreement was cancelled, it does not in itself alter the motive of the Chinese company or the Chinese leadership entering into and constructing such large agreements.

Importantly, as the agreement on the acquisition of the four oil licenses was settled during Hu Jintao's visit to Nigeria in April 2006, this visit could then be seen as an indicator of economic interests, as it offers evidence that the Chinese leadership supported the NOCs' commercial interests. Still, given that the large Eximbank loan was provided subsequent to the Hu Jintao visit and that a strategic partnership was settled during Obasanjo's visit to Beijing in 2005 that could influence the Nigerian elite to favor the Chinese NOCs in the 2006 agreement, there is also evidence of strong state interests. Thus, when looking at the overall factors, the 2006 agreement provides evidence that state and economic interests coincide.

*Domestic stability (*weiwen*)*

This key decision provides no evidence of concerns with domestic stability in Nigeria in the sense of the impact of activities in Nigeria, including the killing of Chinese workers, on Chinese domestic stability. While there are citations pointing to close ties between China and Africa (as seen earlier), because the infrastructure projects were never started and no Chinese workers were harmed, overall, there is no evidence of the concern with domestic stability here.

Conclusion, Key Decision 1

The large Eximbank loan for the building of Nigerian infrastructure, including refineries, hydropower plants, and railways, in conjunction with the awarding of oil licenses to Chinese companies, provides evidence of state interests. China seeks to combine infrastructure, aid flows (the Eximbank loan), and visits to obtain the deals providing access to natural resources. While most of the agreements ultimately stalled, this does not in itself alter the motives behind the agreement from the Chinese side.

How does the analysis here compare to the quantitative analysis? In 2006, when there was an intensification of visits between the two countries, Chinese contributions to the development of Nigerian infrastructure, and donation of aid, the qualitative analysis reflects an increase in the importance of state interests. The quantitative analysis suggests the dominance of economic interests relative to state interests and concerns with domestic stability in 2005 (ratio of 10.1:1). Even if state interests are relatively more important in 2006 (ratio of 1.6:1) than in 2005, economic interests still dominate in absolute numbers. Thus, the results from the quantitative and qualitative analyses are inconsistent.

There will always be some inconsistencies between different types of evidence. The question is whether they are in overall agreement or not. Importantly, in addition to state interests, there is evidence of strong economic interests, as Hu Jintao's visit to Nigeria in 2006 was followed up by the acquisition of four oil stakes by CNPC in the 2006 licensing round, stakes which were very promising and, thus, deemed profitable. Overall, the evidence that economic and state interests coincide is therefore more credible in this key decision.

Key Decision 2: Sinopec acquires addax, 2009

Here, we focus on Sinopec's purchase of Addax in 2009, carefully considering the characteristics and motivations behind this acquisition. This is another case that can contribute to our understanding of whether Chinese foreign policy toward Nigeria is dominated by state interests, economic interests, or concerns with domestic stability (*weiwen*). If state interests dominate, we would see that the acquisition was backed up with aid, state visits, and statements from political leaders and that the company was paying a premium to the market price. Should economic interests dominate, we would see that Sinopec obtains access to important reserves or particular deepwater assets and that the aim is to obtain technology. We would see that its shareholders regarded the transaction as profitable. Should concerns with domestic stability (*weiwen*) dominate, we would see evidence of Chinese workers being targeted in Nigeria, statements made by state leaders, and comments on Chinese social media reflecting concerns with Chinese worker safety in Nigeria.

Acquisition of Addax

On August 18, 2009, SIPC (Sinopec International Petroleum Exploration and Production Corporation), a wholly owned subsidiary of Sinopec Corporation, completed a 100 percent acquisition of Addax (Addax Petroleum Corporation). Addax, an independent oil and gas-producer founded in 1994, is based in Switzerland and listed on the Toronto Stock Exchange with a secondary listing on the London Stock Exchange. The core assets in the Addax portfolio are located in Nigeria. At the time of this acquisition, Addax was a very well-run company, and the financials for December 31, 2008, report a 56 percent profit margin.[53] In the words of Addax CEO Jean Claude Gandur, in its 2009 second quarterly report, Addax reported a "quarterly record for performance."[54] This further reinforces the impression that, at the time of the acquisition, Addax was a very promising company.

The total price of the transaction was \$7.17 billion (table 4.2). The deal was announced on June 24, 2009, and finalized on August 18, 2009.[55] The total enterprise value of the transaction was \$9 billion, including net interest-bearing debt.[56]

Table 4.2 Acquisition of Addax

Announced date	June 24, 2009
Completed date	August 18, 2009
Acquired %	100%
Deal value	$7.17 billion
Acquirer company	SIPC (Sinopec International Petroleum Exploration and Production Corp.)
Vendor company	Addax Petroleum

Rather than financing the transaction with debt, SIPC financed the acquisition with internal funds. Sinopec's takeover of Addax in June 2009 was the single largest offshore acquisition by a Chinese oil company to that date.

Economic interests

Looking at Addax's assets, the reserve growth for Addax in deepwater assets and the Kurdistan assets was significant. Notably, in particular, its offshore deepwater exploration projects were especially promising with significant development potential.[57] According to Sinopec, "with the acquisition Sinopec achieved a breakthrough in oil and gas exploration,"[58] as it added important oil reserves to Sinopec's holdings. In the words of Chairman Fu Chengyu, the acquisition of Addax Petroleum was a "transitional acquisition" that would accelerate its international growth and help it expand in West Africa and Iraq, in line with its strategic objectives.[59] In the words of an industry publication, the goal of the Chinese government is to access the African market and compete with the Western firms there and in particular the "Big Five": Total, BP, Chevron, Shell, and Exxon Mobil.[60] The acquisition of Addax would thus help Sinopec enter the Nigerian market, which is otherwise dominated by IOCs. In the words of Sinopec, the acquisition was particularly motivated by access to technology as "Addax has great potential deepwater exploration projects."[61] The acquisition would also help Sinopec upgrade its technology.

Still, the acquisition can be seen as carrying high risk, including political risks, as Nigeria is a politically sensitive region subject to frequent changes in political leadership. Moreover, there was risk due to the problems with vandalism in the oil-producing areas, in particular in the Niger Delta. Furthermore, some of Addax's projects carry risk because some of its drilling rights in Nigeria are disputed and because some of the contracts in Iraq with the government of the autonomous Kurdish area have been denounced by the Iraqi minister in Baghdad responsible for the oil industry in the country.[62] In addition, the acquisition includes deepwater assets, which are assumed to carry high risk.[63] Thus, all in all, this can be considered a high-risk acquisition, demonstrating that Sinopec was not very risk-averse in this acquisition.

With the acquisition, Sinopec paid a 47 percent premium to Addax's share price at the time of the acquisition. While this might be an indicator that Sinopec overpaid, a significant premium is typically paid in company takeovers. Moreover, there were possibly potential synergies that could account for the willingness to pay a premium, as Sinopec could add Addax's assets to its other assets in Nigeria and gain access to deepwater technology.[64] Thus, the size of the premium alone cannot be used to say anything about whether this was a case of state interest.

Finally, an indicator of economic interest would be the share price. However, the share prices of all three large Chinese oil companies increased from the day that the offer was announced on June 5, 2009, until August 18, 2009, when the deal closed. The share price of Sinopec increased by 14.3 percent, the CNPC share price increased by 23.9 percent, and the CNOOC share price increased by 16.1 percent. Based on that background, Sinopec's increase around the time of the acquisition was not unique.[65] All in all, it is difficult to draw conclusions from the Sinopec share price development in the given period.

Still, summing up, one Chinese informant observes that

> the Addax acquisition reflected that Sinopec wanted to earn money and that it was for profit. In general, companies seek to evaluate whether it is a good investment – and then they make the acquisition. Western companies do that, and so do Chinese companies.[66]

From "oil for infrastructure" to "Addax model"

For the past decade, China's dealings in Nigeria broadly followed a pattern called the "oil-for-infrastructure" model, according to which loans were offered to develop infrastructure in exchange for access to natural resources. Moreover, the agreements were between two governments and underwritten by Chinese finance as state-to-state deals. But, as we saw under the previous Key Decision, in Nigeria, there is high political risk because of how political power rotates between the Christian South and the Muslim North and given the high level of corruption in the country. For example, CNPC's acquisitions in 2006 under the oil-for-infrastructure scheme were later cancelled. Instead, a new model for transactions was presented: the "Addax model." This was a financial acquisition of a shareholder company and not linked to other types of agreements, which demonstrates how Sinopec, in order to gain access to Nigerian oil resources, rather than offering access to construction of infrastructure, has shifted to acquiring stakes in established companies. It also demonstrates that Chinese companies have learned that trading oil assets for cash is a more successful way to gain access to Nigerian oil. Lastly, being an acquisition of a publicly traded company, it could signify that Chinese companies have grown more comfortable with the scrutiny that also follows from this.

While President Yar'Adua visited Beijing in February 2008, and a new Eximbank loan was indeed signed in 2009, neither the visits nor the donations of loans were clearly linked to Sinopec's acquisition of Addax. Thus, there is no evidence of state interests here.

Conclusion, Key Decision 2

This case provides evidence of economic interests. The acquisition by Sinopec was deemed profitable, and the share prices of Sinopec rose in conjunction with the sale. There is no evidence of state interests here, nor of concerns with domestic stability. The dominance of economic interests could be consistent with a greater role played by NOCs. Moreover, while it could be consistent with the Chinese state's desire to boost economic growth, the lack of visits to back up the acquisition indicates that it is more consistent with NOC interests.

How does the analysis here compare to the quantitative analysis? In 2009, when Sinopec acquired Addax, the data reflect the importance of economic interests (ratio of 1.81:1). Even if the data reflect a relative increase in the importance of state interests that year, economic interests still dominate in absolute numbers. The quantitative analysis suggests that concerns with domestic stability (*weiwen*) are relatively stronger in 2009, even if overall economic interests still dominate. This year, economic interests as compared to concerns with domestic stability had a ratio of 12:4, and state interests as compared to concerns with domestic stability had a ratio of 2.8:1 – both are increases relative to the previous and later years. Still, the analysis here does not indicate any ramifications in China of Sinopec's acquisition. Thus, overall, both the analysis here and the quantitative analysis provide evidence of economic interests. The two methods are therefore corroborated.

Key Decision 3: Chinese workers, 2012

Here, we focus on how attacks on Chinese workers in Nigeria in recent years have affected Chinese foreign policy. We focus in particular on the killing of Chinese workers by extremist groups in 2012 and examine the response of the Chinese leadership. If state interests dominate, then limits would become apparent in terms of when the state will become involved in order to protect national interests. If economic interests dominate, then the risk to the Chinese workers renders the investments less safe, that is, there is less potential for profit. However, investments will continue despite the associated risks. If concerns with domestic stability (*weiwen*) dominate, the deaths of Chinese workers in Nigeria would put pressure on the Chinese leadership to mediate, and we would expect statements made by state leaders and comments on Chinese social media reflecting concerns with Chinese worker safety in Nigeria.

Kidnappings in Nigeria

In recent years, the kidnapping and killing of oil workers abroad, including in African countries such as Nigeria, has received considerable attention domestically in China, including in the social media. Although official statistics are unavailable, an estimated 50,000 Chinese people reside in Nigeria (2010).[67] The Niger Delta has been hampered by insurgence and unrest since 2005, which has had a negative impact on oil production and the stability of the country. A number of militant rebel groups that target the IOCs have emerged. Some of these groups, including the Movement for the Emancipation of the Niger Delta (MEND), have attacked oil installations and kidnapped foreign oil workers in recent years (figure 4.8). In the period from 2007–09, these attacks cut Nigerian oil production by 20 percent, amounting to a $4.4 billion loss of national income.[68] In the period from 2009–11, this amounted to $10.9 billion in lost oil revenues.[69] Since early 2006, these attacks have resulted in more than 200 foreigners being kidnapped in the Niger Delta. Numerous Western oil companies have left Nigeria in recent years as a result of the attacks and kidnapping of oil workers. There is no evidence of the abduction of Chinese nationals prior to 2007.

This vandalism has also affected Chinese investments in Nigeria, as attacks by MEND caused at least 500,000 bpd in lost production for Chinese companies in 2006 after the violence began.[70] This has led the Chinese government to focus on the safety of investing in the Nigerian oil industry. In March 2007, for example, NDRC released a list of nine countries it considered most suitable for investment by Chinese oil companies. Nigeria was not on this list of countries in Africa, while the list included Morocco, Libya, and Niger.[71] In September 2011, the Chinese embassy website featured warnings that the deteriorating security situation constituted a serious threat to the safety of Chinese citizens and institutions, with possible implications for Chinese nationals living in Nigeria.[72]

There have been numerous instances of religious violence in Nigeria since 1980. In recent years, Boko Haram, an Islamist fundamentalist group with links to al-Qaeda, set up a branch in Nigeria and, in 2012, repeatedly targeted Chinese nationals. Since 2009, more than 10,000 people have been killed by Boko Haram and 1.5 million people have been displaced.[73] According to the US Africa Command (AFRICOM), Boko Haram has links to al-Qaeda in the Islamic Maghreb (AQIM).[74] In this manner, Islamic sects and sectarian violence in Nigeria link the country to terrorism and to the threat of the rise of al-Qaeda on the African continent.

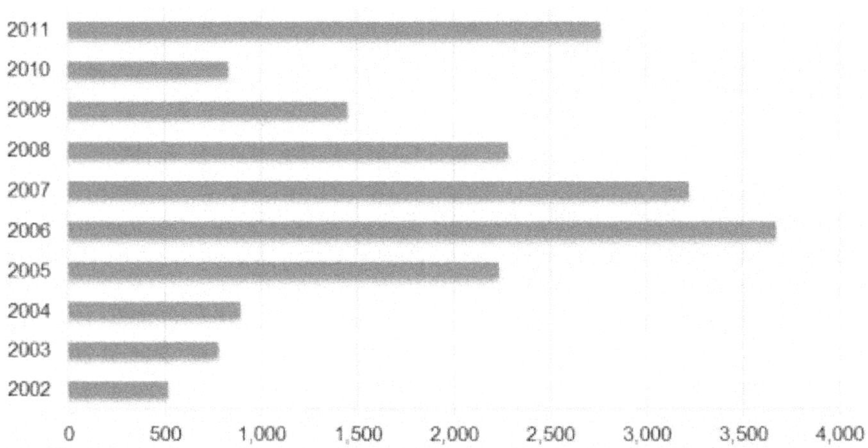

Figure 4.8 Incidents of pipeline vandalism in Nigeria, 2002–11

Table 4.3 Abductions of Chinese workers in Nigeria (since 2002)

Date	*Occasion*	*Actor*	*Casualties*
Jan. 5, 2007	5 Chinese engineers kidnapped – all later rescued	MEND	0
Jan. 25, 2007	9 Chinese workers kidnapped in southern Nigeria – all later rescued	Unidentified armed men	0
March 17, 2007	2 Chinese nationals abducted in Anambra State	Unidentified armed men	0
May 6, 2008	3 Chinese engineers kidnapped in Cross River State – all later released	Unidentified gunmen	0
Oct. 7, 2012	1 Chinese cook working with a construction company killed in Maiduguri, Borno state	Boko Haram	1
Oct. 19, 2012	1 Chinese construction worker (CGC) killed in Maiduguri, Borno state	Boko Haram	1
Nov. 7, 2012	4 Chinese construction engineers (CCECC) attacked in Benishek, Borno State – 2 were killed, 2 escaped	Boko Haram	2
Feb. 2013	3 Chinese doctors killed in Potiskum, Yobe	Boko Haram	3
Jan. 27, 2014	1 Chinese construction worker (rail project) killed and 2 others wounded in Kaduna State	Unidentified gunmen	1
Jan. 25, 2014	9 Chinese oil workers kidnapped in Bayelsa State, southern Nigeria – all later rescued	Unidentified armed men	0

Since 2007, nine Chinese workers have been killed in Nigeria, in addition to 30 who were kidnapped or attacked. Of these, five were killed in 2012, three in 2013, and one in 2014, as illustrated in table 4.3. Boko Haram claimed responsibility for the five deaths in 2012 and the killing of three Chinese doctors in 2013. As 2012 was the year featuring the highest number of killings of Chinese nationals, we focus on the incidents in that year. We focus in particular on the incidents in October 2012, when two Chinese nationals were killed, and the incident in November 2012 in which two Chinese nationals were killed. Both these incidents took place in Borno State in northern Nigeria, the Boko Haram stronghold. Moreover, there was an incident in 2013 in which Boko Haram killed three Chinese doctors in Nigeria. However, given that there were more abductions and casualties among Chinese workers in Nigeria in 2012, we focus on the events of that year together.

*Domestic stability (*weiwen*)*

The key decision in focus here is the 2012 incidents and how the Chinese leadership responded to the killing and abduction of Chinese nationals in 2012. On October 7, the Chinese embassy in Nigeria announced that a Chinese national was among the victims killed by Boko Haram in Maiduguri in northern Nigeria.[75] The local police, who launched an investigation into the killing, suggested that the Chinese might not actually have been the target.[76]

After the killing in Maiduguri on October 22, 2012, the second killing of a Chinese national in October, China's Foreign Ministry spokesman, Hong Lei, stated that China paid "great attention" to this killing. The Chinese government also lodged a diplomatic complaint with Nigeria about these killings of Chinese nationals. The Chinese embassy in Nigeria submitted a formal protest "that Nigeria take concrete measures to ensure the safety of Chinese nationals and institutions in the country."[77]

Then, after the abduction of four Chinese workers and the killing of two others on November 7, 2012, Foreign Ministry spokesperson, Hong Lei, said, "The Foreign Ministry instructed the Chinese Embassy in Nigeria to handle the incident urgently . . . and that effective measures would be taken to ensure the safety of Chinese nationals and institutions in Nigeria."[78] Thus, the Chinese embassy in Nigeria urged substantial measures to protect the safety of Chinese personnel and institutions in Nigeria. But no Chinese delegation was sent to Nigeria at the time. Importantly, contrary to the hypothesis presented here, there were no discussions on the Chinese social media *Weibo* (微波) about the activities of Chinese companies in Nigeria, even after the killings in 2012. While one might speculate whether Chinese companies would be pulling out of Nigeria because of the terrorist threat, written Chinese materials do not answer this question. While Boko Haram killed more than 780 people in Nigeria in 2012,[79] in the killing of Chinese workers that year, there is no indication that the attacks were actually targeted against China or Chinese nationals, as, for example, the killing of a cook in October 2012 occurred together with the killing of a non-Chinese individual.

Yet my own interviews conducted in Beijing as part of this project cast light on the implications of the killing of Chinese workers for the Chinese companies in Nigeria and the question posed earlier. According to a Chinese informant, while a company like CNPC is concerned about the existence of extremist groups in Nigeria and the killing of Chinese workers there, it will not withdraw from Nigeria.[80] When considering whether to exit the country, factors related to economic feasibility become important.[81] According to another Chinese informant, the killing of oil workers in Nigeria had no impact on the decision as to whether CNOOC would remain in Nigeria,[82] leaving no evidence that Chinese NOCs would be pulling out of Nigeria in response to the attacks.

Conclusion, Key Decision 3

This case shows how the killing of Chinese nationals in Nigeria, particularly in 2012 but also including the attacks against and kidnapping of 30 Chinese nationals over an 11-year span, have had no domestic impact and limited consequences for foreign policy and the investment decisions of Chinese companies in Nigeria. No particular delegation has been sent to Nigeria by the Chinese government to resolve the situation. No high-level presence was initiated, and there is no evidence of the domestic politicization of the Chinese role in Nigeria. Moreover, there is no evidence that the domestic audience was aware of the incidents, as no evidence has been found on *Weibo*. Finally, there was also no evidence found that armed rebel groups in Nigeria have targeted Chinese interests in order to apply pressure on the Nigerian government, possibly because even if there is domestic instability in Nigeria, there is no ongoing civil war. Even so, Chinese companies have taken steps to handle security on the ground in their own ways, including the hiring of security companies to protect Chinese oil installations. Thus, the key decision examined here indicates evidence of economic interests.

How does the analysis here compare to the quantitative analysis? In 2012, when the Chinese oil workers were killed, the quantitative results surprisingly show that the importance of domestic stability decreases. In 2012, economic interests dominate relative to concerns with domestic stability (ratio of 35.7:1), up from 2011 (ratio of 20.4:1). In 2012, state interests become more important relative to concerns with domestic stability (ratio of 9.8:1), up from 2011 (ratio of 3.7: 1). Still, the analysis here demonstrates that no ramifications of the killings of and attacks on Chinese nationals are found domestically. Similarly, the activities of the Chinese companies in Nigeria are unaffected. Chinese companies did not move out of Nigeria, and there were no ramifications for foreign policy. Thus, the results from the qualitative and quantitative analyses are consistent.

Conclusion

In the case of Nigeria, the Chinese companies were expected to have an incentive to become involved because of the potential profits to be made from the large amounts of oil available. At the same time, the Chinese government attributes strategic importance to Nigeria. For this reason, we expect evidence of both state and economic interests.

The qualitative analysis shows that in the case of the large oil-for-infrastructure agreement in 2006–07, state and economic interests coincide; in the case of the Sinopec acquisition of Addax, economic interests dominate; and in the case of the killing of Chinese workers, economic interests dominate.

The quantitative analysis shows that for all three key decisions, economic interests dominate. Examining the case of the large oil-for-infrastructure agreement in 2006–07 more closely, given that, in addition to evidence of strong state interests, there is evidence of strong economic interests, the evidence that state and economic interests coincide is more credible. This means that the qualitative and quantitative analyses are in overall agreement. As the quantitative and qualitative analyses thus provide evidence of both state and economic interests, the empirical expectation presented earlier is supported.

Notes

1 Gregory Mthembu-Salter, "Elephants, Ants and Superpowers: Nigeria's Relations with China," South African Institute of International Affairs (SAIIA), China in Africa Project, Occasional Paper 42, September 2009.
2 For general and introductory works on the Nigerian oil and gas industry, see, for example, Sarah Ahmad Khan, *Nigeria: The Political Economy of Oil* (Oxford, UK: Oxford University Press, for the Oxford Institute for Energy Studies, 1994); Mark C. Thurber, Ifeyinwa M. Emelife, and Patrick R.P. Heller, "NNPC and Nigeria's Oil Patronage Ecosystem," in *Oil and Governance: State-Owned Enterprises and the World Energy Supply*, eds. David G. Victor, David R. Hults and Mark C. Thurber (Cambridge, UK: Cambridge University Press, 2012), 701–52.
3 See, for example, Mthembu-Salter, "Elephants, Ants and Superpowers"; Ian Taylor, "China's Relations with Nigeria, The Round Table," *The Commonwealth Journal of International Affairs* 96 (392) (2007): 631–45.
4 For a non-Nigeria specific example of this argument, see "China's Quest for Resources, Opportunities, and Influence in Africa," in *China into Africa. Trade, Aid, and Influence*, ed. Robert Rotberg (Washington, DC: Brookings Institution Press, 2008), 1–21.
5 See, for example, Alex Vines, Lillian Wong, Marcus Weimer and Indira Campos, "Thirst for African Oil," in *Asian National Oil Companies in Nigeria and Angola*, A Chatham House Report (London, UK: Chatham House, August 2009).
6 Theodore H. Moran, *China's Strategy to Secure Natural Resources: Risks, Dangers and Opportunities* (Washington, DC: Peterson Institute for International Economics, July 2012), 1–2.
7 Deborah Brautigam, *The Dragon's Gift. The Real Story of China in Africa* (Oxford, UK: Oxford University Press, 2010); Margaret Egbula and Qi Zheng, "China and Nigeria: A Powerful South – South Alliance," OECD, *West African Challenges* 5 (November 2011); Mthembu-Salter, "Elephants, Ants and Superpowers"?
8 Gregory Mthembu-Salter, "China's Engagement in the Nigerian Oil Sector," Policy Briefing, SAIIA, November 2009, 1–4.
9 Djeri-wake Nabine, "The Impact of Chinese Investment and Trade on Nigeria Economic Growth," African Trade Policy Centre (ATPC)Work in Progress, 77 (Addis Ababa: African Trade Policy Centre, 2009).
10 Egbula and Zheng, "China and Nigeria."
11 Egbula and Zheng, "China and Nigeria."
12 Egbula and Zheng, "China and Nigeria."
13 Joshua Cooper Ramo, *The Beijing Consensus* (London, UK: The Foreign Policy Centre, 2004); *The Economist*, "Aid 2.0," August 13, 2011, accessed December 15, 2019, www.economist.com/node/21525899; Alexandra Gillies, "Obasanjo, the Donor Community and Reform Implementation in Nigeria," *The Round Table: The Commonwealth Journal of International Affairs* 96 (392) (2007): 569–86.
14 Nigerian National Petroleum Corporation, "History of the Nigerian Petroleum Industry," accessed December 15, 2015, www.nnpcgroup.com/NNPCBusiness/Businessinformation/OilGasinNigeria/IndustryHistory.aspx.
15 For more, see *U.S. Energy Information Administration (EIA)*, "Nigeria," accessed December 15, 2015, www.eia.gov/countries/country-data.cfm?fips=ni; Environmental Resources Managers Ltd., *Niger Delta Environmental Survey Final Report Phase I; Volume I: Environmental and Socio-Economic Characteristics* (Lagos: Niger Delta Environmental Survey, September 1997), 195.

16 *People's Daily*, "China, Nigeria Sign Oil Supply Pact," July 9, 2005; *Business Monitor International*, "Nigeria Oil & Gas Report Q1," Q1 2013, 43.
17 *U.S. EIA*, "Nigeria."
18 China's Land Resources Statistical Yearbooks [中国国土资源统计年鉴], Ministry of Land of the People's Republic of China [中华人民共和国国土资源部], various years.
19 See the Appendix for details.
20 Egbula and Zheng, "China and Nigeria."
21 Robert A. Lobban, *Global Security Watch: Sudan* (Santa Barbara, CA: Praeger, 2010), 75.
22 U.S. House of Representatives, "Boko Haram – Emerging Threat to the U.S. Homeland," Committee on Homeland Security, Subcommittee on Counterterrorism and Intelligence, November 30, 2011, accessed December 15, 2015, https://homeland.house.gov/files/Testimony%20Pham.pdf, 5.
23 Toyin Falola and Adebayo O. Oyebade, *Hot Spot: Sub-Saharan Africa* (Santa Barbara, CA: Greenwood, 2010), 33.
24 Henceforth, unless otherwise noted, all monetary figures refer to U.S. dollars ($). National Bureau of Statistics of the People's Republic of China, *China Statistical Yearbooks 2003–2012*.
25 Economist Intelligence Unit, "Nigeria, Country Report," October 2013, 12; United Nations Statistical Division, Commodity Trade Statistics Database, accessed December 15, 2015, http://comtrade.un.org/db/.
26 Economist Intelligence Unit, "Nigeria, Country Report," October 2013, 12.
27 *China Commerce Yearbook 2011* [中国商务年鉴], 北京: 中国商务出版社 (Beijing: China Commerce and Trade Press).
28 U.S. EIA, "Nigeria."
29 U.S. EIA, "Nigeria."
30 U.S. EIA, "Nigeria."
31 U.S. EIA, "Nigeria."
32 U.S. EIA, "Nigeria."
33 "Decade" refers to the ten-year period under investigation here, 2003–12.
34 Lillian Wong, "The Impact of Asian National Oil Companies in Nigeria," *Nigerian Muse*, *Ocnus.Net*, December 30, 2008. According to other sources (Egbula and Zheng, "China and Nigeria"), however, the strategic partnership was agreed to in 2005 during President Obasanjo's trip to Abuja in 2005 and only formally signed during Hu Jintao's visit to Nigeria in April 2006.
35 Vines et al., "Thirst for African Oil," 11.
36 According to Vines et al., CNPC had misunderstood the process, believing that they had secured blocks in the course of the earlier talks and so failed to bid at the auction (Vines et al., "Thirst for African Oil," 15).
37 Vines et al., "Thirst for African Oil," 16.
38 Vines et al., "Thirst for African Oil."
39 Vines et al., "Thirst for African Oil."
40 He Wan [何琬] and Zheng Ying [[郑迎迎], 中国与非洲的石油贸易与合作, ["Sino – African Oil Trade and Cooperation"], *国际经济合作 (International Economic Cooperation)*, November 20, 2007; Taylor, "China's Relations with Nigeria, The Round Table," 631–45, 635.
41 According to Vines et al., this was agreed on the margins of the FOCAC Summit in Beijing in November 2006 (Vines et al., "Thirst for African Oil," 24).
42 Vines et al., "Thirst for African Oil," 23.
43 Vines et al., "Thirst for African Oil," 23.
44 Vines et al., "Thirst for African Oil," 17–18.
45 Xu Yi (徐翼), 胡锦涛访非展开能源外交 ["Hu Visits Africa to Expand Energy Diplomacy"], *中华工商时报* (*China Business Times*), April 30, 2006.

46 Wang Wei [汪巍], 非洲石油市场开发策略 ["Strategy for Development of the African Oil Market"], *中国石油石化* (*China Petroleum and Petrochemical Industry*), October 15, 2009.
47 *China Daily*, "China, Nigeria to Build Strategic Partnership," April 15, 2005.
48 Whereas Obasanjo is a Yoruba from the Christian south, Yar'Adua is a Fulani Hausa and Muslim from the north (Mthembu-Salter, "Elephants, Ants and Superpowers").
49 Vines et al., "Thirst for African Oil."
50 Vines et al., "Thirst for African Oil," 18.
51 Vines et al., "Thirst for African Oil," 25–7.
52 Interviews with Chinese informants, 2014. A number of Chinese-language articles note the high level of risk in Nigeria due to its administrative, economic, and legal systems, as well as risk due to wars, ethnic conflicts, and so forth. See, for example, Shi Lingtao [史凌涛], 非洲地区石油工业投资环境 ("The African's Petroleum Industry's Investment Environment"), *国际石油经济* (*The International Petroleum Economy*) 12 (10) (October 20, 2004).
53 *Wall Street Journal*, "Sinopec Acquisition of Addax Petroleum," June 24, 2009, accessed December 15, 2015, http://wsj.dealogic.com/SINOPEC-Addax-627331.html.
54 Thomson Streetevent, Addax Petroleum Corporation, "Final Transcript, Addax Petroleum Corporation Earnings Conference Call," July 27, 2009, 1–31, 2.
55 China Petroleum and Chemical Corporation [Sinopec], *Yearbook 2010* [中石油石化工集团公司年鉴], 北京：中国石化出版社 (Beijing: China Petrochemical Press), 3; Peter K. Ogden, "Addax Petroleum Corporation – Selling to Sinopec for Cdn$52.80/sh," *National Bank Financial*, June 25, 2009, 1–4, 2.
56 *The Economist*, "Sinopec Buys Addax: Bottom of the Barrel," June 25, 2009.
57 Gavin Wylie, "Addax Petroleum Inc," *Scotia Capital*, July 28 2009.
58 China Petroleum and Chemical Corporation [Sinopec] *Yearbook 2010* [中石油石化工集团公司年鉴], 北京：中国石化出版社 (Beijing: China Petrochemical Press), 98.
59 Tian Li (田力), 成功收购 Addax 石油公司, 中石化海外并购迈出重要一步 ["The Successful Acquisition of Addax Petroleum, an Important Step for Sinopec's Overseas M&A"], *中国石油和化工* (*China Petroleum and Chemical Industry*), September 5, 2009.
60 Wang Wei [汪巍], 非洲石油市场开发策略 ["Strategy for Development of the African Oil Market"], *中国石油石化* (*China Petroleum and Petrochemical Industry*), October 15, 2009.
61 Tian Li (田力), 成功收购 Addax 石油公司, 中石化海外并购迈出重要一步 ["The successful acquisition of Addax Petroleum, an important step for Sinopec's overseas M&A"], *中国石油和化工* (*China Petroleum and Chemical Industry*), September 5, 2009.
62 *Economist*, "Sinopec Buys Addax: Bottom of the Barrel," June 25, 2009.
63 Ogden, "Adax Petroleum Corporation – Selling to Sinopec for Cdn$52.80/sh," 1.
64 *Thomson Streetevent*, "Addax Petroleum Corporation – final transcript," Addax Petroleum Corporation Earnings Conference Call, July 27, 2009, 1–31, 5.
65 Hong Kong dollars.
66 Interview with Chinese informant, 2014.
67 Whereas in 1930, there were four Chinese citizens living in Nigeria, in 1965, that number had grown to 200. Egbula and Zheng, "China and Nigeria"; Vines et al., "Thirst for African Oil," 8.
68 *Epoch Times [大纪元]*, 又有9名中国工人在尼日利亚遭到绑架 ["Nine Chinese Workers Have Been Abducted in Nigeria"], January 26, 2007, accessed December 15, 2015, www.epochtimes.com/gb/7/1/26/n1603988.html.
69 *Reuters*, "Nigeria Loses $10.9bn to Oil Theft," July 30, 2013.
70 Taylor, *China's Relations with Nigeria*, 639.
71 Taylor, *China's Relations with Nigeria*.

72 Embassy of the People's Republic of China in the Federal Republic of Nigeria [中华人民共和国驻尼日利亚联邦共和国大使馆], 驻尼日利亚使馆召开安全形势座谈会 ("The Embassy in Nigeria Holds Conference on the Security Situation in Nigeria"), September 1, 2011, accessed December 15, 2015, http://ng.china-embassy.org/chn/hzqzqw/t853844.html.
73 Council of Foreign Relations Backgrounder, "Boko Haram," March 5, 2015, accessed December 15, 2015, www.cfr.org/nigeria/boko-haram/p25739.
74 Mark Doyle, "Africa's Islamist Militants 'Co-ordinate efforts,'" *BBC*, June 26, 2012.
75 Centre for Chinese Studies, Stellenbosch University, *The Weekly China Briefing* (Stellenbosch: University of Stellenbosch, October 12, 2012), accessed December 15, 2015, www.ccs.org.za/wp-content/uploads/2012/10/Weekly-China-Briefing-12-October-2012.pdf.
76 Centre for Chinese Studies, Stellenbosh University, *The Weekly China Briefing. Xinhua*, "Chinese Killed by Boko Haram Suspects in Northern Nigeria," October 8, 2012.
77 *Agence France-Presse*, "China Lodges Protest over Killing in Nigeria," October 22, 2012.
78 Office of the Commissioner of the Ministry of Foreign Affairs of the People's Republic of China in Macao Special Administrative Region, "Foreign Ministry Spokesperson Hong Lei's Regular Press Conference on November 8, 2012," accessed December 15, 2015, www.fmcoprc.gov.mo/eng/gsxwfb/lxjzzfh/t987276.html.
79 *AP*, "At Least 15 Are Reported Killed in Nigeria," December 29, 2012.
80 Interview with Chinese informant, 2014.
81 Interview with Chinese informant, 2014.
82 Interview with Chinese informant, 2014.

References

Agence France-Presse (AFP). "China Lodges Protest over Killing in Nigeria." October 22, 2012.

Associated Press. "At Least 15 Are Reported Killed in Nigeria." December 29, 2012.

Brautigam, Deborah. *The Dragon's Gift. The Real Story of China in Africa*. Oxford, UK: Oxford University Press, 2010.

Business Monitor International. "Nigeria Oil & Gas Report Q1." 2013.

Centre for Chinese Studies. *The Weekly China Briefing*. South Africa: University of Stellenbosch, October 12, 2012. Accessed 12/15/2015. www.ccs.org.za/wp-content/uploads/2012/10/Weekly-China-Briefing-12-October-2012.pdf.

China Commerce and Trade Press 北京: 中国商务出版社. China Commerce Yearbook 2011 [中国商务年鉴], 北京: 中国商务出版社. Beijing: China Commerce and Trade Press.

China Daily, "China, Nigeria to Build Strategic Partnership." April 15, 2005.

China Petroleum and Chemical Corporation [Sinopec]. *Yearbook 2010* [中石油石化工集团公司年鉴], 中国石油编委会 (Sinopec Editorial Team), 北京：中国石化出版社 (Beijing: China Petrochemical Press), 2010.

Council of Foreign Relations. "Boko Haram." Background report. March 5, 2015. Accessed 12/15/2015. www.cfr.org/nigeria/boko-haram/p25739.

Doyle, Mark. "Africa's Islamist Militants 'Co-ordinate Efforts'." *BBC*, June 26, 2012.

The Economist. "Aid 2.0." August 13, 2011. Accessed 12/15/2015. www.economist.com/node/21525899.

The Economist. "Sinopec Buys Addax: Bottom of the Barrel." June 25, 2009.

Economist Intelligence Unit, "Nigeria, Country Report." October 2013.

Egbula, Margaret and Qi Zheng. "China and Nigeria: A Powerful South – South Alliance." OECD, *West African Challenges* 5 (November 2011): 3–19.

Embassy of the People's Republic of China in the Federal Republic of Nigeria [中华人民共和国驻尼日利亚联邦共和国大使馆]. 驻尼日利亚使馆召开安全形势座谈会 ("The Embassy in Nigeria holds Conference on the Security Situation in Nigeria.") September 1, 2011. Accessed 12/15/2015. l.

Environmental Resources Managers Ltd. "Niger Delta Environmental Survey Final Report Phase I; Volume I: Environmental and Socio-Economic Characteristics, Lagos." Niger Delta Environmental Survey, September 1997.

Epoch Times [大纪元]. 又有名中国工人在尼日利亚遭到绑架 ["Nine Chinese Workers have been Abducted in Nigeria."] January 26, 2007. Accessed 12/15/2015. www.epochtimes.com/gb/7/1/26/n1603988.html.

Falola, Toyin and Adebayo O. Oyebade. *Hot Spot: Sub-Saharan Africa*. Santa Barbara, CA: Greenwood, 2010.

Gillies, Alexandra. "Obasanjo, the Donor Community and Reform Implementation in Nigeria." *The Round Table* 96 (392) (2007): 569–86.

He Wan [何琬] and Zheng Ying [郑flfl]. 中国与非洲的石油贸易与合作 ["Sino – African Oil Trade and Cooperation"]. *国际经济合作* (International Economic Cooperation), November 20, 2007.

Khan, Sarah Ahmad. *Nigeria: The Political Economy of Oil*. Oxford, UK: Oxford University Press for the Oxford Institute for Energy Studies, 1994.

Lobban, Robert A. *Global Security Watch: Sudan*. Santa Barbara, CA: Praeger, 2010.

Ministry of Land of the People's Republic of China [中华人民共和国国土资源部]. *China's Land Resources Statistical Yearbook* [中国国土资源统计年鉴]. Various years.

Moran, Theodore H. *China's Strategy to Secure Natural Resources: Risks, Dangers and Opportunities*. Washington, DC: Peterson Institute for International Economics, July 2012.

Mthembu-Salter, Gregory. "China's Engagement in the Nigerian Oil Sector." Policy Briefing No. 11, South African Institute of International Affairs (SAIIA), November 2009.

Mthembu-Salter, Gregory. "Elephants, Ants and Superpowers: Nigeria's Relations with China." South African Institute of International Affairs (SAIIA), China in Africa Project, Occasional Paper No. 42, September 2009.

Nabine, Djeri-wake. "The Impact of Chinese Investment and Trade on Nigeria Economic Growth." African Trade Policy Centre (ATPC), Work in Progress (77), Addis Ababa: ATPC: 2009.

National Bureau of Statistics of the People's Republic of China. *China Statistical Yearbooks 2003–2013*. Beijing: National Bureau of Statistics, various years.

Nigerian National Petroleum Corporation. "History of the Nigerian Petroleum Industry." Accessed 12/15/2015. www.nnpcgroup.com/NNPCBusiness/Businessinformation/OilGasinNigeria/IndustryHistory.aspx.

Office of the Commissioner of the Ministry of Foreign Affairs of the People's Republic of China in Macao Special Administrative Region. "Foreign Ministry Spokesperson Hong Lei's Regular Press Conference on November 8, 2012." Accessed 12/15/2015. www.fmcoprc.gov.mo/eng/gsxwfb/lxjzzfh/t987276.html.

Ogden, Peter K. "Addax Petroleum Corporation – Selling to Sinopec for Cdn$52.80/sh." *National Bank Financial*, June 25, 2009.

People's Daily. "China, Nigeria Sign Oil Supply Pact." July 9, 2005.

Ramo, Joshua C. *The Beijing Consensus*. London, UK: The Foreign Policy Centre, 2004.

Reuters. "Nigeria Loses $10.9bn to Oil Theft." July 30, 2013.

Rotberg, Robert. "China's Quest for Resources, Opportunities, and Influence in Africa." In *China into Africa. Trade, Aid, and Influence*, edited by Robert Rotberg, 1–21. Washington, DC: Brookings Institution Press, 2008.

Shi Lingtao [史凌涛]. 非洲地区石油工业投资环境 ("The African's Petroleum Industry's Investment Environment"). *国际石油经济* (*The International Petroleum Economy*) 12 (10) (October 20, 2004).

Taylor, Ian. "China's Relations with Nigeria, The Round Table." *The Commonwealth Journal of International Affairs* 96 (392) (2007): 631–45.

Thomson Streetevents. "Addax Petroleum Corporation – Final Transcript, Addax Petroleum Corporation Earnings Conference Call." July 27, 2009.

Thurber, Mark C., Ifeyinwa M. Emelife and Patrick R.P. Heller. "NNPC and Nigeria's Oil Patronage Ecosystem." In *Oil and Governance: State-Owned Enterprises and the World Energy Supply*, edited by David G. Victor, David R. Hults and Mark C. Thurber, 701–52. Cambridge, UK: Cambridge University Press, 2012.

Tian Li (田力). 成功收购 Addax 石油公司, 中石化海外并购迈出重要一步 [The Successful Acquisition of Addax Petroleum, an important step for Sinopec's overseas M&A]. *中国石油和化工 (China Petroleum and Chemical Industry)*, September 5, 2009.

United Nations Statistical Division, Commodity Trade Statistics Database. Accessed 12/15/2015. http://comtrade.un.org/db/.

U.S. Energy Information Administration (EIA). "Nigeria." Accessed 12/15/2015. www.eia.gov/countries/country-data.cfm?fips=ni.

U.S. House of Representatives Committee on Homeland Security, Subcommittee on Counterterrorism and Intelligence. "Boko Haram – Emerging Threat to the U.S. Homeland." November 30, 2011. Accessed 12/15/2015. https://homeland.house.gov/files/Testimony%20Pham.pdf.

Vines, Alex, Lillian Wong, Marcus Weimer and Indira Campos. "Thirst for African Oil, Asian National Oil Companies in Nigeria and Angola." A Chatham House Report. London, UK: Chatham House, August 2009.

The Wall Street Journal. "Sinopec Acquisition of Addax Petroleum." June 24, 2009. Accessed 12/15/2015. http://wsj.dealogic.com/SINOPEC-Addax-627331.html.

Wang Wei [汪巍]. 非洲石油市场开发策略. ["Strategy for Development of the African Oil Market"]. *中国石油石化* (*China Petroleum and Petrochemical Industry*), October 15, 2009.

Wong, Lillian. "The Impact of Asian National Oil Companies in Nigeria." *Ocnus.Net, Nigerian Muse*, December 30, 2008.

Wylie, Gavin. "Addax Petroleum Inc." *Scotia Capital*, July 28, 2009.

Xinhua News Agency. "Chinese Killed by Boko Haram Suspects in Northern Nigeria." October 8, 2012.

Xu Yi (徐翼). 胡锦涛访非展开能源外交 ["Hu visits Africa to Expand Energy Diplomacy"]. *中华工商时报* (*China Business Times*), April 30, 2006.

5 Angola

Independent NOCs impacting foreign policy

Background

The state of China-Angola relations

There are three periods in Sino-Angolan relations. The first period, from 1975 to 1983 prior to the establishment of diplomatic ties, was characterized by "mostly traumatic" relations between Beijing and the Movimento Popular de Libertação de Angola (MPLA). Sino-Angolan relations date back to the years of the anticolonial struggle. In this period, China supported all three major liberation movements in the country: MPLA, the União Nacional para a Indêpendencia Total de Angola (UNITA), and the Frente Nacional para Libertação de Angola (FNLA).[1] In November 1975, MPLA seized power and declared Angola's independence.[2] In the subsequent period, relations were strained between Beijing and MPLA, given the former's previous support to the two rival independence movements. In fact, the Chinese leadership refused to recognize Angola's independence, and diplomatic relations between the two were only established in 1983 (figure 5.1 for map of Angola).[3]

The second phase, from 1983 until the end of the civil war in 2002, was characterized by a gradual rapprochement, facilitated in part by leadership changes in both countries, that is, Deng Xiaoping in China in 1978 and Dos Santos in Angola in 1979.[4] In this period, many trade agreements were signed between the two parties. In fact, at the end of the decade, Angola became China's second-largest trading partner in Africa (after South Africa).

Finally, in the third phase, from 2002 to the present, relations have been characterized by increasing complementarity in terms of trade and cooperation. In this period, large loans have been given to Angola by China in return for access to natural resources for Chinese NOCs, giving rise to a so-called "Angola model." Moreover, the large loans have been seen as enabling Angola to develop without respect to Western principles of "good governance." Many leadership visits have been conducted in this period and a strategic partnership has been established.

Literature on Angola

There are three predominant perspectives on the topic of the activities of Chinese energy companies in Angola: a liberal/*political economy perspective*, a realist/*foreign policy* perspective, and a *globalist* perspective.

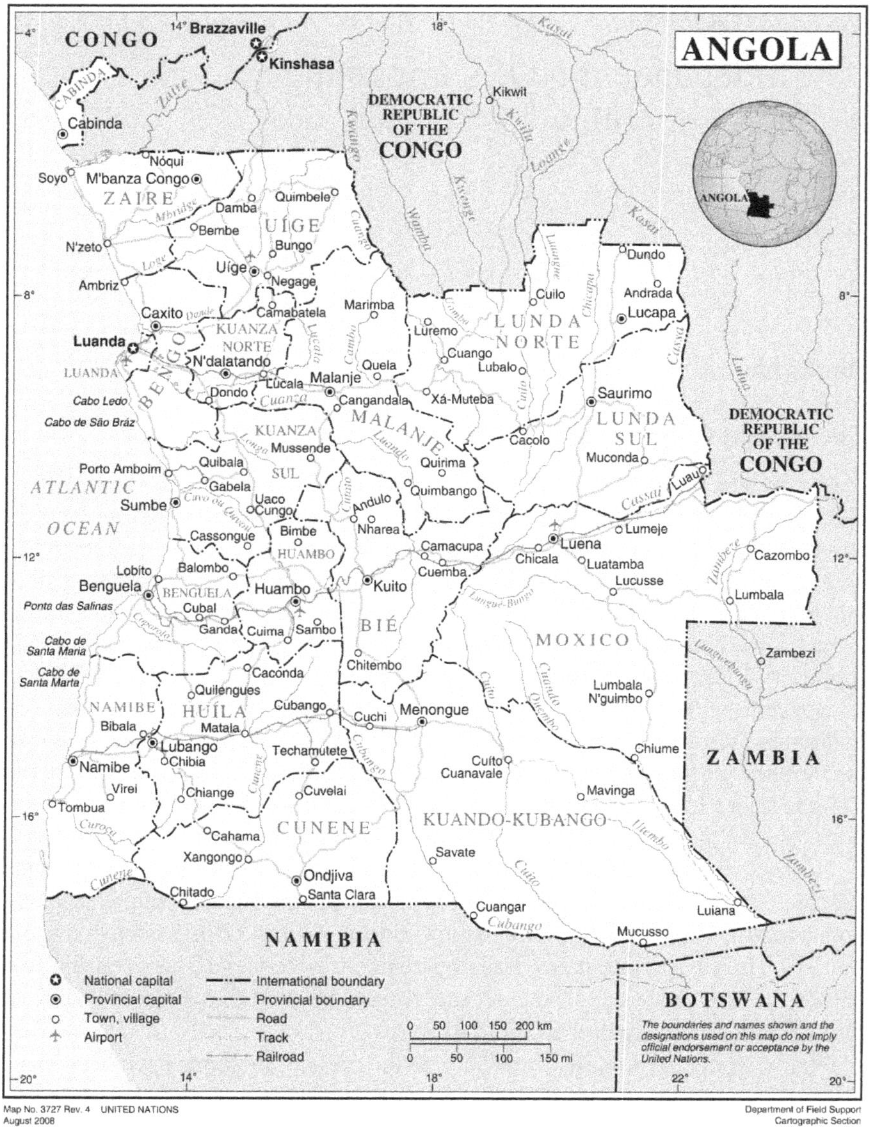

Figure 5.1 Map of Angola

From the political economy perspective, the focus is on bureaucratic politics in Angola and the role of Angolan elites in the management of the oil industry.[5] In fact, due in part to its oil riches, Angola is seen as an example of a failed state.[6] The oil sector in Angola suffers from corruption and a lack of transparency, and the national oil company, Sonangol, has primarily been at the service of the presidency and its rentier ambitions.[7] Lucy Corkin argues that the ease with which Chinese companies obtain access to resources in Angola is related to the companies' connections to the presidency and the constellations of the different interest groups operating in the Angolan state.[8]

From a *foreign policy* perspective, the activities of Chinese companies in Angola are used by the Chinese government as part of an expansionist strategy of the Chinese state. Here Chinese companies are seen as an extension of the state. The general idea is that access to finance and provision of government loans help the Chinese companies to acquire important assets in Angola. These government-backed loans can help the Chinese NOCs gain access to resources, which, in turn, can help the Chinese government ensure its energy security.[9] Moreover, the Chinese leadership uses the Chinese NOCs to expand its influence in Angola.

In contrast, part of the literature on the activities of Chinese companies in Angola stresses the autonomy of the companies.[10] For example, Alex Vines and Indira Campo argue that Chinese NOCs in Angola should be seen as autonomous entities.[11] Similarly, Marcus Power and Ana C. Alves argue that one should open up the box of China and look at the relationship between the companies and the state and that the companies are relatively autonomous in certain acquisitions.[12]

Finally, there is a *globalist* perspective that focuses on the Angola model, which examines the developmental consequences of access to Chinese aid and finance. In 2004, Angola was about to accept an International Monetary Fund (IMF) loan, when the offer of an Eximbank loan with no conditions regarding governance enabled Angola to turn down the IMF loan, together with the conditions accompanying it.[13] This is illustrative of how Chinese loans have come to be seen as an alternative to cooperating with the IMF, as the Chinese concessional loans given to build infrastructure can enable the recipient country to develop, regardless of its political system and without having to adhere to norms of good governance. In this way, Chinese investments are seen as constituting a challenge to the so-called Western development model.[14] In contrast, from the Angolan perspective, China is seen as a model for how poor countries can develop. At the time, Angola experienced an acute need for funding for the reconstruction after the Angolan Civil War, and Chinese loans helped meet some of this need. Also, it is noted that the structural adjustment programs of the IMF and the World Bank (WB) for African countries in the 1960–70s had adverse effects.[15] However, it is also noted that Angola is open to investments from countries other than China.[16] Thus, Angola's choosing to accept the loan from the Eximbank instead of the IMF loan was not a case of the choice of a development model but rather because the loan facilitated greatly needed development in the country.

Thus, as seen earlier, there are three standard takes on the topic of the activities of Chinese companies in Angola. First, through a political economy lens, the Chinese corporate activities in Angola offer a case of Chinese maneuvering in the Angolan bureaucracy and winning over the elites to ensure resource acquisitions. From a foreign policy perspective, the Chinese companies are used as tools by the Chinese state to obtain important oil resources and are part of an expansionist strategy of the Chinese state. Moreover, the extension of credit lines helps the

Chinese leadership to obtain political influence in Angola. Third is a globalist perspective, according to which the activities of the Chinese companies in Angola have positive developmental effects.

These contributions have several limitations. First, they are limited to materials written in English. Second, the existing literature either studies the activities of the Chinese companies as an expression of state control or not. Whereas most of the literature referred to previously assumes that the Chinese state and/or Chinese companies are engaged in Angola for state interests, the analysis here opens up the question of the extent to which this is the case and considers the tension between the two. The assessment here therefore examines whether state interests, economic interests, or concerns with domestic stability dominate the activities of the Chinese companies in Angola and thus proceeds in a different manner. Moreover, given access to materials written in Chinese, this analysis includes the perspective from Chinese academics and decision-makers as reflected in the Chinese state media, together with my own interviews with Chinese business and state representatives. Thus, the study here will be more thorough and comprehensive.

History of Chinese oil companies in Angola

The entrance of Chinese NOCs into Angola is relatively new, with Sinopec being the first Chinese NOC to acquire an asset in Angola in 2004.[17] Since 2004, Sinopec has invested at least $3.6 billion in Angola and formed several joint ventures, including one with BP and others with companies such as Petrobras and ENI. In total, Chinese companies own stakes in 11 oil blocks in the country (none as the sole owner). Of the three majors, however, only Sinopec has invested in Angola; CNOOC and CNPC have yet to make any investments in the country.

Angola is an important source of Chinese oil imports. In the period from 2004–09, Angola accounted for 13–16 percent of all Chinese oil imports, making the country one of the largest suppliers of oil to China.[18] In 2011, Angola supplied 12.27 percent of Chinese oil imports (623,000 bpd).[19]

Angola's strategic importance

The limited strategic importance that Angola holds for China is reflected in the following. First, in terms of the *level of political relations*, China and Angola established relations on January 12, 1983, and the two countries established a strategic partnership in November 2010 (战略伙伴关系/*zhanlue huoban guanxi*) during Vice President Xi Jinping's visit to Angola.[20] Unlike the Chinese ambassadors to both South Africa and Egypt, with whom China also has strategic partnerships, the ambassador to Angola does not have ministerial-level status. There have been a relatively limited number of visits from each side in recent years, and most of these have been from Angola to China (see the Appendix). Moreover, on the issue of Taiwan, Angola has consistently supported Beijing over Taiwan. Lastly, Angola can be deemed attractive to China because of its relative political stability.

Second, in terms of the role of *CCP regime stability*, no extremist or separatist groups have established a branch in the country, unlike in the countries in the northern part of Africa, such as the Sahel Belt, including Nigeria and Mali. In contrast to Sudan, there is no evidence of links to Islam or al-Qaeda in Angola. Some security issues remain in the wake of the country's 27-year civil war, which ended in 2002, particularly in the disputed oil-rich Cabinda exclave, where separatist groups remain active. However, there is no evidence of links between these groups and al-Qaeda. There is no evidence of fatalities involving Chinese nationals in Angola in recent years. As of 2012, approximately 259,000 Chinese live in Angola.[21] While there is evidence of Chinese nationals being involved in crime, these incidents are unrelated to extremist activities; they are related instead to kidnappings, armed robberies, and prostitution.[22]

Third, in terms of the *salience of territory*, there are no ethnic ties to China, which holds for all of the countries in Africa. In terms of *strategic location*, Angola is located on the west coast of Africa and has important access to the Atlantic Ocean, which means that the shipping routes to North American and European markets are shorter than those to the Middle Eastern and Asian markets. Even so, Angola's access to the sea makes it attractive as a trade partner. In terms of infrastructure, Angola's infrastructure is still hampered by its 27-year civil war and is in need of further development. There are three main ports as well as several export terminals (see figure 5.2 for the infrastructure in Angola).[23] Angola has one refinery, in Luanda, and is in the process of building another in Lobito.[24] However, for a country with a large coastline covering 1.2 million km^2 (24th in the world), the transport infrastructure can be characterized as inadequate.[25] Still, despite its infrastructure inadequacies, Angola's strategic location makes the country geopolitically important to China.

Fourth, in terms of the role of the *other great power*, Angola is not a US alliance partner, and the United States does not have military bases in Angola (neither does China). There appears to be a sense of ambivalence marking Angola-US relations. During the Cold War, Angola was the site of a proxy war waged by the United States, Cuba, and the Soviet Union, and the United States blocked Angola's admission to the UN in 1976. In fact, the United States supported the FNLA and UNITA before and after independence.[26] More recently, however, the United States has been paying increasing attention to Angola, including visits by senior leaders (e.g., Secretary of State Hilary Clinton in 2009). UN sanctions have never been launched against Angola. Still, the fact that Angola is of some importance to the United States renders the country of some strategic importance to China.

Fifth, in terms of *bilateral trade*, Angola and South Africa have competed for the status as China's largest trading partner on the African continent, South Africa having been China's largest trading partner until 2005 and since 2010, while China traded more with Angola in the period from 2006–09. Bilateral trade has grown in recent years from $1.2 billion in 2002 to $37.5 billion in 2012, as figure 5.3 illustrates.

China accounted for 20.8 percent of Angola's imports and 45.8 percent of all Angolan exports in 2012, being the largest source of both imports and exports.[27]

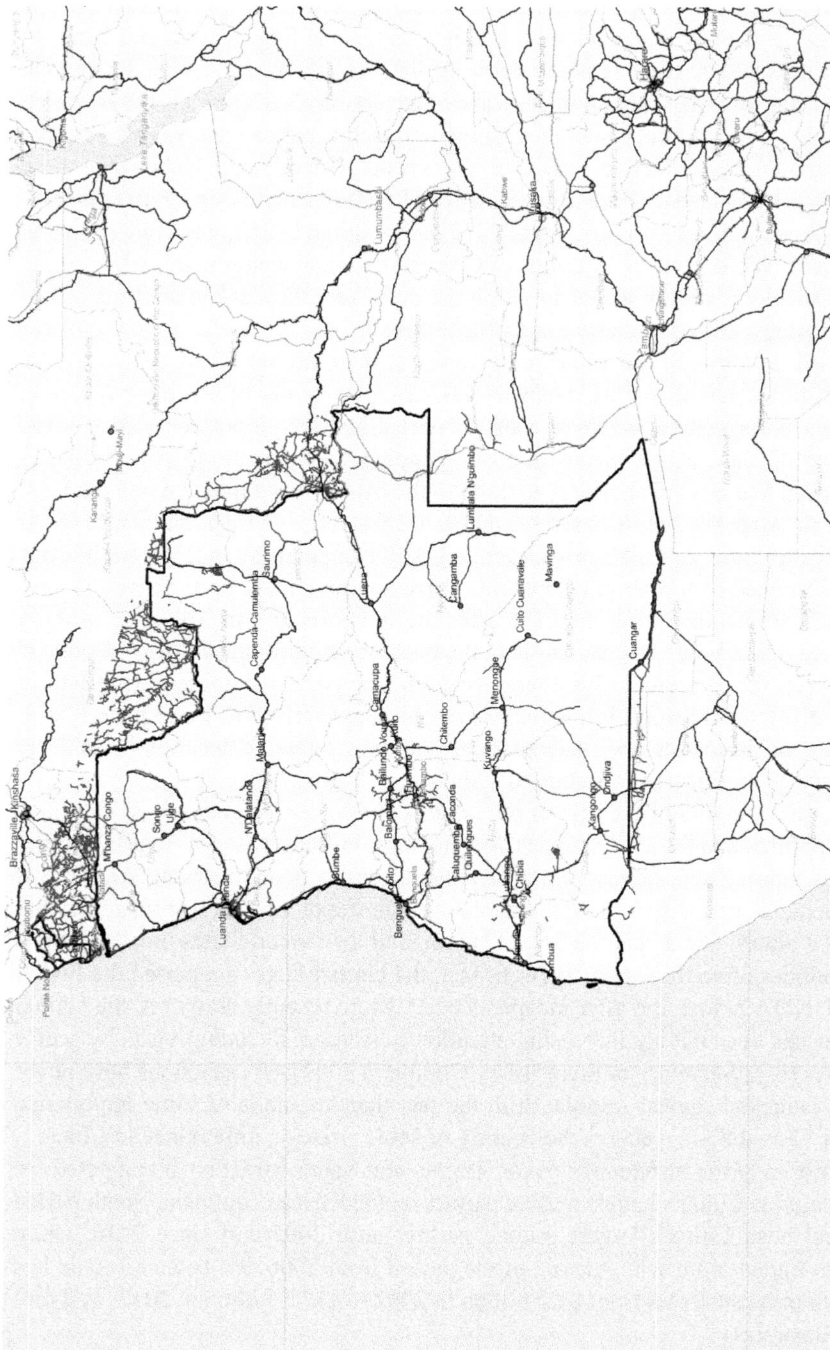

Figure 5.2 Angola, infrastructure

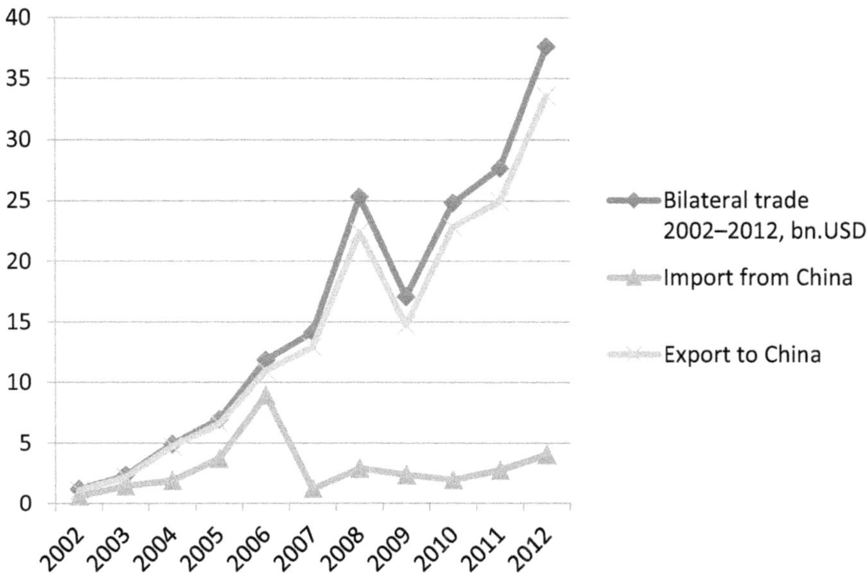

Figure 5.3 Sino-Angolan bilateral trade, 2002–12

Table 5.1 Level of strategic importance: Angola (for more detail, see Appendix)

Country	*1. Level of political relations*	*2. Role for CCP regime stability*	*3. Salience of territory*	*4. Role for other great power*	*5. Bilateral trade*	*Total*
Angola	1	0	1	1	2	1

China is now the largest source of Angolan imports, up from fourth largest in 2007 ($1.2 billion) and second largest in 2008 ($2.9 billion).

As becomes apparent after computing the preceding components, and as table 5.1 illustrates, visits have been relatively limited between the two countries, and no extremist groups have become established in the country. Moreover, in terms of strategic location, Angola is of limited importance. Even if there is high bilateral trade, overall, Angola is of limited strategic importance to China.

Oil and gas levels

Angola has very rich gas and oil reserves together with high production. In terms of oil, as of 2014, Angola has proven reserves of 10.47 billion barrels of crude oil.[28] This figure is the second-largest in Sub-Saharan Africa, after Nigeria, and ranks 18th in the world. Most of the Angolan oil is light to medium and has low sulfur content, rendering it well-suited for export to the United States, China, and other large importers. In 2013, Angola's oil production accounted for 1.83 million bpd, ranking the country as the world's 16th-largest oil producer; in 2012, it was Africa's third largest oil producer, after Nigeria and Algeria.[29]

In terms of gas, Angola's natural gas reserves are estimated at 366.14 billion m^3 in 2014, ranked 35th in the world and second in Sub-Saharan Africa after Nigeria.[30] Its production of natural gas in 2012 was 752.10 million m^3 (67th in the world).[31] Angola's first LNG terminal at Soyo started operations in June 2013.[32]

Thus, relatively speaking, Angola can therefore be said to possess very rich gas and oil reserves together with high production.

The empirical expectation

As the preceding data illustrate, Angola is a country of limited strategic importance and has abundant reserves of oil. Based on these characteristics and together with the history of the case, the empirical expectation is that *economic interests are the dominant motivating force* in Angola. It is thus predicted that, in Angola, Chinese companies have an incentive to be involved because of the large quantities of oil in order to maximize profits, but as the Chinese government attributes limited strategic importance to the country, the state will not seek to pursue its state interests there. The companies will be in the driver's seat, and there will be evidence of economic interests.

Quantitative content analysis

For Angola, as presented earlier, the hypothesis is that economic interests dominate. The quantitative analysis of the Chinese state media shows that 80 percent of the articles for Angola have a preponderance of economic interests over the ten-year period under investigation. Thus, the activities are driven by commercial interests, and the preceding hypothesis is supported. Still, looking at how the discourse develops over the course of the period under examination, we see many fluctuations: as figure 5.4 shows, economic interests dominate relative to state interests and concerns with domestic stability, except for in the years 2006 (ratio of 0.8:1) and 2009 (ratio of 0.97:1). Thus, in the years 2006 and 2009, state interests and concerns with domestic stability actually dominate relative to economic interests. Furthermore, economic interests peak relative to state interests/concerns with domestic stability in the years 2003–04 (ratios of 2.8:1–3.0:1) and 2007 (ratio of 3.7:1). Still, in most years, the quantitative evidence supports the hypothesis.

When we zoom in and examine particular ratios, such as the ratio of economic interests to state interests, we see that, for the whole decade, economic interests are stronger relative to state interests. Economic interests peak in 2004 (ratio of 7.1:1), 2007 (ratio of 8.1:1), and 2010 (ratio of 5.2:1), as figure 5.5 shows. The strength of economic interests in 2007 can be explained by the refinery deal that year, as we will see in Key Decision 2 later in this chapter. State interests are relatively strong relative to economic interests in 2006 (ratio of 2.2:1) and 2008–09 (ratios of 1.5:1–2.1:1). The importance of state interests in 2006 would follow

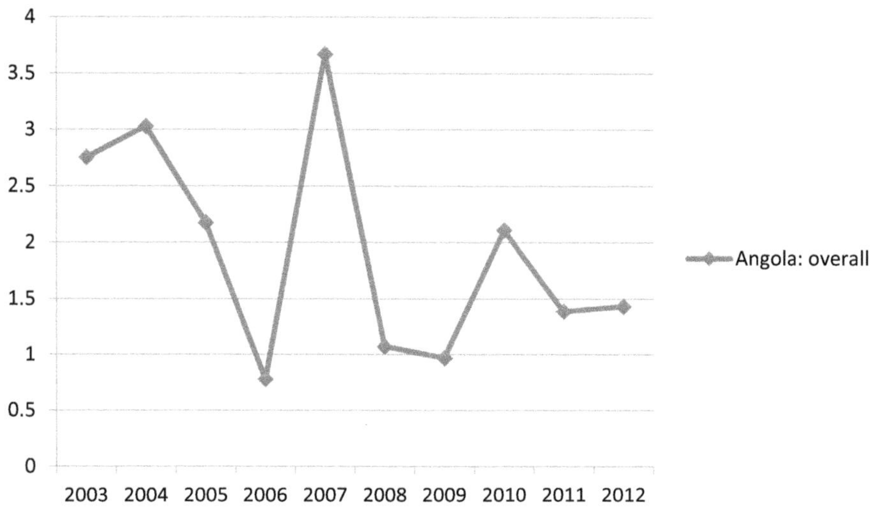

Figure 5.4 Ratio of economic interests to state interests/domestic stability

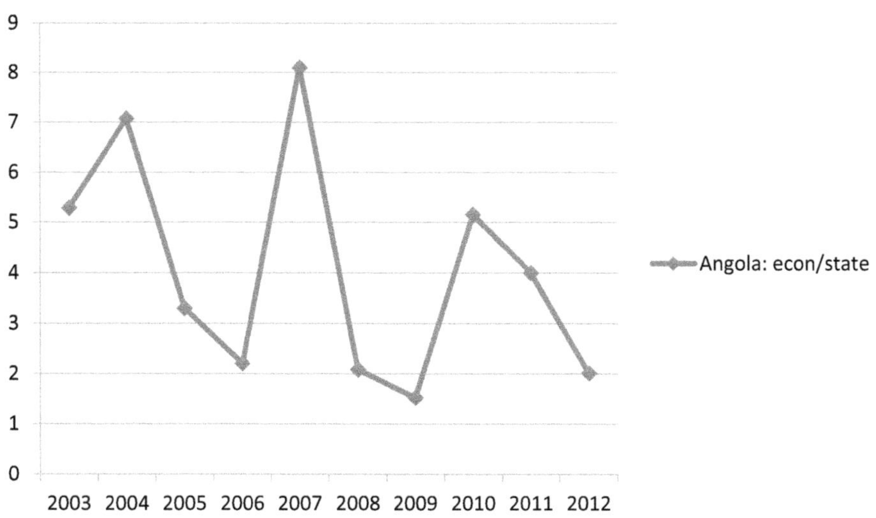

Figure 5.5 Ratio of economic interests to state interests

from Wen Jiabao's visit to Angola that year. Moreover, in 2008, President dos Santos visited Beijing twice.

Probing the relationship between economic interests and concerns with domestic stability (*weiwen*), as figure 5.6 illustrates, we see that that economic interests peak in 2006 (ratio of 68.5:1). In other years, the concern with domestic stability has greater importance, particularly in the years 2009–12 (ratios of 2.0:1–5.2:1).

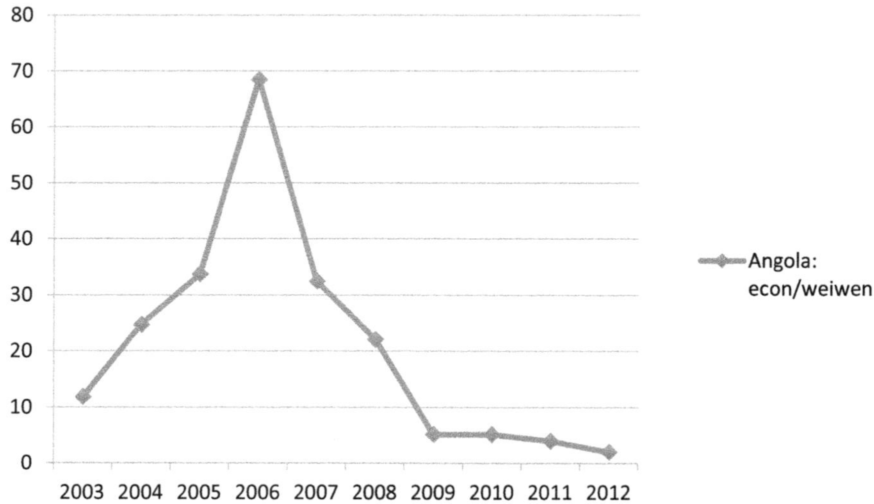

Figure 5.6 Ratio of economic interests to domestic stability

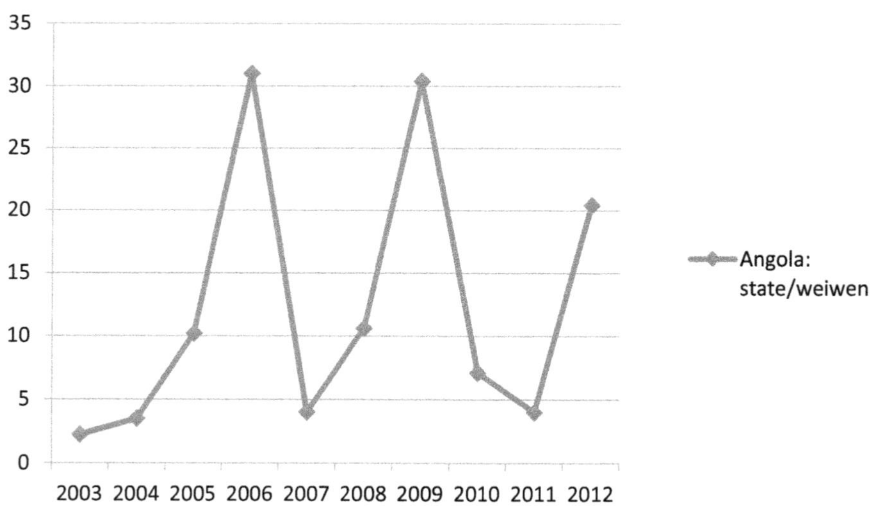

Figure 5.7 Ratio of state interests to domestic stability

Finally, looking at the ratio of state interests to concerns with domestic stability (*weiwen*), as illustrated in figure 5.7, we see that, overall, over the course of this period, state interests are stronger than concerns with domestic stability. Still, concerns with domestic stability have greater importance in the years 2003–04 (ratios of 2.2:1–3.5:1), in 2007 (ratio of 4:1), and in 2010–11 (ratios of 4.0:1–7.1:1).

The preceding results generally confirm the hypothesis presented here that economic interests are expected to dominate in most years. The remainder of this chapter explores the extent to which the results from the quantitative analysis are corroborated by the results from the qualitative analysis, to which we now turn.

Qualitative analysis

This section focuses on three key decisions illuminating important aspects of the activities of Chinese companies in Angola. They have been selected to allow for analysis over time. I focus on the Eximbank loan to Angola in 2004, an agreement in 2006–07 on the construction of a refinery in Angola, and Sinopec and CNOOC's failed attempt to acquire an asset in 2009–10. An alternative key decision could be Sinopec's purchase of the stakes of SSI in Block 18 in Angola in 2010, but since this is an internal company transaction, it is not included here. The preceding three key decisions are argued to be particularly significant and representative in terms of the activities of Chinese companies in Angola in the period under investigation. Thus, analyzing these decisions contributes to our understanding of whether Chinese foreign policy toward Angola is dominated by state interests, economic interests, or concerns with domestic stability (*weiwen*).

Key Decision 1: the Eximbank loan to Angola

This section focuses on the Eximbank loan to Angola in 2004, particularly the characteristics of the loan and whether it was given in conjunction with other agreements and/or resource acquisitions. If state interests dominate, we would see the donation of aid, loans, and credit lines to enable the building of infrastructure. Such loans aim to help Chinese companies win important resource deals. This, in turn, would be linked to visits from political leaders. If economic interests dominate, we would see evidence that as most of the loans are tied, most of the work will be granted to Chinese companies – ultimately employing Chinese workers and using Chinese materials – thus helping the Chinese economy to grow. If concerns with domestic stability (*weiwen*) dominate, we would see evidence of Chinese oil workers killed in Angola, statements made by state leaders, and comments on Chinese social media reflecting concerns with Chinese worker safety in Angola.

State interests

After 27 years of civil war (1975–2002), Angola had an urgent need for financing to carry out infrastructure investments and kick-start the economy, especially in the agricultural, transportation, and housing sectors. At the time, however, because of their debt record and rejection of IMF's loan conditions, Angola experienced difficulty attracting investments. From the Angolan perspective, the loans offered by the Chinese government were very welcome: they offered lower interest rates and longer repayment schedules than commercial loans and, not least, had "no political strings" attached.

In 2002, the Chinese government first provided a $150 million loan from the China Construction Bank and Eximbank for infrastructure development.[33] Then, in 2003, the Chinese Ministry of Trade signed an agreement for new economic and commercial cooperation with the Angolan Ministry of Finance.[34] Overall, from 2002 to 2007, Eximbank and the Angolan government have entered into three major financial deals amounting to $4.5 billion. The first deal, approved on March 21, 2004, was a $2 billion financing package for public investment projects, earmarked for infrastructure construction and rehabilitation, to be repaid over 12 years at an interest rate of Libor plus 1.5 percent with a grace period of up to three years.[35] In July 2007, a further extension of $500 million was signed for "complementary actions" to projects tied to the first phase. In September 2007, an additional $2 billion loan was given, to be repaid over 15 years at Libor plus 1.25 percent.[36]

The combined loan of $4.5 billion was to be partly repaid in oil, with provision of 10,000 bpd in the first two years and to increase to 40,000 bpd in 2009.[37] The logic behind the repayments in oil is to ensure a secure, long-term oil supply. According to one Chinese informant, "Chinese banks ask such a strong guarantee as oil to do business in Angola because there is high risk."[38]

In addition to repayment in oil, a characteristic was that, in principle, Eximbank loans require that all projects that receive financing are undertaken by a Chinese company. In the Angolan case, however, it was negotiated that 30 percent of the contract value was to be allocated to the Angolan private sector in order to encourage Angolan participation in the reconstruction process, that is, "Angolanization."[39]

Thirdly, a characteristic is that the loan must be used for the development of the recipient country, industrial development and infrastructure in particular.[40]

In 2005, the China International Fund (CIF) provided another loan of $2.9 billion to Angola.[41] As the CIF has subsequently been plagued by mismanagement and corruption and most of its construction projects came to a halt in September 2007, we will not address this loan and its significance further here.

The Angola model

The particular loans given to Angola have given rise to an "Angolan model" characterized by financial assistance secured by Chinese access to natural resources, which, in turn, is tied to the use of Chinese contractors. The Eximbank provide a loan to be used for the building of infrastructure in the recipient country. In turn, this is backed by agreements to supply oil. Controversially, however, this money often returns to China indirectly, as Eximbank loans must be used to pay Chinese companies employing Chinese workers. In this way, in practice, the loans help China to develop, as the employment of Chinese workers and use of Chinese materials benefit the Chinese economy.

The Angola model can be characterized in the following way: "we give the money to the Angolan government, and then the Angolan government gives us natural resources. It is a money-for-natural-resources conversion model."[42] In the words of a Chinese oil industry publication, the loans are seen as the embodiment of a model that reflects the pragmatic nature of China's assistance and fits into the notion of "win-win co-operation" and the model of "mutual benefit."[43] During Premier Wen Jiabao's visit to Angola in June 2006, he declared Angola to be a partner and that "we want to . . . carry out mutually beneficial cooperation in the energy field."[44] Importantly, the second tranche of the oil-backed Eximbank loan was also agreed upon during Wen Jiabao's visit.

Angolan Ambassador to China João Manuel Bernardo referred to Beijing as "a true friend of Africa" and said that "Africa can [now] develop by its own effort with China's help . . . without any political conditions."[45] Thus there is satisfaction with the Chinese aid and the oil-for-loan cooperation model from the Angolan side, which indicates that the recipient appreciates its Chinese partner.[46]

Economic interests: bidding for Block 18

In mid-2003, Shell put its 50 percent stake in Block 18 up for sale, allegedly because of rising exploration costs and unsuccessful drilling. This block contains deep-water oil assets with the highest reserves and production volume among projects of similar type.

On April 9, 2004, India's Oil and Natural Gas Corporation (ONGC) bid $623 million for Shell's 50 percent stake in BP-operated Block 18 in Angola.[47] By August 2004, while BP had approved the deal, Sonangol still had not done so. In October, however, Sinopec made a counter offer of $725 million that Sonangol accepted two months later. Surprisingly, Sonangol exerted its preemptive right and instead allowed Sinopec in. Thus, in February 2005, Sonangol transferred the stake to Sinopec (SSI) (table 5.2).[48] One reason for this transaction might be that Sinopec's $725 million bid was higher than ONGC's $623 million. Importantly, the acquisition was accompanied by the $2 billion Eximbank loan. This was higher than the loan that the Indian government offered of $200 million to help develop Angola's railways.[49]

For Sinopec, the acquisition was its first stake in the Angolan oil industry, giving the company access to most of the Sinopec/SSI-produced oil in that block. Finally, because the stake would be managed in partnership with BP, a company with advanced technology, the acquisition would help Sinopec gain access to new

Table 5.2 Sinopec's acquisition of a stake in Block 18

Announced date	October 2004
Completed date	February 2005
Acquired %	50%
Deal value	$725 million
Acquirer company	Sinopec (SSI)
Vendor company	Royal Dutch Shell
Stake	Block 18, Angola

oil technology. Says a Chinese informant, because "Chinese technology is lagging behind (比较落后/*bijiao luohou*) the joint venture (JV) [between BP and Sinopec] is good as a platform for sharing technology."[50] Finally, in Block 18, BP had carried much of the investment, for which reason the acquisition did not require extensive investments from Sinopec.[51]

State interests

The acquisition was finalized shortly after the signing of the first tranche of the credit line in March 2004 from the Eximbank loan. Although there is no clear link between the extension of the loan and Chinese access to the oil stake, it would appear as though the loans and long-term crude supply deals helped Sinopec acquire the stake, resulting in Sinopec's entry into the Angolan oil industry.

*Concerns with domestic stability (*weiwen*)*

In terms of the concerns with domestic stability, a total of 259,000 Chinese live in Angola (as of 2012),[52] and many Chinese companies are involved in Angolan infrastructure projects. In recent years, there have been growing concerns about violence against Chinese nationals. In contrast to Nigeria, Angola has fewer problems with organized, collective resistance in the oil industry. Moreover, Angola's oil is generally located offshore. However, there are risks associated with Angola's main oil-producing region, the Cabinda Province.[53] This, however, has not had any ramifications for the Chinese nationals in Angola. Thus, there is no evidence of concerns with domestic stability (*weiwen*).

Conclusion, Key Decision 1

As seen in the preceding case, there is a puzzling simultaneity of events, as an important business deal on an important, promising stake in the Angolan oil industry, Block 18, is settled immediately after the donation of the Eximbank loan. Moreover, statements from political leaders and important political visits take place to back up the acquisition. The Eximbank loan in 2004–05 favored the Chinese state, as it helped Chinese companies close numerous deals, among them the oil stake in Block 18 in Angola. The building of infrastructure was also offered to enable the acquisition. In this sense, the political agreements are bait to "catch" oil deals. There is, therefore, evidence that rather than the bid for the oil stake in Block 18 and the loan being unrelated, these two events are closely linked, intended to aid the Chinese companies to enter the competitive Angolan oil industry. In the words of a Chinese academic, there is "fierce competition . . . and huge amounts of money and certain political conditions related to investments in Angolan infrastructure are needed."[54] Therefore, Chinese concessional loans might be seen as a way to ensure important state objectives and thus as a foreign policy tool. This key decision to extend the Eximbank loan thus reflects state interests.

Still, there was an important visit by Wen Jiabao to Angola in 2006 during which the oil-backed Eximbank loan was enlarged, which could be seen as an indicator of economic interests, as the visit by Wen Jiabao and the loan can be seen as helping Sinopec pursue its interest. Moreover, the deep-water oil block, Block 18, that Sinopec acquired had the highest reserves and production volume among projects of similar type and could thus be regarded as promising. Finally, the acquisition of the stake in Block 18 helped Sinopec acquire important technology and "catch up" with Western companies. As there is also evidence of economic interests in addition to state interests, state and economic interests coincide in this key decision.

How does the analysis here compare to the quantitative analysis? The results from the quantitative analysis show that economic interests dominate relative to state interests/domestic stability in 2004 (ratio of 3.0:1) and in 2005 (ratio of 2.2:1). Similarly, when studying economic interests relative to state interests, economic interests are seen to dominate both in 2004 and 2005 (ratio of 7.1:1 and ratio of 3.3:1, respectively). In terms of the concerns with domestic stability, no such evidence is found. Overall, the results from the quantitative analysis are not consistent with the qualitative analysis here, as they indicate that state and economic interests coincide.

While there will always be some inconsistencies between different types of evidence, the question is whether they are in overall agreement. Still, based on the preceding, the evidence that state and economic interests coincide is more credible.

Key Decision 2: refinery, 2006–07

Here, we focus on the 2006 agreement for Sinopec (SSI) to build a refinery in Angola, which was part of a larger agreement reached in conjunction with Sinopec being awarded stakes in the 2006 licensing round. In 2007, however, the negotiations for the refinery stalled, and Sinopec withdrew from the project. We examine the significance of this for Chinese foreign policy and whether there was evidence of state interests, economic interests, or concerns with domestic stability (*weiwen*). If state interests dominate, the donation of credit lines would influence the Angolan executive to favor China to build the refinery. This would be important as bait to win access to oil acreage and would be backed up by visits. Should economic interests dominate, we would see that the refinery was a way to gain access to technology. If concerns with domestic stability dominate, we would see evidence of workers killed in Angola, statements made by state leaders, and comments on Chinese social media reflecting concerns with Chinese worker safety in Angola.

Lobito refinery

Angola has only one refinery, situated near Luanda. It was constructed in 1955 and has a capacity of 39,000 bpd, supplying a mere 10 percent of Angola's petroleum

Table 5.3 The Sonaref Refinery

Announced date	March 16, 2006
Failed date	March 2007
Acquired %	30%
Deal value	$3.5 billion
Acquirer company	Sinopec (SSI)
Vendor company	Sonangol
Stake	Sonaref refinery

requirements.[55] As of 2014, Angola imports 80 percent of its refined products.[56] The plan for the new Sonaref refinery was presented in May 2001. It would be placed in the port city of Lobito south of Luanda, an attractive location given its location on the Atlantic coast and its large port capable of handling large numbers of ships.[57] Increased refining capacity could help meet domestic demand, allow the country to eliminate petrol imports, and augment the export capacity for refined products.[58]

Sonangol had struggled to find partners to finance the project. Some IOCs questioned the economic viability of the project also given rising oil prices at the time. Some Asian companies, such as ONGC and Sinopec (SSI), were more positive about building the refinery. These firms, however, lacked deepwater technology and experience.

An agreement was eventually signed with Sinopec (SSI) to jointly examine plans for the refinery, despite its lack of deepwater technology. The refinery would have a processing capacity of 200,000 bpd, and Sinopec was to provide the full funding for the project of $3.5 billion.[59] It was projected to start operations in 2010 (see table 5.3).

State interests

Vice Premier Zeng Peiyan visited Luanda on February 25–27, 2005, at which time he met with President dos Santos and Sonangol Chairman Manuel Vicente. Zeng Peiyan signed a total of nine cooperation agreements with Angola, four of which were oil-related, including oil from Sonangol to Sinopec over seven years, with 40,000 bpd due in the first three years.[60] The two parties also signed an understanding on the joint construction of the new Sonaref refinery.[61]

On March 16, 2006, following up on the deals signed during Zeng Peiyan's 2005 visit, a partnership agreement was signed to develop a refinery. According to this agreement, Sinopec was to fund the entire project, which amounted to an investment of $3.5 billion. Sonangol would hold 70 percent of the shares in this project and Sinopec the remaining 30 percent.[62] The refinery would be able to process heavy crudes[63] and would almost triple the existing Angolan refining capacity. Even so, Angola was expected to remain dependent on imports for the foreseeable future. According to the agreement, 80 percent of the output would be reserved for export to foreign markets.[64]

In January 2007, however, the refinery negotiations stalled between Sonangol and Sinopec, and in March, Sinopec announced its decision to withdraw from the project, citing concerns about the current market for refined products.[65] On March 14, Sonangol declared that it would manage the project on its own. As Sonangol Chairman Manuel Vicente explained, "We will go it alone."[66] What were the reasons for this?

There was disagreement over how big a share of the output was to be exported, as well as which markets the Sonaref refinery's products would target. According to the agreement, 80 percent of Sonaref's production would be exported to foreign markets.[67]

The Angolan government disapproved of the plan later, as the domestic market regularly experiences shortages of refined products and as the government wished for most of the production to remain in the domestic and African markets rather than in an overseas market. In fact, Sonaref aimed to control 50 percent of the regional market.[68]

On February 23, 2007, the Sonangol chairman said that the company had reached a point where it could not make concessions; "we cannot construct a refinery just to make products for China."[69] From the Chinese side, some sources indicate that Sinopec was not genuinely interested in the refinery project from the outset;[70] the company had only become involved with the refinery project given that the Angolan government had linked the refinery project to the concession Blocks 15/06, 17/06, and 18/06 in the 2006 licensing round. According to Chang Hexi, the Chinese economic counselor in Luanda, Chinese negotiators deliberately obstructed the negotiations.[71] For Sinopec, it would be more commercially viable to export crude oil from Angola rather than exporting more expensive refined products, particularly as sufficient refining capacity is available in China. Moreover, a refinery was being built in South Africa that would compete with the Sonaref refinery. Furthermore, as petrol prices are controlled and highly subsidized in Angola, the prospects for turning a profit were very low.[72] Finally, the financial viability of the project and the risk to which it exposes the investor were questioned.[73] In the words of one Chinese scholar, "There was high risk involved in building the refinery," and – adding to the risk – "to build a refinery is not an easy thing for Sinopec given that it lacks experience and knowledge."[74] Thus, we see that Sinopec was not interested in the project, as it was not seen as financially viable and carried high risk.[75]

Based on the preceding evidence, it is reasonable to conclude that economic interests dominated this case. The question, then, is why economic interests dominate and whether this is more consistent with NOC or state interests. As reflected in interviews with various company representatives in Angola, the Chinese leadership was very interested in the Lobito refinery.[76] It offered a way of guaranteeing oil imports to China – thus contributing to oil security. A total of 80 percent of the oil refined at the Lobito refinery was to be exported to the Chinese market, which would favor China at the expense of the local Angolan market.[77] In contrast, from Sinopec's side, the refinery was high risk, and it was unlikely that Sinopec would be able to profit from this venture. Thus, Sinopec withdrew from the deal. It would therefore appear as though Sinopec's original motive to build the refinery was to promote the development between the two countries but that it later withdrew because of its own business interests. This would be consistent with a greater role for NOCs in Chinese foreign policy.

Visit to Angola

Shortly after the May 2006 bidding round, Premier Wen Jiabao visited Angola in June 2006, at which time he offered a $9 billion loan for infrastructure improvements in return for petroleum and a number of cooperation agreements, particularly in the fields of health, technical assistance, and reconstruction.[78] This came immediately after Sinopec, through SSI, won stakes in Blocks 15/06, 17/06, and 18/06 in the May 2006 licensing round. These three offshore oil blocks hold proven reserves of 3.2 billion barrels. At the time, the bids paid for this round were the highest ever offered for oil assets.[79]

One of the prerequisites at the time of the acquisition of shares in Block 15/06, 16/06, and 18/06 – and in accordance with the agreement signed during Vice Premier Zeng Peiyan's 2005 visit – was the agreement for the Sonaref refinery signed between Sinopec and Sonangol on March 16, 2006.[80] There would appear to be some correlation between the two events.

During Chinese PM Wen Jiabao's visit to Angola in June 2006, Angolan President dos Santos described their bilateral relations as being "mutually advantageous," "pragmatic," and with no "political preconditions."[81] Thus, there is evidence of the appreciation of the recipient, which is evidence of state interests. This reflected China's general foreign policy principle *vis-à-vis* Africa, showing how the Chinese side was seeking to promote South-South development. During this visit, Premier Wen Jiabao declared that Sino-African cooperation is mutually beneficial and that it benefits African countries, as it can alleviate the Western monopoly.[82] While Premier Wen made no explicit statements concerning the refinery during the visit to Angola, for the premier to visit Angola while negotiations for the Sonaref refinery were ongoing can be seen as an indication that the Chinese government supported the construction of the refinery. All these indications make the ultimate failure of the refinery deal all the more surprising.

*Concerns with domestic stability (*weiwen*)*

No evidence is found of any link to the concern with domestic stability (*weiwen*), as no Chinese workers ever actually worked on the Angolan refinery (which ultimately failed).

Conclusion, Key Decision 2

Even if the Angolan government was very interested in the Sonaref refinery and they had experienced difficulties finding an investor, and thus were keen on Sinopec's interest in building the Sonaref refinery, the planned Lobito refinery failed.

While this failure demonstrated that Sonangol was unwilling to give in to Sinopec's demands, there is evidence that, in fact, the collapse of the refinery was the result of withdrawal on the part of the Chinese. Sinopec abandoned the project because the refinery was not considered to be profitable. Thus, this key decision demonstrates how Sinopec will only invest in commercially viable projects. Sinopec was risk-averse and driven by its commercial interests. An important visit by Wen Jiabao took place in June 2006, intended to enable the agreement on the refinery. But despite his statements declaring the importance of building the refinery and an additional offer of a $9 billion loan for infrastructure improvements, the refinery project failed. Thus, this is a case in which the company appears to be acting independently of the Chinese state and pursuing its own interests, which ultimately had consequences for foreign policy. In other words, this decision by Sinopec would point to the NOCs playing a role for Chinese foreign policy. This action did not favor the state, however, as Chinese companies subsequently lost important bids for promising stakes, as seen in Key Decision 3. Moreover, it can be seen as damaging Chinese security interests, as it might allow for less oil to be imported to China. It was also a blow to otherwise stable bilateral relations. Thus, the key decision considered here – the withdrawal from the Sonaref refinery in 2007 – reflects economic interests. While Wen Jiabao made important statements reflecting state interests, in assessing the overall weight of different sources and focusing on the political relationship, this key decision shows evidence of economic interests.

How does the analysis here compare to the quantitative analysis? Whereas economic interests clearly dominated prior to 2006, state interests became more important in 2006–07. In fact, in 2006, state interests and the concern with domestic stability came to dominate relative to economic interests (ratio of 0.8:1). In the year 2006, state interests peaked relative to concerns with domestic stability (ratio of 33.0:1). Thus, the decrease in economic interests is caused by stronger state interests. With the finalization of the important deal for the oil refinery in Angola in 2006 supported by Premier Wen Jiabao's visit, the quantitative analysis thus reflects this increase in the importance of state interests. In 2007, however, when the refinery deal collapsed, economic interests became more important (ratio of 3.7:1). This reflects the withdrawal of Sinopec from the project because of commercial concerns. Lastly, it is worth noting that the quantitative analysis produces no evidence of the activities of the Chinese companies in Angola having any significant impact on domestic stability in China. In this key decision, the quantitative results and qualitative analysis are thus consistent, as both reflect a dominance of state interests in 2006 and both show evidence of economic interests in 2007.

Key Decision 3: Sinopec and CNOOC's failure, 2009–10

After the failed refinery deal, Sinopec and CNOOC attempted to acquire an asset in Angola in 2009, which also ultimately failed. Here, we scrutinize this failed attempt, as doing so will contribute to the understanding of whether Chinese foreign policy toward Angola is dominated by economic interests, state interests, or concerns with domestic stability (*weiwen*). If state interests dominate, we would see the existence of credit lines in conjunction with acquisitions and that acquisitions would be made in conjunction with formation of, for example, strategic partnerships. If economic interests dominate, Sinopec and CNOOC would gain access to important reserves, including deepwater assets. If concerns with domestic stability dominate, we would see statements made by state leaders and comments on Chinese social media reflecting concerns with Chinese worker safety in Angola.

Economic interests

In 2009, Sinopec and CNOOC sought to acquire a minority stake in an oil block in Angola, Block 32 (see table 5.4). Even if it was only a minority stake, because this investment was blocked subsequent to the failed refinery deal in 2006–07 and therefore had importance for Sino-Angolan relations, it is worth considering more thoroughly.[83]

Block 32, operated by Total, is an offshore (ultra-deep) block and had at the time yielded 12 discoveries.[84] It is estimated to have 1.5 billion barrels of oil reserves and is considered "highly prospective." Production was expected to start in 2012.

On July 17, 2009, Sinopec and CNOOC placed a joint bid for a 20 percent stake in Block 32 owned by Marathon Oil, a US-based integrated oil company.[85] The consideration for the 20 percent stake was $1.3 billion. Marathon Oil was to retain a 10 percent stake in Block 32.[86]

The joint bid by CNOOC and Sinopec was supposedly higher than bids by other bidders, including ONGC and Petrobras. CNPC had also made a separate bid. On December 11, 2009, however, the CNOOC – Sinopec bid was blocked when Sonangol exercised its right of first refusal on the interest. Instead, Sonangol acquired the stake for $1.3 billion, and the deal closed on February 9, 2010. Interestingly, the 20 percent interest in Block 32 was subsequently transferred in 2010 to its subsidiary, China Sonangol.[87] This points to a linearity of interest between Sonangol and China Sonangol.[88]

It would appear as though Sonangol's intervention was based on market considerations, as the stake, supposedly, was being sold at a price lower than its real value, which was estimated at US$ 1.4–1.6 billion.[89] However, as Sonangol ended up transferring the stake to China Sonangol, it would appear that instead of the intervention being motivated by economic interests, it was a consequence of

Table 5.4 The failed acquisition of Block 32

Announced date	July 17, 2009
Failed	Dec. 11, 2009
Acquired %	20%
Deal value	$1.3 billion
Acquirer company	CNOOC and Sinopec
Vendor company	Marathon Oil
Stake	Block 32

Sinopec's withdrawal from the Sonaref project in 2007 and thus a way to block the entrance of "Chinese" companies into Angola and therefore motivated by security interests.[90] The acquisition would have been a significant addition to Sinopec's oil assets in Angola by adding access to another 1.5 bn barrels of proven reserves and 130,000 bpd. Further, it was an offshore field (ultra-deep water), which had been a strategic priority for Sinopec in recent years in order to gain more deepwater technology. According to a Chinese industry magazine, "Chinese companies are very interested in acquiring deep-sea oilfields in order to grasp the deep-sea technology."[91] With this acquisition, Sinopec and CNOOC aimed to purchase a stake in an established portion of the industry and obtain access to important technology.

Finally, as this is a stake in an oil block operated by Total (30 percent) and the other shareholders included experienced IOCs, such as Marathon (30 percent) and ExxonMobil (15 percent), this stake would enable CNOOC and Sinopec to gain access to advanced technology, particularly with regard to deepwater technology, and to learn management techniques from Western companies.[92] It is worth noting that regardless of the failure of the acquisition, the motives on the part of the Chinese companies remain unchanged today.

Another indicator of economic interest would be the share price of the two companies. It is worth noting that the share prices of all of the large NOCs increased the day after the acquisition was announced (July 20). Sinopec's share price increased 1.6 percent, CNOOC's share price increased 4.5 percent, and CNPC's share price increased 3.6 percent. Based on this information, the Sinopec and CNOOC increases around the time of the acquisition were not unique. Thus, it is difficult to draw conclusions from the Sinopec and CNOOC share price developments in the given period.

State interests

Vice President Xi Jinping visited Angola in November 2010 to meet with President dos Santos. During the visit, a strategic partnership was established between the two countries, and seven cooperation agreements were signed in the spheres of the economy, technology, energy, and mining.[93] During the visit, aid worth approximately $9.4 million was donated to Angola.[94] Xi emphasized the existence of a "traditional friendship between China and Angola (中安传统友谊/*zhong an chuantong youyi*)," and Xi referred to "Angola cooperation," where "energy, credit and engineering are bundled together."[95]

While Sinopec had unsuccessfully bid on a number of projects in the years up to 2010, it appears as though, after Xi's visit and the establishment of the strategic partnership, another Chinese company, China Sonangol, was finally able to acquire the stakes in the aforementioned Blocks 31 and 32. The visit was followed up by further credit lines from Eximbank and new loans from CDB. Thus, there are intricate links between the different parts of the activities, such as the deals, visits, and loans. The frequency of the visits made by senior leaders, not only from Angola to China but also from China to Angola, increased in the period after 2007, and Xi Jinping's visit in 2010 was particularly remarkable.

Additional credit lines and new loans have been extended in recent years. For example, in August 2009, a new $6.6 billion Eximbank loan was granted for infrastructure development, which was tied to an oil supply contract. This money can function as bait in order to win important resource acquisitions.

It is worth noting that a strategic partnership was established in 2010, new credit lines were offered, and the block that CNOOC and Sinopec unsuccessfully bid for in 2009 was acquired by China Sonangol in 2010. This confluence of events reinforces the impression that there is a linearity of interest between Sinopec/SSI and China Sonangol, as China Sonangol thus profited from the intervention of the leadership in Beijing.[96]

*Domestic stability (***weiwen***)*

The activities of the Chinese oil companies in Angola are not found to have any consequences for domestic stability in the year under scrutiny.

Conclusion, Key Decision 3

The key decision under investigation here was the unsuccessful attempt of CNOOC and Sinopec to acquire a stake in Block 32 in Angola in 2009. On the one hand, this case provides evidence of economic interest, as Sinopec and CNOOC's transaction would have given the company access to important reserves and technology (deepwater assets) and thus would be considered profitable. This reflects the determination of Sinopec and CNOOC to enter the Angolan oil sector and acquire new technological expertise in deep-sea exploration. Surprisingly, in a later turn of events, the block was transferred to China Sonangol. This is also a case of how, in the period leading up to China Sonangol's obtaining the stake in Block 32, leadership visits between the two countries intensified. A strategic partnership was formed during Xi Jinping's visit in 2010, and additional loans from CDB and Eximbank were extended. It would be difficult to argue that the goings-on in Angola in those years took place outside of government oversight, given the Xi Jinping visit in 2010. All in all, the key decision examined here thus provides evidence of state interests.

How does the analysis here compare to the quantitative analysis? Whereas economic interests dominated prior to 2009, state interests and concerns with domestic stability became more important in 2009. In fact, in 2009, state interests dominate relative to economic interests (ratio of 0.97:1). Thus, in 2009, the results from the quantitative and qualitative analyses are consistent. Then, in 2010, economic interests come to dominate relative to state interests/domestic stability (ratio of 2.1:1). Still, the key decision considered here focuses on 2009. Thus, in this key decision, the quantitative results and qualitative analysis are consistent (for 2009).

Conclusion

In the case of Angola, the Chinese companies were expected to have an incentive to become involved because of the large quantities of oil. But as the government attributes little strategic importance to the region, the Chinese state will not seek to pursue its state interests there; the companies will be in the driver's seat. We therefore expect to find evidence of economic interests in the Angolan case.

The qualitative analysis reveals that state and economic interests coincide in the case of the Eximbank loan; in the case of the refinery deal, economic interests dominate; and in the case of Sinopec and CNOOC's failed acquisition in 2009, state interests dominate. The quantitative analysis corroborates the results, with the exception of the Eximbank loan in 2004. Here, it is argued that the evidence that state and economic interests coincide in the 2004 instance is more credible, as there is also evidence of strong state interests in addition to economic interests. This means that the qualitative and quantitative analyses are in overall agreement.

The empirical expectation presented is therefore only partially supported, as the results from the quantitative and qualitative analyses produce evidence of both economic and state interests.

Notes

1 Indira Campos and Alex Vines, *Angola and China: A Pragmatic Partnership* (London, UK: Center for Strategic and International Studies, March 2008); Thomas Collelo, ed., *Angola: A Country Study* (Washington, DC: Federal Research Division, Library of Congress, 1991), xxii; Piero Gleijeses, *Conflicting Missions: Havana, Washington, and Africa, 1959–1976* (Chapel Hill, NC: University of North Carolina Press, 2002), 9.

2 Harmala Kaur, "China and the Angolan National Liberation Movement," *China Report* 13 (19) (1977); Steven F. Jackson, "China's Third World Foreign Policy, Angola and Mozambique 1961–93," *The China Quarterly* 142 (June 1995): 388–422; Keith Somerville, *Angola, Politics, Economics and Society* (London, UK: Frances Pinter, 1986).

3 Gleijeses, *Conflicting Missions*, 9; Ian Taylor, *China and Africa: Engagement and Compromise* (London, UK: Routledge, 2006).

4 Lucy Corkin, *Uncovering African Agency: Angola's Management of China's Credit Lines* (Ashgate: Surrey, 2013).

5 Ana Cristina Alves, "Chinese Economic Statecraft: A Comparative Study of China's Oil-Backed Loans in Angola and Brazil," *Journal of Current Chinese Affairs* 42 (1) (2013): 99–130.

6 This relates to a more general take on the *resource curse* within this literature. For more, see Paul Collier and Anke Hoeffler, "Resource Rents, Governance, and Conflict," *Journal of Conflict Resolution* 49 (4) (August 2005): 625–33.

7 Ricardo Soares de Oliveira, "Business Success, Angola-Style: Postcolonial Politics and the Rise and Rise of Sonangol," *Journal of Modern African Studies* 45 (4) (2007): 595–619.

8 Corkin, *Uncovering African Agency*.

9 See, for example, Serge Michel and Michel Beuret, *China Safari: On the Trail of Beijing's Expansion in Africa* (New York, NY: Nation Books, 2009).

10 E.g., see Corkin, *Uncovering African Agency*; Lucy Corkin, *China and Angola, Strategic Partnership or Marriage of Convenience* (Bergen: Chr. Michelsen Institute, 2011), 1–4; Alves, "Chinese Economic Statecraft," 99–130; Ana Cristina Alves, "The Oil Factor in Sino – Angolan Relations at the Start of the 21st Century," South African Institute of International Affairs, Occasional Paper No. 55, February 2010.

11 Alex Vines, Lillian Wong, Marcus Weimer, and Indira Campos, "Thirst for African Oil," in *Asian National Oil Companies in Nigeria and Angola*, A Chatham House Report, (London: Chatham House, August 2009). As seen in Chapter 4, this links up to

a more general debate in the literature about the extent to which Chinese companies are independent. For a view of the Chinese companies as relatively autonomous, see Bo Kong, *China's International Petroleum Strategy* (Santa Barbara, CA: Praeger, 2010); Erica S. Downs, "Business Interest Groups in Chinese Politics: The Case of the Oil Companies," in *China's Changing Political Landscape: Prospects for Democracy*, ed. Cheng Li (Washington, DC: Brookings Institution, 2008), 121–41.

12 Marcus Power and Ana Cristina Alves, "Introduction: China and Angola's Partnership," in *China and Angola: A Marriage of Convenience*? eds. Marcus Power and Ana C. Alves (Cape Town, Africa: Pambazuka Press, 2012), 1–9.

13 Princeton N. Lyman, "China's Rising Role in Africa," Presentation to the US–China Commission, July 21, 2005.

14 Joshua Cooper Ramo, *The Beijing Consensus* (London: The Foreign Policy Centre, 2004).

15 See, for example, Fantu Cheru and Cyril Obi, "Chinese and Indian Engagement in Africa: Competitive or Mutually Reinforcing Strategies?" *Journal of International Affairs* 64 (2) (Spring–Summer 2011): 91–110.

16 Campos and Vines, *Angola and China*, 1–28.

17 *Energy Compass*, "Angola: China's Complex Connections," August 14, 2009, 1; China Sonangol International Ltd, "Our Business," accessed December 15, 2015, www.chinasonangol.com/oil_and_gas.html; Vines et al., "Thirst for African Oil," 33. 1.

18 *China's Land Resources Statistical Yearbook 2010* [中国国土资源统计年鉴], Ministry of Land of the People's Republic of China [中华人民共和国国土资源部]. Beijing, 2010.

19 U.S. Energy Information Administration (EIA), "Angola," accessed December 15, 2015, www.eia.gov/countries/country-data.cfm?fips=AO.

20 Ministry of Foreign Affairs of the People's Republic of China [中华人民共和国外交部], 中华人民共和国和安哥拉共和国关于建立战略伙伴关系的联合声明 ("People's Republic of China and the Republic of Angola a Joint Statement on the Establishment of a Strategic Partnership"), November 21, 2010, accessed December 15, 2015, www.fmprc.gov.cn/chn/pds/ziliao/1179/t770825.htm.

21 *Visão*, "Angola Cerca de 259.000 Chineses Vivem No Pais," April 25, 2012.

22 *BBC*, "Angola Deports China 'Gangsters,'" August 25, 2012.

23 U.S. EIA, "Angola Energy Profile: Second-Largest Oil Producer in Sub-Saharan Africa Behind Nigeria – Analysis," January 4, 2013, accessed December 15, 2015, www.eurasiareview.com/04012013-angola-energy-profile-second-largest-oil-producer-in-sub-saharan-africa-behind-nigeria-analysis/.

24 *Business Monitor International*, "Angola Infrastructure Report – Q4 2011," 9.

25 *Business Monitor International*, "Angola Infrastructure Report – Q4 2011," 9.

26 Collelo, ed., *Angola: A Country Study*, 199.

27 Central Intelligence Agency (CIA), "Import Partners of Angola – CIA World Factbook 2012," accessed December 15, 2015, www.cia.gov/library/publications/the-world-factbook/fields/2061.html#ao; Central Intelligence Agency (CIA), "Export Partners of Angola – CIA World Factbook 2012," accessed December 15, 2015, www.cia.gov/library/publications/the-world-factbook/fields/2050.html#ao.

28 U.S. EIA, "Angola."

29 U.S. EIA, "Angola." *Platts Oilgram Price Report*, "Angola Sees 2011 Output at 1.9 Million B/d," December 14, 2010.

30 U.S. EIA, "Angola."

31 U.S. EIA, "Angola."

32 *Petroleum Economist*, "Sonangol: Africa's Rising Star," October 2013.

33 Alves, "The Oil Factor."

34 Campos and Vines, *Angola and China*, 6.

35 The London Interbank Offered Rate (Libor) is an interest rate at which banks can borrow funds, in marketable size, from other banks in the London interbank market.

36 Corkin, *Uncovering African Agency*, 81–2.
37 United Nations Office for the Coordination of Humanitarian Affairs, *Angola: Cautious Optimism for 2005* (New York, NY: United Nations, January14, 2005.
38 Interview with Chinese informant, 2014.
39 Still, there seems to be consensus that even this 30 percent mark is generally not reached. See Alves, "The Oil Factor"; Campos and Vines, *Angola and China*; Interview with Chinese informant, 2014.
40 Interview with Chinese informant, 2014. Alves, "The Oil Factor"; Corkin, *Uncovering African Agency*, 63; Interview with Chinese informant, 2014.
41 China International Fund is owned by the Dayuan International, which also owns part of China Sonangol. For more, see Lee Levkowitz, Marta M. Ross and J.R. Warner, "The 88 Queensway Group. A Case Study in Chinese Investors' Operations in Angola and Beyond," July 10, 2009, U.S. – China Economic & Security Review Commission; Vines et al., "Thirst for African Oil," 50–6.
42 Interview with Chinese informant, 2014.
43 Yang Yang [杨扬]. 走出去: 目标锁定非洲 – 中国石油多元化海外战略重点透析 ["The Going Out Strategy: Aiming at Africa – Reevaluation of China's Overseas Oil Diversification Strategy"], *中国石油和化工* (*China Petroleum and Chemical Industry*), August 6, 2006.
44 Yang Yang [杨扬], 走出去: 目标锁定非洲 – 中国石油多元化海外战略重点透析 ["The Going Out Strategy: Aiming at Africa – Reevaluation of China's Overseas Oil Diversification Strategy"], August 6, 2006.
45 *Xinhua News Agency*, "Angolan Ambassador: China's African Policy Trustworthy," January 24, 2006.
46 See also *All Africa*, "Angola: Ambassador Considers Relations with China Excellent," November 15, 2007.
47 Moran, "China's Strategy to Secure Natural Resources," 14.
48 Alves, "The Oil Factor."
49 *International Herald Tribune*, "China Buys More Angolan Crude than Saudi," March 19, 200.
50 Interview with Chinese informant, 2012.
51 Interview with Chinese informant, 2012.
52 *Visão*, "Angola Cerca de 259.000 Chineses Vivem No Pais," April 25, 2012.
53 Kang Sheng [亢升]. 中国与安哥拉石油业的合作风险及规避措施 ["Risks and Preventive Measures for the Cooperation between China and Angola's Oil Industries"], 西亚非洲 (*West Asia and Africa*), January 10, 2010.
54 Kang Sheng [亢升]. 中国与安哥拉石油业的合作风险及规避措施 ["Risks and Preventive Measures for the Cooperation between China and Angola's Oil Industries"], 西亚非洲 (*West Asia and Africa*), Jan. 10, 2010.
55 U.S. EIA, "Angola."
56 U.S. EIA, "Angola."
57 *Stratfor Global Intelligence*, "Cooperation and Competition in Angola-South Africa Relations," December 6, 2010, accessed December 15, 2015, www.stratfor.com/analysis/cooperation-and-competition-angola-south-africa-relations.
58 U.S. EIA, "Angola."
59 Christina Katsouris, "Angola: Sonangol Keeps Firm Grip," *Energy Compass*, February 9, 2006.
60 *All Africa*, "Angola; Angola and China Sign Cooperation Agreements," February 25, 2005.
61 In addition to other agreements. For more, see *Afrol News*, "China, Angola Sign 9 Cooperation Agreements," March 7, 2005.
62 Other sources indicate that the construction of the refinery would cost $9 billion. See *Stratfor Global Intelligence*, "Cooperation and Competition in Angola-South Africa

Relations." *Business Monitor International*, "Market Overview – Angola, Energy Market Overview Q4 2013," September 6, 2013.
63 Jacinta Moran, "Angola Again Raises Oil Output in November," *Platts Oilgram Price Report*, December 9, 2009.
64 *Stratfor Global Intelligence*, "Cooperation and Competition in Angola-South Africa Relations."
65 The Economist Intelligence Unit, "Angola Industry: Sinopec Drops out of Lobito Refinery Project," May 30, 2007.
66 *Platts Oilgram Price Report*, "Sonangol to Build Refinery without Sinopec," March 16, 2007.
67 *Stratfor Global Intelligence*, "Cooperation and Competition in Angola-South Africa Relations."
68 Alves, "The Oil Factor," 19.
69 *Stratfor Global Intelligence*, "Cooperation and Competition in Angola-South Africa Relations."
70 Interview, Luanda, Angola, 2014.
71 Centre for Chinese Studies, "China's Engagement of Africa: Preliminary Scoping of Africa Case Studies," Stellenbosch, South Africa: University of Stellenbosch, November 2007, accessed December 15, 2015, www.ccs.org.za/wp-content/uploads/2009/04/rf_paper_final.pdf.
72 Centre for Chinese Studies, "Oil, Energy and Power in Sino-Angolan Relations," *The China Monitor* 54 (August 2010), accessed December 15, 2015, www.ccs.org.za/wp-content/uploads/2010/09/China_Monitor_AUGUST_2010.pdf.
73 Alves, "The Oil Factor," 20; Centre for Chinese Studies, "Oil, Energy and Power in Sino-Angolan Relations."
74 Interview with Chinese informant, 2014.
75 Interviews, Luanda, Angola, 2014.
76 Interviews, Luanda, Angola, 2014.
77 Interviews, Luanda, Angola, 2014.
78 *BBC*, "Angola: China's African Foothold," June 20, 2006.
79 See, for example; Yang Honghui [杨宏会]. 外国石油公司动态 ["Foreign Oil Companies"], *国际石油经济 (The International Petroleum Economy)*, June 20, 2006.
80 Alves, "Taming the Dragon: China's Oil Interests in Angola."
81 *All Africa*, "Angola: President's Speech during China Premier's Visit," June 20, 2006.
82 *China Economic Herald [中国经济导报]*. 中非合作：石油不是惟一 ("China–Africa Cooperation: Oil is not the only dimension"), November 7, 2006.
83 China Petroleum and Chemical Corporation [Sinopec] *Yearbook 2011* [中石油石化工集团公司年鉴], 北京: 中国石化出版社 (Beijing, China: China Petrochemical Press, 2011), 153. See also *Shanghai Daily*, "Sinopec Buys Angola Stake," March 30, 2010; *Energy Risk*, "China Secures Big Angola Oil Deal," March 29, 2010.
84 *Oil Daily*, "Sonangol Buys Marathon Stake," December 14, 2009; *Stratfor Global Intelligence*, Re: [Africa] Fwd: [OS] ANGOLA/CHINA/ENERGY- "Angola Blocks Sale of Marathon Field Stake to China," September 10, 2009, accessed December 15, 2015, https://wikileaks.org/gifiles/docs/49/4976461_-africa-fwd-os-angola-china-energy-angola-blocks-sale.html.
85 Noah Brenner, "Marathon Wraps up Block 32 Sale," *Upstream,* February 9, 2010.
86 *Oil & Gas Journal*, "CNOOC, Sinopec Sign $1.3 billion Deal for Angola Block," July 20, 2009; Marathon, "Marathon announces $1.3 billion sale of 20 percent interest in Angola bloc 32," Press Release, July 17, 2009, accessed December 15, 2015, www.marathon.com/News/Press_Releases/Press_Release/?id=1308708.
87 Sully Manope, "Marathon Leaves Angola Entirely, Cashes Out with $2 Billion," *Africa Oil and Gas Report*, September 20, 2013.

88 China Sonangol is a joint venture between a private fund based in Hong Kong, Dayuan International (30 percent), and Angola's national oil company, Sonangol (70 percent).
89 Ana C. Alves, "Energy in Angola in 2011," Center for Studies and Scientific Research (CEIC), Luanda: Catholic University of Angola (UCAN), October, 2011. According to Sonangol President Mr. Vincente, Sonangol in fact only paid US$ 1.0 billion for the asset (Sully Manope, "Marathon Leaves Angola Entirely, Cashes Out With $2 Billion."
90 Wang Peng [王鹏]. 新五大海外能源投资项目详解 ["Presentation of Five New Investments in Energy Projects Abroad"], *化工管理* (*Management of the Chemical Industry*), October 1, 2011. *Oil & Gas Journal,* "Sonangol to buy offshore Angola interest from Marathon," September 16, 2013.
91 *China Metal Bulletin [中国金属通报],* 相关行业 ("Related Industries"), August 18, 2008.
92 Other shareholders include Sonangol (20 percent) and Galp (5 percent).
93 Ministry of Foreign Affairs of the People's Republic of China [中华人民共和国外交部], 中华人民共和国和安哥拉共和国关于建立战略伙伴关系的联合声明 ("People's Republic of China and the Republic of Angola, a Joint Statement on the Establishment of a Strategic Partnership"), November 21, 2010.
94 *Xinhua News Agency*, "CDB will Continue to Support China–Africa Pragmatic Cooperation," November 21, 2010.
95 Embassy of the People's Republic of China in Angola [中华人民共和国驻安哥拉共和国大使馆], 习近平与驻安哥拉中资企业代表座谈并发表讲话 ["Xi Jinping Met with Representatives from Chinese Companies in Angola and Gave a Speech"], November 21, 2010, accessed December 15, 2015, http://ao.chineseembassy.org/chn/zt/xjpfzx/t770897.html.
96 In support of this interpretation, in the words of Sinopec, "Sonangol Sinopec International Ltd. (SSI) belongs to Sinopec International Petroleum Exploration and Production Corporation (SIPC)" (Jiang Chunhui, "Sunlight of Dawn Shining upon Africa," *Sinopec Weekly*, accessed December 15, 2015, www.sinopecweekly.com/content/2011-03/04/content_945822.html. Moreover, Sinopec's annual reports show that the word for Sinopec (中石化) is used both to denote SSI as well as SSI's stakes in Angola (18, 15/06, 17/06 and 18/06) as well as the stakes held by China Sonangol. See, for example China Petroleum and Chemical Corporation [Sinopec] *Yearbook 2011* [中石油石化工集团公司年鉴], 北京: 中国石化出版社 (Beijing: China Petrochemical Press, 2011). See also Levkowitz et al., "The 88 Queensway Group". For an assessment according to which China Sonangol and Sinopec are considered separate, see Ana C. Alves, "*Energy in Angola in 2011*."

References

Afrol News. "China, Angola Sign 9 Cooperation Agreements." March 7, 2005.

All Africa. "Angola: Ambassador Considers Relations with China Excellent." November 15, 2007.

All Africa. "Angola; Angola and China Sign Cooperation Agreements." February 25, 2005.

All Africa. "Angola: President's Speech During China Premier's Visit." June 20, 2006.

Alves, Ana C. "Chinese Economic Statecraft: A Comparative Study of China's Oil-Backed Loans in Angola and Brazil." *Journal of Current Chinese Affairs* 42 (1) (2013): 99–130.

Alves, Ana C. "Energy in Angola in 2011." Center for Studies and Scientific Research (CEIC), Catholic University of Angola (UCAN), October 2011.

Alves, Ana C. "The Oil Factor in Sino – Angolan Relations at the Start of the 21st Century." South African Institute of International Affairs, Occasional Paper No. 55, February 2010.

Alves, Anna. "Taming the Dragon: China's Oil Interests in Angola." In *China and Angola: A Marriage of Convenience?* Edited by Marcus Power and Ana C. Alves, 1–9, 105–23. Cape Town, Africa: Pambazuka, 2012.

BBC. "Angola: China's African Foothold." June 20, 2006.

BBC. "Angola Deports China 'Gangsters'." August 25, 2012.

Brenner, Noah. "Marathon Wraps up Block 32 Sale." *Upstream*, February 9, 2010.

Business Monitor International. "Angola Infrastructure Report – Q4 2011."

Business Monitor International. "Market Overview – Angola, Energy Market Overview Q4 2013." September 6, 2013.

Campos, Indira and Alex Vines. *Angola and China: A Pragmatic Partnership*. London, UK: Center for Strategic and International Studies, March 2008.

Central Intelligence Agency (CIA). "Export Partners of Angola." *CIA World Factbook 2012*. Accessed 12/15/2015. www.cia.gov/library/publications/the-world-factbook/fields/2050.html#ao.

Central Intelligence Agency (CIA). "Import Partners of Angola." *CIA World Factbook 2012*. Accessed 12/15/2015. www.cia.gov/library/publications/the-world-factbook/fields/2061.html#ao.

Centre for Chinese Studies. *China's Engagement of Africa: Preliminary Scoping of Africa Case Studies*. South Africa: University of Stellenbosch, November 2007. Accessed 12/15/2015.

Centre for Chinese Studies. "Oil, Energy and Power in Sino – Angolan Relations." *The China Monitor* 54 (August 2010). Accessed 12/15/2015. www.ccs.org.za/wp-content/uploads/2010/09/China_Monitor_AUGUST_2010.pdf.

Cheru, Fantu and Cyril Obi. "Chinese and Indian Engagement in Africa: Competitive or Mutually Reinforcing Strategies?" *Journal of International Affairs* 64 (2) (Spring 2011): 91–110.

China Economic Herald [中国经济导报]. 中非合作：石油不是惟一 ("China – Africa Cooperation: Oil is not the only Dimension"), November 7, 2006.

China Metal Bulletin [中国金属通报]. 相关行业 ("Related Industries"), August 18, 2008.

China Petroleum and Chemical Corporation [Sinopec]. *Yearbook 2011* [中石油石化工集团公司年鉴], 中国石油编委会 (Sinopec Editorial Team), 北京: 中国石化出版社 (Beijing: China Petrochemical Press), November 2011.

China Sonangol International Ltd. "Our Business." Accessed 12/15/2015. www.chinasonangol.com/oil_and_gas.html.

Collelo, Thomas, ed. *Angola: A Country Study*. Washington, DC: Federal Research Division, Library of Congress, 1991.

Collier, Paul and Anke Hoeffler. "Resource Rents, Governance, and Conflict." *Journal of Conflict Resolution* 49 (4) (August 2005): 625–33.

Corkin, Lucy. *China and Angola, Strategic Partnership or Marriage of Convenience*. Bergen, Norway: Christian Michelsen Institute, 2011.

Corkin, Lucy. *Uncovering African Agency: Angola's Management of China's Credit Lines*. Surrey: Ashgate, 2013.

Downs, Erica S. "Business Interest Groups in Chinese Politics: The Case of the Oil Companies." In *China's Changing Political Landscape: Prospects for Democracy*, edited by Cheng Li, 121–41. Washington, DC: Brookings Institution, 2008.

Economist Intelligence Unit. "Angola Industry: Sinopec Drops Out of Lobito Refinery Project." May 30, 2007.

Embassy of the People's Republic of China in Angola [中华人民共和国驻安哥拉共和国大使馆]. 习近平与驻安哥拉中资企业代表座谈并发表讲话 ["Xi Jinping Met with Representatives from Chinese Companies in Angola and Gave a Speech"], November 21, 2010. Accessed 12/15/2015. http://ao.chineseembassy.org/chn/zt/xjpfzx/t770897.html.

Energy Compass. "Angola: China's Complex Connections." August 14, 2009.

Energy Risk. "China Secures Big Angola Oil Deal." March 29, 2010.

Gleijeses, Piero. *Conflicting Missions: Havana, Washington, and Africa, 1959–1976*. Chapel Hill, NC: University of North Carolina Press, 2002.

International Herald Tribune. "China Buys More Angolan Crude than Saudi." March 19, 2006.

Jackson, Steven F. "China's Third World Foreign Policy, Angola and Mozambique 1961–93." *The China Quarterly* 142 (June 1995): 388–422.

Jiang, Chunhui. "Sunlight of Dawn Shining upon Africa." *Sinopec Weekly*. Accessed 12/15/2015. www.sinopecweekly.com/content/2011-03/04/content_945822.html.

Kang Sheng [亢升]. 中国与安哥拉石油业的合作风险及规避措施 ["Risks and Preventive Measures for the Cooperation between China and Angola's Oil Industries"]. 西亚非洲 *(West Asia and Africa)*, January 10, 2010.

Katsouris, Christina. "Angola: Sonangol Keeps Firm Grip." *Energy Compass*, February 9, 2006.

Kaur, Harmala. "China and the Angolan National Liberation Movement." *China Report* 13 (19) (1977): 19–33.

Kong, Bo. *China's International Petroleum Strategy*. Santa Barbara, CA: Praeger, 2010.

Levkowitz, Lee, Marta M. Ross and J.R. Warner. "The 88 Queensway Group. A Case Study in Chinese Investors' Operations in Angola and Beyond." U.S. – China Economic & Security Review Commission, July 10, 2009.

Lyman, Princeton N. "China's Rising Role in Africa." Presentation to the US – China Commission, July 21, 2005.

Manope, Sully. "Marathon Leaves Angola Entirely, Cashes Out With $2Billion." *Africa Oil and Gas Report*. September 20, 2013.

Marathon. "Marathon Announces $1.3 Billion Sale of 20 Percent Interest in Angola Bloc 32." *Press Release*, July 17, 2009. Accessed 12/15/2015. www.marathon.com/News/Press_Releases/Press_Release/?id=1308708.

Michel, Serge and Michel Beuret. *China Safari: On the Trail of Beijing's Expansion in Africa*. New York, NY: Nation Books, 2009.

Ministry of Foreign Affairs of the People's Republic of China [中华人民共和国外交部]. 中华人民共和国和安哥拉共和国关于建立战略伙伴关系的联合声明 ("People's Republic of China and the Republic of Angola, a Joint Statement on the Establishment of a Strategic Partnership"), November 21, 2010. Accessed 12/15/2015. www.fmprc.gov.cn/chn/pds/ziliao/1179/t770825.html.

Ministry of Land of the People's Republic of China [中华人民共和国国土资源部]. *China's Land Resources Statistical Yearbook 2010* [中国国土资源统计年鉴],2010.

Moran, Jacinta. "Angola Again Raises Oil Output in November." *Platts Oilgram Price Report*, December 9, 2009.

Moran, Theodore H. *China's Strategy to Secure Natural Resources: Risks, Dangers and Opportunities*. Washington, DC: Peterson Institute for International Economics, July 2012.

Ministry of Foreign Affairs of the People's Republic of China [中华人民共和国外交部]. 中华人民共和国和安哥拉共和国关于建立战略伙伴关系的联合声明 ("People's

Republic of China and the Republic of Angola, a Joint Statement on the Establishment of a Strategic Partnership"), November 21, 2010. Accessed 12/15/2015. www.fmprc.gov.cn/chn/pds/ziliao/1179/t770825.html.

Oil Daily. "China Offers Billions for Angola Acreage." May 10, 2006.

Oil Daily. "Sonangol Buys Marathon Stake." December 14, 2009.

Oil & Gas Journal. "CNOOC, Sinopec Sign $1.3 billion Deal for Angola Block." July 20, 2009.

Oil & Gas Journal. "Sonangol to Buy Offshore Angola Interest from Marathon." September 16, 2013.

Petroleum Economist, "Sonangol: Africa's Rising Star." October 2013.

Platts Oilgram Price Report. "Angola Sees 2011 Output at 1.9 Million B/d." December 14, 2010.

Platts Oilgram Price Report, "Sonangol to Build Refinery without Sinopec." March 16, 2007.

Power, Marcus and Ana Cristina Alves. "Introduction: China and Angola's Partnership." In *China and Angola: A Marriage of Convenience?* Edited by Marcus Power and Ana C. Alves, 1–9. Cape Town, Africa: Pambazuka, 2012.

Ramo, Joshua C. *The Beijing Consensus*. London, UK: The Foreign Policy Centre, 2004.

Shanghai Daily. "Sinopec Buys Angola Stake." March 30, 2010.

Soares de Oliveira, Ricardo. "Business Success, Angola-Style: Postcolonial Politics and the Rise and Rise of Sonangol." *Journal of Modern African Studies* 45 (4) (2007): 595–619.

Somerville, Keith. *Angola, Politics, Economics and Society*. London, UK: Frances Pinter, 1986.

Stratfor Global Intelligence. "Cooperation and Competition in Angola-South Africa Relations." December 6, 2010. Accessed 12/15/2015. www.stratfor.com/analysis/cooperation-and-competition-angola-south-africa-relations.

Stratfor Global Intelligence. Re: [Africa] Fwd: [OS] ANGOLA/CHINA/ENERGY- "Angola Blocks Sale of Marathon Field Stake to China." September 10, 2009. Accessed 12/15/2015. https://wikileaks.org/gifiles/docs/49/4976461_-africa-fwd-os-angola-china-energy-angola-blocks-sale.html.

Taylor, Ian. *China and Africa: Engagement and Compromise*. London, UK: Routledge, 2006.

U.S. EIA. "Angola." Accessed 12/15/2015.

U.S. EIA. "Angola Energy Profile: Second-Largest Oil Producer in Sub-Saharan Africa Behind Nigeria – Analysis." January 4, 2013.

United Nations Office for the Coordination of Humanitarian Affairs. "Angola: Cautious Optimism for 2005." New York, NY, January 14, 2005.

Vines, Alex, Lillian Wong, Marcus Weimer and Indira Campos, "Thirst for African Oil. Asian National Oil Companies in Nigeria and Angola." A Chatham House Report. London, UK, August 2009.

Visão. "Angola Cerca de 259.000 Chineses Vivem No Pais." April 25, 2012.

Wang Peng [王鹏]. 新五大海外能源投资项目详解 ["Presentation of Five New Investments in Energy Projects Abroad"]. *化工管理* (*Management of the Chemical Industry)*, October 1, 2011.

Xinhua News Agency. "Angolan Ambassador: China's African Policy Trustworthy." January 24, 2006.

Xinhua News Agency. "CDB will Continue to Support China – Africa Pragmatic Cooperation." November 21, 2010.

Yang Honghui [杨宏会]. 外国石油公司动态 ["Foreign Oil Companies"]. *国际石油经济 (The International Petroleum Economy*), June 20, 2006.

Yang Yang [杨扬]. 走出去: 目标锁定非洲 – 中国石油多元化海外战略重点透析 ["The Going Out Strategy: Aiming at Africa – Reevaluation of China's Overseas Oil Diversification Strategy"], *中国石油和化工 (China Petroleum and Chemical Industry)*, August 6, 2006.

6 Sudan

A change of foreign policy

Background

The state of China-Sudan relations

There are three phases in Sino-Sudanese (political) relations. The first phase was from 1956–59, since relations were established in 1956, when Sudan initially supported Taiwan (until 1959).[1] Sudan was among the countries to support China's bid for UN Security Council membership in 1971. Still, the first phase, which lasted until the late 1980s, can be characterized as a relatively quiet period of relations.

The second phase started in June 1989 with the National Islamic Front (NIF) military coup when the Islamic Al-Ingaz regime (later the NCP) seized power in Sudan. The country subsequently faced international sanctions.[2] This period, from 1989 until the separation of Sudan into two countries in 2011, was characterized by civil wars, and the regime was hampered by fiscal problems. Still, China's relations with Sudan continued to develop in this period. Leadership visits were frequent, important economic agreements were settled between the two countries, and this is when the Chinese NOCs, with CNPC in the lead, came to Sudan and helped develop its oil infrastructure and expand oil exploration, as presented in the following.

The third phase began with South Sudan's independence on July 9, 2011, when Sudan was divided into two countries (see figure 6.1 for map of Sudan). Since then, relations have developed even further with many visits and the donation of aid to both Sudan and the new state, South Sudan (see the following qualitative analysis for more detail).

Overall, it is worth noting that despite the absence of a formal strategic partnership, the two countries have very close relations.

Literature on Sudan

In the literature that addresses the activities of Chinese energy companies in Sudan, three perspectives can be distinguished: a liberal/political economy perspective, a realist/foreign policy perspective, and a globalist perspective.

From the *political economy* perspective, the role played by oil in domestic Sudanese politics is examined, looking at how Sudan's economic growth has

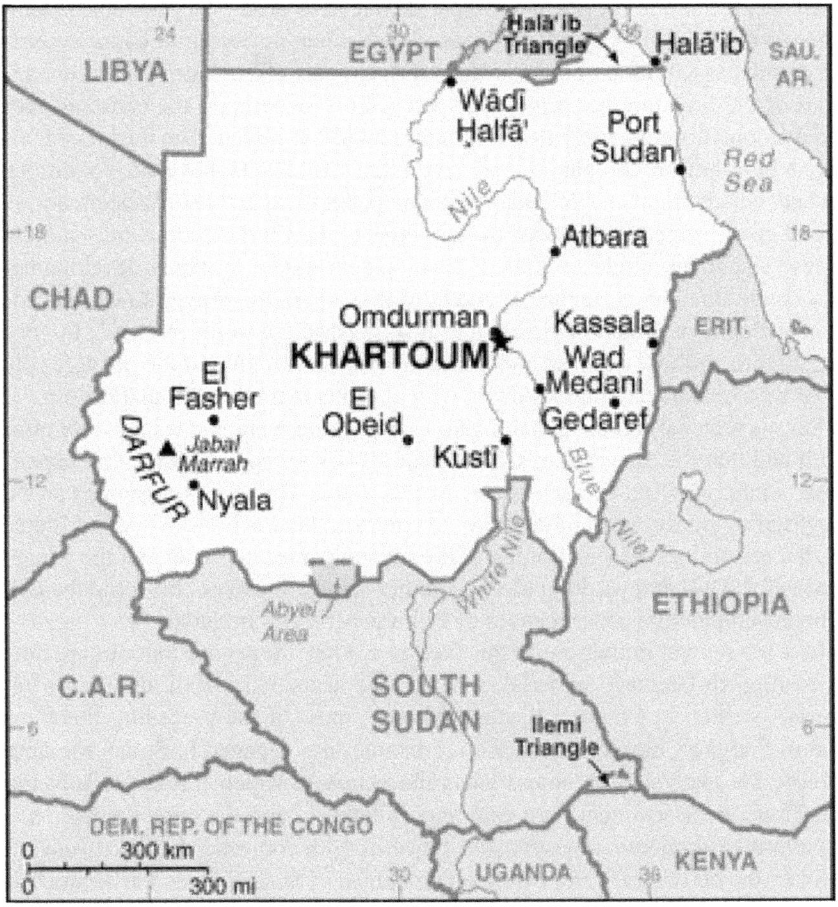

Figure 6.1 Map of Sudan

primarily benefited a small northern elite.[3] This literature focuses on relations between Beijing's ruling NCP and different elites within the Sudanese state,[4] a relationship that builds on a longer history of political and economic dominance by ruling elites that has resulted in the marginalization of southern Sudan.[5]

When looking at the activities of the Chinese NOCs, the most dominant perspective is as a case of *foreign policy*. Here, the Chinese strategy is seen as motivated by the defense of economic interests (oil) driven by power calculations by the Chinese state.[6] Given the distrust of the Chinese government of international energy markets, the Chinese leadership helps its NOCs to venture abroad in order to obtain contracts on equity oil, which can help the Chinese leadership ensure a safe energy supply and thus energy security.[7] Here, the Chinese oil companies are seen as part of the Chinese state. Another part of the debate on the activities of Chinese oil companies in Sudan looks at the NOCs as relatively independent. Business considerations draw the companies overseas, where they are able to earn higher profits and enjoy greater autonomy than when operating in Chinese territory, and the assumption of the Chinese NOCs as part of the state is questioned.[8]

Part of the literature has a *globalist* perspective, examining the consequences for development of the activities of Chinese NOCs in Sudan. The business deals offered by Chinese companies and credit lines in Sudan have no conditions attached, which might enable Sudan to develop, but irrespective of Western norms of good governance.[9] In this way, the activities of the Chinese companies and the Chinese leadership might promote a development model in which development is *not* conditioned on principles of good governance. In this way, a so-called Chinese development model is visible that is an alternative to the West's.[10] In contrast, both the official Chinese and Sudanese positions highlight the positive role played by China in economic growth, which results in a win-win relationship.[11]

Thus, as seen earlier, the general take is that Chinese companies are only after the oil and that the activities of Chinese companies are merely part of an expansionist strategy of the Chinese state. In this sense, Chinese companies can be thought of as an extension of the state. In contrast, there is a small body of literature that scrutinizes the functioning of the oil companies in Sudan and the consequences for IOCs and world markets. Another standard take on this topic focuses on the developmental consequences of Chinese activities in Sudan.

There are several limitations to this literature. First, these contributions are limited to English-language material, whereas the account in hand also draws on materials written in Chinese. Second, whereas most of the preceding literature assumes that the Chinese state and/or companies are engaged in Sudan for state interests, the analysis here investigates the extent to which this is actually the case. Thus, the assessment here examines whether – and the extent to which – state interests, economic interests, and concerns with domestic stability (*weiwen*) dominate the activities of the Chinese companies in Sudan. Thus, I will proceed in a different manner than the existing literature.

History of Chinese oil companies in Sudan

Oil exploration first started Sudan in 1956 after the country became independent. Subsequently, in the period from 1959 to 1972, a number of Western companies were welcomed to the country, including Agip, Conoco, Shell, British Petroleum (BP), and Chevron, and a number of licenses were issued. Figure 6.2 shows key oil infrastructure in Sudan and South Sudan.[12]

CNPC has made a number of acquisitions in Sudan. In fact, since 1996, CNPC has invested at least $15 billion in Sudan in exploration activities and infrastructure development.[13] In fact, Sudan has become the main location for investments made by Chinese oil companies. Overall, Chinese oil companies control 75 percent of the oil in Sudan, CNPC with the largest Chinese operations. The Sinopec operations are smaller: CNPC has shares in 20 oil blocks and Sinopec in two oil blocks. CNOOC is not currently operating in Sudan.

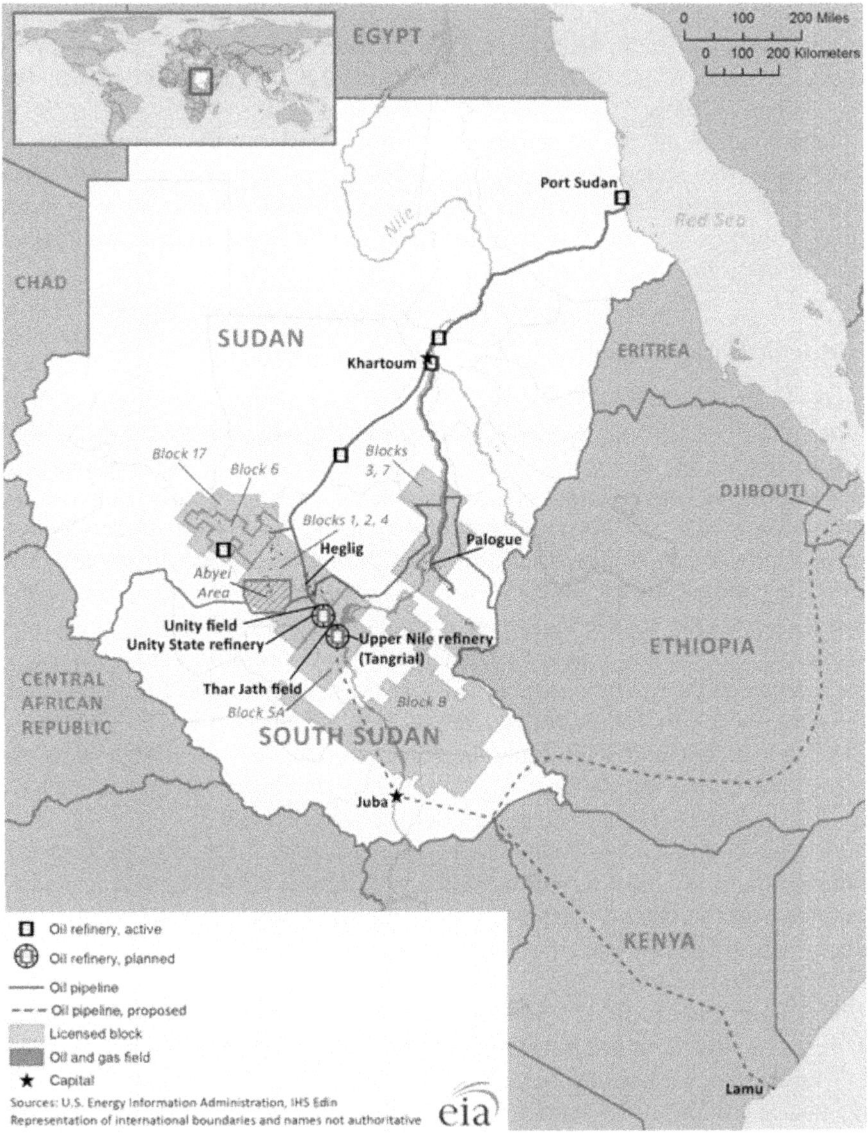

Figure 6.2 Sudan oil concession map

Sudan provided China with 5.6 percent of its total oil imports in the period from 1999 to 2009.[14] In 2011, Sudan accounted for 5.12 percent of Chinese oil imports – the second largest African supplier and seventh largest in the world.[15] In 2013, however, the export of Sudan and South Sudan oil to China plummeted; it accounted for only 2 percent of China's total crude oil imports that year.[16] For the Sudan and South Sudan oil exports, however, China is far and away the leading export market. In 2013, 86 percent of Sudan and South Sudan's total oil output was exported to China.[17] Of this, Sudan exported 49,000 bpd and South Sudan 65,000 bpd to China.[18]

In terms of equity oil, 32 percent of China's overseas equity oil production in 2006 came from Sudan.[19] According to a company representative, the equity share belonging to CNPC from each stake produced in Sudan (40 percent of production) is shipped to China.[20] It is worth noting that Sudanese crude is well-suited for Chinese refineries.

Strategic importance[21]

Sudan holds great strategic importance for China for the following reasons. First, in terms of the *level of political relations*, the two countries established diplomatic relations in 1959 (after Sudan gained independence in 1956). China and Sudan have not entered into a strategic partnership, and the Chinese ambassador to Khartoum does not have ministerial-level status, in contrast to the Chinese ambassadors to both South Africa and Egypt, for example, with whom Sudan has strategic partnerships.[22] China and Sudan are seen as sharing a particular South-South cooperation founded on a common colonial history.[23] Lastly, Sudan has supported China's bid to assume a position at the UN. There have been many visits between the two countries in recent years, most from Sudan to China (see the Appendix). From the Chinese side, the only presidential-level visit was by President Hu Jintao in 2007. From the Sudanese side, there have been two such visits since 2000. From the South Sudan side, there has been a single presidential-level visit, when President Kiir visited Beijing in April 2012.

Second, in terms of the role of *CCP regime stability*, there have been strong links to Islam in Sudan throughout history. After the 1989 *coup d'état*, Sudan came to host a number of Islamist terrorist groups. Islamic Sharia law was introduced across the entire territory, and the country became radicalized in political and religious terms. In particular, Sudan had close links to al-Qaeda in the 1990s. From 1991 to 1996, Osama bin Laden found refuge in Sudan after being expelled in 1991 from Saudi Arabia.[24] After 1996, however, when bin Laden fled to Afghanistan, the links to al-Qaeda grew weaker. Since 2001, the link to Islam in Sudan has withered.[25] Thus, while an extremist group linked to al-Qaeda clearly had a branch in Sudan until 1996, the extent to which there has been one since is unclear. Still, there have been multiple occasions in which Chinese nationals working in Sudan have been killed in recent years (see Key Decision 2 for more detail). Finally, in terms of Taiwan, Sudan supported Taiwan in the first three years after Sudanese independence in 1956, from 1956 to 1959. In 1959, Sudan then shifted its support to China.

Third, in terms of *salience of territory*, there are no ethnic ties to China. In terms of *strategic location*, Sudan is located on the east coast of Africa and has important access to the Red Sea. This Red Sea access is of strategic importance

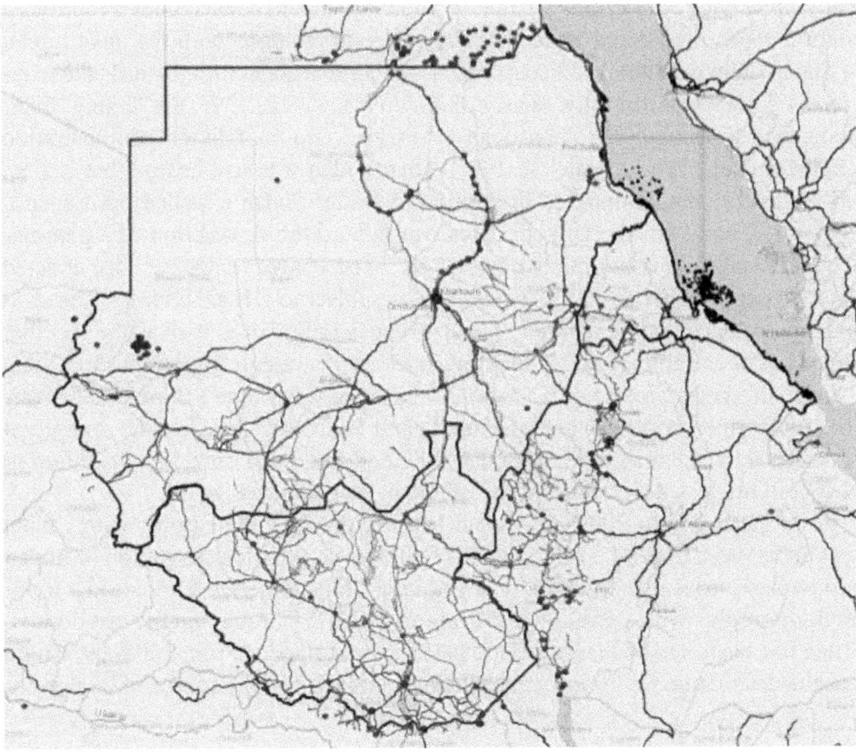

Figure 6.3 Infrastructure: Sudan

with respect to transport to Asia compared to the West African coast, as the shipping time is shorter. There are two major ports: Port Sudan and Suakim. In terms of infrastructure, Sudan has two main crude oil pipelines transporting oil to the main export terminal in Bashair, in addition to several smaller pipelines.

Sudan also has five refineries: the two larger operations – Khartoum Refinery and Port Sudan Refinery – and three smaller topping plants: El Obeid, Shajirah, and Abu Gabra.[26] There are also a number of petrochemical plants, including the Petrochemical Project, built by CNPC in 2002. Most of the infrastructure in Sudan, including river, road, pipeline, and railway systems, are in need of improvement. Given that Sudan, relative to other African countries, has a relatively sound oil-related infrastructure and that it has been built by CNPC renders Sudan of strategic importance to China.

Fourth, in terms of the role of the *other great power*, Sudan is not a US alliance partner. Moreover, while the United States launched the US Africa Command (AFRICOM) in February 2007 to ensure a military presence in Africa, neither the United States nor China has military bases in Sudan or South Sudan. At the same time, many visits between Sudan and China have taken place in recent years, although not at the presidential level. Sudan–US relations have fluctuated dramatically in recent years. From the time of Sudanese independence until the military coup in 1989, the United States maintained good relations with the government of Sudan. However, the 1989 coup and Sudan's subsequent turn toward Islam signaled a dramatic shift in that relationship. On August 12, 1993, the United States designated Sudan a "state sponsor of terrorism," and the Clinton administration labeled Sudan a "rogue state" in 1995, when Sudan was still hosting bin Laden. US–Sudan relations improved briefly in 1996 after Sudan expelled bin Laden.[27] Soon after, however, the United States was behind the destruction of a pharmaceutical plant in Khartoum in August 1998.[28] The United States has also enacted sanctions against Sudan,[29] and the country is subject to UN sanctions.[30] The strategic importance that the United States attributes to Sudan as well as the fact that Sudan has been subject to UN sanctions render it of strategic importance to China.

Fifth, in terms of *bilateral trade*, in 2011, Sudan was China's third largest overall trade partner in Africa, behind Angola and South Africa. After the separation of Sudan into Sudan and South Sudan, bilateral trade fell from $11.54 billion to $3.73 billion, less than a third of the previous year (figure 6.4).

In the period from 2002–11, Sudan had a growing trade surplus with China, peaking at more than $7.5 billion in 2011. However, after the separation of Sudan into two countries, the situation reversed, and China experienced instead a modest trade surplus with Sudan of $0.62 billion in 2012. Throughout the last decade, China has been Sudan's largest trade partner. In the period from 2005–09, China was the destination for 76 percent of Sudan's exports and the source of 22 percent

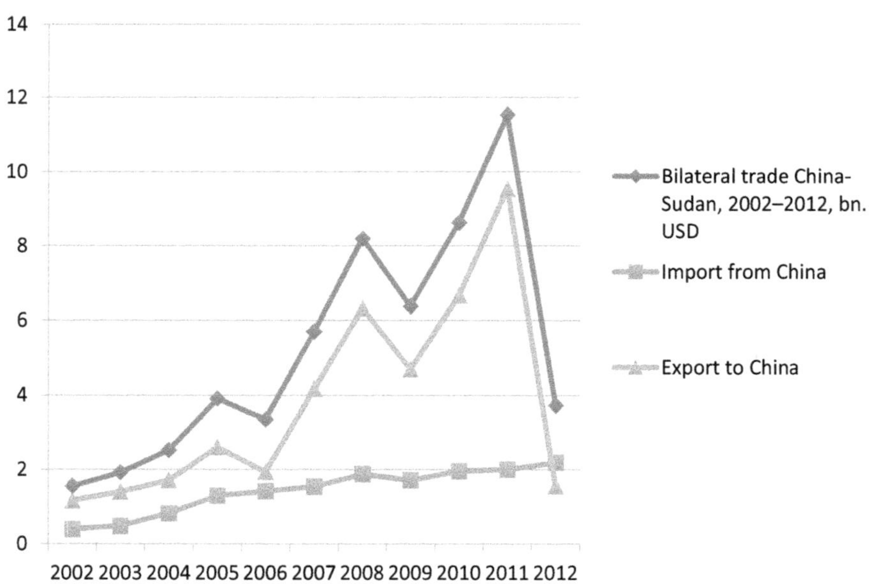

Figure 6.4 Sino-Sudanese bilateral trade, 2002–12

Table 6.1 Level of strategic importance: Sudan (for more detail, see the Appendix)

Country	*1. Level of political relations*	*2. Role for CCP regime stability*	*3. Salience of territory*	*4. Role for other great power*	*5. Bilateral trade*	*Total*
Sudan	0	2	2	2	1 (2011)	2

of its imports.[31] In 2012, after the separation of the two countries, China still accounted for 18.1 percent of Sudanese imports, but exports from Sudan fell sharply in 2011 (to less than 4 percent).[32] Thus, up until 2011, the bilateral trade between the two countries was significant.

In summary, and as illustrated in table 6.1, Sudan is of great strategic importance to China. This is reflected by the high number of visits that have taken place between the two countries, the (previous) existence of an extremist group in the country, and the fatalities among Chinese nationals in the country. Sudan's importance relates to the country's strategic location and important Chinese-built infrastructure. Finally, even if bilateral trade is relatively limited, the fact that Sudan is of great strategic importance to the United States and that it has been subjected to UN sanctions renders the country strategically important to China.

Sudan's level of oil and gas

As of January 1, 2014, Sudan and South Sudan combined had proven oil reserves of 5.0 billion barrels (25th in the world). Sudan had 1.5 billion barrels and South Sudan 3.5 billion barrels of proven oil reserves.[33] Sudan and South Sudan combined were Sub-Saharan Africa's third-largest oil producer until 2012, behind Nigeria and Angola. In 2010, Sudan produced 500,000 bpd. In 2012, after the separation, both countries combined produced a mere 115,000 bpd due to South Sudan's shutting down its oil production and the armed conflict between north and south.[34] Since South Sudan resumed its oil production in 2012–13, their combined oil production has increased. It is worth noting that, given the lack of exploration activity during the north-south civil war, future oil and gas discoveries are likely.[35]

In terms of gas, Sudan and South Sudan combined are rich in natural gas with reserves estimated at 84.95 billion m^3 (56th in the world).[36] However, neither Sudan nor South Sudan has any gas production, and gas exploration has been limited.

Thus, relatively speaking, Sudan has neither particularly rich oil and gas reserves nor high production.

The empirical expectation

As becomes apparent when considering the preceding data, Sudan is a country that is attributed high strategic importance by the Chinese leadership and only has little oil. Based on these characteristics and the history of the case, the hypothesis is that state interest is the dominant driver in Sudan. The empirical expectation is that in Sudan, *the companies have little incentive to be involved because of the limited availability of oil. As the Chinese government attributes high strategic importance to the country, it pursues its state interests there. Thus, state interests/ domestic stability (*weiwen*) dominate.*

Quantitative analysis

As presented earlier, the hypothesis for the case of Sudan is that state interests dominate. The quantitative analysis of the Chinese state media shows that 80 percent of the articles on Sudan display a preponderance of economic interests over the ten-year period under investigation. Thus, the activities are driven by commercial interests and the preceding hypothesis is not supported. Looking over this period, the quantitative analysis shows that the level of economic interests fluctuates: overall, over the course of the period, economic interests dominate relative to state interests and concerns with domestic stability, except in the years 2008 (ratio of 0.7:1) and 2009 (ratio of 0.9:1), as figure 6.5 illustrates. Economic interests are particularly strong relative to state interests and domestic stability in 2003 (ratio of 6.9:1) and 2012 (ratio of 3.5:1). Thus, a dramatic development takes place over the ten-year period, as illustrated in figure 6.5. Still, in most years, the quantitative evidence supports the preceding hypothesis.

Zooming in and studying the particular ratios, that is, the ratio of economic to state interests, we see that, with the exception of the year 2008, when state interests were stronger, economic interests dominated relative to state interests (ratio of 0.8:1), as figure 6.6 illustrates. This is significant, as this was the year of the

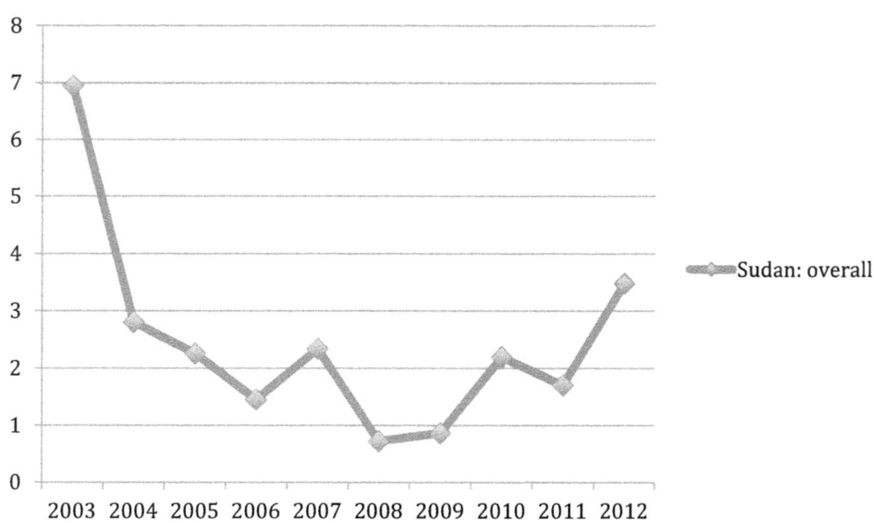

Figure 6.5 Ratio of economic interests to state interests/domestic stability[37]

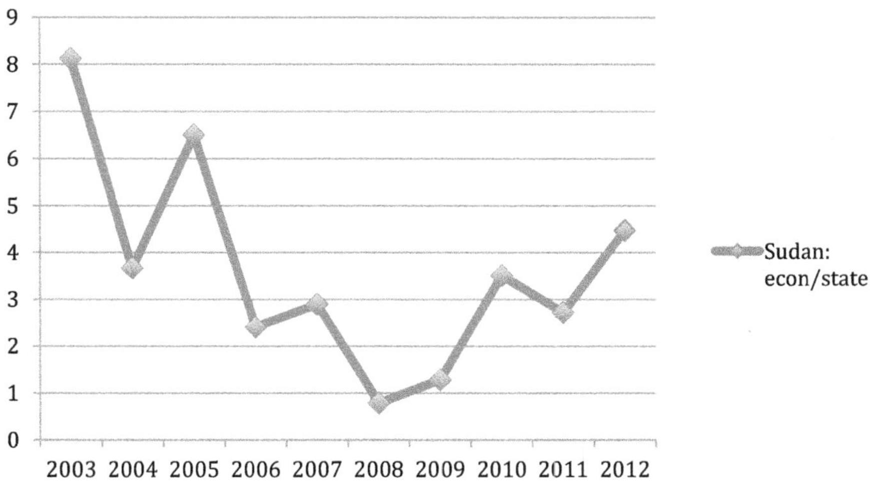

Figure 6.6 Ratio of economic interests to state interests

Beijing Olympics. It would be consistent with a greater role for security interests and for these interests to dominate foreign policy.

When examining the relationship between economic interests and concerns with domestic stability (*weiwen*), we see that economic interests generally dominate the period. Still, concerns with domestic stability are relatively stronger in the years 2005–10, as figure 6.7 illustrates. In particular, the concerns with domestic stability have relatively more importance in the years 2005 (ratio of 3.5:1), 2006 (ratio of 3.7:1), and 2009 (ratio of 2.7:1). In 2008, there was a serious incident when five Chinese workers were killed in Sudan. This is also somewhat reflected in the results, as the concern with domestic stability was relatively strong that year (ratio of 9.3:1). Surprisingly, the kidnapping of 29 workers in 2012 would not appear to be reflected in the results, as they show a dominance of economic interests (ratio of 15.6:1).

Finally, examining the ratio of state interests to concerns with domestic stability, we see that overall state interests dominated, except for in 2005, when concerns with domestic stability dominated (ratio of 0.5:1), as illustrated in figure 6.8. In fact, in 2008, state interests peaked relative to concerns with domestic stability (ratio of 11.8:1). This would be consistent with the importance attributed to the Beijing Olympics that year and its importance as a factor in foreign policy. Still, whereas many analyses have noted the concern with domestic stability around 2008, this analysis can also show that there is actually more evidence of a dominance of state interests at the time.

Overall, the preceding results are surprising and disprove the hypothesis presented in this book that state interests are expected to dominate. Instead, we find evidence of the dominance of economic interests, except for in the years 2008 and 2009. The remainder of this chapter examines why this is the case and discusses the significance.

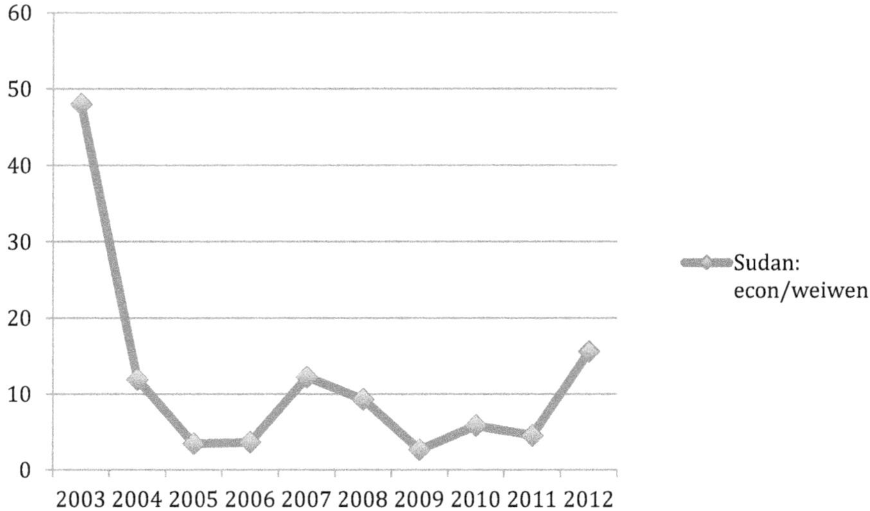

Figure 6.7 Ratio of economic interests to domestic stability

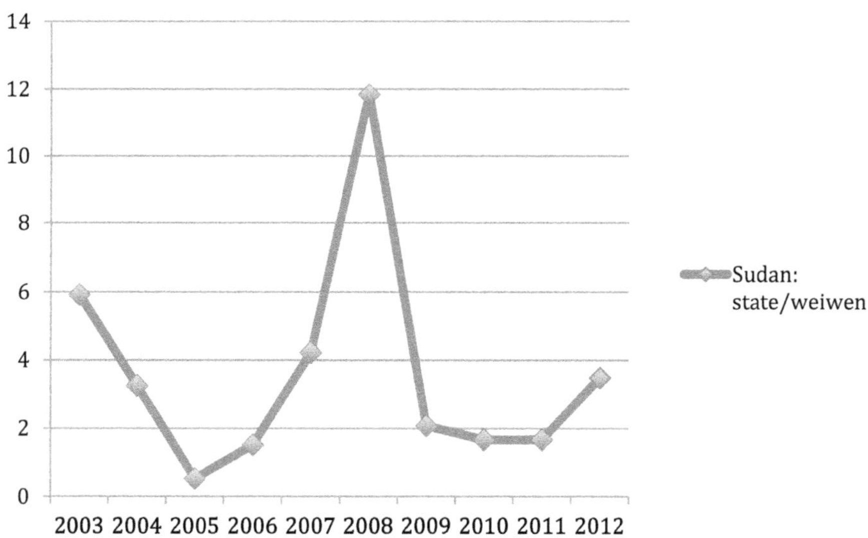

Figure 6.8 Ratio of state interests to domestic stability

Qualitative analysis: 3 Key Decisions

We now scrutinize three key decisions, as a focus on these will illuminate important aspects of the activities of Chinese companies in Sudan. The three key decisions are deemed to be the most significant and representative in terms of the activities of Chinese companies in Sudan over the last decade, and they allow for an analysis across time. First, we consider how Hu Jintao puts pressure on Sudanese President Bashir in 2006–07. Second, we focus on the response from the Chinese leadership to the killing of Chinese workers in Sudan in 2008. Third, we focus on how the Chinese leadership responded to the oil production shutdown by South Sudan in January 2012 following the separation of Sudan into two countries in 2011. Another possibility would have been to focus on a particular acquisition by CNPC. Still, it is held that the three key decisions outlined earlier offer a richer analysis. An analysis of these key decisions will help us understand if Chinese foreign policy toward Sudan is dominated by state interests, economic interests, or concerns with domestic stability (*weiwen*).

Key Decision 1: change in foreign policy, 2006–07

Here, the focus is on a key shift in policy in 2006–07 by the Chinese government, which was a change from China's traditional non-interference stance to a more interventionist stance. Here, we focus on this policy change and the motivations behind it, as doing so will help us understand if the activities of the Chinese companies in Sudan are dominated by economic interests, state interests, or concerns with domestic stability (*weiwen*). If state interests dominate, Hu Jintao would pressure Bashir to ensure that the international crisis was weathered. We would see new agreements on credit lines, infrastructure development, aid, and visits to persuade the Sudan government to follow China's lead. We would see clear statements from the political leadership that would support these actions. If economic interests dominate, then Beijing would not put pressure on Sudan in 2006–07 based on the idea that the economic risk that the Chinese energy companies would incur when interfering was too high to bear. If concerns with domestic stability dominate, the deaths of Chinese workers abroad would put pressure on the leadership to mediate. We would see statements made by state leaders and comments on Chinese social media reflecting concerns with Chinese worker safety in Sudan.

Change of foreign policy, 2006

In late 2006, Beijing started applying pressure on Khartoum to modify its behavior and press for the peaceful resolution of the Darfur conflict.[38] The Darfur conflict was characterized as a genocide by the United States in 2004.[39] At the time, there were attempts in the UN to enact sanctions against Sudan, but several countries, including China, abstained. At this time, there was only a limited peacekeeping force in Sudan under the mandate of the African Union Mission in Sudan (AMIS). In response, in November 2006, UN Secretary General Kofi Annan presented the "Annan plan," which would deploy a joint UN-African Union (AU) force into Sudan in three phases to ensure peace (this eventually became UNSC resolution 1769). This allowed the UN to boost AMIS and simultaneously augment the UN presence in steps. Sudanese President Bashir was opposed to this, as he did not want to allow the joint AU-UN peacekeeping force into Sudan, which he argued would attempt to recolonize Sudan.[40] China was initially opposed to the Annan plan but ended up supporting it in late 2006. The resolution was passed with three abstentions, including China. Eventually, as seen in the following, the Chinese leadership intervened at the very highest level and pressured the Sudanese leader to accept the hybrid UN-AU force. Why did it do so?

State interests

On February 2–3, 2007, President Hu Jintao visited Khartoum. Prior to this trip, the Chinese leadership made an effort to defend its economic relations with Sudan. Zhou Wenzhong, China's deputy foreign minister, articulated the traditional position when asked about China's relations with Sudan in the context of the Darfur crisis: "Business is Business. We try to separate business from politics."[41] During the visit, Assistant Foreign Minister Zhai Jun voiced the Chinese government's opposition to sanctions. An MFA spokesman explained that "China would use its diplomatic influence to encourage a settlement of the Darfur crisis, but . . . China would not publicly pressure Sudan or threaten it with sanctions."[42] Thus, Hu Jintao refrained from making any public statements about Darfur in the course of his visit to Sudan.

According to other sources, including Zhang Dong, the Chinese ambassador in Khartoum, Presidents Bashir and Hu held a meeting behind closed doors during the visit to discuss the issue. It was leaked to the media that, in the course of this meeting, Hu urged Bashir to accept the hybrid UN-AU force and that his "government should work more earnestly to get the rebels who did not sign the Darfur peace agreement to join the peace process."[43] This received extensive coverage in Chinese media reports and was offered as evidence that China had adopted a new policy toward Sudan.[44]

Moreover, Hu offered four principles during the trip on how to deal with the Darfur issue, affirming that "it is imperative to improve the situation in Darfur and the living conditions of the people."[45] This can be seen as support from Hu for the Annan plan. That same month, Chinese Ambassador to the UN Wang Guangya highlighted the pressure China was putting on Sudan, explaining that "China doesn't usually send messages, but this time [during] Chinese President Hu Jintao's recent visit to Sudan they did . . . it was a clear, strong message."[46] In other words, in this instance, there is evidence of the dominance of state interests.

In addition to Hu Jintao's visit, there were also other types of pressure put on Sudan from the Chinese side. Previously, in October 2006, President Hu appealed to President Bashir publicly at the Forum on Chinese-Africa Cooperation to agree to the deployment of UN peacekeeping troops to Darfur. During the UNSC meeting in New York on November 16, 2006, China agreed to the deployment of a hybrid AU-UN peacekeeping mission (the Annan plan). Finally, on a more concrete level, the NDRC released its list of priority countries for investment in March 2007, which now excluded Sudan, although this did not stop the CNPC from acquiring further assets there.[47]

Shift in China's position, 2006–07

The pressure must have grown too strong for President Bashir, and on June 12, 2007, in a joint statement with the AU and UN, Sudan declared that it had explicitly accepted the third phase of the Annan proposal:[48] the deployment of the AU-UN force to enter Darfur. Subsequently, on July 31, 2007, during its term as the UNSC chair, China supported the new resolution: UNSC Resolution 1769, which authorized the deployment of a joint AU-UN peacekeeping force to Darfur under a Chapter 7 mandate, in a new mission to be known as the UN-AU Mission in Darfur (UNAMID). This almost tripled the size of the peacekeeping force in Darfur. It would consist of UN and AMIS troops numbering 19,555 troops, including 360 military observers and 3,772 police. In return, the resolution did not assert pressure or impose sanctions on Sudan.

In September 2007, Liu Guijin declared that the diplomacy by the Chinese leadership had been successful in leading the Sudanese government to approve the hybrid AU-UN peacekeeping force to the Darfur region.[49] The passage of Resolution 1769 was seen as a result of China's active persuasion or subtle diplomacy: the Chinese leadership played a key role in cooperating with the UN, the AU, and the Sudanese government. That President Hu Jintao had pressured Sudan to accept the UN-AU force, something which would otherwise be considered part of domestic politics, illustrates how Beijing shifted its policy from its traditional refusal to become involved in the internal affairs of other countries. Moreover, it signified a shift in the Chinese position on what constituted legitimate UN intervention.[50] A change did take place, as China interfered in matters that would otherwise be considered part of domestic politics and within the policy of non-interference.

After the agreement was reached, problems mounted regarding its implementation. While UNSC Resolution 1769 had been passed, no more than half of the planned 26,000 peacekeepers had arrived on the ground by mid-2008. This was mainly due to opposition from Khartoum.[51] During a January 2008 AU meeting in Addis Ababa, Chinese Assistant Foreign Minister Zhai Jun declared, "The world is running out of patience with what's going on in Darfur."[52] In February 2008, Liu Guijin publicly urged the Sudanese government to remove any hindrance to the full UNAMID deployment.[53] At this time, in February 2008, Bashir dispatched the Sudanese militia to burn down more towns in Darfur in order to obstruct and delay the deployment of the force.[54]

Later, in June 2008, just months before the Beijing Olympics, at a point when the conflict in Darfur had not been settled and the UN-AU force had not yet been fully deployed, Sudan's vice president Ali Uthman Muhammad Taha visited Beijing and met with Hu Jintao. During the visit, President Hu Jintao was reported to have put pressure on Sudan to settle the conflict in Darfur. Still, new economic deals were also signed during Taha's visit.[55]

Concern with international opinion

A number of motives led Beijing to adopt a new foreign policy. The role of Western public opinion became pertinent as in the early months of 2007, human rights activists in the United States and Europe tried to organize a boycott of the 2008 Beijing Summer Olympics. The campaign was led by US actress Mia Farrow, who described the conflict in Darfur as "genocide by Arab Janjaweed militia of black villagers in Darfur." The campaign and potential boycott of the 2008 Olympics would have represented a major political embarrassment to China. Having been awarded the 2008 Olympics had a great significance for the Chinese leadership. In the words of Wang Wei, the senior Beijing Olympics official, "winning the host rights means winning the respect, trust and favor of the international community."[56] Special Representative Liu Guijin said that linking political issues such as Darfur to the Beijing Olympics went against the spirit of the event.[57] "The Olympic Games are not to be politicized."[58] Liu stressed that non-politicization constitutes the very spirit of the Olympics. Chinese Foreign Ministry spokesperson Jiang Yu protested that the activists were "exploiting the Olympic Games to put pressure on China."[59] The Olympics was intended as an arena for China to be recognized as an equal among other states. Thus, even if the Olympics was "just" a sports event, the Chinese envisioned it to be an important showcase for the world to "see" China. One Chinese informant notes that "The Beijing Olympics being called Genocide Olympics was not acceptable for the Chinese people."[60] This would bring shame on the Chinese nation.

In March 2007, the Beijing Olympics and a possible boycott were discussed in the US Congress. The next month, Chairman of the US Senate Foreign Relations Committee Joseph Biden and 96 other senators wrote a letter urging the Chinese leadership to use its influence to solve the Darfur conflict, warning that the Beijing Olympics would be in jeopardy if it did not change its stance on Sudan. Furthermore, on May 9, 2007, more than 100 US House of Representatives members sent a letter to the Chinese government about the upcoming Olympics.[61] In fact, the threat of the upcoming Olympics becoming known as the "Genocide Olympics" pushed Beijing to change its foreign policy. Thus, the change can be ascribed to concern with international opinion.

Economic interests

The criticism had an "economic image," however, in the sense that several investment groups made changes to their investment portfolios following the mounting criticism of China resulting from its involvement in Sudan. In May 2007, Fidelity Investments, the world's largest mutual fund firm, sold 90.6 percent of its American depositary receipt holdings in PetroChina amid pressure from US activist groups on institutional investors to divest their PetroChina shares because of CNPC's involvement in Sudan. Thus, the decision to adopt a new stance toward Sudan shows how the threat of a 2008 Olympic boycott and repercussions from loss to China's "international face" is considered more important to the Chinese leadership than the risk of economic losses, the loss of a political ally such as Bashir, and the risk to national security of losing a chunk (approximately 6 percent) of the country's oil imports. This view of the Chinese leadership is connected to Chinese history and the century of humiliation.[62]

Indicators of state interest

There is a certain rhythm in terms of how the visits by Chinese leaders to Sudan were carried out. They were often a result of pressure, either foreign or domestic, and used to "soothe" criticism – or push for certain things (not) to happen. In the case of the Darfur crisis, for example, Hu Jintao traveled to Sudan in February 2007 to put pressure on Bashir, thereby breaching the principle that has otherwise been the cornerstone of Chinese foreign policy since the founding of the Chinese republic: non-interference in the domestic affairs of other countries. Moreover, China's assistant foreign minister with responsibility for Africa, Zhai Jun, visited Sudan in April 2007, meeting with Bashir and visiting Darfur refugee camps.

On May 10, 2007, the Chinese government appointed Liu Guijin as a special representative of African Affairs with a mandate to solve the Darfur crisis. Liu visited Sudan several times in 2007. During Liu's June visit, he indicated that the Chinese leadership had privately put pressure on Bashir to solve the Darfur conflict, sometimes using "very direct language."[63] Liu said that China "did not believe in 'patronizing' the Sudanese but instead wished to engage them on an equal footing."[64]

Another indicator of state interests is the flow of aid. During a May 2007 visit, Liu announced that China would extend humanitarian aid of $10 million to displaced people in Darfur, the third of four batches that the Chinese government had promised since 2005, and would commit 315 engineers to Darfur to help with development work.[65] In total, China had provided $30 million in development assistance to Sudan since 2005. During Hu Jintao's visit to Sudan in February 2007, China canceled $70 million of debt, in addition to some $14 million that had been totally written off.[66]

Another indicator of state interests is whether aid is appreciated by the recipient. For Sudan, the relationship with China had political benefits in the form of protection from UNSC resolutions and arms imports and led to the construction of important infrastructure, including the first refinery, which made Sudan independent of the import of refined products. In 1999, when Sudan went from an oil-importing country to an oil-exporting country, the Sudanese president emotionally declared, "Sudan finally has its own oil industry, and the one making the greatest contribution to its creation is China."[67] Generally speaking, the two parties refer to each other as "friends" (朋友/*pengyou*)[68] and "brothers" (兄弟/*xiongdi*)[69] and to the existence of a "traditional friendship" between the two sides.[70] President Bashir is quoted in a Chinese oil industry publication as saying, "with the support of our Chinese brothers we constructed the Khartoum refinery. This is a witness to the deep and traditional friendship between Sudan and China and that China and Sudan stand together as third world countries."[71] This all reflects how "the other party" appreciated the role of China in Sudan.

*Domestic stability (*weiwen*)*

If there is evidence of the concern with domestic stability, then concern with domestic media would be an important factor influencing the Chinese foreign policy. The Olympics – given the connection to national pride and thus to nationalism and ultimately to CCP survival – arguably became a matter of national security. In order to ensure domestic stability, China therefore had to satisfy a domestic need for the citizens to "feel" national pride. It would not look good to the Chinese public if foreign countries were to boycott the Olympics. This case demonstrates how the occurrence of certain events related to national security can provoke Beijing to adopt new policy. However, while the concerns with domestic stability are present here, state interests remain dominant. Importantly, there is no evidence of Chinese workers killed in this instance.

Conclusion, Key Decision 1

In the case of the foreign policy shift in 2006, international opinion and foreign pressure played a key role in Beijing taking a "responsible" position on Darfur. Beijing sought to avoid criticism and project an image of it working actively to solve the Darfur crisis. The Chinese leadership was facing a situation in which it did not want the country to be seen as an irresponsible power by blocking international efforts to prevent genocide in Darfur. The pressure placed by Hu Jintao on President Bashir reflected how the concern with international image overshadowed economic interests. It demonstrates that the Chinese leadership was willing to sacrifice its economic interests to ensure its security interests. Thus, this key decision provides evidence of state interests.

The 2006 policy shift had ramifications for Chinese companies operating in Sudan. Prior to the Darfur crisis, the companies had been left on their own and, in fact, according to CNPC, the company's operations in Sudan had been its most profitable overseas activities.[72] The Chinese companies were treated according to Arab "gentleman" custom, receiving preferential treatment in return for "no interference."[73] But when the Chinese president interfered in domestic politics, thus transgressing what had previously been an unwritten agreement, the Chinese companies operating in Sudan suffered: "It was because politics got in the way."[74] Moreover, CNPC lost large sums of money during this period, because of production stoppages and militia attacks.

This was evidence that politics had attained a primacy over oil interests and that when the state pursued its interest and the CCP "interfered" politically, this occurred at the expense of the companies. The events in Darfur in 2006–08 came to have consequences for the Chinese companies operating in Sudan, as a change becomes evident around Darfur. Prior to the incident, the Chinese companies had been more independent, whereas they clearly fell under greater pressure from Beijing afterward.[75]

This case demonstrates a policy change on the part of the Chinese leadership, a move away from the policy of non-interference. This key decision can be viewed as a case in which China adapts to international norms and is an instance where external advocacy triggered a normative change in the Chinese leadership. It provides evidence of China showing greater flexibility regarding the principle of sovereignty and illustrates that international and institutional cooperation has become an important element in Chinese foreign policy. Moreover, it reflects how a peaceful international environment would seem attractive to China.[76] At the same time, it would also signify an attitudinal change to UN peacekeeping, as the Chinese leadership with its intervention showed support for a larger UN peacekeeping force to be placed in Darfur.[77]

Thus, in the period leading up to the Olympics, an international campaign launched against the Chinese government led it to change its foreign policy *vis-à-vis* Sudan. This key decision thus provides evidence of how the independent activities of the NOCs and profitable commercial activities in Sudan came to have negative ramifications for Chinese foreign policy, given the possible repercussions from a boycott of the Beijing Olympic Games for the Chinese "image." Chinese scholar Zhu Feng has commented that "[t]hese state-owned companies have become very powerful interest groups. They even hijacked China's foreign policy in Sudan."[78] The key decision under study here thus shows that NOCs play a role in Chinese foreign policy.

How does the analysis here compare to the quantitative analysis? The results from the quantitative analysis show that whereas economic interests dominate relative to state interests and concerns with domestic stability before 2006, state interests and concerns with domestic stability become more important in 2006–07 (ratios of 1.5–2.3:1), and in fact, state interests/domestic stability dominate economic interests in 2008 (ratio of 0.7:1). Thus, in the years 2006–08, when the Sudan/Darfur issue was indeed most relevant for the People's Republic of China (PRC), the data reflects this increase in the importance of state interests. Thus, the results from the quantitative and qualitative analyses are corroborated (for 2008).

Key Decision 2: kidnapping of Chinese workers, 2008

This section focuses on the risks to domestic stability arising from the threats to the security of Chinese workers and the impact this has for Chinese foreign policy. If state interests dominate, then the state will become involved if Chinese nationals are kidnapped in order to protect the national interest. We see aid, state visits, and declarations from political leaders supporting this. If economic interests dominate, then the risk to the Chinese workers in terms of fatalities and kidnappings compromises the investments, potentially reducing profits; however, the investments would continue despite the risks involved. If concerns with domestic stability (*weiwen*) dominate, then the killing of Chinese nationals in Sudan puts pressure on the Chinese leadership to mediate, as the safety of Chinese workers abroad is linked to the ability of the Chinese state to maintain domestic stability. We will see statements made by Chinese state leaders and comments on Chinese social media emphasizing the significance of the deaths of Chinese workers in Sudan for Chinese domestic stability.

Kidnapping of Chinese workers in 2008

Chinese companies have increasingly been concerned with the risks associated with their investments, including their workers. In the years following the recent

Table 6.2 Abductions of Chinese workers (2004–13)[1]

Date	*Occasion*	*Actor*	*Casualties*
March 14, 2004	2 Chinese engineers working on water projects in Kordofan kidnapped	Sudan Liberation Army (SLA)	0
October 18, 2008	9 CNPC employees (China Petroleum Engineering Construction Co.) in Heglig, Southern Kordofan, kidnapped; 5 were killed and 4 rescued	JEM/Al-Qaeda	5
November 27, 2010	1 Chinese oil worker working for an oil company in Southern Kordofan kidnapped	Heiban tribe	0
October 3, 2011	1 Chinese oil worker killed during attack on oilfield in South Kordofan	Unidentified armed men	1
January 28, 2012	29 Chinese construction workers (Sinohydro) kidnapped in South Kordofan State	Northern wing of SPLM	0
January 2013	4 Chinese workers working on development projects in North Darfur (1 engineer and 3 drivers) and 11 Sudanese workers kidnapped	JEM or SLA-Minnawi	0

Source: Author's production

1 In addition to the preceding, in October 2007, JEM attacked an oilfield run by the GNPOC in Defra, Kordofan, and kidnapped two foreign and three Sudanese workers (no Chinese) with no casualties. On December 11, 2007, JEM attacked Chinese oil installations (oilfield run by GNOPC in Southern Kordofan) with no casualties.

"Going Out" strategy, a growing number of Chinese workers have been stationed abroad. As of February 2012, some 850,000 Chinese were working abroad, many in risk-prone areas in Asia, the Middle East, and Africa.[79] In Sudan, there are have been up to 10,000 Chinese workers. Table 6.2 shows abductions of Chinese workers in Sudan from 2004–2013.[80]

The key decision considered here is the response from the Chinese leadership to the most serious abduction of Chinese workers in Sudan in 2008, together with another occurrence in 2012.

On October 18, 2008, nine CNPC employees, including three engineers and six other workers, were kidnapped at a worksite in southern Kordofan near the Abeyi region while doing contract work for the GNPOC. The abduction, which led to the deaths of five Chinese workers (the four others were rescued), was undertaken by rebels affiliated with the Justice and Equality Movement (JEM).[81] After the rebel attack, the JEM commander asserted that "China supports the Khartoum government militarily and helps to marginalize our region. But our case is with the government in Khartoum."[82] Thus, for the rebels, including groups such as JEM, the target was not really China itself; rather, it was the central government in Khartoum. But even if the target was not China, the attacks on Chinese oil workers had ramifications extending far beyond Sudan. As the Chinese government was seen as supporting the Sudanese government, however, CNPC was seen as a relevant target.[83]

For our purposes here, how did the Chinese government respond? While there had been previous abductions in Sudan, the severity of this incident and the publicity it subsequently received in China rendered this case different. Four things happened: first, Chinese Ambassador to Sudan Li Chengwen and CNPC Deputy General Manager Wang Dongjin paid visits to the rescued workers.[84] Second, on October 24, Liu Guijin, the Chinese government's special representative on the Darfur issue, was sent to Khartoum to mediate. Third, on October 28, 2008, the Chinese ambassador to the UN, Zhang Yesui, condemned the murder of Chinese workers in Sudan at a UNSC meeting on Darfur.[85] Fourth and finally, on October 30, 2008, 12 days later, while several workers were still missing, the Chinese government sent a delegation headed by the MFA together with officials with the Ministry of Commerce (MOFCOM) and CNPC to Sudan to pay a visit to the four rescued Chinese workers, who were receiving treatment in a Khartoum hospital.

Maintaining the safety of Chinese workers when they are abroad and serving the interests of the nation – that is, protecting oil imports and, thus, the energy supply – is very important to the Chinese public. In the words of one Chinese informant, "in Sudan, when workers are killed, this puts pressure on Chinese leaders."[86]

It later became evident that the Sudanese government appreciated the help they received from their Chinese "brother." On November 3, 2008, for example, the Sudanese minister of the interior stated that the kidnapping and killing of Chinese workers was aimed at damaging the relations between Sudan and China, ruling out that the criminals would be successful: "The Chinese companies and persons are participating positively in the process of development in Sudan not only in the petroleum sphere but also in a lot of other spheres where their role cannot be ignored."[87] Thus, the recipient country supports and appreciates the activities of the Chinese NOCs in Sudan.

Still, the 2008 incident offers evidence of the domestic politicization of the Chinese role in Sudan that took place when armed Darfurian and allied rebel groups targeted Chinese interests in order to apply pressure on Khartoum. But as we have noted, the target is not China; it is Khartoum. A Chinese informant says, "[T]he killing of the Chinese workers in Sudan is really just part of the conflict between the North and South."[88] As reasoned in a Chinese academic article, the "2008 kidnapping incident is evidence that the Darfur rebel groups want the Chinese government to put pressure on the Sudanese government to ensure that . . . authority and resources are shared with the South."[89]

Consequently, there is increased concern among Chinese companies about the high risk associated with corporate investments, including company workers, with respect to the activities in Sudan.[90] Still, according to one Chinese informant, the CNPC decision about whether to remain in Sudan was not influenced by a security risk assessment.[91] Even if the killing of Chinese workers in Sudan was not targeted at China, it has domestic consequences for China, as protecting the lives of its workers is important for maintaining social stability. Thus, it touches on concerns with regime legitimacy, which is ultimately linked to the survival of CCP rule.

The 2012 incident

Another incident occurred in 2012. On January 28, rebels from SPLA-North (SRF) in South Kordofan State at El Abbasiya, kidnapped 29 Chinese employees of Sinohydro, a hydropower engineering and construction company, who were working on a road project. This incident was triggered by the domestic conflict between Sudan and South Sudan. All of the Chinese workers were released unharmed two weeks later.

In response, a number of things happened. First, diplomats from Sudan participated in emergency discussions in Beijing, resulting in a delegation being dispatched to Sudan on January 30, 2012. After the incident, Deputy Foreign Minister Xie Hangsheng said that China "attaches great importance to protecting nationals overseas" and is "deeply shocked" by the abduction in Sudan.[92] In fact, it appears as though the abductions were intended as bait, in the sense that the rebels hoped Beijing would use its influence to get Sudan to halt its military attacks and let aid reach South Kordofan.

While the official media generally played down this kidnapping, the incident stirred up considerable attention in the Chinese social media (*Weibo*). *Weibo* was full of questions about why China, despite its rising economic and military power, does not intervene more forcefully to protect its citizens who are victimized abroad. While four Chinese oil workers were killed in Sudan in 2008, this incident caused greater attention. The *Global Times*, which is affiliated with the *People's Daily*, published an editorial urging "better protection" for Chinese working in Africa, calling for Chinese companies to pay more attention to – and pay more for – security rather than merely looking to the government for help. It stated that "China is not powerful enough at this time to protect every Chinese citizen scattered around the vast continent."[93]

This, thus, illustrates that the Chinese government is concerned with the safety of Chinese workers, as protecting the lives of its workers abroad is vital to maintaining domestic stability.

Conclusion, Key Decision 2

The deaths of the Chinese workers in Sudan in 2008 (and the kidnapping in 2012) touch on the ability of the Chinese state to ensure domestic stability. This key decision shows how these incidents caused a considerable stir domestically in China. This instance thus provides evidence of how the activities of Chinese SOEs abroad affect foreign policy. Whereas the driver was external in the case of Sudan in 2008, the driving force here is domestic and about securing domestic stability. Thus, this key decision provides evidence of concern with domestic stability. Similarly, several studies in the *People's Daily* show how the concern with domestic stability increased overwhelmingly around 2008–09.

How does the analysis here compare to the quantitative analysis? In 2008, state interests and concerns with domestic stability are more dominant relative to economic interests (ratio of 0.7:1). However, looking singularly at the ratio of state interests to concerns with domestic stability in 2008, state interests dominate (ratio of 11.8:1). Thus, whereas the killing of Chinese workers in Sudan in 2008 is important and causes concerns regarding domestic stability, the Chinese leadership is more driven by state interests in this year, the reason being the Olympics and the crisis in Darfur. Thus, the results here provide evidence of state interests.

There is evidence of some state interests that the qualitative analysis is missing, the reason being that steps undertaken by the Chinese leadership to ensure domestic stability in the face of killed Chinese workers in Sudan can also be motivated by concerns with national security and, thus, the security interests of the state. In fact, state interests and the concern with domestic stability (*weiwen*) have the same driver. Thus, what might be seen as evidence of state interests might in turn be evidence of the concern with domestic stability. Still, considering the overall evidence, in this instance, the evidence of concerns with domestic stability is more credible.

Key Decision 3: the 2012 oil shutdown

This section focuses on the almost year-long South Sudan oil production shutdown in 2012 that cost CNPC $3 billion due to damaged oil installations and lost imports. It looks at the response to these events of the Chinese companies operating in Sudan and the Chinese government. If state interests dominate, we would expect the Chinese government to put pressure on both Sudan and South Sudan to resume the operations in both countries. Indicators of this would be visits, the flow of aid, statements from political leaders, and so forth. If economic interests dominate, then we would see that, despite running substantial losses, the Chinese leadership would not interfere to help the companies. If concerns with domestic stability (*weiwen*) dominate, we would expect the lack of supplies to cause a domestic crisis in China. Moreover, we would expect statements made by state leaders and comments on Chinese social media reflecting concerns with Chinese worker safety in Sudan.

Oil production shutdown, 2012

After two civil wars, including more than two decades of conflict, Sudan separated into two countries on July 9, 2011, after a referendum held in South Sudan in which 98 percent of the Southern Sudanese population supported South Sudanese independence.

While the Comprehensive Peace Agreement (CPA) had a template in 2005 for how oil revenue was to be shared equally between north and south, there was no post-independence oil-sharing mechanism or determination of transit fees. There were two particular points on which the two parties disagreed: the fee that South Sudan should pay to use the infrastructure in the north and the compensation to Sudan for the lost income, as 75 percent of its previous oil reserves were now in South Sudan. In terms of the former, whereas Sudan had asked for $36/barrel for the transit fee through the north's pipeline, South Sudan demanded $0.41/barrel, which, according to industry analysts, is more in line with international standards.[94] In terms of the latter, Dr. Mohammed Sabir, head of Sudan's economic delegation to talks in Addis Ababa in January 2012, announced that South Sudan owed Sudan $900 million in oil export revenue for the period since independence, that is, since July 2011.[95] From December 2011 to January 2012, Sudan blocked the export of South Sudanese oil from Port Sudan by blocking two oil tankers and denied access to the port for two shipments of oil.[96] All in all, South Sudan accused Khartoum of withholding some 1.4 million barrels of its oil, which was worth $815 million, at Bashair Harbor.[97]

On January 22, 2012, in response to the stolen oil, South Sudan incrementally shut down its entire oil production of 350,000 bpd, even though this jeopardized its own economic survival (the shutdown was completed on February 8). The situation then escalated. In April 2012, Sudan dropped bombs on South Sudan, including Bentiu.[98] In return, South Sudan seized the contested Heglig oilfield (Blocks 1/2/4) on April 10, resulting in the heaviest fighting since 2005 (Heglig is situated in South Kordofan in Sudan but is claimed by South Sudan). On April 20, 2013, after some ten days, South Sudanese forces left Heglig. The Heglig oil facility, CNPC's key installation in Sudan, sustained roughly $3 billion of damages as a result of the fighting.[99]

On September 27, 2012, the two parties reached an agreement regarding oil transit under the mediation of the AU at a summit between President Al Bashir of Sudan and South Sudanese President Salva Kiir Mayardit in Addis Ababa, Ethiopia. While the AU mediated the negotiations, China played an active role behind the scenes. With the agreement, South Sudan would resume its oil production and would be granted access to use oil transportation and processing facilities in Sudan. Moreover, a demilitarized buffer zone was established between the two countries.[100]

State interests

The problem for Beijing after the division of Sudan into two countries was that the goodwill in terms of investments in Sudan over the course of the last decade was wasted, in the sense that the oil was located in the south of the country. CNPC has invested some $15 billion in Sudanese oil infrastructure, including pipelines and a refinery.[101] How did the Chinese government respond to South Sudan's blocking of oil tankers and oil? In November 2011, Chinese Ambassador to Sudan Luo Xiaoguang called Khartoum's aforementioned blockage of oil tankers "very serious and unjustified."[102] On November 29, 2011, Chinese MFA spokesman Hong Lei called for the governments of South Sudan and Sudan to find a "flexible" and "pragmatic" resolution to the dispute.[103] Later, in December 2011, when discussions between the two sides broke down and the North threatened to disrupt the passage of oil from the South, Pagan Amum, the secretary-general of the Sudan People's Liberation Movement (SPLM), spoke to Chinese ambassador Luo Xiaoguang: "The ambassador . . . wanted to ensure that oil keeps flowing. . . . We talked about threats to our national interest and their national interests."[104] Still, no major initiatives were initiated from the Chinese side to solve the conflict between the two sides.

After the oil shutdown, Foreign Ministry Spokesperson Liu Weimin declared in a statement posted on the ministry website in January 2012 that China remains committed to aiding efforts to broker a peaceful resolution to the dispute between the two sides. "Chinese oil companies and their partners have major projects in both Sudan and South Sudan. Their legitimate rights and interests should receive significant protection."[105]

Then, after the disaster involving the destruction of CNPC's installations in April 2012, the Chinese government initiated efforts in May 2012 to broker the conflict. On April 6, 2012, Chen Xiaodong, director-general of the Chinese MFA's Department of West Asian and North African Affairs, issued the following statement:

> The Foreign Ministry takes this very seriously and has used various opportunities to urge the governments of the two countries to ensure the stable and sustained nature of oil cooperation and to genuinely protect the personnel and property of Chinese enterprises as well as their legal rights and interests.[106]

But no direct criticism was voiced by the Chinese side and no actual pressure was placed on the two sides to solve the conflict. Thus, following the tradition of Chinese foreign policy, in this instance, Beijing stuck to its policy of "studied neutrality" or "non-interference."

Beijing was trying to maintain good relations with both Juba and Khartoum at the same time. A number of visits were conducted to ensure that oil would continue to flow. On August 8, 2011, Foreign Minister Yang Jiechi visited Khartoum to meet with President Bashir and was clear in the Chinese government's support of Sudan and that China sought to remove the distortions that accompanied UNSC Resolution 1593 related to the International Criminal Court (ICC), as President Bashir was the target of ICC arrest warrants for alleged war crimes and genocide in the Darfur region.[107] President Bashir said during the meeting that "China is Sudan's real friend and good partner. It supports Sudan in exploiting oilfields and has helped train many Sudanese talents."[108] Thus, even if Sudan lost its oil reserves, China still regarded Sudan as a strategic partner and would continue to support Sudan, both in international fora and in terms of Sudan's development. If Beijing can help broker a peace between the two countries that would more or less maintain the status quo – China being able to continue to use the existing pipeline infrastructure built for Chinese money – then this would be in Beijing's interest.

However, when oil for Sinopec's shipment bound for China was held up for several days by Sudan in December 2011, Special Representative Liu Guijin traveled immediately to both Juba and Khartoum to mediate in the negotiations between the two parties, warning that oil must keep flowing "because the consequences of stopping . . . will be disastrous to everyone."[109] Still, Liu's statements during his visits to Khartoum and Juba can be seen along the traditional lines of non-interference.

The Chinese government has sought to maintain good relations with both countries by providing loans and aid to both after the separation in 2011. Accordingly, during Foreign Minister Yang Jiechi's visit to Sudan in December 2011, China gave a $15.55 million interest-free loan.[110] China has also continued to provide aid to the South Sudanese side. In mid-2007, China's aid to Southern Sudan increased in the form of funding for projects such as hydropower, road construction, hospitals, and schools, the total value of which is unclear.[111] During President Kiir's visit to Beijing in April 2012, a new loan scheme to fund infrastructure – the exact amount of this is also unclear – was announced.[112, 113]

*Domestic stability (*weiwen*)*

There is evidence that the oil shutdown put pressure on the Chinese leadership to mediate, but since no Chinese oil workers were killed in relation to the oil shutdown, the analysis gives no evidence of concerns with domestic stability in this case.

Conclusion, Key Decision 3

The 2012 oil shutdown has had major significance for the Chinese leadership, as it led to sizable financial losses for the Chinese companies. As a result, it would be in the interest of the Chinese government to negotiate a solution to the conflict. Immediately after the CNPC installations were damaged in April 2012, the Chinese government initiated efforts to broker the conflict, dispatching envoy Zhong Jianhua to the region. The idea was that Beijing could ensure stability in Sudan through its role as a trusted broker, given its commercial interests and credibility on both sides. At the same time, while an envoy and the MFA indeed went to Khartoum and Juba, there were no senior visits to Sudan or South Sudan after 2011 to apply pressure to avoid a crisis, including the oil shutdown.

The Chinese president did not travel to the region, nor were any official statements issued by the Politburo. Moreover, aid was limited. Thus, the Chinese response was relatively subdued. The CNPC was simply left to fend for itself, despite suffering major losses. This demonstrates how it is only when national security – the pride of the nation – is at stake, as in the case of the Olympics, that Beijing intervenes. The companies being left on their own thus shows how the political leadership will not necessarily help out when companies find themselves in trouble, even when problems with major financial consequences occur. Thus, despite the oil shutdown, the Chinese decision was to simply remain on the sidelines, and non-interference once again came to characterize Chinese foreign policy toward the two Sudans. This instance illustrates how economic interests again came to dominate the activities of the companies abroad in the sense that economic interests were not serious enough for the Chinese state to interfere.

How does the analysis here compare to the quantitative analysis? In 2012, economic interests again strongly dominate relative to state interests/domestic stability (ratio of 3.5:1). Similarly, in 2012, economic interests dominate relative to concerns with domestic stability (ratio of 15.6:1) and state interests (ratio of 4.5:1). Thus, the results from the quantitative and qualitative analyses are corroborated.

Conclusion

In the case of Sudan, the companies have little incentive to become involved because of the limited availability of oil. As the government attributes high strategic importance to the country, it pursues its state interests. Thus, the empirical expectation is that state interests/concerns with domestic stability (*weiwen*) will dominate.

The qualitative analysis produced evidence of state interests, concerns with domestic stability, and economic interests, but this evidence varied over time. The analysis shows that in the case of the 2006–08 foreign policy change, state interests dominated. In the case of the Chinese nationals killed in 2008, concerns with domestic stability dominated. Finally, in the case of the oil shutdown in 2012, economic interests dominated. Interestingly, I find particular evidence of the concern with domestic stability in 2008, which is a novel finding.

The quantitative analysis corroborates these results, except in the case of the oil workers killed in 2008. Still, it is argued that, in fact, the evidence of concerns with domestic stability is more credible in this instance. Thus, the two methods are generally corroborated. In conclusion, the quantitative and qualitative analyses only partly support the empirical expectation, as the results show evidence of both economic interests and state interests/domestic stability (*weiwen*).

Notes

1 Ali Abdalla Ali, *The Sudanese – Chinese Relations Before and After Oil* (Khartoum: Sudan Currency Printing Press, 2006).
2 Awad al-Jaz, "The Oil of Sudan: Challenges and Achievements," in *The Kenana Handbook of Sudan*, ed. Peter G. Hopkins (London: Kegan Paul, 2007), 671–82, 673.
3 See, for example, Stephanie Beswick, *Sudan's Blood Economy* (Rochester, NY: University of Rochester Press, 2004). Here, Sudan is looked upon as a case of the "resource curse."
4 Daniel Large, "China's Sudan Engagement: Changing Northern and Southern Political Trajectories in Peace and War," *The China Quarterly* 199 (September 2009): 610–26.
5 Daniel Large and Luke A. Patey, "Sudan Looks East: Introduction," in *Sudan Looks East. China, India and the Politics of Asian Alternatives*, eds. Daniel Large and Luke A. Patey (Woodbridge: James Currey, 2011), 1–34, 2–4.

6 Serge Michel and Michel Beuret, *China Safari: On the Trail of Beijing's Expansion in Africa* (New York, NY: Nation Books, 2009), 8, 254.
7 Robert Rotberg, ed., *China into Africa. Trade Aid and Influence* (Washington, DC: Brookings Institution Press, 2008).
8 See, for example, BinBin Jiang, "China National Petroleum Corporation (CNPC): A Balancing Act Between Enterprise and Government," in *Oil and Governance: State-Owned Enterprises and the World Energy Supply*, eds. David G. Victor, David R. Hults and Mark C. Thurber (Cambridge: Cambridge University Press, 2011), 379–417.
9 See, for example, Ricardo Soares de Oliveira, "Making Sense of Chinese Oil Investment in Africa," in *China Returns to Africa: A Rising Power and a Continent Embrace*, eds. Chris Alden, Daniel Large, and Ricardo Soares de Oliveira (London, UK: Hurst & Co., 2008), 83–110.
10 E.g., Daniel Large, "From Non-Interference to Constructive Engagement? China's Evolving Relations with Sudan," in *China Returns to Africa. A Rising Power and a Continent Embrace*, eds. Chris Alden, Daniel Large, and Ricardo Soares de Oliveira (London, UK: Hurst & Co., 2008), 275–94, 291.
11 Laura M. James, "The Oil Boom and Its Limitations in Sudan," in *Sudan Looks East. China, India and the Politics of Asian Alternatives*, eds. Daniel Large and Luke A. Patey (Woodbridge: James Currey, 2011), 52–69, 52.
12 Chen Wenxian [陈文仙], 苏丹：受全球石油投资 者青睐 ["Sudan–Highly Esteemed by Global Oil Investors"], 中国石化报 (*China Petrochemical News*), February 24, 2005. For more, see Sherief El Tuhami, "Oil in Sudan: Its Discovery and Industrial Development," in *The Kenana Handbook of Sudan*, ed. Peter Gwynvay Hopkins (London, UK: Kegan Paul, 2007), 657–70, 657.
13 Interview with Chinese informant, 2014. However, according to other sources, for example, Carmody, since 1996, the Chinese government has made an estimated $20 billion of investments in Sudan (Padraig Carmody, *Globalization in Africa: Recolonization or Renaissance?* [London, UK: Lynne Rienner, 2010], 77).
14 China's Land Resources Statistical Yearbook 2010 [中国国土资源统计年鉴], Ministry of Land of the People's Republic of China [中华人民共和国国土资源部].
15 *U.S. Energy Information Administration (EIA)*, "Country Analysis Brief: Sudan and South Sudan," September 2, 2014, accessed December 15, 2015, www.eia.gov/countries/country-data.cfm?fips=su.
16 *U.S. EIA*, "Country Analysis Brief: Sudan and South Sudan."
17 *U.S. EIA*, "Country Analysis Brief: Sudan and South Sudan."
18 *U.S. EIA*, "Country Analysis Brief: Sudan and South Sudan."
19 Erica S. Downs, "The Fact and Fiction of Sino-African Energy Relations," *China Security* 3 (3) (2007): 42–68, 46.
20 Interview with Chinese informant, 2012.
21 This section focuses on Sudan and South Sudan in the period 2002–13. In July 2011, the country was divided into Sudan and South Sudan. Here, I primarily present Sudan. Details about South Sudan are included where relevant.
22 Interview with Chinese informant, 2012.
23 Interview with Chinese informant, 2012.
24 Toyin Falola and Adebayo O. Oyebade, *Hot Spot: Sub-Saharan Africa* (Santa Barbara, CA: Greenwood, 2010); *Hotspot,* 157.
25 Robert A. Lobban, *Global Security Watch: Sudan* (Santa Barbara, CA: Praeger, 2010), 135–7.
26 *U.S. EIA*, "Country Analysis Brief: Sudan and South Sudan."
27 Robert O. Collins, *A History of Modern Sudan* (Cambridge: Cambridge University Press, 2008).
28 Collins, *A History of Modern Sudan*, 272–302.

29 Richard Barltrop, *Darfur and the International Community: The Challenges of Conflict Resolution in Sudan* (London: I.B. Tauris, 2011), 114.
30 In fact, since July 2004, UNSC has passed ten resolutions regarding Darfur, five of them under Chapter Seven of the UN Charter. China abstained from many of the votes in the UNSC, including UNSC Res. 1044, 1054, 1556, 1564, 1591, and 1593. In this sense, China has been a supporter of Sudan in the UN forum. See Key Decision 1 for more detail on the specific resolutions.
31 *United Nations Statistical Division*, Commodity Trade Statistics Database, accessed December 15, 2015, http://comtrade.un.org/db/.
32 *Central Intelligence Agency (CIA)*, "Export Partners of Sudan," CIA World Factbook 2013, accessed December 15, 2015, www.cia.gov/library/publications/resources/the-world-factbook/geos/su.html; *CIA*, Import Partners of Sudan," CIA World Factbook 2013, accessed December 15, 2015, www.cia.gov/library/publications/resources/the-world-factbook/geos/su.html.
33 *U.S. EIA*, "Country Analysis Brief: Sudan and South Sudan."
34 *U.S. EIA*, "Country Analysis Brief: Sudan and South Sudan."
35 Luke A. Patey, "Crude Days Ahead? Oil and the Resource Curse in Sudan," *African Affairs,* 109 (437) (2010): 617–36.
36 *U.S. EIA*, "Country Analysis Brief: Sudan and South Sudan."
37 6.9:1 = approx. 14 percent. This means that for every one reference to concern with domestic stability (*weiwen*) / state interest, there are 6.9 references to economic interests.
38 Lobban, *Global Security Watch – Sudan*, 94, 100.
39 Later in 2005, the United States retreated from its definition of genocide (Michel and Beuret, *China Safari*, 154–5).
40 *Sudan Tribune*, "Sudan Accepts UN Package for Darfur, Willing to Ceasefire," December 27, 2006.
41 Howard French, "China in Africa: All Trade, With No Political Baggage," *New York Times*, August 8, 2004.
42 *International Herald Tribune*, "Hu to Seek Darfur Deal During Visit to Sudan," January 25, 2007.
43 Alfred De Montesquiou, "China's Hu Presses Sudan for Progress on Darfur," *Associated Press*, February 3, 2007.
44 Interview with Chinese informant, 2014.
45 The four principles were (1) respect Sudan's sovereignty and territorial integrity, 2) solve the issue by peaceful means, 3) take into consideration the overall situation and from a long-term perspective respect and address each other's reasonable concerns, and 4) it is imperative to improve the situation in Darfur and living conditions of local people (*Xinhua News Agency*, "Hu Puts Forward Four-Point Principle on Solving Darfur Issue," February 3, 2007).
46 *Sudan Tribune*, "China Told Sudan to Adopt UN's Darfur Plan – Envoy," February 7, 2007.
47 Richard McGregor, "Iran, Sudan and Nigeria off China Incentive List," *Financial Times,* March 2, 2007.
48 *Xinhua News Agency*, "Common language helps resolve Darfur issue," October 2, 2007.
49 *BBC*, "Envoy Says China Plays 'Unique' Role in Settling Darfur Issue," September 8, 2007.
50 Interview with Chinese informant, 2014.
51 Ian Taylor, "China's Peacekeeping Efforts in Africa: Assessing the Contributions, Future Prospects, and Challenges," in *Peacekeeping in Africa: The Evolving Security Architecture*, eds. Thierry Tardy and Marco Wyss (London, UK: Routledge, 2014): 93–112, 103.

52 *Sudan Tribune*, "China Issues a Warning to Sudan over Darfur Crisis," January 30, 2008.
53 Ian Taylor, "The People's Republic of China," in *The International Politics of Mass Atrocities. The case of Darfur*, eds. David R. Black and Paul D. Williams (London: Routledge, 2010), 176–94.
54 Human Rights Watch, "Failing Darfur, Q&A: Crisis in Darfur," September 2008, accessed December 15, 2015, www.hrw.org/sites/default/files/features/darfur/fiveyearson/qanda.html.
55 *Xinhua News Agency,* "Sudan, China Sign Deals on Stronger Agricultural Co-op," June 11, 2008.
56 Elizabeth C. Economy and Adam Segal, "China's Olympic Nightmare," *Foreign Affairs*, 97 (July–August 2008): 47–56.
57 Permanent Mission of the People's Republic of China to the UN, "China's SR on Darfur Holds a Briefing in Beijing," March 7, 2008, accessed December 15, 2015, www.china-un.org/eng/chinaandun/securitycouncil/regionalhotspots/africa/darfur/t468259.html.
58 Embassy of the People's Republic of China in India, "Special Representative of the Chinese Government on the Darfur Issue Holds a Briefing for Chinese and Foreign Journalists," May 29 2007, accessed December 15, 2015, http://in.chineseembassy.org/eng/zgbd/t325291.html.
59 *Reuters,* "China Confirms Will Send Engineers to Darfur," May 8, 2007.
60 Interview with Chinese informant, 2014.
61 Eric Reeves, "Darfur: The 'Genocide Olympics'? Campaign Roars into High Gear," *Sudan Tribune*, May 10, 2007.
62 For more on this issue, see Peter H. Gries, *China's New Nationalism: Pride, Politics, and Diplomacy* (Berkeley, CA: University of California Berkeley Press, 2004); Peter H. Gries and Stanley Rosen, eds., *State and Society in 21st Century China: Crisis, Contention and Legitimation* (New York, NY: Routledge, 2004).
63 Alec Russell and William Wallis, "China Puts Private Pressure on Sudan," *Financial Times*, June 19, 2007.
64 Nora Boustany, "Envoy Lauds China's Role in Diplomacy with Sudan," *Washington Post*, September 7, 2007.
65 Wang Xiangjiang [王湘江], 世界军事新闻剪影 ["Outline of World Military News"], *世界军事年鉴* (*World Military Yearbook*), January 1, 2008.
66 *BBC*, "Chinese Ambassador Says Sudan Is a Major Trade Partner with His Country," November 11, 2007.
67 Wu Fugui [吴富贵], 中国石油健儿建功苏丹 ("CNPC's heroes' achievements in Sudan"), *国际人才交流* (*International Talent*), May 6, 2003.
68 See, for example, Zeng Bin [曾彬]. 苏丹总统巴希尔视察中国石油六区项目 ["Sudan's President al-Bashir Inspected CNPC's Six Oil Projects"], *中国石油报* (*China Petroleum Report*), March 12, 2007).
69 See, for example, Wang Dongmei [王冬梅] and Li Zhanbin [李占彬]. 中国石油：用真诚奉献在异国创造和谐 ["CNPC: Creating Harmony Abroad through Sincere Devotion"], *工人日报* (*Workers' Daily*), January 16, 2008.
70 See, for example, Li Zhongfa [李忠发]. 中苏合作给苏丹带来石油与和平 ["Sino-Sudan Cooperation Brings Oil and Peace to Sudan"], *新华每日电讯 (Xinhua Daily Telegraph)*, November 19, 2009.
71 Li Tianxing [李天星]. 友谊长存, 携手发展" – 写在中国石油苏丹项目投产10周年之际 ["Friendship Forever, Joining Hands in Development," written at the ten-year anniversary of the operation of CNPC's Sudan project], *中国石油企业 (Chinese Oil Companies),* November 15, 2009.
72 Interview with Chinese informant, 2014.
73 Interview with Chinese informant, 2012.
74 Interview with Chinese informant, 2012.

75 Interview with Chinese informant, 2012.
76 Hu Jintao's concept of the "harmonious world" (和谐世界/*hexie shijie*) is grounded in the recognition that an interdependent, harmonious world is a precondition for China's peaceful development (Yee Sienho, "Towards a Harmonious World: The Roles of the International Law of Co-Progressiveness and Leader States," *Chinese Journal of International Law* 7 (2008): 99–105.
77 Pan Zhongying, "China's Changing Attitude to UN Peacekeeping," *International Peacekeeping* 12 (1) (2005), 87–104, 98.
78 Richard McGregor, "Chinese Diplomacy 'Hijacked' by Companies," *Financial Times,* March 17, 2008.
79 *Financial Times*, "A Chinese Puzzle; South Sudan Tests Beijing's Long-Term Foreign Policy Stance," February 22, 2012.
80 *Central Intelligence Agency (CIA)*, "The World Factbook, Sudan," accessed December 15, 2015, www.cia.gov/library/publications/the-world-factbook/geos/su.html.
81 Winnie Lee, "Chinese Oil Workers Kidnapped in Sudan," *Platts Oilgram News*, October 21, 2008.
82 *Al-Shaq al-Awsat* (BBC), October 25, 2008, "Sudan: Rebel Says Chinese Hostages Moved to Area Government Forces Cannot Reach."
83 Zong Kunpeng [宗鲲鹏] and Yan Qi [闫琦]. 绑架劫持事件的分阶段安全应对措施探讨 ["Investigation of Safety Measures in Response to Kidnapping Incidents"], *中国安全生产科学技术* (*Science and Technology of China's Safety Production*), August 15, 2010.
84 *Xinhua News Agency*, "China's Workgroup Visits Rescued Chinese Workers from Kidnapping in Sudan," November 1, 2008.
85 *Xinhua News Agency*, "Chinese UN Ambassador Condemns Killing of Chinese Workers in Sudan," October 29, 2008.
86 Interview with Chinese informant, 2012.
87 E. Zheng, "Minister of Interior: Sudan's Police Has List of Criminals Kidnapping Chinese Workers," *Xinhua News Agency*, November 3, 2008.
88 Interview with Chinese informant, 2014.
89 Jin Danni (金丹妮). 中国石油公司在苏丹的发展历史研究 ["Research on the Development History of Chinese Oil Companies in Sudan"], *西安石油大学学报* (*Journal of Xian Petroleum University*), August 15, 2012.
90 Interview with Chinese informant, 2014. See, for example, Zong Kunpeng [宗鲲鹏] and Yan Qi [闫琦]. 绑架劫持事件的分阶段安全应对措施探讨 ["Investigation of Safety Measures in Response to Kidnapping Incidents"], *中国安全生产科学技术 (Science and Technology of China's Safety Production*), August 15, 2010.
91 Interview with Chinese informant, 2014; Interview with Chinese informant, 2012.
92 Andrew Higgins, "Abduction of Chinese Workers in Sudan Ignites Criticism," *Washington Post*, February 2, 2012.
93 Andrew Higgins, "Abduction of Chinese Workers in Sudan Ignites Criticism," *Washington Post,* February 2, 2012.
94 Bai Yang [白洋]. "兄弟"反目只为石油 ["Brothers' Quarrel just for Oil"], *中国石化报* (*China Petrochemical News*), February 17, 2012; *Petroleum Economist*, "Both Sudans Pay High Price for Output Shut-in," July 2012.
95 *Petroleum Economist*, "Continuity Vital as Two Sudans Prepare to Talk," September 2011. Other accounts state $727 million, $815 million, or $1 billion of unpaid fees, including charges for oil processing, transit fees, and cost of transport as well as fees for use of the Port *(BBC*, "South Sudan Reportedly Owes Sudan over 900m Dollars," January 15, 2012).
96 *BBC*, "China Appeals to Sudan, South Sudan to Resolve Conflict Over Oil Exports," December 1, 2011; Bai Yang [白洋]. "兄弟"反目只为石油 ["Brothers" Quarrel Just for Oil], *中国石化报 (China Petrochemical News),* February 17, 2012.

97 Government of Republic of South Sudan (GoRSS), "Government of Sudan Poisons Negotiation Atmosphere in Addis by Stealing 1.4 Million Barrels of South Sudan Oil Just Days Before," Press Release, January 17, 2012.
98 Eric Watkins, "Crisis Looms in South Sudan," *Oil & Gas Journal,* February 6, 2012.
99 Interview with Chinese informant, 2014; *Platts Oilgram News*, "Sudan Eyes Oil Output Increase at Heglig," May 8, 2013.
100 For more, see *U.S. EIA*, "Country Analysis Brief: Sudan and South Sudan."
101 Interview with Chinese informant, 2014.
102 *Sudan Tribune*, "South Sudan Threatens to Suspend Oil Production if North Imposes Charges Unilaterally," November 30, 2011.
103 *Xinhua News Agency*, "China Calls for Friendly Resolution to Oil Export Dispute between South Sudan, Sudan," November 29, 2011.
104 Andrew Higgins, "Oil-Thirsty China Stuck Deep in Sudanese Muck," *Seattle Times*, December 25, 2011.
105 Song Yen Ling and Jacinta Moran, "China Seeks Protection for Sudan Operations," *Platts Oilgram News*, April 25, 2012; *Sudan Tribune*, "Sudan; China Reiterates Call for Restraint between North and South on Oil Dispute," January 21, 2012.
106 *BBC*, "China Says Sudan-South Sudan Tensions Affect Oil Cooperation," April 18, 2012.
107 *BBC*, "China, Sudan Hold Talks in Khartoum on Ways to Strengthen Ties," August 9, 2011.
108 *Xinhua News Agency*, "Sudan, China Pledge to Strengthen Ties," August 9, 2011.
109 Andrew Higgins, "Oil Interests Push China into Sudanese Quagmire," *Washington Post,* December 25, 2011; *BBC/Al-Sahafah*, "China to Set Up Emergency Plan to Help Sudan Overcome Economic Crisis," October 26, 2011; *Sudan Vision*, "China Envoy in Khartoum to Mediate Oil Dispute," December 7, 2011.
110 *Wikileaks*, [Africa] "China Oil Deals w/ Sudan and RSS, China Chases Sudan Oil Tie-ups," August 9, 2011, *Upstream*, accessed December 15, 2015, www.upstreamonline.com/live/article271427.ece.
111 *BBC*, "Chinese Diplomat Spells Out Steps to Build Ties with South Sudan," July 10, 2011; *Xinhua News Agency*, "China Starts Training Petroleum-Related Workers in South Sudan – Agency," July 11, 2011.
112 *Africa News*, "South Sudan; South Sudan to Benefit from a Major Chinese Loan Scheme," April 24, 2013; Interview with Chinese informant, 2014.
113 Prior to President Kiir's visit to Beijing in April 2012, the Southern Sudan diplomats vied for Chinese economic support to build the pipeline to Lamu. While the visit was not successful in obtaining the fi nancial assistance from Beijing, according to my own research, Eximbank will off er a loan to fi nance the pipeline (Interview with Chinese informant, 2014).

References

Africa News. "South Sudan; South Sudan to Benefit from a Major Chinese Loan Scheme." April 24, 2013.

Al-Shaq al-Awsat (*BBC*). "Sudan: Rebel Says Chinese Hostages Moved to Area Government Forces Cannot Reach." October 25, 2008.

Ali, Abdalla Ali. *The Sudanese – Chinese Relations before and after Oil*. Khartoum: Sudan Currency Printing Press, 2006.

Awad, al-Jaz. "The Oil of Sudan: Challenges and Achievements." In The *Kenana Handbook of Sudan*, edited by Peter G. Hopkins, 671–82. London, UK: Kegan Paul, 2007.

Bai Yang [白洋]. "兄弟"反目只为石油 ["'Brothers' Quarrel just for Oil"], *中国石化报* (*China Petrochemical News*), February 17 2012.

Barltrop, Richard. *Darfur and the International Community: The Challenges of Conflict Resolution in Sudan*. London, UK: I.B. Tauris, 2011.
BBC. "China Appeals to Sudan, South Sudan To Resolve Conflict Over Oil Exports." December 1, 2011.
BBC. "China Says Sudan-South Sudan Tensions Affect Oil Cooperation." April 18, 2012.
BBC. "China, Sudan Hold Talks in Khartoum on Ways to Strengthen Ties." August 9, 2011.
BBC. "Chinese Ambassador Says Sudan Is a Major Trade Partner with His Country." November 11, 2007.
BBC. "Chinese Diplomat Spells out Steps to Build Ties with South Sudan." July 10, 2011.
BBC. "Envoy Says China Plays 'Unique' Role in Settling Darfur Issue." September 8, 2007.
BBC. "South Sudan Reportedly Owes Sudan over 900m Dollars." January 15, 2012.
BBC/Al-Sahafah. "China to Set Up Emergency Plan to Help Sudan Overcome Economic Crisis." October 26, 2011.
Beswick, Stephanie. *Sudan's Blood Economy*. Rochester, NY: University of Rochester Press, 2004.
Boustany, Nora. "Envoy Lauds China's Role in Diplomacy with Sudan." *The Washington Post*, September 7, 2007.
Carmody, Padraig. *Globalization in Africa: Recolonization or Renaissance?* London, UK: Lynne Rienner, 2010.
Central Intelligence Agency (CIA). "Export Partners of Sudan." *CIA World Factbook 2013*. Accessed 12/15/2015. www.cia.gov/library/publications/resources/the-world-factbook/geos/su.html.
Central Intelligence Agency (CIA). "Import Partners of Sudan." *CIA World Factbook 2013*. Accessed 12/15/2015. www.cia.gov/library/publications/resources/the-world-factbook/geos/su.html.
Central Intelligence Agency (CIA). "The World Factbook, Sudan." Accessed 12/15/2015. www.cia.gov/library/publications/the-world-factbook/geos/su.html.
Chen, Wenxian [陈文仙]. 苏丹: 受全球石油投资者青睐 ["Sudan – Highly Esteemed by Global Oil Investors], *中国石化报* (*China Petrochemical News*), February 24, 2005.
Collins, Robert O. *A History of Modern Sudan*. Cambridge, UK: Cambridge University Press, 2008.
De Montesquiou, Alfred. "China's Hu Presses Sudan for Progress on Darfur." *Associated Press*, February 3, 2007.
Downs, Erica S. "The Fact and Fiction of Sino – African Energy Relations." *China Security* 3 (3) (2007): 42–68.
Economy, Elizabeth C. and Adam Segal. "China's Olympic Nightmare." *Foreign Affairs* 97 (July–August 2008): 47–56.
Embassy of the People's Republic of China in India. "Special Representative of the Chinese Government on the Darfur Issue Holds a Briefing for Chinese and Foreign Journalists." *Press Release*, May 29 2007. Accessed 12/15/2015. http://in.chineseembassy.org/eng/zgbd/t325291.html.
Falola, Toyin and Adebayo O. Oyebade. *Hot Spot: Sub-Saharan Africa*. Santa, Barbara, CA: Greenwood Press, 2010.
Financial Times. "A Chinese Puzzle: South Sudan Tests Beijing's Long-Term Foreign Policy Stance." February 22, 2012.
French, Howard. "China in Africa: All Trade, With No Political Baggage." *New York Times*, August 8, 2004.

Government of Republic of South Sudan (GoRSS). “Government of Sudan Poisons Negotiation Atmosphere in Addis by Stealing 1.4 Million Barrels of South Sudan Oil Just Days Before.” *Press Release*, January 17, 2012.

Gries, Peter Hays. *China's New Nationalism: Pride, Politics, and Diplomacy*. Berkeley, CA: University of California Berkeley Press, 2004.

Gries, Peter Hays and Stanley Rosen. “Introduction: Popular Protest and State Legitimation in 21st Century China.” In *State and Society in 21st Century China: Crisis, Contention and Legitimation*, edited by Peter H. Gries and Stanley Rosen, 1–23. New York, NY: Routledge, 2004.

Higgins, Andrew. “Abduction of Chinese Workers in Sudan Ignites Criticism.” *The Washington Post*, February 2, 2012.

Higgins, Andrew. “Oil Interests Push China into Sudanese Quagmire.” *The Washington Post*, December 25, 2011.

Higgins, Andrew. “Oil-Thirsty China Stuck Deep in Sudanese Muck.” *Seattle Times*, December 25, 2011.

Human Rights Watch. “Failing Darfur, Q&A: Crisis in Darfur.” September 2008. Accessed 12/15/2015. www.hrw.org/sites/default/files/features/darfur/fiveyearson/qanda.html.

International Herald Tribune. “Hu to Seek Darfur Deal during Visit to Sudan.” January 25, 2007.

James, Laura M. “The Oil Boom and Its Limitations in Sudan, 2011.” In *Sudan Looks East: China, India and the Politics of Asian Alternatives*, edited by Daniel Large and Luke A. Patey, 52–69. Woodbridge, UK: James Currey, 2011.

Jiang, Binbin. “China National Petroleum Corporation (CNPC): A Balancing Act Between Enterprise and Government.” In *Oil and Governance: State-Owned Enterprises and the World Energy Supply*, edited by D.G. Victor, David R. Hults and Mark C. Thurber, 379–417. Cambridge, UK: Cambridge University Press, 2012.

Jin Danni (金丹妮). 中国石油公司在苏丹的发展历史研究 [“Research on the Development History of Chinese Oil companies in Sudan”], *西安石油大学学报* (*Journal of Xian Petroleum University*), August 15, 2012.

Large, Daniel. “China's Sudan Engagement: Changing Northern and Southern Political Trajectories in Peace and War.” *The China Quarterly*, 199 (September 2009): 610–26.

Large, Daniel. “From Non-Interference to Constructive Engagement? China's Evolving Relations with Sudan.” In *China Returns to Africa. A Rising Power and a Continent Embrace*, edited by Chris Alden, Daniel Large and Ricardo Soares de Oliveira, 275–94. London: Hurst & Co., 2008.

Large, Daniel and Luke A. Patey. “Sudan Looks East: Introduction.” In *Sudan Looks East: China, India and the Politics of Asian Alternatives*, edited by Daniel Large and Luke Patey, 1–34. Woodbridge, UK: James Curry, 2011.

Lee, Winnie. Platts Oilgram News. “Chinese Oil Workers Kidnapped in Sudan.” *Platts Oilgram News*, October 21, 2008.

Li Tianxing [李天星]. 友谊长存, 携手发展” – 写在中国石油苏丹项目投产10周年之际 [”Friendship Forever, Joining Hands in Development.” Written at the 10-year Anniversary of the Operation of CNPC's Sudan Project], *中国石油企业* (Chinese Oil Companies), November 15 2009.

Li Zhongfa [李忠发]. 中苏合作给苏丹带来石油与和平 [“Sino – Sudan Cooperation Brings Oil and Peace to Sudan”], *新华每日电讯 (Xinhua Daily Telegraph*), November 19, 2009.

Ling, Song Yen and Jacinta Moran. “China Seeks Protection for Sudan Operations.” *Platts Oilgram News*, April 25, 2012.

Lobban, Robert A. *Global Security Watch: Sudan*. Santa Barbara, CA: Praeger, 2010.

McGregor, Richard. "Chinese Diplomacy 'Hijacked' by Companies." *Financial Times*, March 17, 2008.

McGregor, Richard. "Iran, Sudan and Nigeria off China Incentive List." *Financial Times*, March 2, 2007.

Michel, Serge and Michel Beuret. *China Safari: On the Trail of Beijing's Expansion in Africa*. New York, NY: Nation Books, 2009.

Ministry of Land of the People's Republic of China [中华人民共和国国土资源部], *China's Land Resources Statistical Yearbook 2010* [中国国土资源统计年鉴], 2010.

National Bureau of Statistics of the People's Republic of China 2003–13. *China Statistical Yearbook*. Beijing: National Bureau of Statistics, various years.

Pan Zhongying. "China's Changing Attitude to UN Peacekeeping." *International Peacekeeping* 12 (1) (2005): 87–104.

Patey, Luke A. "Crude Days Ahead? Oil and the Resource Curse in Sudan." *African Affairs* 109 (437) (2010): 617–36.

Permanent Mission of the People's Republic of China to the UN. "China's SR on Darfur Holds a Briefing in Beijing." March 7, 2008. Accessed 12/15/2015. www.china-un.org/eng/chinaandun/securitycouncil/regionalhotspots/africa/darfur/t468259.html.

Petroleum Economist. "Both Sudans Pay High Price for Output Shut-in." July 2012.

Petroleum Economist. "Continuity Vital as Two Sudans Prepare to Talk." September 2011.

Platts Oilgram News. "Sudan Eyes Oil Output Increase at Heglig." May 8, 2013.

Reeves, Eric. "Darfur: The 'Genocide Olympics?' Campaign Roars into High Gear." *Sudan Tribune*, May 10, 2007.

Reuters. "China Confirms Will Send Engineers to Darfur." May 8, 2007.

Rotberg, Robert, ed. *China into Africa. Trade, Aid, and Influence*. Washington, DC: Brookings Institution Press, 2008.

Russell, Alec and William Wallis. "China Puts Private Pressure on Sudan." *Financial Times*, June 19, 2007.

Soares de Oliveira, Ricardo. "Making Sense of Chinese Oil Investment in Africa." In *China Returns to Africa: A Rising Power and a Continent Embrace*, edited by Chris Alden, Daniel Large and Ricardo Soares de Oliveira, 83–110. London, UK: Hurst & Co., 2008.

Sudan Tribune. "China Issues a Warning to Sudan over Darfur Crisis." January 30, 2008.

Sudan Tribune. "China Told Sudan to Adopt UN's Darfur Plan – Envoy." February 7, 2007.

Sudan Tribune. "South Sudan Threatens to Suspend Oil Production if North Imposes Charges Unilaterally." November 30, 2011.

Sudan Tribune. "Sudan Accepts UN Package for Darfur, Willing to Ceasefire." December 27, 2006.

Sudan Tribune. "Sudan; China Reiterates Call for Restraint Between North and South on Oil Dispute." January 21, 2012.

Sudan Vision. "China Envoy in Khartoum to Mediate Oil Dispute." December 7, 2011.

Taylor, Ian. "China's Peacekeeping Efforts in Africa: Assessing the Contributions, Future Prospects, and Challenges." In *Peacekeeping in Africa: The Evolving Security Architecture*, edited by Thierry Tardy and Marco Wyss, 93–112. London: Routledge, 2014.

Taylor, Ian. "The People's Republic of China." In *The International Politics of Mass Atrocities. The case of Darfur*, edited by David R. Black and Paul D. Williams, 176–94. London, UK: Routledge, 2010.

Tuhami, Sherief E. "Oil in Sudan: Its Discovery and Industrial Development." In *The Kenana Handbook of Sudan*, edited by Peter G. Hopkins, 657–70. London, UK: Kegan Paul, 2007.

United Nations Statistical Division, Commodity Trade Statistics Database. Accessed 12/15/2015. http://comtrade.un.org/db/.

U.S. Energy Information Administration (EIA). "Country Analysis Brief: Sudan and South Sudan." September 2, 2014. Accessed 12/15/2015. www.eia.gov/countries/country-data.cfm?fips=su.

Wang Dongmei [王冬梅] and Li Zhanbin [李占彬]. 中国石油：用真诚奉献在异国创造和谐 [CNPC: Creating Harmony Abroad Through Sincere Devotion], *工人日报* (*Workers' Daily*), January 16, 2008.

Wang Xiangjiang [王湘江], 世界军事新闻剪影 ["Outline of World Military News"], *世界军事年鉴* (*World Military Yearbook*), January 1 2008.

Watkins, Eric. "Crisis Looms in South Sudan." *Oil & Gas Journal*, February 6, 2012.

Wikileaks, [Africa]. "China Oil Deals w/ Sudan and RSS, China Chases Sudan Oil Tie-ups." August 9, 2011; *Upstream*, Accessed 12/15/2015. www.upstreamonline.com/live/article271427.ece.

Wu Fugui [吴富贵], 中国石油健儿建功苏丹 ("CNPC's Heroes' Achievements in Sudan"), *国际人才交流* (*International Talent*), May 6 2003.

Xinhua News Agency. "China Calls for Friendly Resolution to Oil Export Dispute Between South Sudan, Sudan." November 29, 2011.

Xinhua News Agency. "China Starts Training Petroleum-Related Workers in South Sudan – Agency." July 11, 2011.

Xinhua News Agency. "China's Workgroup Visits Rescued Chinese Workers from Kidnapping in Sudan." November 1, 2008.

Xinhua News Agency. "Chinese UN Ambassador Condemns Killing of Chinese Workers in Sudan." October 29 2008.

Xinhua News Agency. "Common Language Helps Resolve Darfur Issue." October 2, 2007.

Xinhua News Agency. "Hu Puts Forward Four-Point Principle on Solving Darfur Issue." February 3, 2007.

Xinhua News Agency. "Sudan, China Pledge to Strengthen Ties." August 9, 2011.

Xinhua News Agency. "Sudan, China Sign Deals on Stronger Agricultural Co-op." June 11, 2008.

Yee Sienho. "Towards a Harmonious World: The Roles of the International Law of Co-Progressiveness and Leader States." *Chinese Journal of International Law* 7 (2008): 99–105.

Zeng Bin [曾彬]. 苏丹总统巴希尔视察中国石油六区项目 ["Sudan's President al-Bashir Inspected CNPC's Six Oil Projects"], *中国石油报* (*China Petroleum Report*), March 12, 2007.

Zheng, E. "Minister of Interior: Sudan's Police Has List of Criminals Kidnapping Chinese Workers." *Xinhua News Agency*, November 3, 2008.

Zong Kunpeng [宗鲲鹏] and Yan Qi [闫琦]. 绑架劫持事件的分阶段安全应对措施探讨 ["Investigation of Safety Measures in Response to Kidnapping Incidents"], *中国安全生产科学技术* (*Science and Technology of China's Safety Production*), August 15, 2010.

7 Tunisia

Chinese companies involved for profit

Background

The state of China and Tunisia relations

Only one phase can be distinguished in Sino-Tunisian relations. While Tunisia became independent in 1956, Tunisia–China historical relations date back to the establishment of relations in 1964, when Premier Zhou Enlai visited Tunisia (see figure 7.1 for map of Tunisia). On September 26, 1967, relations between the two countries were suspended, and China closed its embassy in Tunisia because of disagreement over the "one China" policy, as the Tunisian president had suggested a need to accept the existence of "two Chinas."[1] On October 8, 1971, relations were reestablished (复馆)[2] when China offered Tunisia $40 million in credits for infrastructure projects.[3] Since then, relations can be characterized as having had a "smooth" development (发展顺利/*fazhan shunli*).[4] Leaders from the two countries have visited one another, and the two countries have signed numerous trade agreements.

Literature on Tunisia

As Tunisia has very little oil and activities undertaken by Chinese NOCs in Tunisia are limited, it is hardly surprising that the existing secondary literature on the topic of the activities of the Chinese NOCs in Tunisia is limited. Still, two dominant perspectives can be distinguished – focused in large part on general Sino-Tunisian relations – either a *political economy* perspective or the Chinese position *vis-à-vis* the Tunisian Revolution. From a *political economy* perspective, some scholars praise the economic performance of the Ben Ali regime,[5] and some examine the impact of oil on the Tunisian economy.[6] There is literature relating to the Chinese position regarding the Tunisian Revolution. Jonathan Pollack argues that China is no longer insulated from the upheaval in the Middle East, that its investments there are at risk in some instances, and that the CCP leadership sees parallels between the Arab uprisings and pressures for political change within China.[7] Still, no direct implications of these events (i.e., Tunisian Revolution) for China and Chinese domestic stability have been seen.

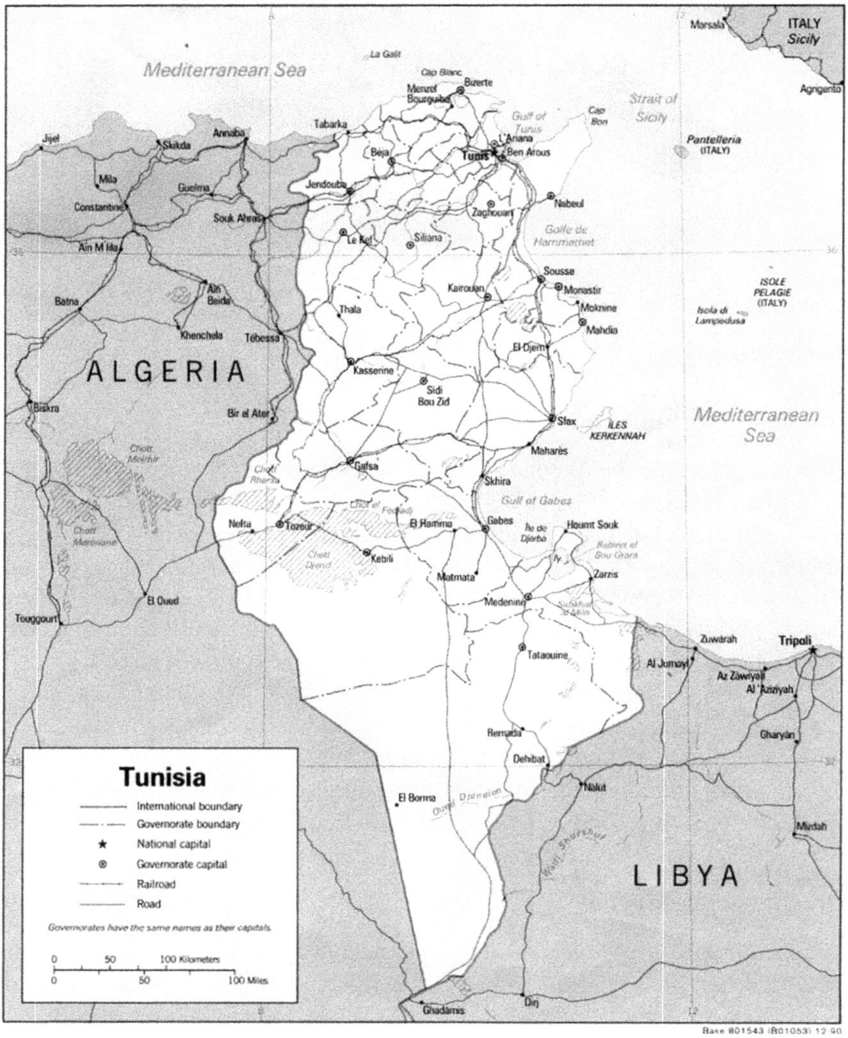

Figure 7.1 Map of Tunisia

As seen earlier, the standard take on the activities of Chinese companies in Tunisia is to focus on the impact of the Arab uprisings on Chinese domestic stability. This literature has several limitations: first, and most important, the secondary literature is very limited, as there is very little written about the Chinese companies engaged in Tunisia. Second, the preceding contributions are limited to materials written in English, whereas this analysis includes materials written in Chinese. The analysis here therefore proceeds differently. The remainder of this chapter will illuminate whether the conclusions reached here stand in contrast to the standard image of the strategy behind Chinese activities in Tunisia found in much of the secondary literature.

History of Chinese oil companies in Tunisia

Oil production began in Tunisia 1966 in the southern part of the country in the main fields of El Borma and Ashtart. At the end of 2009, more than 40 companies held an interest in at least one exploration block in Tunisia, including the IOCs, BG Group Plc (UK), ETAP (Tunisia), ENI S.p.A./Agip (Italy), and PA Resources AB (Sweden).

Two Chinese energy companies are currently operating in Tunisia: Sinochem and CNPC. Sinochem is the fourth largest Chinese oil company.[8] It has only recently ventured into overseas exploration and production and remains in the shadow of the three big oil companies: CNPC, Sinopec, and CNOOC.

In Tunisia, overall, CNPC thus has two assets: the SLK stake and the NK oil license, although only the SLK stake is producing. Sinochem has two assets in Tunisia, Oudna and Isis, the latter of which is no longer producing. Neither Sinopec nor CNOOC have sites in Tunisia. Sinopec unsuccessfully looked to make an acquisition in Tunisia in 2002–03 (as we will see in Key Decision 1).[9]

Overall, Tunisia has provided China with a very limited share of its total oil imports from 1999–2009 (less than 1 percent).

Strategic importance

Tunisia is of limited strategic importance to China for the following reasons. First, in terms of the *level of political relations*, the two countries established relations on January 10, 1964, during Premier Zhou Enlai's visit to Tunisia. China closed its embassy in Tunisia in September 1967, first reestablishing relations in October 1971 (复馆/*fu guan*).[10] China and Tunisia have not entered a strategic partnership, and the ambassador to Tunis does not enjoy ministerial-level status, as opposed to the ambassadors from China to both South Africa and Egypt, with whom China has strategic partnerships. The number of visits between China and Tunisia in recent years has been very limited; since establishing relations in 1964, there has only been one presidential-level visit (President Jiang Zemin in 2002). There have been no presidential-level visits from Tunisia (see the Appendix) in the same period. This speaks to the limited strategic importance attributed to Tunisia. With respect to the Taiwan question, Tunis has consistently supported Beijing over Taiwan.

Second, in terms of the role for *CCP regime stability*, there is evidence that three extremist Islamic organizations have cells operating in Tunisia: Tunisian Combatant Group, the Tunisian Islamic Front, and al-Qaeda in the Islamic Maghreb (AQIM).[11] AQIM has conducted several attacks in Tunisia since 2002,[12] but none of these have targeted Chinese nationals. Throughout its history, Tunisia has had strong links to Islam. Under the Bourguiba rule from 1956–87,[13] the leadership supported the Islamist movement indirectly in order to counterbalance the left.[14] Then, under the Ben Ali regime in the period from 1987–2011, the dominant Islamist group in Tunisia, En Nadha, was banned.[15] During the course of the Arab uprisings, in January 2011, the Tunisian military took power, and En Nadha's leaders, who had been living in exile, were welcomed home. In the parliamentary elections in October 2011, En Nadha won 41 percent of the seats and formed the largest parliamentary group.[16] Thus, the Islamist groups have experienced a revival in Tunisia in recent years. What is important for the purposes of this discussion is that while there are extremist groups in Tunisia linked to al-Qaeda, there have not been any fatalities involving Chinese nationals in Tunisia.

Third, in terms of the *salience of territory*, there are no ethnic ties to China. In terms of *strategic location*, Tunisia has 30 ports along the Mediterranean Sea, including eight large commercial ports and one for oil transshipment. Tunisia is a predominantly Muslim country and part of the Maghreb in Northwest Africa. Moreover, Tunisia and its neighbors serve as a buffer between Europe and the countries of the Sahel and the Horn of Africa. Tunisia has a relatively sound and developed infrastructure. The country has one refinery, with an oil distillation capacity of 34,000 bpd.[17] In terms of oil and gas infrastructure, Tunisia has one oil pipeline, Gabes–Tunis, and one gas pipeline, the TransMed.[18]

Fourth, in terms of the role of the *other great power*, neither the United States nor China has any military bases in Tunisia. Since 2001, the United States has held more joint military exercises with Tunisia than any of the other Maghreb countries[19] and has provided aid in the form of military assistance to Tunisia. In fact, the United States became Tunisia's most important source of economic assistance after France.[20] In return, Tunisia has sought to help the United States in the international war on terror. The Ben Ali regime supported the US operations in Afghanistan with Tunisian agents and arrested more than 600 Tunisians in the period 2005–07 for trying to travel to Iraq.[21] Thus, while Tunisia is not formally a US alliance partner, the two nations have nevertheless had very close relations over the last two decades. Tunisia has never been subjected to UN sanctions. The importance attributed to Tunisia by the United States renders the country of some strategic importance to China. Tunisia has traditionally imported most of its arms from the Western powers, especially the United States,[22] apparently having become dependent on the United States as its primary arms supplier.

Fifth, the bilateral trade between China and Tunisia has increased in recent years, from $0.18 billion in 2002 to $1.57 billion in 2012, as figure 7.2 shows.

As presented earlier, the Tunisian trade deficit with China amounted to $0.89 billion in 2011 and $1.21 billion the following year.

China accounted for 6.0 percent of Tunisia's imports in 2012 and a very limited share of Tunisia's exports – less than 3.1 percent.[23] Still, China is Tunisia's most important economic partner in Asia, with investments amounting to more than $3 billion in the period from 2000 to 2012.[24]

As documented earlier, and as table 7.1 illustrates, Tunisia is of little strategic importance to China. There have been very few visits between China and Tunisia, there is no strategic partnership between Tunisia and China, and bilateral trade has

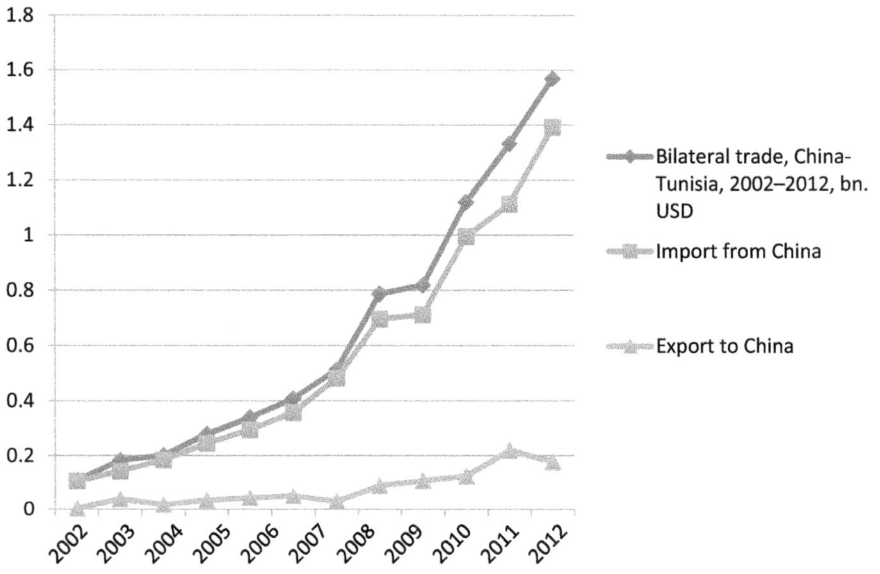

Figure 7.2 Sino-Tunisian bilateral trade, 2002–12

Table 7.1 Level of strategic importance: Tunisia (for more detail, see the Appendix)

Country	*1. Level of political relations*	*2. Role for CCP regime stability*	*3. Salience of territory*	*4. Role for other great power*	*5. Bilateral trade*	*Total*
Tunisia	0	1	1	0	0	0

been limited. At the same time, the existence of an extremist branch linked to al-Qaeda on the territory renders it of some relevance for CCP regime stability; moreover, Tunisia is of strategic importance to the United States. Overall, however, the preceding documents that Tunisia is of limited strategic importance to China.

Oil and gas levels

The Tunisian oil and gas reserves are relatively limited, as is its oil and gas production.

In terms of oil, Tunisia had proven oil reserves of 0.43 billion barrels (47th in the world) and production of 0.067 million oil bpd in 2014 (56th in the world).[25] The production of petroleum and other liquids had been steadily declining from a peak of 120,000 bpd in the years 1982–84.[26] In fact, Tunisia became a net oil importer in 2000 for the first time since the 1970s, the main reason for the declining production being the depletion of the two biggest fields, El Borma and Ashtart.[27]

In terms of gas, Tunisia has proven gas reserves of 63.13 billion m^3 (2014) (58th in the world), about two-thirds of which are located offshore. In 2014, Tunisian production amounted to 1.93 billion m^3 (55th in the world).[28] Tunisia does not export natural gas.

Thus, relatively speaking, the Tunisian oil and gas reserves are relatively limited, as is the country's production of both oil and gas.

The empirical expectation

As the preceding data indicates, Tunisia is a country with limited oil reserves and a country that only holds a limited strategic importance to China. Thus, the hypothesis is that neither strategic importance nor economic interests are the dominant driving forces in Tunisia. Based on the characteristics presented earlier and the history of the case, the specific empirical expectation is that *the companies have little incentive to become involved because of the limited availability of oil. And as the government attributes little strategic importance to Tunisia, the state will not seek to pursue its interests there. Consequently, neither state nor economic interests dominate.*

Quantitative analysis

The quantitative analysis of the Chinese state media related to the Tunisian case shows that, over the course of the ten-year period, economic interests dominate. Thus, economic interests are the dominant motive behind the companies' activities, and the preceding hypothesis is not supported. It should be noted, however, that the quantitative analysis is based on a mere 34 articles from the CNKI database. Consequently, the quantitative analysis for the Tunisian case is rather unstable, but this is a fact determined by the nature of the evidence.

Looking over the decade under investigation, overall, the results indicate dominant economic interests. But the level of economic interests varies: in 2003, the ratio of economic interests to state interests/domestic stability peaks (ratio of 19.2:1), as figure 7.3 shows. For all of the other years, economic interests still dominate relative to state interests/domestic stability but more modestly (ratios of 1.1–7.7:1). Thus, a pronounced shift is seen over the course of the decade, as illustrated in figure 7.3.

Zooming in and scrutinizing particular ratios, such as the ratio of economic interests to state interests, we see that whereas, overall, economic interests dominate relative to state interests over the course of the decade, the dominance of economic interests over state interests peaks in 2003 (ratio of 23.3:1) and again in 2012 (ratio of 9.3:1). This is shown in figure 7.4.

Turning to the relationship between economic interests and the concern with domestic stability (*weiwen*), we see that, over the course of the ten-year period, economic interests clearly dominate. As figure 7.5 demonstrates, in the year 2003, economic interests peak relative to domestic stability (ratio of 107.2:1). Similarly, economic interests are strong relative to concerns with domestic stability in the period 2005–07 (ratios

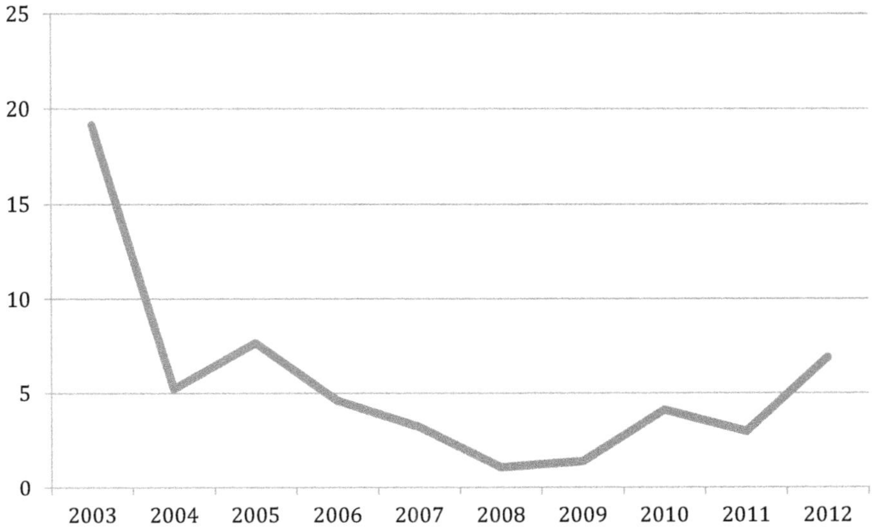

Figure 7.3 Ratio of economic interests to state interests/domestic stability

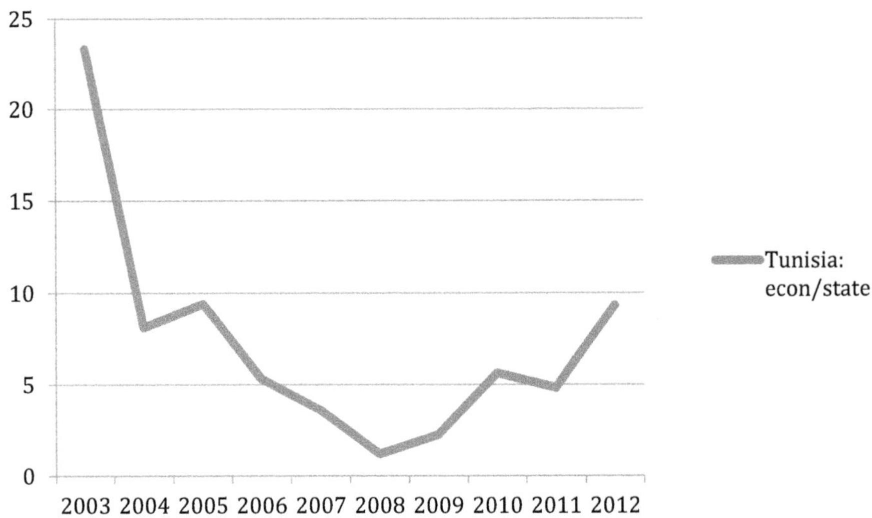

Figure 7.4 Ratio of economic interests to state interests

of 28.8–41.3:1) and in 2012 (ratio of 26.1:1). Concerns with domestic stability are only remarkable in 2009 (ratio of 3.6:1) and 2011 (ratio of 7.7:1).

Finally, examining the ratio of state interests to concerns with domestic stability (*weiwen*), we see that, overall, state interests dominate over the course of the

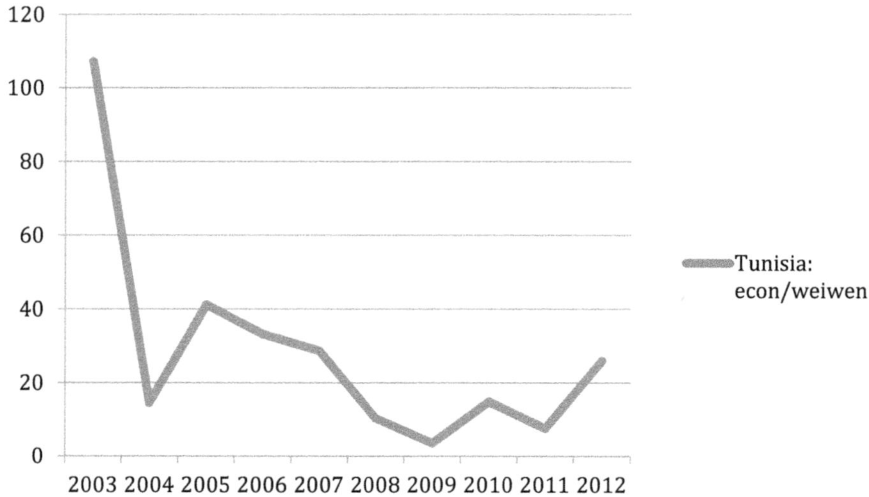

Figure 7.5 Ratio of economic interests to domestic stability

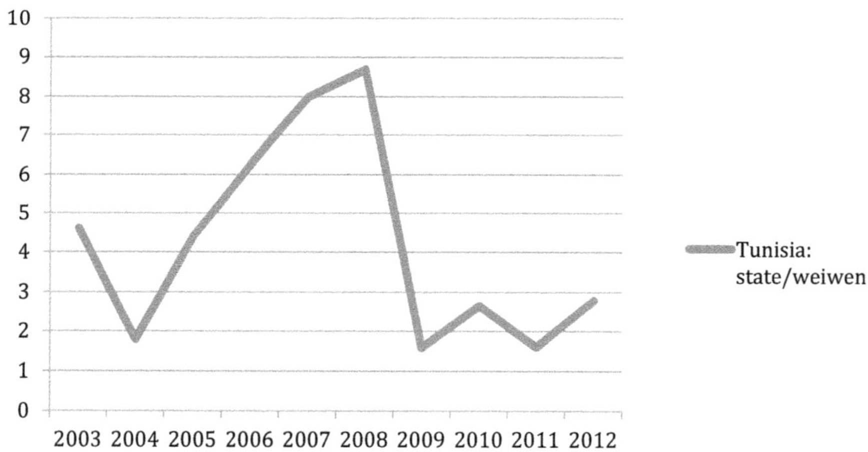

Figure 7.6 Ratio of state interests to domestic stability

decade. As figure 7.6 demonstrates, state interests are most dominant in the years 2006–08 (ratios of 6.3:1–8.7:1). Still, concerns with domestic stability are relatively strong in 2004 (ratio of 1.8:1) and in the period 2009–12 (ratios of 1.6:1–2.8:1).

Overall, the preceding results are rather surprising. They disprove the hypothesis presented earlier that neither state nor economic interests are expected to dominate. Instead, we find evidence that economic interests dominate. The remainder of this chapter explores the extent to which the results from the quantitative analysis are corroborated by the results from the qualitative analysis.

Qualitative analysis

This section focuses on three key decisions that illuminate important aspects of the activities of Chinese companies in Tunisia and their possible impact on Chinese foreign policy. They have been selected to allow for analysis over time. The following focuses first on the acquisition made by Sinochem in 2003, second on the acquisition by CNPC in 2004, and third, the decision made by the Chinese leadership to maintain the policy of non-interference in the wake of the Tunisian Revolution in 2011. These three key decisions are the most significant and representative in terms of the activities of Chinese companies in Tunisia over the last decade. Note also that the limited activities of Chinese NOCs in Tunisia and the limited strategic importance attributed to Tunisia by the Chinese leadership mean that there are few activities there and, thus, few data entries, making the three key decisions outlined earlier the most significant in the last decade. Analyzing them therefore helps us to understand whether Chinese foreign policy toward Tunisia is dominated by state interests, economic interests, or concerns with domestic stability (*weiwen*).

Key Decision 1: Sinochem, 2003

The key decision examined here is Sinochem's acquisition of Atlantis (Atlantis Holding Norway AS). As Atlantis owned contractual blocks in Tunisia, among facilities in other countries, Sinochem thereby acquired important assets in Tunisia. I include Sinochem, even if it is only the fourth largest Chinese oil and gas company, as Sinochem's activities are some of the most significant in terms of the activities of Chinese NOCs in Tunisia. If state interests dominate in this particular key decision, then we would see donation of aid in conjunction with visits from Chinese state leaders. If economic interests dominate, we would see that the acquisition would be considered profitable. If concerns with domestic stability dominate, we would see evidence of Chinese oil workers killed in Tunisia, as well as statements made by state leaders and comments on Chinese social media reflecting concerns with Chinese worker safety in Tunisia.

Acquisition of Atlantis, March 2003

On February 20, 2003, Sinochem acquired Atlantis from Norwegian Petroleum Geo-Service (PGS). Headquartered in Dubai of the UAE, Atlantis has a total of 12 licensing contracts, including oil and gas concessions, in Tunisia, Oman, and the United Arab Emirates (UAE).[29]

The negotiations for Sinochem's acquisition of Atlantis started on January 22, 2002, and were finalized on February 20, 2003 (see table 7.2). The rationale for the sale of Atlantis was a contemplated merger of PGS and Veritas, based in Houston, Texas, an international seismic company that would create the world's second largest provider of geophysical data to the energy sector with a market capitalization of about $1 billion. The proceeds from the sale of Atlantis were to be used to pay off PGS's short-term debt, which was a prerequisite for the merger to go

Table 7.2 Acquisition of Atlantis

Announced date	Jan. 22, 2002
Completed	Feb. 20, 2003
Deal value	$105 million
Acquirer company	China Petroleum & Chemical Corp. (Sinochem)
Vendor company	Petroleum Geo-Service (PGS)
Target	Atlantis Holding Norway

ahead.[30] Negotiations between PGS and Sinochem were initiated in late 2001. The transaction was dependent on regulatory approval from the UAE and Oman. PGS, however, failed to obtain approval in time from the UAE, and on July 31, 2002, Veritas issued a statement declaring that the PGS deal was "formally terminated." Consequently, PGS was unable to merge with Veritas. This had consequences for the acquisition price. From the outset of the negotiations between Atlantis and Sinochem in late 2001, the reported $215 million price tag was to include the assumed debt and drilling costs and development work done by Atlantis between January 22 and the final day of the sale.[31] However, when the deal was completed in February 2003, the final transaction price was $105 million.[32] Thus, this price was a considerably lower value than an earlier estimate.

In addition to waiting it out on PGS, Sinochem made another smart move in the negotiations. Early in the negotiations, Sinopec and Sinochem were to buy the asset in partnership, each taking a 50 percent share. For Sinochem, the acquisition would help it to become an integrated oil company; for Sinopec, the acquisition would help it to expand internationally. The agreement for the acquisition of Atlantis was signed on January 24, 2003. On February 18, 2003, however, Sinopec announced that it was no longer interested in buying a 50 percent stake in the Atlantis oil subsidiary: "We have changed our minds to partner with them [Sinochem] because we have reviewed our strategies and decided we want to invest less in building gas reserves for now."[33] Thus, given that the acquisition of Atlantis was Sinochem's first overseas upstream asset, a joint bid with Sinopec, a more experienced Chinese oil company that already had upstream assets overseas, convinced Atlantis to sell the stake to Sinochem. However, after the agreement was settled in January 2003, Sinopec could pull out.

Economic interests

The acquisition of Atlantis included the offshore Isis field, which is a deepwater oil and gas field located offshore in the Gulf of Gabes. In 2003–04, Isis was the third largest oil producer in the country. The acquisition also included the oilfield Oudna, which Atlantis had an exploration license for, but no oil had been found. The Oudna field is estimated to contain 11.5 million barrels of oil.[34] Thus, all in all, Atlantis had promising assets.

The acquisition of Atlantis was Sinochem's first major overseas oil and gas investment, giving it control over Atlantis's two stakes in Tunisia, Isis, and Oudna.

For Sinochem, in the words of the company vice president, Han Gensheng, "It [Atlantis, ed.] is Sinochem's first major overseas oil and gas investment, as it extends its business from trading to oil and gas exploration and production to beef up the firm's competitive edge."[35] Sinochem selected Atlantis because of its attractive risk premium.[36] It was a case of a joint venture with a Western partner and, thus, an opportunity to acquire technology. Moreover, the stake had the Swedish company Lundin as an operator. Lundin is a company that utilizes advanced technology in deepwater explorations. According to Sinochem Chief Geologist Zeng Xingqiu, "Chinese oil firms are still in primary school in terms of their experience in operating overseas projects."[37] The production and development of both Isis and Oudna had been aided by advances in subsea production technology. In the words of a Sinochem employee, Sinochem's oilfield in Tunisia was using "advanced new technologies," including the large *Ikdam* Floating Production Storage Offloading (FPSO) unit and the world's biggest jet pump.[38] For Sinochem, acquiring a stake in this site thus offered a way to obtain advanced technology and improve its technological capabilities.

Acquiring Atlantis would mean that Sinochem would become an integrated oil company with its own oilfield, thus forming an industrial platform for the development of its oil business.[39] Moreover, the acquisition would allow Sinochem to expand its crude production rate by 15,000–20,000 bpd, a high priority for the company.[40]

Lastly, the acquisition of Atlantis would also enable Sinochem to achieve its long-standing aim of getting a foot in the door in North Africa, a key region for Sinochem Corporation to implement its expansion toward upstream business. All this points to evidence of economic interests in this acquisition.

The share price of Sinochem relative to the other three large Chinese oil companies can be seen as an indicator of economic interests. Looking at the period from when the acquisition was announced on January 22, 2002, until it closed on February 20, 2003, the Sinochem share price moved relatively similarly compared to the other Chinese companies. PetroChina was up 17.3 percent, CNOOC up 32.1 percent, Sinopec up 37.7 percent, and Sinochem up 23.3 percent. Thus, one sees here that since all of the Chinese oil companies increased at about the same rate, it was not a unique characteristic of Sinochem in this period.

State interests

In April 2002, President Jiang Zemin visited Tunisia and met with President Zine El Abidine Ben Ali.[41] As reflected in various Chinese articles, there are friendly and cooperative relations (友好合作关系/*youhao hezuo guanxi*) between the two countries, and they have strategic, cooperative relations (伙伴合作关系/*huoban hezuo guanxi*).[42] Another Chinese article referring to the visit states that "China [through the visit, ed.] displays its energy diplomacy," and that President Jiang's visit speaks to a content of economic cooperation. The article opposes how the United States arbitrarily casts a number of sovereign states as rogue states or places them on an "axis of evil" blacklist, stating that "China is both Libya's but also the whole Muslim world's trustworthy friend (值得信赖的朋友/*zhidexinlai de pengyou*)."[43] This is evidence of an agenda of South-South cooperation with emphasis on mutual development as well as opposition to the United States. Still, even if President Jiang Zemin visited Tunisia in 2002, a visit during which several economic agreements were signed,[44] there is no evidence that this acquisition was connected to the visit.

In terms of aid, since the establishment of diplomatic relations, China has provided financial assistance to Tunisia and sent medical teams.[45] In the period from 2000–11, China has provided Tunisia with aid amounting to 0.02 percent of GNI.[46] Thus, Tunisia received a relatively limited amount of the Chinese aid to Africa.

*Domestic stability (*weiwen*)*

No evidence of the concerns with domestic stability (*weiwen*) was found.

Conclusion, Key Decision 1: evidence of economic interests

This key decision reflects economic interests, as there are indications that, at the time of the acquisition, it seemed to be a profitable investment. The development of the field has allowed Sinochem to develop its technology and given Sinochem opportunity to expand abroad. At the same time, there is evidence of state interests. The acquisition was made immediately after President Jiang Zemin's visit in 2002, and aid was given to Tunisia. Still, there is no explicit evidence of any link between the Jiang Zemin visit and the acquisition being made and thus no evidence of the acquisition being a result of the interest of the Chinese leadership. This, together with the aid given being very limited, rather than this acquisition reflecting state interests, overall, it produces evidence of economic interests. Sinochem is involved in Tunisia to earn a profit and does so irrespective of the political leadership in Beijing. This would then indicate that Sinochem independently pursued the asset in Tunisia. This could be consistent with a greater role for NOCs in foreign policy.

How does the analysis here compare to the quantitative analysis? The quantitative analysis shows how economic interests dominated in 2003. Moreover, as economic interests dominated relative to concerns with domestic stability in 2003 (ratio of 107.2:1), no evidence is found here of concerns with domestic stability. Thus, overall, the analysis here confirms the results from the quantitative analysis, as the analysis produces evidence of economic interests. Thus, the two methods are corroborated.

Key Decision 2: CNPC, 2004

The key decision for CNPC to acquire the major oilfield Sidi el-Kilani (SLK) was made in 2004. If state interests dominate in this key decision, then we would see the donation of aid and credit lines in conjunction with visits from political leaders, and there would be evidence of visits by Chinese state leaders.

If economic interests dominate, we would see that the acquisition would be considered profitable. If concerns with domestic stability (*weiwen*) dominate, we would see Chinese oil workers being targeted, statements made by state leaders, and comments on Chinese social media reflecting concerns with Chinese worker safety in Tunisia.

The CNPC acquisitions: Sidi El Kilani (SLK)

On October 12, 2004, the China National Petroleum Corporation International Ltd. (CNPCI), a CNPC subsidiary, acquired two assets from the Kuwait Foreign Petroleum Exploration Company (KUFPEC): a 50 percent stake in the North Kairouan exploration permit (NK) and a 22.5 percent interest in the Sidi el Kilani mining concession (SLK).[47] Here, we will focus on this key decision, namely, the CNPC acquisition of the SLK stake in 2004. Importantly, neither CNPCI nor KUFPEC are listed on stock exchanges. Moreover, it is unclear whether other companies were interested in the acquisition of SLK at the time; nor is there information available on the acquisition price.

In July 1984, KUFPEC, a Kuwait Petroleum Corp (KPC) subsidiary, was granted two licenses for onshore acreages in the Kairouan region in northeast Tunisia, the South Kairouan and North Kairouan licenses. The latter was a 30 percent stake in the NK Block in partnership with Elf (15 percent) and ETAP (55 percent). Elf later pulled out of the Kairouan Nord acreage, selling its 15 percent stake to KUFPEC, thus raising its stake to 45 percent.

The SLK block is Tunisia's third largest oilfield as well as the country's third biggest onshore oilfield and provides high quality light sweet oil (39 API crude oil).[48] Production at SLK started in September 1991, but the field's real production began when SLK went onstream in 1993. Its output peaked in 1997 at 15,000 bpd but has since declined.[49]

The NK exploration license was renewed on several occasions, the fourth extension covering the period 2008–10.[50] And even if the license was expired, it appears that KUFPEC and CNPC still hold the NK interest.[51] As NK is not producing and it is unclear that it has great prospects, we focus here on SLK.

According to KUFPEC, the SLK site benefited from attractive infrastructure, as a 125 km crude oil export pipeline runs from SLK to the port of La Skhira, near Sfax, which was built at a cost of $15 million and completed in 1999.[52] In the period up to the acquisition in late 2003, the SLK field had produced over 44 million barrels of oil. Up until 1994, the field had generated $28.6 million of revenue. Thus, the investment to develop the SLK has recouped KUFPEC's earlier investment. As KUFPEC representative Al-Rahmani commented, "We discovered and now operate Sidi el-Kilani. We are very proud of it."[53] Thus, at the time of the CNPC acquisition, SLK appeared to be a promising oil stake.

The stake was also interesting to CNPCI from a technological perspective. The development of SLK benefited from an improved understanding of fractured reservoir models, which had a positive influence on exploration of the field. A Chinese scholar notes how, compared with the Western multinational companies in terms of size, technology, and capital, the Chinese oil companies are still lagging considerably behind (还有相当大的差/*haiyou xiangdang de cha*).[54] Particularly, in terms of deepwater oil development technologies, Chinese oil companies are not as developed, which seriously hampers their offshore oil development activities in Africa. Thus, the acquisition of SLK has enabled CNPC, in partnership with ETAP, to learn advanced technology with regard to onshore oil exploration. This would be evidence of economic interests.

State interests

In June 2004, Politburo member Zeng Qinghong visited Tunisia to meet with Tunisian Prime Minister Mohamed Ghannouchi, at which time eight cooperation agreements were signed, including three economic agreements.[55] According to a Chinese scholar, the visit signified "turning a new page" (开新的一页/*kai xin de yi ye*) in their bilateral relations.[56] An industry publication mentions the CNPC acquisitions in Tunisia in the same year,[57] and a Chinese academic article specifically commenting on the Zeng Qinghong visit notes that Chinese oil companies active in Africa and in their cooperation with the Tunisian side seek to ensure that this cooperation is "win-win."[58]

On the Tunisian side, there was an interest in extending preferential policies and in providing favorable conditions to China. The Tunisian leadership expressed interest in attracting further investments and emphasized that the cooperation between the two parties is mutually beneficial and can serve as an example for North Africa of a "model case" (一个范例/*yi ge fanli*).[59] This reflects the recipient's appreciation, then, which is also evidence of state interests.

*Domestic stability (*weiwen*)*

No evidence of any concern with domestic stability is found, and the activities in Tunisia in the year under study have had no domestic ramifications in China.

Conclusion, Key Decision 2

There is evidence of economic interests, as the SLK acquisition was profitable and the SLK stake was still under development. CNPC is involved in Tunisia to earn a profit, even if Tunisian oil reserves are limited. At the same time, Zeng Qinghong's visit indicates a link between CNPC's acquisition of the two stakes and the visit.[60] Thus, even if no aid is given, this key decision reflects state interests.

How does the analysis here compare to the quantitative analysis? The quantitative analysis shows how, in 2004, economic interests dominate relative to state interests/domestic stability (ratio of 5.2:1). Even if state interests are relatively more important in 2004 compared to 2003 (with a ratio of economic interests relative to state interests/domestic stability of 19.1:1), economic interests still dominate in absolute numbers. Thus, in this instance, the results from the quantitative and qualitative analyses are not consistent.

Still, important economic agreements were announced during Zeng Qinghong's visit to Tunisia in 2004, which would be an indicator of economic interests, as the visit could be seen as support to CNPC to pursue its own interests. Moreover, the stakes that CNPC acquired in 2004 were promising, the SLK stake being the largest oil find in Tunisia in ten years and Tunisia's third largest oilfield and third largest onshore oilfield. As here, in addition to state interests, there is thus evidence of economic interests, the evidence that state and economic interests coincide is more credible.

Key Decision 3: the Tunisian Revolution, 2011

The key decision examined here is the Tunisian Revolution in 2011 and its implications. We consider the Chinese leadership's decision to maintain the policy of non-interference over the course of the Tunisian Revolution and the possible implications for the Chinese companies operating in Tunisia. If state interests dominate, we would see the Chinese leadership putting pressure on the Tunisian government to protect Chinese investments in Tunisia. If economic interests dominate, we would see evidence of the Tunisian Revolution and eventual financial losses not having any impact on foreign policy – the Chinese leadership would not pressure the recipient country's government to favor Chinese companies in the country. If concerns with domestic stability (*weiwen*) dominate, we would see that the killing of Chinese workers in Tunisia would put pressure on the Chinese leadership to mediate. We would see statements made by state leaders and comments on Chinese social media reflecting concerns with Chinese worker safety in Tunisia.

The Jasmine Revolution, 2011

Chinese academic business magazines describe the Arab uprisings during this period as "rebel waves" (反叛浪潮/*fanpan langchao*).[61] The so-called "Jasmine Revolution" in Tunisia in January 2011 began in a remote part of Southern Tunisia on December 17, 2010, with the self-immolation of Mohammed Bouazizi, supposedly in protest against the police. It then spread to Egypt, where President Hosni Mubarak was ultimately forced to step down in June 2011, before spreading to Jordan, triggering mass demonstrations protesting rising prices, and proceeding to Libya in 2011 and other countries in the years thereafter. A Chinese oil industry publication describes how a number of foreign oil companies in Libya had to stop production and evacuate employees, which also had negative consequences for the Chinese companies operating there.[62] Moreover, the oil industry magazine states that if the chaos (混乱/*hunluan*) in Tunisia, Egypt, and Libya would continue, it would spread deeper into the Middle East, potentially affecting the world's energy supply. In the context of the Arab Spring, Tunisia is, in fact, referred to as a "domino" (第一块多米诺/*diyi kuai duominuo*).[63]

Faced with the political turmoil in North Africa, one Chinese scholar notes that Chinese oil enterprises overseas need to do "risk management" when investing, as nearly 60 percent of the countries, particularly in Africa and the Middle East, in which Chinese oil companies invest in oil projects are politically unstable.[64] This is backed up by the CNPC, which similarly emphasized the need for the company to do better "risk management."[65] There was also an economic effect: Arab stock exchanges losing nearly $50 billion in the last week of January 2011 alone as political unrest escalated in Tunisia and Egypt as a result of investor concerns with the prospects for further instability throughout the region.[66]

*Domestic stability (*weiwen*)*

The Chinese leadership and companies alike were worried that the Arab uprisings and instability in North Africa could adversely affect its own economic interests in the region. According to one Chinese informant,

> We were worried that it would lead to more regime changes. It is what we call the butterfly effect. The question is how you deal with this kind of tremendous political change when you have economic interests on the ground. But both Chinese investors and policy makers lacked an understanding of political issues.[67]

But given that the investments of Chinese oil companies in Tunisia were limited, there was in fact, no effect. The companies stayed, and no Chinese oil workers were killed.

There was concern that the Arab uprisings could lead to similar protests and produce similar consequences domestically in China. The CCP leadership might see parallels between the Arab Spring and pressures for political change in China, explaining why CCP would not permit public expressions of support for the Arab Spring.[68] Consequently, subsequent to the uprisings, media censorship was enacted in China, and the spread of information via the Internet and social media was contained. The Jasmine Revolution therefore received limited news coverage, and the leadership clamped down on foreign reporters. In response to the Tunisian Revolution, the *Global Times* warned against "colour revolutions" in places such as Tunisia and Egypt, stating that they would not bring about the kind of democracy hoped for by Western nations:

> democracy is still far away for Tunisia and Egypt. . . . But when it comes to political systems, the Western model is only one of a few options. It takes time and effort to apply democracy to different countries, and to do so without the turmoil of revolution.[69]

As a tool, in response to the Arab Spring, Beijing shipped two batches of humanitarian aid to Tunisia in April 2011.[70]

Overall, however, the Tunisian Revolution did not have any implications for China. None of the Chinese workers died; the Arab Spring stabilized and did not spread to China.

Conclusion, Key Decision 3

The Tunisian Revolution has not resulted in financial losses for Chinese companies. Chinese investments were not affected, neither those of Sinochem nor the CNPC.[71] The Chinese government sent aid to Tunisia, and the Chinese ambassador held talks with the Tunisian side, which is indicative of state interest. At the same time, the Chinese leadership maintained its policy of non-interference during the Arab Uprisings, in its stance both toward Tunisia and toward countries such as Libya and Syria. Overall, this key decision, namely, to maintain the foreign policy of non-interference, even in the face of risk, thus reflects economic interests.

How does the analysis here compare to the quantitative analysis? The quantitative analysis shows that economic interests dominated relative to state interests and concerns with domestic stability in 2011 (ratio of 3.0:1). Still, the concerns with domestic stability in that year were more important relative to state interests (ratio of 1.6:1) than in the previous year (ratio of 2.6:1). Even so, economic interests dominate in absolute numbers. Thus, the quantitative analysis does not reflect the greater importance of concerns with domestic stability and state interests, as we would expect. This key decision is therefore actually a case of the two methods reaching the same conclusion: economic interests dominated this key decision.

Conclusion

The expectation in the case of Tunisia was that the Chinese oil companies would have little incentive to be involved because of the limited availability of oil. And as the Chinese government attributes little strategic importance to Tunisia, the state will not seek to pursue its economic interests there. The empirical expectation is, therefore, that in the case of Tunisia, we expect neither state nor economic interests to dominate.

The results from the quantitative analysis show that, overall, economic interests dominate over the course of the decade. Still, it is worth noting that the quantitative findings for Tunisia are rather unstable, as they are based on a mere 34 articles. But this is a fact determined by the nature of the evidence.

The qualitative analysis shows that economic interests dominated the Sinochem acquisition in 2003. In the CNPC acquisition in 2004, state and economic interests coincided. And economic interests dominated the Tunisian Revolution in 2011. Comparing the results from the two methods, looking at the 2004 CNPC acquisition, evidence that state and economic interests coincide is more credible. As the qualitative and quantitative analyses produce evidence of both state and economic interests, the empirical expectation is supported.

Notes

1 David H. Shinn and Joshua Eisenman, *China and Africa: A Century of Engagement* (Philadelphia: University of Pennsylvania Press, 2012), 237; Alaba Ogunsanwo, *China's Policy in Africa 1958–71* (Cambridge: Cambridge University Press, 1974), 190.

2 China Science and Technology Information [中国科技信息], "Tunisia Investment Guide" (突尼斯投资指南), August 8, 2002.
3 Shinn and Eisenman, *China and Africa,* 190.
4 China Science and Technology Information [中国科技信息]. "Tunisia Investment Guide" (突尼斯投资指南), August 8, 2002.
5 See, for example, Stephen J. King, "Structural Adjustment and Rural Poverty in Tunisia," in *The Arab Revolts: Dispatches on Militant Democracy in the Middle East*, eds. David McMurray and Amanda Ufheil-Somers (Bloomington, IN: Indiana University Press, 2013), 39–44.
6 See, for example, Konrad Schliephake, *Oil and Regional Development: Examples from Algeria and Tunisia* (New York, NY: Praeger Publishers, 1977), v.
7 Jonathan D. Pollack, "China: Unease from Afar," in *The Arab Awakening: America and the Transformation of the Middle East*, eds. Kenneth M. Pollack, Daniel I. Byman et al. (Washington, DC: Brookings Institution Press, 2011), 298–310, 301.
8 China Petroleum & Chemical Corp. (Sinochem) was created in 1950. It is China's largest trading company, the largest fertilizer importer and manufacturer, and the most important chemical service provider. Sinochem is China's fourth largest oil company (*Fortune*, "Global 500 2014, Sinochem," accessed December 15, 2015, http://fortune.com/global500/sinochem-105/).
9 *KUFPEC's Annual Report 2012*, 30th Report, accessed December 15, 2015, www.kufpec.com/Reports/KUFPEC%20Annual%20Reports/Annual%20Report%202011.pdf.
10 China Science and Technology Information [中国科技信息]. "Tunisia Investment Guide" (突尼斯投资指南), August 8, 2002.
11 Jeffrey A. Coupe and Hamadi Redissi, "Tunisia," in *The Middle East*, ed. Ellen Lust (Los Angeles, CA: Sage, 2014), 789–829, 825.
12 Coupe and Redissi, "Tunisia," 825–6.
13 Tunisia gained its independence from France in 1956.
14 Azzedine Layachi, "Islam and Politics in North Africa," in *The Oxford Handbook of Islam and Politics*, eds. John Esposito and Emad El-din Shahin (Oxford, UK: Oxford University Press, 2013), 352–78, 360–1.
15 Ian O. Lesser, *Security in North Africa: Internal and External Challenges* (Santa Monica, CA: Rand, Project Air Force, 1993), 61–2; Kenneth Perkins, *A History of Modern Tunisia* (Cambridge: Cambridge University Press, 2004), 210.
16 Michael J. Willis, "Islamic Movements in Algeria, Morocco and Tunisia," in *The Oxford Handbook of Islam and Politics*, eds. John Esposito and Emad El-din Shahin (Oxford, UK: Oxford University Press, 2013), 532–43.
17 *U.S. Energy Information Administration (EIA)*, "Tunisia," accessed December 15, 2015, www.eia.gov/countries/country-data.cfm?fips=TS&trk=p1.
18 *U.S. EIA*, "Tunisia."
19 Christopher Alexander, *Tunisia: Stability and Reform in the Modern Maghreb* (London: Routledge, 2010), 99.
20 Coupe and Redissi, "Tunisia," 825.
21 Coupe and Redissi, "Tunisia."
22 Alexander, *Tunisia*, 97.
23 Observatory of Economic Complexity, "Import Origins of Tunisia 2011," accessed December 15, 2015, http://atlas.media.mit.edu/explore/tree_map/hs/import/tun/show/all/2011/html.
24 Coupe and Redissi, "Tunisia"; Austin Strange, Bradley C. Parks, Michael J. Tierney, Andreas Fuchs, Axel Dreher, and Vijaya Ramachandran, "China Development Finance to Africa: A Media-Based Approach to Data Collection," Center for Global Development, Working Paper 323, April 2013, 1–67.
25 *U.S. EIA*, "Tunisia."

26 *U.S. EIA*, "Tunisia."
27 *U.S. EIA,* "Tunisia."
28 *U.S. EIA,* "Tunisia."
29 *Sinochem*, "Atlantis Holding Norway AS," accessed December 15, 2015, http://english.sinochem.com/g935/s1798/t4340.aspx.
30 Felicia Loo Pei Pei, "China's Sinochem Still in Quest for Atlantis," *International Oil Daily,* August 1, 2002.
31 Sam Dale and James Irwin, "Sinochem's Atlantis Deal Runs into Trouble," *International Oil Daily*, May 10, 2002.
32 *Petroleum Geo-Services*, "PGS Closes Sale of Its Atlantis Subsidiary to Sinochem," February 20, 2003, accessed December 15, 2015, www.pgs.com/Pressroom/Press_Releases/PGS_Closes_Sale_of_its_Atlant/html.
33 Karen Teo, "Sinopec Drops out of Sinochem," *International Oil Daily*, February 18, 2003.
34 *Economist Intelligence Unit*, "Oil and Gas: Tunisia," December 1, 2006.
35 Chen Aizhu, "China's Sinochem Still in Talks to Buy PGS Unit," *Reuters,* January 10, 2002.
36 *Reuters*, "China's Sinochem Still in Talks to Buy PGS Unit."
37 Eric Ng, "Sinochem Forges Local Alliances for Foreign Bids," *South China Morning Post*, September 23, 2005.
38 Yang Tingsheng [杨廷胜], Sun Dongfang [孙东方], and Li Xuehong [李雪红]. Oudna海上油田射流泵采油技术 ["The Jet Pump at the Offshore Oudna Oilfield's Extraction Technology"], *油气田地面工程* (*Oil and Gas Fields Surface Engineering*), September 1, 2010.
39 *Sinochem Group*, "The First Phase of the Acquisition of Atlantis by Sinochem Ended," March 4, 2003.
40 Sam Dale and Felicia Loo Pei Pei, "Sinochem Drives Hard Bargain on Atlantis," *International Oil Daily*, May 23, 2002.
41 Ministry of Foreign Affairs of the People's Republic of China, "President Jiang Zemin Held Talks with Tunisian President," April 18, 2002, accessed December 15, 2015, www.fmprc.gov.cn/mfa_eng/wjb_663304/zzjg_663340/xybfs_663590/gjlb_663594/2893_663786/2895_663790/t16438.html.
42 China Science and Technology Information [中国科技信息]. "Tunisia Investment Guide" (突尼斯投资指南), August 8, 2002.
43 Hu Baichuan [胡百川], 第三只眼看中国 ["Looking at China?], *南风窗* (*Southern Window*), May 8, 2002.
44 Ministry of Foreign Affairs of the People's Republic of China, "President Jiang Zemin Held Talks with Tunisian President," April 18, 2002.
45 *International Financing [国际融资]*. 突尼斯投资与经贸风险分析报告 ("Analysis of Investment and Trade Risk in Tunisia"), April 30, 2007.
46 Strange et al., "China Development Finance to Africa," 39.
47 *China National Petroleum Corporation Yearbook 2005* [中国石油天然气集团公司年鉴], Beijing: 石油工业出版社 (Petroleum Industry Press), 46–55.
48 KUFPEC's *Annual Report 2009*, 28th Annual Report, 22, accessed December 15, 2015, www.kufpec.com/Reports/KUFPEC%20Annual%20Reports/Annual%20Report%202011.pdf.
49 KUFPEC's *Annual Report 2009*, 22.
50 KUFPEC's *Annual Report 2009*, 23.
51 China National Petroleum Corporation (*CNPC)* [中国石油], 中国石油在突尼斯 ["CNPC in Tunisia"], accessed December 15, 2015, www.cnpc.com.cn/cnpc/Tunisia/country_index.html).
52 *U.S. EIA*, "Arab Maghreb Union," January 2002, accessed December 15, 2015, www.mafhoum.com/press2/81E18.html.

53 *Dow Jones*, "Meed Special Report on Oil and Gas – KUFPEC Puts Past Losses Behind It," March 25, 1996.
54 Yao Guimei [姚桂梅], 中国与非洲的石油合作 ("China and Africa's Oil Cooperation"), *国际石油经济 (The International Petroleum Economy)*, November 20, 2006.
55 *People's Daily*, "China, Tunisia Sign Eight Cooperation Accords," June 21, 2004.
56 Tang Nengxuan [唐能宣], 中国企业纵横北非 ("Chinese Enterprises in North Africa"), *国际商报 (International Business)*, October 8, 2004.
57 Tang Nengxuan [唐能宣], 中国企业纵横北非 ("Chinese Enterprises in North Africa"), *国际商报 (International Business)*, October 8, 2004.
58 Yao Guimei [姚桂梅]. 中国与非洲的石油合作 ("China and Africa's Oil Cooperation"), *国际石油经济 (The International Petroleum Economy),* Nov. 20, 2006.
59 Tang Nengxuan [唐能宣], 中国企业纵横北非 ("Chinese Enterprises in North Africa"), *国际商报 (International Business)*, October 8, 2004.
60 Tang Nengxuan [唐能宣], 中国企业纵横北非 ("Chinese Enterprises in North Africa"), *国际商报 (International Business)*, October 8, 2004.
61 Hong Yuan Securities Macro Research Team [宏源证券宏观研究团队], 地缘与石油: 2011 年核心风险 ["Regions and Oil: 2011 Key Risk"], *股市动态分析 (Stock Market Trends Analysis),* February 26, 2011.
62 *China Petroleum and Petrochemical Industry* [中国石油石化], "两会"的能源期待 ["Expectations as to the Energy Sector from the Sessions of NPC and CPPCC], March 1, 2011.
63 Zhao Qing [赵青], 中东乱局与中国石油企业"走出去"战略 ["The Riots in the Middle East and the 'Going Out' Strategy of Chinese Oil Companies"], *新远见 (New Vision)*, July 15, 2011.
64 Zhao Qing [赵青], 中东乱局与中国石油企业"走出去"战略 ["The Riots in the Middle East and the 'Going Out' Strategy of Chinese Oil Companies"], *新远见 (New Vision)*, July 15, 2011.
65 *China National Petroleum Corporation Yearbook* [中国石油天然气集团公司年鉴] (Beijing: 石油工业出版社 Petroleum Industry Press, 2011), 166–7.
66 *The International Herald Tribune*, "Wave of Unrest Wipes Billions off Stock Values: Political Instability Sends Investors on a Search for Safety from Turmoil," February 10, 2011.
67 Interview with Chinese informant, 2014.
68 Pollack, "China: Unease from Afar," 298–304.
69 *Global Times*, "Color Revolutions Will Not Bring About Real Democracy," January 30, 2011.
70 *The Majalla*, "The Dragon Eyes the Arab Spring," April 14, 2011.
71 Interview with Chinese informant, 2014.

References

Alexander, Christopher. *Tunisia: Stability and Reform in the Modern Maghreb*. London, UK: Routledge, 2010.

Chen, Aizhu. Reuters. "China's Sinochem Still in Talks to Buy PGS Unit." *Reuters*, January 10, 2002.

China Science and Technology Information [中国科技信息]."Tunisia Investment Guide" (突尼斯投资指南). August 8, 2002.

China National Petroleum Corporation (CNPC) [中国石油]，中国石油在突尼斯 ["CNPC in Tunisia"]. Accessed 12/15/2015. www.cnpc.com.cn/cnpc/Tunisia/country_index.shtml

China National Petroleum Corporation Yearbook [中国石油天然气集团公司年鉴]. Beijing: 石油工业出版社 (Petroleum Industry Press), various years.

China Petroleum and Petrochemical Industry [中国石油石化]. "两会"的能源期待 ["Expectations as to the Energy sector from the Sessions of NPC and CPPCC"]. March 1, 2011.

Coupe, Jeffrey A. and Hamadi Redissi. "Tunisia." In *The Middle East*, edited by Ellen Lust, 789–829. Los Angeles, CA: Sage, 2014.

Dale, Sam and James Irwin. "Sinochem's Atlantis Deal Runs into Trouble." *International Oil Daily*, May 10, 2002.

Dale, Sam and Felicia Loo Pei. "Sinochem Drives Hard Bargain on Atlantis." *International Oil Daily*, May 23, 2002.

Dow Jones. "Meed Special Report on Oil and Gas – KUFPEC Puts Past Losses Behind It." March 25, 1996.

Economist Intelligence Unit. "Oil and Gas: Tunisia." December 1, 2006.

Fortune. "Global 500 2014, Sinochem." Accessed 12/15/2015. http://fortune.com/global500/sinochem-105.

Global Times. "Color Revolutions Will Not Bring About Real Democracy." January 30, 2011.

Hong Yuan Securities Macro Research Team [宏源证券宏观研究团队]. 地缘与石油: 2011年核心风险 ["Regions and Oil: 2011 Key Risk"]. *股市动态分析* (Stock Market Trends Analysis), February 26, 2011.

Hu Baichuan [胡百川]. 第三只眼看中国 ["Looking at China"]. *南风窗 (Southern Window)*, May 8, 2002.

International Financing [国际融资]. 突尼斯投资与经贸风险分析报告 ("Analysis of Investment and Trade Risk in Tunisia"). April 30, 2007.

International Herald Tribune. "Wave of Unrest Wipes Billions off Stock Values: Political Instability Sends Investors on a Search for Safety from Turmoil." February 10, 2011.

King, Stephen J. "Structural Adjustment and Rural Poverty in Tunisia." In *The Arab Revolts: Dispatches on Militant Democracy in the Middle East*, edited by David McMurray and Amanda Ufheil-Somers, 39–44. Bloomington, IN: Indiana University Press, 2013.

KUFPEC's Annual Report 2009, 28th Annual Report. Accessed 12/15/2015. www.kufpec.com/Reports/KUFPEC%20Annual%20Reports/Annual%20Report%202011.pdf

KUFPEC's Annual Report 2012, 30th Annual Report. Accessed 12/15/2015. www.kufpec.com/Reports/KUFPEC%20Annual%20Reports/Annual%20Report%202011.pdf

Layachi, Azzedine. "Islam and Politics in North Africa." In *The Oxford Handbook of Islam and Politics*, edited by John Esposito and Emad El-din Shahin, 352–78. Oxford, UK: Oxford University Press, 2013.

Lesser, Ian O. *Security in North Africa: Internal and External Challenges*. Santa Monica, CA: Rand, Project Air Force, 1993.

The Majalla, "The Dragon Eyes the Arab Spring." April 14, 2011.

Ministry of Foreign Affairs of the People's Republic of China. "President Jiang Zemin Held Talks with Tunisian President." April 18, 2002. Accessed 12/15/2015. www.fmprc.gov.cn/mfa_eng/wjb_663304/zzjg_663340/xybfs_663590/gjlb_663594/2893_663786/2895_663790/t16438.html.

National Bureau of Statistics of the People's Republic of China, 2003–13. *China Statistical Yearbook*. Beijing: National Bureau of Statistics, various years.

Ng, Eric. "Sinochem Forges Local Alliances for Foreign Bids." *South China Morning Post*, September 23, 2005.

Observatory of Economic Complexity. "Import Origins of Tunisia 2011." Accessed 12/15/2015. http://atlas.media.mit.edu/explore/tree_map/hs/import/tun/show/all/2011/.

Ogunsanwo, Alaba. *China's Policy in Africa, 1958–71*. Cambridge, UK: Cambridge University Press, 1974.

Pei, Felicia Loo Pei. "China's Sinochem Still in Quest for Atlantis." *International Oil Daily*, August 1, 2002.

People's Daily. "China, Tunisia Sign Eight Cooperation Accords." June 21, 2004.

Perkins, Kenneth. *A History of Modern Tunisia*. Cambridge, UK: Cambridge University Press, 2004.

Petroleum Geo-Services. "PGS Closes Sale of Its Atlantis Subsidiary to Sinochem." *Press Release*. February 20, 2003. Accessed 12/15/2015. www.pgs.com/Pressroom/Press_Releases/PGS_Closes_Sale_of_its_Atlant

Pollack, Jonathan D. "China: Unease from Afar." In *The Arab Awakening: America and the Transformation of the Middle East*, edited by Kenneth M. Pollack, Daniel I. Byman et al., 298–310. Washington, DC: Brookings Institution, 2011.

Schliephake, Konrad. *Oil and Regional Development: Examples from Algeria and Tunisia*. New York, NY: Praeger Publishers, 1977.

Shinn, David H. and Joshua Eisenman. *China and Africa: A Century of Engagement*. Philadelphia, PA: University of Pennsylvania Press, 2012.

Sinochem. "Atlantis Holding Norway AS." Accessed 12/15/2015. http://english.sinochem.com/g935/s1798/t4340.aspx.

Sinochem Group. "The First Phase of the Acquisition of Atlantis by Sinochem Ended." March 4, 2003.

Tang Nengxuan [唐能宣]. 中国企业纵横北非 ("Chinese Enterprises in North Africa"), *国际商报* (International Business). October 8, 2004.

Teo, Karen. "Sinopec Drops out of Sinochem." *International Oil Daily*, February 18, 2003.

U.S. EIA. "Tunisia." Accessed 12/15/2015. www.eia.gov/countries/country-data.cfm?fips=TS&trk=p1

U.S. Energy Information Administration (EIA), "Arab Maghreb Union." January 2002. Accessed 12/15/2015. www.mafhoum.com/press2/81E18.html.

Willis, Michael J. "Islamic Movements in Algeria, Morocco and Tunisia." In *The Oxford Handbook of Islam and Politics*, edited by John Esposito and Emad El-din Shahin, 532–43. Oxford, UK: Oxford University Press, 2013.

Yang Tingsheng [杨廷胜], Sun Dongfang [孙东方] and Li Xuehong [李雪红]. Oudna海上油田射流泵采油技术 ["The Jet Pump at the Offshore Oudna Oilfield's Extraction Technology"]. *油气田地面工程 (Oil and Gas Fields Surface Engineering)*, September 1, 2010.

Yao Guimei [姚桂梅]. 中国与非洲的石油合作 ("China and Africa's Oil Cooperation"), *国际石油经济 (The International Petroleum Economy)*, November 20, 2006.

Zhao Qing [赵青]. 中东乱局与中国石油企业"走出去"战略 ["The Riots in the Middle East and the 'Going Out' Strategy of Chinese Oil Companies"], *新远见 (New Vision)*, July 15, 2011.

8 Mini-cases

This chapter focuses on a number of mini-cases, namely Kazakhstan, Canada, Uzbekistan, and Denmark, which have been selected from the whole universe of countries.

The mini-cases here are structured in the same manner as the regular cases, the only difference being that they are shorter in length and do not contain a literature review of the activities of the Chinese NOCs in the country in question. The purpose of the mini-cases is exploratory; they can be read as a supplement to the main cases. The analysis of these mini-cases examines the extent to which the conclusions that I find for Africa can be generalized across regions.[1]

Kazakhstan

Background

The state of Sino-Kazakh relations

Three phases can be distinguished in China-Kazakh relations (see figure 8.1.1 for map of Kazakhstan). The first is from 1992–97, starting when the two countries established diplomatic relations on January 3, 1992. Since then, many agreements have been signed between the two parties, including important boundary agreements.[2] The second phase, from 1997–2001, was characterized by an increased number of leadership visits and increased trade.

During the third phase, from 2002 onward, leadership visits have increased, and bilateral trade has surged. During this time, there has been a focus on the economic development of Xinjiang and the strengthening of the role of the SCO.[3] Overall, there has been a process of increasing engagement of China with Kazakhstan.

History of Chinese oil companies in Kazakhstan

China and Kazakhstan officially began cooperating on energy in September 1997, when, during a visit by Premier Li Peng, the two countries signed a number of

Figure 8.1.1 Map of Kazakhstan

agreements concerning petroleum cooperation, among other things, that CNPC would acquire a 60.3 percent stake in AktobeMunaiGaz for $4.3 billion.[4] Moreover, CNPC proposed building two pipelines. The first was the China-Kazakhstan pipeline, a 3,040 km oil pipeline from the port of Atyrau in northern Kazakhstan to Alashankou on the Chinese border in Xinjiang, ultimately aimed for the Dushanzi oil refinery in Xinjiang (Sino-Kazakh Oil Pipeline Co. Ltd.).[5] A second pipeline was to stretch from the Uzen region of Kazakhstan to the Turkmenistan border and onward to Iran. This project ultimately failed after running up against US embargoes against Iran.[6] Overall, during Li Peng's visit, CNPC proposed the investment of a total of $9 billion in the development of the field and pipeline construction in Kazakhstan.

CNPC is the Chinese oil company with the largest number of oil assets in Kazakhstan. It has nine stakes, and Sinopec and CITIC each operate a single stake in the country.[7] CNOOC has no stakes in Kazakhstan.[8]

In 2013, Kazakhstan was the eighth largest source of China's oil imports, with 4 percent that year.[9] In terms of the destinations for Kazakhstan's oil and gas exports, 16 percent of the oil and gas produced in Kazakhstan in 2012 was exported to China, the second largest export destination.[10]

Strategic importance

Kazakhstan holds great strategic importance for China, as table 8.1.1 illustrates. Many visits have taken place between the two countries, they enjoy a comprehensive strategic partnership, and bilateral trade is high. The existence of extremist groups linked to al-Qaeda in Kazakhstan renders the country of great importance for CCP regime stability. Lastly, the territory is highly salient given the country's geographic proximity to China and its extensive infrastructure. All of this renders Kazakhstan of high strategic importance to China.[11]

Oil and gas levels

Kazakhstan has proven oil reserves of 30 billion barrels (12th in the world as of late 2012).[12] In 2012, Kazakhstan produced 1.64 billion bpd, ranking it 18th in the world that year.[13] Although 62 percent of the territory is potentially oil-rich, only 50 percent of it has been explored (as of 2012).[14]

In terms of gas, Kazakhstan's domestic hydrocarbon reserves amount to 2.41 trillion m^3 of gas, the 14th largest reserves in the world.[15] In 2012, Kazakhstan produced 11.35 billion m^3 of natural gas, ranking them 38th in the world that year.

Thus, Kazakhstan holds very large oil and gas reserves, together with a high production of both oil and gas.

The empirical expectation

As the compiled data indicate, Kazakhstan is a country of high strategic importance to China and one with significant oil reserves and production. For this reason, the hypothesis is that both economic and state interests will dominate in Kazakhstan. Based on the characteristics presented earlier and the history of the case, the empirical expectation regarding Kazakhstan is as follows: *The companies are expected to have an incentive to become involved because of the large quantities of available oil. At the same time, the government attributes strategic importance to the country. The hypothesis is, therefore, that in the case of Kazakhstan, we will expect evidence of both state and economic interests.*

Table 8.1.1 Level of strategic importance: Kazakhstan (for more detail, see the Appendix)

Country	*1. Level of political relations*	*2. Role for CCP regime stability*	*3. Salience of territory*	*4. Role for other great power*	*5. Bilateral trade*	*Total*
Kazakhstan	2	2	2	1	2	2

Quantitative content analysis

For Kazakhstan, as presented earlier, the hypothesis is that we will find evidence of both state and economic interests. The quantitative analysis of the Chinese state media shows that 90 percent of the articles have a preponderance of economic interests over the ten-year period under investigation. Thus, the activities are driven by commercial interests, and the preceding hypothesis is not supported. Still, when considering the entire period, the results show that the level of evidence of economic interests found in the articles fluctuates: as illustrated in the following, economic interests dominate relative to state interests/concerns with domestic stability over the course of the period, except for the year 2003 (ratio of 0.5:1). Economic interests are also strong relative to state interests/domestic stability in the years 2005 (ratio of 7.0:1), 2007 (ratio of 7.7:1), and 2012 (ratio of 10.4:1). State interests and concerns with domestic stability hold greater importance in the years 2006 (ratio of 1.5:1), 2008 (ratio of 2.4:1), and 2011 (ratio of 1.4:1). Thus, a pronounced development takes place over the ten-year period. This is illustrated in figure 8.1.2.

Zooming in and scrutinizing particular ratios, including the ratio of economic to state interests, figure 8.1.3 shows, that, overall, economic interests dominated relative to state interests over the course of the decade, except for the year 2003 (ratio of 0.6:1). The importance of state interests in 2003 would follow from Hu Jintao's visit to Astana that year. Economic interests dominated strongly relative to state interests in the years 2004–05 (ratios of 7.8:1–8.7:1), 2007 (ratio of 8.6:1), 2009 (ratio of 10.8:1), and 2012 (ratio of 14.2:1). In addition to the year 2003, state interests held greater importance in 2006 (ratio of 1.3:1), 2008 (ratio of 2.6:1), and 2011 (ratio of 1.6:1). The importance of state interests in 2006 and 2008 would follow from the fact that President Nazarbayev visited Beijing these two years. State interests being strong could follow from Hu Jintao's visit to Astana in 2011.

Looking at the relationship between economic interests and concerns with domestic stability (*weiwen*), as figure 8.1.4 shows, we see that, overall, economic interests dominated relative to concerns with domestic stability over the course of the decade and particularly in the years 2005 (ratio of 36.1:1), 2007 (ratio of 75.5:1), and 2012 (ratio of 38.3:1). In other years, concerns with domestic stability were stronger, with ratios ranging between 2.2:1 and 24.0:1.

Finally, when considering the ratio of state interests to concerns with domestic stability (*weiwen*), as figure 8.1.5 shows, over the course of the period, state interests dominated relative to concerns with domestic stability, except for the year 2009. Here, concerns with domestic stability dominated relative to state interests (ratio of 0.8:1). State interests were particularly strong in the years 2006–08 (ratios of 6.0:1–9.1:1) and again in 2011 (ratio of 7.4:1). In addition to 2009, concerns with domestic stability had relatively greater importance in 2003–05 (ratios of 2:1–4.1:1) and in 2012 (ratio of 2.7:1).

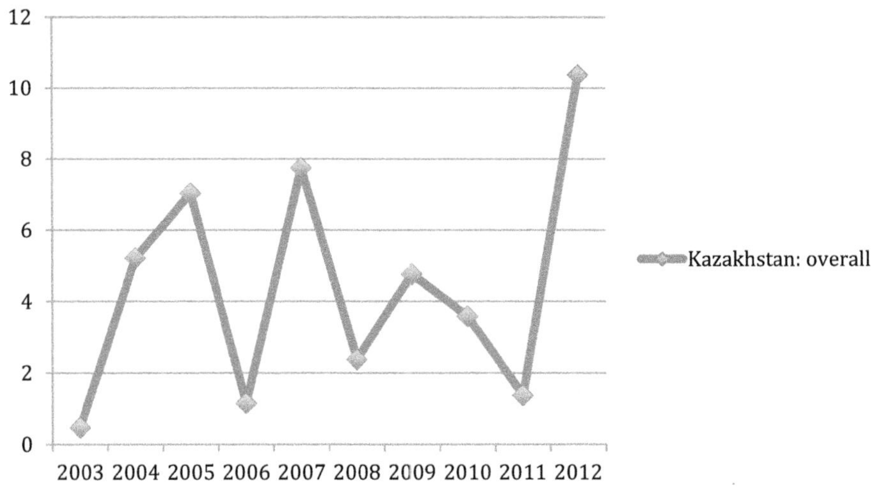

Figure 8.1.2 Ratio of economic interests to state interests/domestic stability

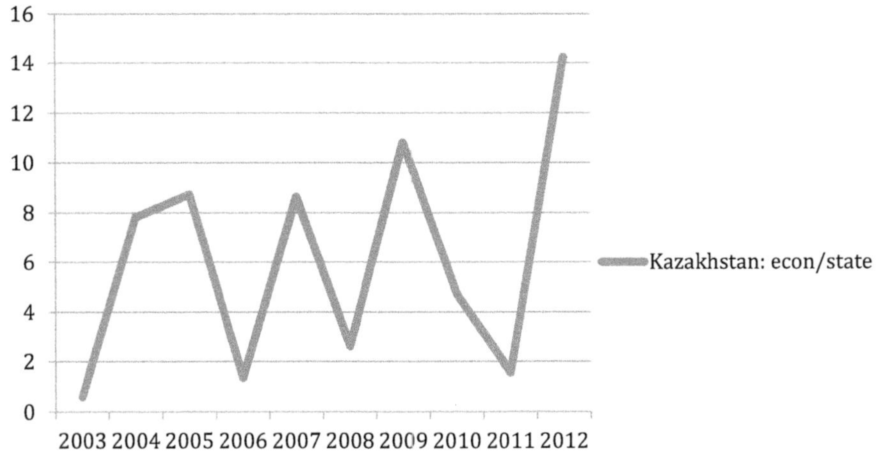

Figure 8.1.3 Ratio of economic interests to state interests

Overall, the preceding results are surprising and disprove the hypothesis presented in this book that economic and state interests will dominate equally. Here, we find dominance of economic interests, except for the year 2003. The remainder of this chapter seeks to answer why this is the case.

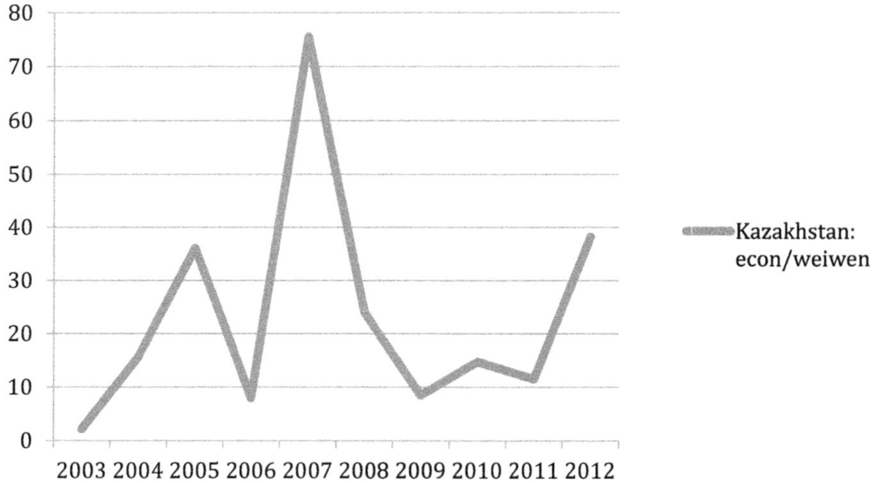

Figure 8.1.4 Ratio of economic interests to domestic stability

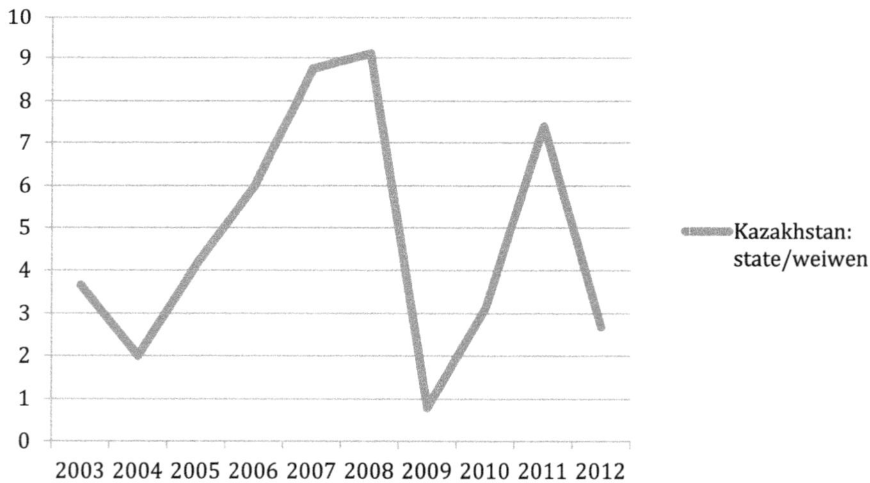

Figure 8.1.5 Ratio of state interests to domestic stability

Qualitative analysis

Here, we focus on three key decisions that are considered the most significant and representative in terms of the activities of Chinese companies in Kazakhstan over the decade (2003–2012). First, we focus on CNOOC and Sinopec's failed attempt to enter the Kazakh oil industry in 2003. Second, we focus on CNPC's acquisition of PetroKazakhstan in 2005. Third, we focus on the link between instances involving ethnic separatists in Kazakhstan and their implications for Chinese companies operating in Kazakhstan. While the analysis could have focused on the building of the China-Kazakhstan pipeline agreed to in 1997, because this analysis is limited to the post-2002 period, we do not focus on that here. The analysis of these three key decisions will help us understand if Chinese foreign policy toward Kazakhstan is dominated by state interests, economic interests, or concerns with domestic stability.

Key Decision 1: failure in 2003

We focus here on CNOOC and Sinopec's failed attempt to enter the Kazakh oil industry. On March 7, 2003, CNOOC and Sinopec announced their joint bid for a 16.7 percent share of the Agip KCO international consortium owned at the time by British Gas (BG Group) for $1.23 billion[16] ($615 million each). The Agip KCO consortium exploits several Caspian Sea sites and is responsible for developing the offshore Kashagan Reservoir. The Kashagan offshore field in the northern section of the Caspian Sea is possibly the largest oilfield outside of the Middle East, with estimated reserves of 13 billion barrels of oil, and is considered to be the most important of the Caspian areas.[17]

On March 7, 2003, CNOOC and Sinopec announced their joint bid for a 16.7 percent share of the Agip KCO international consortium (see table 8.1.2). In fact, Sinopec and CNOOC made their respective bids independent of one another. The consortium partners had the pre-emptive right and were able to block the bid by matching the price to BG within 60 days of the offer,[18] and on May 12, 2003, the consortium partners blocked CNOOC's bid.[19] Four days later, Sinopec's bid was blocked by the consortium partners.[20]

Why would the consortium members block the Chinese companies' bids? From the perspective of the consortium partners, the Chinese firms would add little to the capacity of the consortium, whereas Sinopec and CNOOC would gain access to some of the world's most advanced oil exploration and extraction techniques. The Chinese firms would likely have pushed for an eastern pipeline option to

Table 8.1.2 CNOOC and Sinopec's failed acquisition

Announced date	March 7, 2003
Failed	May 2003
Acquired %	16.7%
Deal value	$1.23 billion
Acquirer company	CNOOC and Sinopec
Vendor company	British Gas (BG)
Project	Agip KCO international consortium

China in order to ship some of the Kashagan oil northeast to the Aktyubinsk-Urumqi pipeline in order to maximize the capacity of the latter.[21] One view was, if China entered the consortium, the Chinese companies would push for a way to divert oil from Western countries to China. According to other sources, however, the bids were blocked not because of the IOCs but instead because of the Kazakhstan government's intervention.[22]

According to the first interpretation, the IOCs therefore played a nasty trick to block a bid by Chinese companies to preserve their interests. According to the other interpretation, the Kazakhstan government was to blame. Irrespective of which interpretation is correct, CNOOC and Sinopec failed to gain access to the Kashagan structure in Kazakhstan.[23]

Economic interests

According to investment analysts, the price that Sinopec and CNOOC offered was not "cheap, only fair."[24] It was attractive compared to CNOOC's average finding cost of $1/boe and the costs of its previous overseas acquisitions.[25] The stake would give the two Chinese companies access to technology without overpaying. Moreover, the Kashagan field is one of the world's largest unexplored sites and would provide CNOOC and Sinopec with the opportunity to boost their reserves. By becoming part of the large consortium, CNOOC and Sinopec would cooperate with large IOCs, giving them access to both new technology and new management techniques. Thus, the acquisition of the BG shares provides evidence of economic interests. This key decision could be consistent with a greater NOC role and the companies pursuing their interests independently of the government, and also independently of each other, as the bids were made separately.

How does the analysis here compare to the quantitative part of the analysis? In 2003, when CNOOC and Sinopec made their combined bid for the important oil stake, surprisingly, the data do not reflect this increase in the importance of economic interests; in fact, 2003 is the only year in the ten-year period where state interests and concerns with domestic stability overshadow economic interests (ratio of 0.47:1). Looking at state interests relative to concerns with domestic stability, the former dominate (ratio of 2.0:1).

The importance of state interests in 2003 can be explained by President Hu Jintao's visit to Kazakhstan on June 2–4, 2003. Still, in addition to agreements in the security sphere, several economic agreements were signed during this visit, including agreements pertaining to the Kazakhstan-China oil pipeline,[26] which could be seen as an indicator of economic interests. One might wonder why the acquisition did not come to pass when the Chinese president was to arrive in June the same year. As pointed out earlier, however, the fact that the other consortium partners did not approve the acquisitions by CNOOC and Sinopec was more a result of the fact that the IOCs viewed the two Chinese companies as competitors rather than it having to do with the motives of the

Chinese companies. The two methods, therefore, reach different conclusions in this case.

There will always be some inconsistencies between different types of evidence. The question is whether they are in overall agreement or not. In fact, there is evidence of some state interests given Hu Jintao's visit the same year. Still, overall, as the acquisition would allow the companies to gain access to some of the world's most advanced oil techniques, the evidence of economic interests is more credible.

Key Decision 2: CNPC acquires PetroKazakhstan

Here, we focus on CNPC's acquisition of PetroKazakhstan in 2005. On August 22, 2005, it was announced that CNPC would acquire PetroKazakhstan, formerly Hurricane Hydrocarbons, for $4.18 billion, amounting to $55/share (see table 8.1.3). Two months later, on October 27, 2005, the acquisition was finalized.

PetroKazakhstan, the third-largest oil producer in Kazakhstan, is headquartered in Calgary, Canada.[27] In the process leading up to the acquisition, both Indian Oil and Natural Gas Corporation (ONGC) and Russian Lukoil had bid for the stake, with ONGC offering a reported $3.6 billion.[28] After an intensive bidding process with ONGC, CNPC agreed to purchase the company for $4.18 billion. Some analysts regarded this as an overvaluation by CNPC.[29]

Economic interests

This was the largest foreign acquisition undertaken by a Chinese company, and Kazakhstan thus became the second-largest foreign base of CNPC operations, after Sudan. The acquisition gave CNPC control over the Shymkent oil refinery, the refinery in Kazakhstan with the most modern technology.[30] From the Chinese side, the takeover not only provided an extra source for its oil supply, but it could potentially also help improve the efficiency of the proposed Kazakh-China oil pipeline by helping to fill it, as CNPC's own production in Kazakhstan was insufficient. A Chinese industry article emphasizes how the PetroKazakhstan acquisition represented a major advancement of "CNPC's technological development."[31] According to CNPC, the Kazakhstan acquisition represents a "bright point"

Table 8.1.3 CNPC Acquires PetroKazakhstan

Announced date	August 22, 2005
Completed date	October 27, 2005
Acquired %	100%
Deal value	$4.18 billion
Acquirer company	CNPC International Ltd.
Vendor Company	PetroKazakhstan

(亮点/*liangdian*) for the company and offered the company a strategic breakthrough (战略性突破/*zhanluexing tupo*).[32] As one of the motives was to gain access to technology, there is evidence of economic interests.

However, a situation reminiscent of the aforementioned blocking of CNOOC and Sinopec bids emerged in connection with the PetroKazakhstan sale in 2005 when the Kazakh government threatened to utilize its pre-emptive rights. Ultimately, the deal was settled via negotiations, and on July 5, 2006, 33 percent of CNPC's shares in PetroKazakhtan was transferred to KazMunaiGas, while CNPC retained the remaining 67 percent stake.[33] In this manner, CNPC's position was somewhat weakened.

State interests

The analysis here shows that the important acquisition made by CNPC in 2005 is evidence of economic interests, as the acquisition appeared profitable. Still, even if there is no evidence of CNPC receiving loans from either CDB or Eximbank to finance the acquisition, significantly, Hu Jintao visited Kazakhstan in July 2005, at which time a strategic partnership was established. Moreover, no agreements on major economic investment projects were made during the visit.[34] Consequently, overall, this key decision thus provides evidence of state interests.

How does the analysis here compare to the quantitative part of the analysis? The results from the quantitative analysis show a peak in the dominance of economic interests relative to state interests and concerns with domestic stability in 2005 (ratio of 7.0:1). Thus, in this key decision, the results from the quantitative and qualitative analyses are inconsistent.

Again, there will always be some divergence between different types of evidence. The question is whether they agree overall. Importantly, however, while there is evidence of strong economic interests here, as the acquisition appeared profitable, still, looking at the overall evidence, the evidence of state interests is more credible.

Key Decision 3: ethnic separatism in Kazakhstan, 2001

Here, we focus on the link between instances involving ethnic separatists in Kazakhstan and their implications for Chinese companies operating in Kazakhstan, as well as implications for Chinese domestic stability. We also consider whether recent events of ethnic separatists in Xinjiang are linked to events in Kazakhstan. While some Kazakh workers have been killed in recent years in Kazakhstan, there are no reports of Chinese workers ever being killed there. One such instance of Kazakh workers being killed is presented here, namely in December 2011, when oil workers in Kazakhstan were killed.

December 2011 incident

Given the strong links between Uighurs in Xinjiang and Uighurs in Kazakhstan, a link is expected between events in Kazakhstan and Chinese domestic stability. At the same time, no terrorist attack has ever been successfully carried out in Kazakhstan, although Kazakh officials claim they have uncovered and prevented attacks.[35]

In December 2011, 16 oil workers in Kazakhstan were killed, although none of them were Chinese. Oil workers at state-run KazMunaiGas Exploration Production (RDGZ), an oil facility controlled by KazMunaiGas (KMG) in Zhanaozen in Kazakhstan, had rioted after disputes over wages and the firing of almost 1,000 workers.[36] In addition to the 16 people dead, more than 100 were injured. Still, the violence on this occasion did not threaten Chinese investments, as Chinese oil companies have no assets in Zhanaozen – the Chinese joint ventures operate in Aktau. Still, it is worth noting a link between the riots and Chinese investments, as the riots in Kazakhstan were related to a KMG subsidiary, a Chinese oil company operating in Kazakhstan, even if, according to Chinese Foreign Ministry Spokesperson Zhang Hanhuy, no Chinese company had fired oil workers in Kazakhstan.[37] Thus, no Chinese oil workers were killed. Moreover, there is no evidence of this occurrence receiving any domestic attention, as on the Chinese social media (微博/*Weibo*). For this reason, there is not sufficient evidence to claim that the riots in Kazakhstan in December 2011 had implications for domestic stability in China. Instead, this key decision provides evidence of economic interests.

How does the analysis here compare to the quantitative analysis? In 2011, the quantitative analysis shows the dominance of economic interests relative to state interests/concerns with domestic stability (ratio of 1.4:1), even if – in relative numbers – state interests and concerns with domestic stability are more important in 2011 than in both 2010 (ratio of 3.6:1) and 2012 (ratio of 10.4:1). The results for the quantitative and qualitative analyses are thus corroborated.

Conclusion

In Kazakhstan, the Chinese companies were expected to have an incentive to become involved because of the large quantities of available oil and opportunity to maximize profits. At the same time, the government attributes strategic importance to Kazakhstan. On this background, the empirical expectation is evidence of both state and economic interests.

The qualitative analysis here shows that the failure of CNOOC and Sinopec to acquire a stake in the Agip KCO international consortium provides evidence of economic interests. CNPC's acquisition of PetroKazakhstan in 2005 provides evidence of state interests. Finally, rather than the instances of ethnic separatism in Kazakhstan in 2011 being evidence of concerns with domestic stability, they provide evidence of economic interests.

The results from the quantitative analysis corroborate the results from the qualitative analysis except in the case of the failure of CNOOC and Sinopec to acquire a stake in the Agip KCO consortium and in the case of the acquisition of PetroKazakhstan. Still, it is argued that, overall, evidence for economic interests is more credible in the case of the Agip KCO consortium, and evidence of state interests is more credible in the case of the acquisition of Petrokazakhstan.

The empirical expectation is supported by the quantitative and qualitative analyses, which produce evidence of both economic and state interests.

Canada

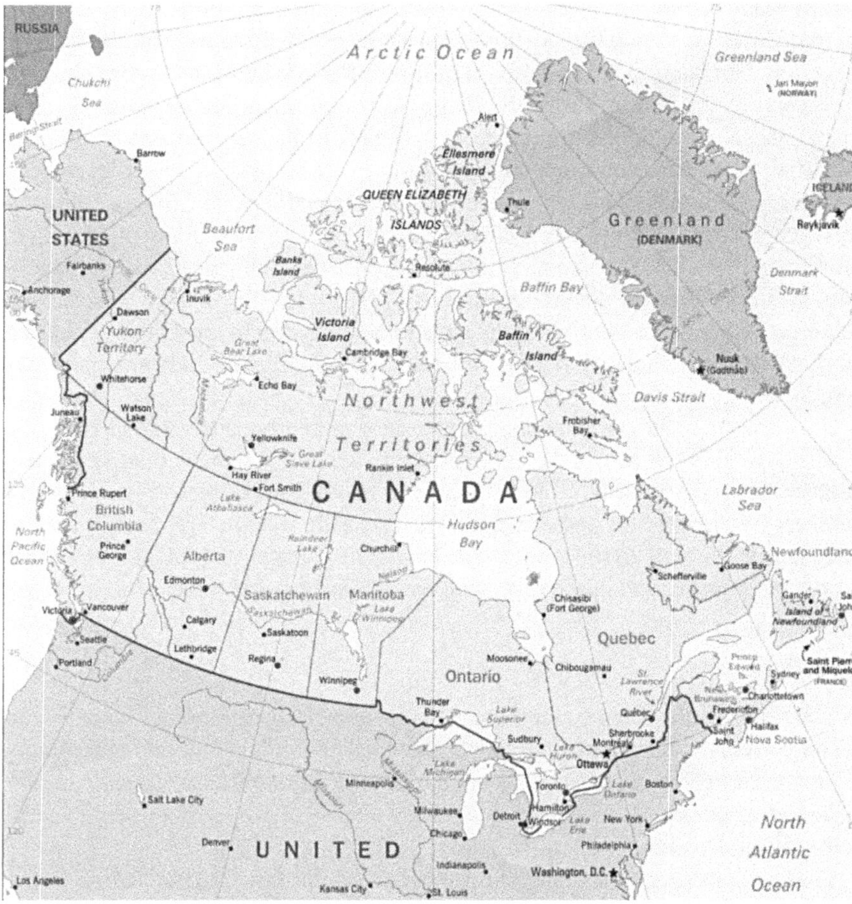

Figure 8.2.1 Map of Canada

Background

The state of Sino-Canadian relations

China and Canada established relations in 1970 when Canada became one of the first Western countries to recognize the People's Republic of China (PRC) (see figure 8.2.1 for map of Canada). Relations developed slowly thereafter. During the first years of Canadian Prime Minister (PM) Stephen Harper's government

(2006–15), relations deteriorated when Harper criticized the Chinese leadership for their human rights record and the Dalai Lama question. The period from 2005–09 was a low point in Sino-Canadian diplomatic and political relations.[38] Since 2009, however, relations have improved and leadership visits have become more frequent. While the two countries signed a strategic partnership agreement in 2005, there is no comprehensive strategic partnership, which reflects the limited strategic importance that China attributes to Canada.

History of Chinese oil companies in Canada

In 1993, CNPC became the first Chinese NOC to acquire an asset in the Canadian energy sector. Since then, all three major Chinese NOCs have become involved in the Canadian energy sector; in fact, they have entered into some of their largest overseas acquisitions there. Sinopec has five stakes, CNOOC has four stakes, and CNPC has two stakes; Sinopec is the Chinese oil company with the most assets in Canada, both oil and gas.[39]

China imports very little oil from Canada, less than 2 percent of total Chinese oil imports in 2013,[40] and less than 1 percent of Canada's oil and gas exports are exported to China, partly as a result of the lengthy transportation time and lacking infrastructure to transport oil and gas to Asian markets.

Strategic importance

Canada is of limited strategic importance to China for the following reasons.[41] There have been relatively few visits between the two sides. At the same time, the proximity to shipping routes, the developed infrastructure, the high bilateral trade figures, and the fact that Canada as a US alliance partner is important territory for the United States, renders the country of some strategic importance. Overall, however, Canada is of limited strategic importance to China, as table 8.2.1 illustrates.

Oil and gas levels

As of early 2013, Canada has proven oil reserves of 173.11 billion barrels (4th in the world) and produces 3.86 million bpd of oil (5th in the world) (as of early 2013).[42] In addition to conventional oil, Canada has oil sands that are estimated to hold approximately 173 billion barrels of oil.[43] Because of increased oil sands production, Canadian production is expected to increase to 6.6 million bpd by 2035.[44]

Table 8.2.1 Level of strategic importance: Canada (for more detail, see the Appendix)

Country	*1. Level of political relations*	*2. Role for CCP regime stability*	*3. Salience of territory*	*4. Role for other great power*	*5. Bilateral trade*	*Total*
Canada	0	0	0	1	2	0

Canada's domestic hydrocarbon reserves amount to 1.93 trillion m^3 of gas (18th in the world as of early 2013).[45] In 2013, Canada produced 143.56 billion m^3 of natural gas (5th in the world as of January 1, 2014).[46] In addition to natural gas, Canada has great unconventional natural gas reserves in the form of CBM, shale gas, and tight gas.[47] Specifically, Canada has 10.99 trillion m^3 of technically recoverable shale gas resources.[48] Thus, as this data shows, Canada has high levels of both oil and gas.

The empirical expectation

On the basis of the preceding data, Canada is only of limited strategic importance to the Chinese leadership but has extensive oil reserves. It is therefore hypothesized that economic interests will be the dominant motive in Canada. Based on the characteristics presented earlier and the history of the case, the empirical expectation is that, in Canada, *Chinese companies have an incentive to become involved because of the large quantities of oil, but as the government attributes little strategic importance to the region, the state will not seek to pursue its interests there. The companies will be in the driver's seat, and there will be evidence of economic interests.*

Quantitative analysis

For Canada, as presented earlier, the hypothesis is that we will find evidence of economic interests. The quantitative analysis of the Chinese state media shows that 89 percent of the articles have a preponderance of economic interests over the ten-year period under investigation. Thus, the analysis indicates that the activities are driven by commercial interests and the preceding hypothesis is supported. Still, when examining the period 2002–12, the results indicate that the level of evidence of economic interests found in the articles fluctuates; overall, economic interests dominated relative to state interests/concerns with domestic stability. Economic interests were particularly strong in the years 2003 (ratio of 20.6:1), 2006 (ratio of 15.6:1), and 2008–09 (ratios of 8.9:1–9.2:1), respectively. State interests and concerns with domestic stability had relatively greater importance in the years 2004–05 (ratios of 2.7:1–3.4:1), 2007 (ratio of 3.0:1), and 2010 (ratio of 2.9:1). Thus, economic interests dominated over the course of the decade, although there is variation in the degree, as illustrated in figure 8.2.2.

Examining particular ratios more closely, such as the ratio of economic interests to state interests (figure 8.2.3), overall, economic interests dominate over the course of the decade. Looking more closely, economic interests peaked in 2003 (ratio of 23.6:1) and 2006 (ratio of 19.45:1). Economic interests were also strong in the years 2008–09 (ratios of 11.88–11.96:1) and 2011–12 (ratios of 8.24–10.45:1). State interests were strong relative to economic interests in 2004 (ratio of 4.33:1), 2007 (ratio of 3.23:1), and 2010 (ratio of 4.14:1). The fact that state interests were relatively stronger in 2010 would follow from state visits made by Hu Jintao and PM Harper to one another that year. Surprisingly, when PM Paul

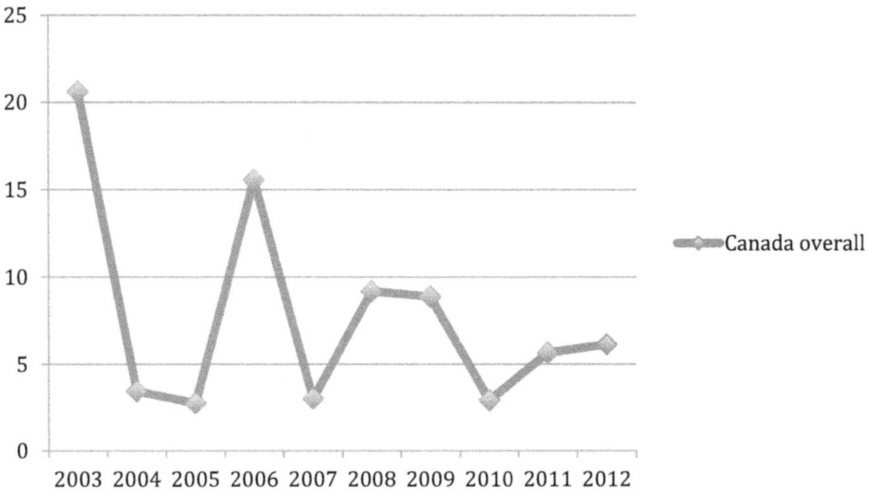

Figure 8.2.2 Ratio of economic interests to state interests/domestic stability

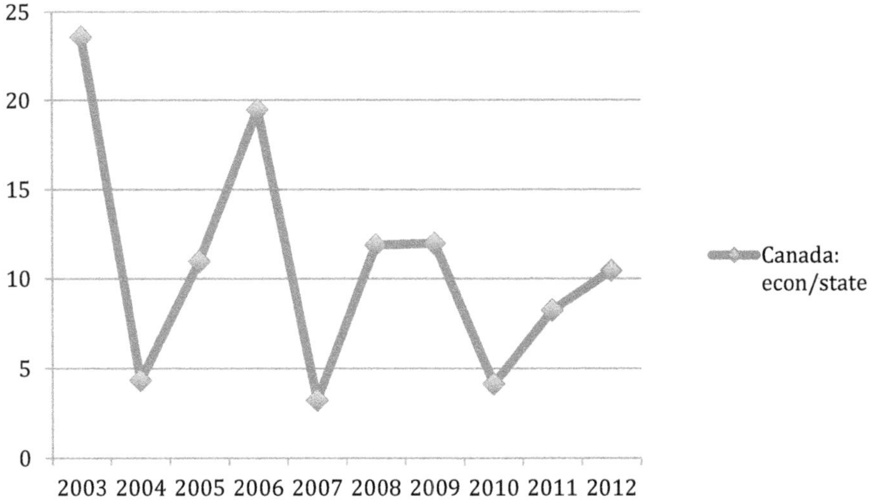

Figure 8.2.3 Ratio of economic interests to state interests

Martin and Hu Jintao made visits to one another in 2005, it is not reflected in the data here. Moreover, when PM Jean Chrétien visited Beijing in 2003, it is not reflected in the results, as they show dominance of economic interests.

Examining the relationship between economic interests and concerns with domestic stability (*weiwen*), figure 8.2.4 shows that overall, in the period from 2002 to 2012, economic interests dominated relative to concerns with domestic

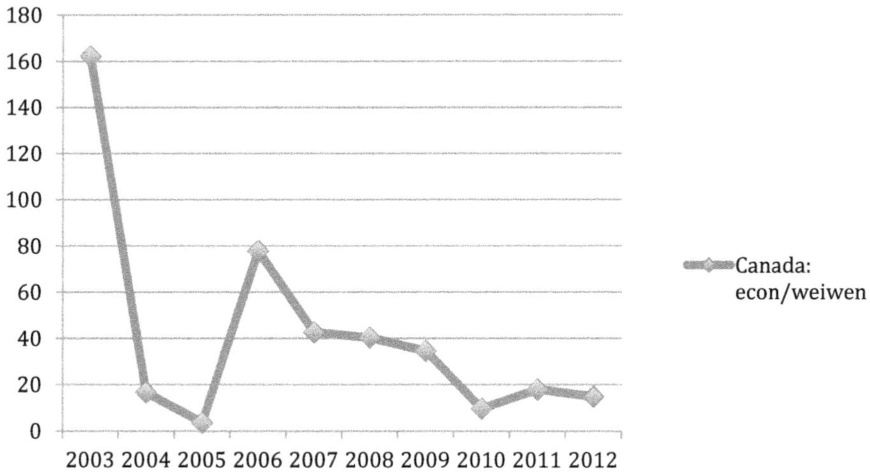

Figure 8.2.4 Ratio of economic interests to domestic stability

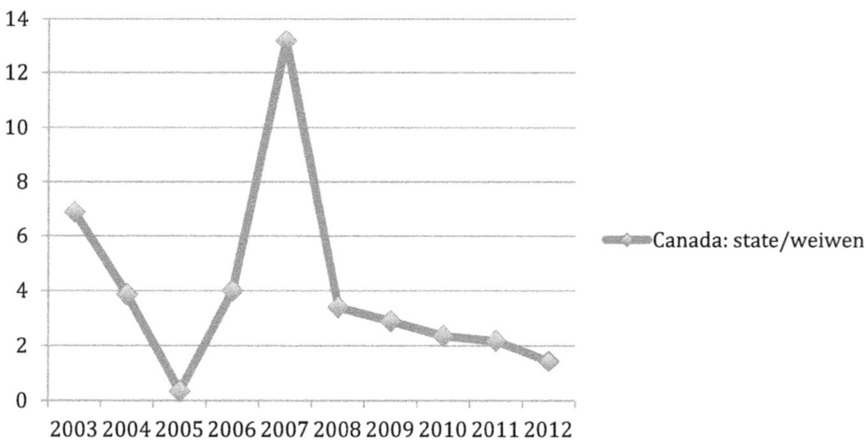

Figure 8.2.5 Ratio of state interests to domestic stability

stability. Economic interests strongly dominated in 2003 (ratio of 162.25:1) and the years 2006–09 (ratios of 34.55–77.8:1). Concerns with domestic stability had more importance in the years 2004–05 (ratios of 3.65:1–16.71:1) and 2010–12 (ratios of 9.74:1–17.94:1).

Finally, turning to the ratio of state interests to concerns with domestic stability (*weiwen*), figure 8.2.5 shows that, over the course of the period, state interests dominate relative to concerns with domestic stability, except in 2005, when concerns with domestic stability actually dominate (ratio of 0.33:1). In 2007, state interests peak (ratio of 13.18:1). In addition to the year 2005, concerns with domestic stability have more importance in 2004 (ratio of 3.9:1), 2006 (ratio of 4:1), and 2008–12 (ratios of 1.42:1–3.4:1).

Overall, the preceding results are hardly surprising. They confirm the hypothesis presented in this book that economic interests are expected to dominate. The rest of this section will explore the extent to which the results from the quantitative analysis are corroborated by the qualitative analysis.

Qualitative analysis

The following focuses on three key decisions, which will illuminate important aspects of the activities of Chinese companies in Canada and their possible impact on Chinese foreign policy. We focus first on the CNPC acquisition of a 60 percent stake in Canada's Athabasca Oil Sands Corporation (AOSC) in 2009; second, CNPC's failed attempt to acquire Encana's gas assets in 2010; and third, the CNOOC acquisition of Nexen, a Canadian company, in 2012. These key decisions have been selected because they allow for analysis of some of the major acquisitions of Chinese NOCs in Canada in the last decade and are spread out over time. Importantly, they allow for analysis of both the oil and gas sectors, even if one of them fails (the Encana deal in 2010), which in itself has no bearing on the motive of the Chinese side. Other possibilities could have been to analyze Sinopec's acquisition of a stake in Syncrude in 2010 or of Talisman in 2012. Still, the three key decisions earlier are seen as the most significant and representative in terms of the activities of Chinese companies in Canada in this ten-year period.[49] Thus, this analysis will help us understand if Chinese foreign policy toward Canada is dominated by state interests, economic interests, or concerns with domestic stability.

Key Decision 1: CNPC acquires AOSC, 2009

On August 31, 2009, AOSC and PetroChina (PetroChina International Investment Company Ltd.), a wholly owned subsidiary of CNPC, reached an agreement whereby PetroChina would acquire a 60 percent interest in AOSC's MacKay River and Dover oil sands projects for $1.75 billion. AOSC would remain the operator of the two projects.[50] The acquisition was completed on February 10, 2010 (see table 8.2.2).[51]

Table 8.2.2 CNPC's acquisition of AOSC

Announced date	August 31, 2009
Completed date	February 10, 2010
Acquired %	60
Deal value	$1741.51 million
Acquirer company	PetroChina Co. Ltd. (Parent: CNPC)
Vendor company	Athabasca Oil Corporation
Project	MacKay River and Dover Oil Sands Projects

AOSC is a privately owned oil sands company headquartered in Calgary; it is focused on the exploration, development, and production of oil sands-related assets, mainly in the Athabasca region of Northern Alberta. AOSC's oil sands assets have been estimated at 10 billion barrels of contingent bitumen resource.[52]

According to research analysts, at the time of the acquisition, AOSC was an attractive investment option – "a top pick," given Athabasca's extensive portfolio of oil resource opportunities and solid balance sheet position.[53]

As part of the agreement, PetroChina agreed to make capital expenditures of more than $250 million for the MacKay and Dover oil sands projects over the next three years, to maintain an Alberta head office for the operating companies, to ensure that most of the senior management positions of the operating companies are held by Canadians, and to continue to organize the operating companies under Canadian law.[54] According to AOSC, the two projects would cost a direct investment of $15–20 billion to develop.[55] The agreement included a financing arrangement, which according to AOSC CEO Bill Gallacher, "was the real carrot for AOSC."[56] As part of the agreement, PetroChina made three loans to Athabasca, amounting to a total of $1.09 billion.[57] In return, PetroChina would reportedly receive approximately 3 billion barrels of oil.[58]

Moreover, on September 9, 2009, CNPC, the parent of PetroChina, received a five-year discounted loan from the China Development Bank (CDB) to help it buy further upstream assets overseas.[59] It is therefore likely that PetroChina's acquisition of a 60 percent interest in AOSC was financed by a CDB loan.

Economic interests

The acquisition of the 60 percent stake was the largest venture by China in the Canadian oil sands to date, and according to CNPC, the acquisition was "a major breakthrough in the unconventional oil sector."[60] The acquisition of AOSC was attractive, as it provided access to AOSC's portfolio of reserves. Moreover, Canada is primarily attractive for Chinese companies because of its large oil sands reserves, which are the largest in the world, and its advanced oil sands technologies.[61] AOSC and PetroChina supposedly intended to use relatively new methods to develop the two oil sands projects, both steam-assisted gravity drainage (SAGD) and cyclic steam stimulation (CSS) techniques.[62] Acquiring oil sands technology from the cooperation with AOSC can help PetroChina further develop oil sands in China. This acquisition will also allow PetroChina to hedge against the risk that conventional oil will be harder and more expensive to find in the future.[63] Finally, the acquisition enables PetroChina to emulate AOSC's extensive management expertise, encompassing both North American and international experts with extensive oil experience from many of the major unconventional oil operators, the IOCS. Thus, overall, this acquisition reflects economic interests, as the acquisition provides access to advanced oil sands technology and the Canadian oil sands market.

State interests

Three weeks before reaching the agreement with AOSC in August 2009, Canada's finance minister Jim Flaherty visited Beijing, together with AOSC executives, and met with First Vice Premier Li Keqiang. This visit can be seen as an indicator of support for the acquisition. Moreover, the Chinese government has made oil sands a high priority,[64] and the Canadian oil sands are attractive in this regard. For example, Xu Chunming, director of the China University of Petroleum, has commented that Canadian oil sands products are very suitable for the Chinese market.[65]

Lastly, there is evidence that the recipient country appreciated the acquisition. Finance Minister Flaherty stated that "we are encouraging Chinese direct foreign investment, so long as there is compliance with the governance concern and other rules that we have with Investment Canada."[66] Still, while this acquisition bears elements of evidence of state interests, overall, the acquisition shows evidence of economic interests.

*Domestic stability (*weiwen*)*

Is there evidence of any impact on Chinese domestic stability? The Chinese leadership has stressed the importance of advanced technology (SAGD) for Chinese companies in relation to Canada.[67] In early 2009, Zhou Yongkang of the CCP Central Committee Political Bureau Standing Committee visited the Liaohe (China) heavy oil site, stating that the CCP Central Committee hopes that they, through "the development of heavy oil cutting-edge technology can achieve sustained and stable oil supply." To the extent that this identifies a link between China's obtaining important oil sands technology abroad in order to develop oil sands domestically, which is important for economic growth and domestic stability, then this offers evidence of concerns with domestic stability (*weiwen*). Still,[68] as this component is conceptualized, this key decision here offers no evidence of any ramifications of the activities of the Chinese companies in Canada for domestic stability in China.

Conclusion, Key Decision 1

Overall, the key decision examined here offers an example of economic interests. It helps CNPC gain access to important oil sands reserves and acquire new technological expertise in oil sands exploration and demonstrates CNPC's determination to enter the most promising area in the Canadian energy sector. Still, CDB provided a loan to PetroChina to finance the investment, visits took place between the two sides, and according to a policy from the Chinese leadership, oil sands are prioritized as a source of energy supply. Even so, assessing the overall weight of different sources, this key decision indicates a dominance of economic interests.

How does the analysis here compare to the quantitative analysis? The quantitative analysis shows that economic interests dominated in 2009 relative to state interests/concerns with domestic stability (ratio of 8.9:1). The acquisition was first approved in February 2010, a year in which economic interests dominated (ratio of 2.9:1), even if state interests and concerns with domestic stability become relatively more important. As the quantitative analysis points to the strength of economic interests in 2009–10, the results from the quantitative and qualitative analyses are thus corroborated.

Key Decision 2: the failed Encana shale gas deal, 2010–11

In June 2010, PetroChina International Investment Company Ltd., a subsidiary of PetroChina Company Ltd., and Encana Corporation signed a memorandum of understanding (MOU), according to which PetroChina would acquire a 50 percent stake in Encana Corporation's shale gas Montney properties: Cutbank Ridge and Horn River in British Columbia and Alberta for $5.5 billion (see table 8.2.3). A subsequent cooperation agreement was signed in February 2011. According to the agreement, PetroChina would fund half of the future capital costs, and Encana would continue to operate the fields.[69] At the time, this deal would be the largest overseas acquisition on record for PetroChina, in fact of any Chinese company, in terms of natural resources abroad.

Encana Corp., based in Calgary, is Canada's largest producer of natural gas. Encana's Cutbank Ridge assets cover approximately 5,300 km^2 of land; the site is located on the border between northern British Columbia and Alberta.[70] At the time, Encana was performing well in terms of revenue and had a relatively high share price.[71]

On June 23–25, 2010, President Hu Jintao visited Canada to meet PM Harper, and the MoU on the agreement for PetroChina parent CNPC to develop some of Encana's lands was announced on the final day of the visit. This would seem to indicate some correlation between the visit and the transaction. The Chinese government website stated that, during the visit, leaders of the two countries reiterated their commitment to develop the China-Canada strategic partnership and announced the goal of $60 bn. in bilateral trade by 2015.[72]

PetroChina's bid for Encana was supported by a loan from CDB, as CNPC received a five-year discounted $30 billion loan on September 9, 2009, from the CDB to fund the acquisition of more upstream assets overseas.[73]

Table 8.2.3 CNPC's failed acquisition of Encana

Announced date	June 25, 2010
Failed	June 21, 2011
Acquired %	50
Deal value	$5.5 billion
Acquirer company	PetroChina
Vendor company	Encana
Project	Montney properties (Cutbank Ridge and Horn River)

Economic interests

The 50 percent stake investment in Encana's Cutbank Ridge assets would give PetroChina its first shale-gas reserves in North America. As Encana is a world leader in the development of shale gas, PetroChina would gain access to the technical understanding of shale gas development. Finally, PetroChina expected the joint venture to provide a platform for entering the North American market, which is indicative of the company's long-term commitment to the North American natural gas business.

Collapse of the deal

In June 2011, the joint venture discussions collapsed after more than a year of negotiations. While the agreement, signed in June 2010, was pending approval from Ottawa under the Investment Canada Act, according to Encana Spokesperson Alan Boras, the federal review played no role in the deal's failure.[74] Rather, it failed because the two sides could not agree on issues such as the joint operating agreement and the valuation of the assets. PetroChina Spokesperson Mao Zefeng said, "The reason is that we felt we couldn't reach agreement on the asset evaluation and the procedure."[75] In terms of the valuation of the acquisition [price, ed.], a Chinese analyst said, "[F]rom the point of view of return on investment, a price of $5.4 bn. is high."[76]

At the time of the acquisition, there was growing concern that shale gas deals were becoming too expensive in North America, as natural gas prices had remained low and the prospects of once-promising shale basins were diminishing. At the time of the acquisition, gas prices had fallen 52 percent from the 2008 average of $8.9. Given that the break-even price for shale gas development is $5/mmBTU, the price of gas falling below $5/mmBTU during the acquisition period (June 2010 – June 2011) could explain why PetroChina lost interest in the project.[77] In this sense, this key decision offers an example of a Chinese oil company not being willing to pay an over price and looking closely at the break-even price of the project when determining whether to pursue an investment.

Another indicator of economic interests would be the PetroChina share price at the time of the acquisition. However, as the share price of PetroChina did not increase dramatically compared to both CNOOC and Sinopec during this period,[78] one cannot conclude that the decision to acquire Encana's assets was a particularly profitable endeavor.

Still, considering all of the factors together, this failed acquisition generally reflects economic interests.

*Domestic stability (*weiwen*)*

There is no evidence of any impact on domestic stability in China.

Conclusion, Key Decision 2

Overall, the key decision examined here is, thus, an example of economic interests. The acquisition would help CNPC develop its shale gas technology and provide access to gas reserves. At the same time, falling shale gas prices made it harder to cover production costs. Thus, PetroChina withdrew because of their concern that the deal was overvalued. There is also evidence of state interests, as Hu Jintao travelled to Ottawa in 2010, where an MoU on the acquisition was signed. For Hu Jintao to sign the MoU on the agreement while visiting Canada is a very strong indication of the Chinese leadership's intentions. The political leadership in Beijing wanted the deal to go through, as the political leaders prioritize shale gas and access to advanced shale gas technology. Moreover, a CDB loan was provided to CNPC to help finance the deal, which would have been PetroChina's largest overseas investment. When PetroChina withdrew from the deal later, it was out of concern that the acquisition would not be profitable. This case then provides evidence that PetroChina pursued its own activities and interests, even when they were out of tune with the policy line from Beijing. This key decision could then point to a greater role being played by the NOCs and a greater role played by NOCs in Chinese foreign policy.

How does the analysis here compare to the quantitative analysis? The quantitative analysis shows that, overall, economic interests dominated relative to state interests and concerns with domestic stability in the period 2010–11. When the acquisition failed in 2011, however, the data reflect the relative increase in the importance of economic interests to state interests/domestic stability (ratio of 5.6:1) from 2010 (ratio of 2.9:1). Thus, the quantitative analysis shows that, in fact, economic interests became relatively more important in 2011. There is no evidence in the years 2010–11 of the activities of the Chinese companies in Canada having consequences for domestic stability in China. Overall, the quantitative analysis reveals a dominance of economic interests in the years 2010–11. Thus, the results from the quantitative and qualitative analyses are consistent.

Key Decision 3: CNOOC's acquisition of Nexen, 2012–13

On July 23, 2012, CNOOC Ltd. – through its subsidiary CNOOC Canada Holding – announced the acquisition of Nexen Inc. for $15.1 billion, and on February 26, 2013, the acquisition of Nexen Inc. was completed (see table 8.2.4).

Nexen is a Canadian firm headquartered in Calgary, Alberta; prior to the acquisition, it was listed on both the New York and Toronto stock exchanges.

With the acquisition, CNOOC assumed Nexen's current debt of approximately $4.3 billion.[79] In total, the transaction amounted to an investment of $20 billion.[80]

CNOOC's acquisition of Nexen was the largest Chinese investment overseas at the time. The acquisition would allow CNOOC access to upstream resources and secure energy supplies for China. It would help expand CNOOC's overseas operations and resource base and the company's entry into both oil and gas fields

Table 8.2.4 CNOOC acquires Nexen

Date of announcement	July 23, 2012
Date of completion	February 26, 2013
Acquired %	100
Deal value	$15.1 billion
Acquirer company	CNOOC Canada Holding
Vendor company	Nexen
Target	Nexen

and would help build a North American business beyond its current role as a financial backer. In this sense, it was a strategy of diversification. The acquisition would increase CNOOC's production by 20 percent and its proven reserves by 30 percent.[81] In addition, the Canadian investment environment is better than that in Central Asia and Africa and comes with lower political risks, as Canada is a stable democracy. Moreover, even in the Canadian context, Nexen is a very advanced company in terms of management practices, which CNOOC could emulate.[82] Finally, according to one Chinese informant, CNOOC was motivated to become involved in Canada to make technological gains.[83]

Another indicator of economic interests would be how the CNOOC share price moved during the time of the acquisition. As CNOOC's share price, from the announcement of the acquisition on July 23, 2012, until it closed on February 26, 2013, fell by 2.46 percent, whereas both the Sinopec and CNPC share prices increased, this could be interpreted as an indicator that the market did not view this as a profitable investment. In fact, some analysts believe that the Chinese overpaid, as CNOOC's offer of $27.50/share represents a premium of 61 percent when compared to the closing price of Nexen's common shares on the NYSE on July 20, 2012, which was viewed as a significant premium.[84] Similarly, in the words of CNOOC, "the purchase price is relatively high."[85] According to one analyst, given that CNOOC had underestimated the risks of monetizing the landlocked oil sands and shale-gas assets in Canada, assets that account for 75 percent of Nexen's proven and probable reserves, CNOOC had actually overpaid by $3–4 billion.[86] Still, when considering the overall evidence, the acquisition reflected economic interests. It enabled CNOOC to acquire important technology, not least technology relevant for developing oil sands operations, and provides access to new oil reserves.

State interests

A number of visits took place leading up to the CNOOC acquisition of Nexen to back up the acquisition. On February 8–9, 2012, PM Harper visited China, and Harper and Natural Resources Minister Joe Oliver both met with the chairmen of the three Chinese oil companies. Five months later, the acquisition was announced. It is also important to note that Chinese Commerce Minister Chen Deming visited Canada in September of the same year.

Domestic stability (**weiwen*****)***

In 2012, there is no evidence found of ramifications of the activities of the Chinese companies in Canada for domestic stability in China.

Conclusion, Key Decision 3

The key decision analyzed here is CNOOC's acquisition of Nexen, a Canadian company. The agreement on the Nexen acquisition was made in 2012 and finalized in 2013. On the one hand, this case provides evidence of economic interests: the transaction gave CNOOC access to important reserves and technology, reflecting CNOOC's determination to enter the most promising area of the sector in Canada and to acquire new technological expertise in oil sands exploration. Still, there is also evidence of state interests, as up to the acquisition in 2012, visits intensified, as seen with Hu Jintao's visit to Canada in 2010 and PM Harper's visit to Beijing in February 2012 immediately before the announcement of the acquisition. This demonstrated the importance attributed by Beijing to the deal, also given that CNOOC's attempt to buy Unocal had failed. Thus, there is evidence of state interests, even if no loans from CDB and Eximbank were offered to back up the acquisition. In addition, Sinopec and later CNPC offered to construct the Northern Gate pipeline. However, while there is thus some indication of state interest, overall, this key decision produces evidence of economic interests.

How does the analysis here compare to the quantitative analysis? The quantitative analysis shows that economic interests dominated relative to state interests/concerns with domestic stability in 2012 (ratio of 6.1:1) and more so than the previous year (ratio of 5.6:1). Thus, overall, the quantitative analysis provides evidence of economic interests in 2012. The results from the quantitative and qualitative analyses are thus corroborated.

Conclusion

In the Canadian case, the Chinese companies were expected to have an incentive to become involved because of the large quantities of oil. But as the Chinese government attributes little strategic importance to Canada, the state is not expected to pursue its state interests there, and the companies will be in the driver's seat. In the case of Canada, the empirical expectation is therefore that economic interests dominate.

The qualitative analysis shows that economic interests dominated both the PetroChina acquisition of AOSC, in the case of the failed attempt to acquire Encana in 2010–11, and in the case of the CNOOC acquisition of Nexen in 2012. The quantitative analysis also reveals a dominance of economic interests over the course of the period. Thus, the quantitative and qualitative analyses corroborate one another, and the presented empirical expectation is supported.

Uzbekistan

Figure 8.3.1 Map of Uzbekistan

Background

The state of China-Uzbekistan relations

Uzbekistan and China established relations on January 2, 1992, since which time relations developed rapidly (see figure 8.3.1 for map of Uzbekisktan). Since 2002, a number of issues between the two countries were settled, including border issues or problems with Uighur separatism (Uighurs are an ethnic group in the country). Since then, the two countries have focused on increasing bilateral trade.[87] Numerous leadership visits have taken place between the two parties, and they have reached many agreements. A strategic partnership was settled in 2012.

History of Chinese oil companies in Uzbekistan

CNPC has been present in Uzbekistan since 2006. Whereas CNPC has two stakes in Uzbekistan, neither Sinopec nor CNOOC have any operations in Uzbekistan.

As a share of Chinese oil and gas imports, Uzbekistan has a small part. It has no oil exports, but exports approximately 10 percent of its natural gas to Kazakhstan, Kyrgyzstan, and Tajikistan and around 12 percent to Russia. Uzbekistan supplies China with a smaller share (500 million m^3) of natural gas via southern Kazakhstan.[88]

Strategic importance

Uzbekistan is a country of high strategic importance to China, as illustrated in table 8.3.1. This comes from the high number of leadership visits between the

Table 8.3.1 Level of strategic importance: Uzbekistan (for more details, see the Appendix)

Country	*1. Level of political relations*	*2. Role for CCP regime stability*	*3. Salience of territory*	*4. Role for other great power*	*5. Bilateral trade*	*Total*
Uzbekistan	1	2	2	2	0	2

two, the existence of an extremist group with links to al-Qaeda in its territory, and its proximity to Chinese territory. Finally, as a former US alliance partner, the country is of high importance to the Chinese regime. Thus, even if bilateral trade is limited, overall, Uzbekistan is a country of high strategic importance to China.

Oil and gas levels

Uzbekistan has oil reserves of 0.59 billion barrels (2012) (44th largest in the world) and oil production of 0.10 million bpd (2012) (49th in the world).[89] Uzbekistan imports oil – mainly from Russia, Kazakhstan, and Turkmenistan (as of 2009). Uzbekistan is expected to be importing 566 million barrels of oil in 2020 and 744 million barrels in 2030.[90] As noted earlier, Uzbekistan does not export oil.

Uzbekistan's total gas reserves amount to 1.84 trillion m^3 (2012) (18th largest in the world), and its total gas production amounts to 63.0 billion m^3 (2012) (13th in the world).[91] In 2012, Uzbekistan was the third largest natural gas producer in Central Asia, behind Russia and Turkmenistan.[92]

The empirical expectation

The data compilation shows that Uzbekistan is of great strategic importance to China but has limited oil reserves and oil production. The hypothesis is, therefore, that state interests will dominate in Uzbekistan. Based on the characteristics presented earlier and the history of the case, the specific empirical expectation is that *the companies have little incentive to become involved because of the limited quantities of oil. At the same time, the government attributes strategic importance to the country. For this reason, the hypothesis is that there will be evidence of state interests.*[93]

Quantitative content analysis

For Uzbekistan, as presented earlier, the hypothesis is that we will find evidence of state interests. The quantitative analysis of the Chinese state media shows that 90 percent of the articles reflect a preponderance of economic interests over the ten-year period under investigation. Thus, the activities in Uzbekistan are driven by commercial interests, and the preceding hypothesis is not supported. Looking more closely at the results from the quantitative analysis, over the course of the ten-year period from 2002–12, overall, economic interests dominated relative to state interests/concerns with domestic stability over the course of the period, except for the year 2006 (ratio of 0.5:1). Economic interests peaked relative to state interests/domestic stability in 2003 (ratio of 6.9:1), 2009 (ratio of 5.8:1), and 2012 (ratio of 11.1:1). State interests and concerns with domestic stability were of relatively greater importance compared to economic interests in the years 2006–08 (ratios of 0.5–2.4:1) and 2010–11 (ratios of 1.3–2.1:1). Thus, with the exception of a single year, 2006, economic interests dominated. Still, there is variation in the degree over the course of the ten-year period, as figure 8.3.2 shows.

Zooming in and scrutinizing particular ratios, such as the ratio of economic interests to state interests, we see that, overall, economic interests dominated relative to state interests over the course of the period, except for the year 2006 (ratio of 0.64:1), as figure 8.3.3 shows. In 2006, in fact, state interests dominated. The dominance of economic interests peaked in 2009 (ratio of 46:1) and 2012 (ratio of 13.0:1). In addition to 2006, state interests were strong relative to economic interests in 2008 (ratio of 1.71:1), 2010 (ratio of 1.43:1), and 2011 (ratio of 3.62:1). Strong state interests in 2010 and 2011 might be explained by Hu Jintao's visit to Tashkent in 2010 and President Karimov's visit to Beijing in 2011.

Focusing on the relationship between economic interests and concerns with domestic stability (*weiwen*), for the period under study, economic interests clearly dominated relative to concerns with domestic stability. Still, economic interests were relatively stronger in 2003–04 (ratios of 77.4–26.7:1) and in 2012 (ratio of 75.5:1), as figure 8.3.4 shows. Concerns with domestic stability were relatively stronger in the years 2005–07 (ratios of 1.8–5.0:1), 2009 (ratio of 6.6:1), and 2011 (ratio of 5.2:1).

Finally, looking at the ratio of state interests to concerns with domestic stability (*weiwen*), as illustrated in figure 8.3.5, over the course of the period, state interests

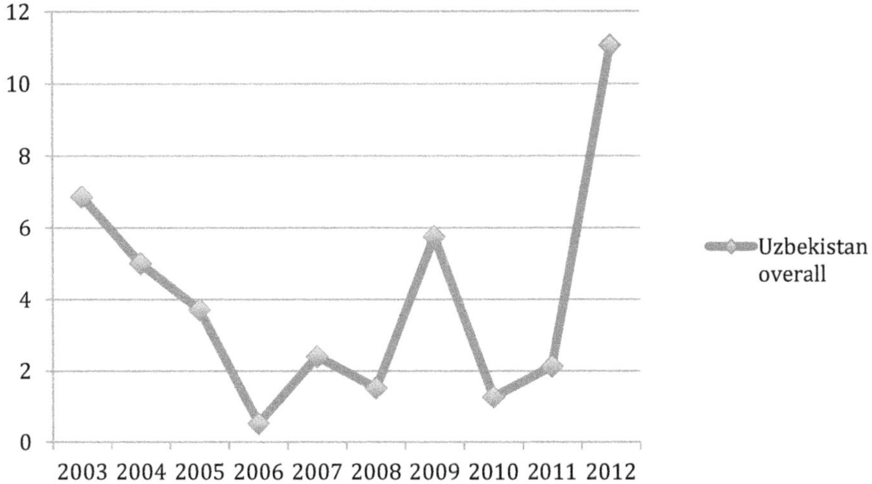

Figure 8.3.2 Ratio of economic interests to state interests/domestic stability

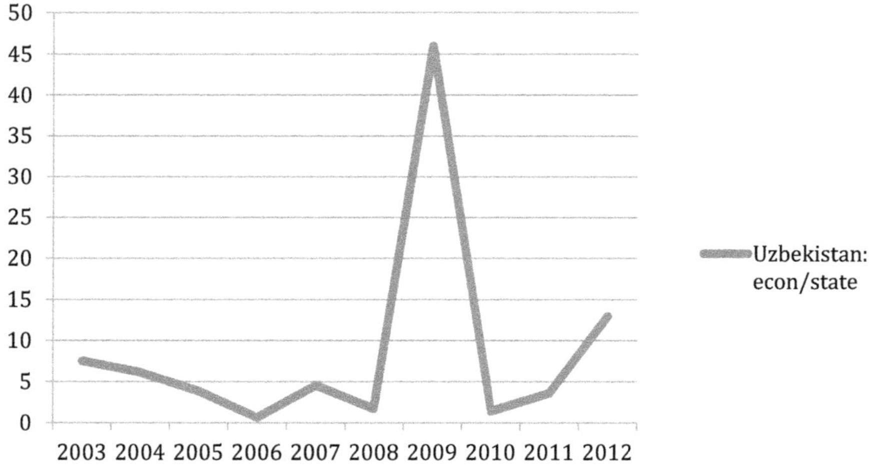

Figure 8.3.3 Ratio of economic interests to state interests

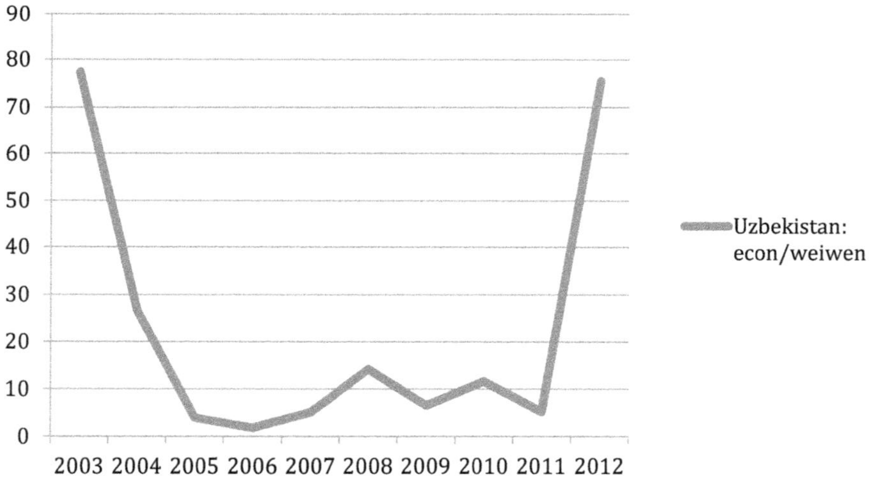

Figure 8.3.4 Ratio of economic interests to domestic stability

dominated relative to concerns with domestic stability, except for the year 2009 (ratio of 0.1:1). Thus, in 2009, concerns with domestic stability dominated relative to state interests. State interests peaked in 2005 (ratio of 27:1). Two state visits to Beijing by President Karimov that year could explain this surge. In addition to the aforementioned year 2009, concerns with domestic stability had greater importance relative to state interests in the years 2004 (ratio of 4.3:1), 2006 (ratio of 4.5:1), 2007 (ratio of 1.1:1), and 2011 (ratio of 1.4:1).

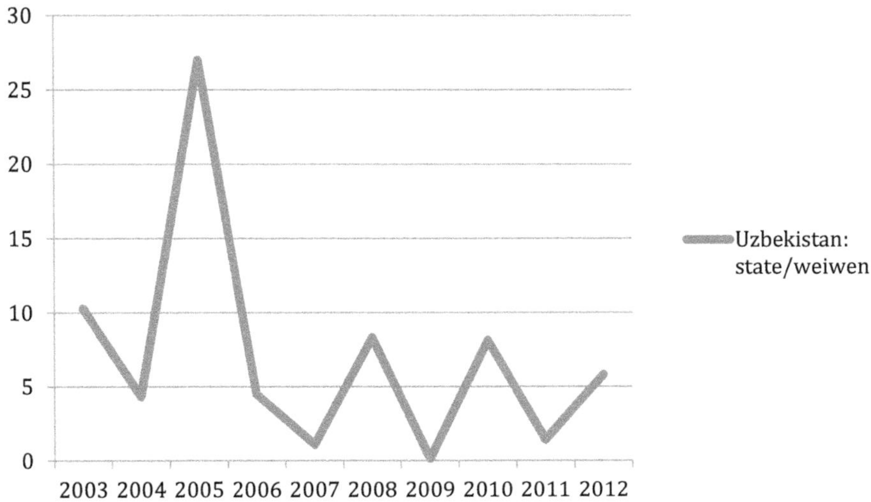

Figure 8.3.5 Ratio of state interests to domestic stability

Overall, the preceding results are somewhat surprising; they do not confirm the hypothesis that state interests will dominate. The remainder of this chapter will seek to cast light on why this is the case.

Qualitative part

Three key decisions are examined in the following, namely CNPC's acquisitions in Uzbekistan in 2004–06, the May 2005 crackdown on the Uzbek population, and the building of the Uzbekistan-China pipeline in 2007. Another possibility would have been to examine the visit by President Karimov to Beijing in 2012 and the negotiation of the strategic partnership, but as no large NOC acquisition was made, this is not addressed here. The argument is that these three key decisions are the most significant and representative in terms of the activities of Chinese companies in Uzbekistan over the last decade. Thus, analyzing them will contribute to the understanding of whether Chinese foreign policy toward Uzbekistan is dominated by state interests, economic interests, or concerns with domestic stability (*weiwen*).

Key Decision 1: CNPC's acquisitions, 2004–06

Here, we focus on the decision regarding large acquisitions made by Beijing to become involved in oil and gas operations in Uzbekistan in 2004. While the focus is on the 2004 visit, as the acquisitions made as a result of the visit are finalized in 2006, I also include here the acquisitions made in 2005 and 2006.

Economic interests

CNPC has been involved in oil and gas operations in Uzbekistan since 2004, when Chinese President Hu Jintao visited Tashkent in June 2004. During this visit, CNPC and the Uzbek oil and gas company Uzbekneftegaz signed an agreement on cooperation in the oil and gas sector.[94] Following up on this visit and after President Islam Karimov's visit to Beijing in May 2005, CNPC announced plans to invest $600 million in oil and gas development in Uzbekistan. Specifically, an agreement was reached on a 50–50 joint venture between CNPC and Uzbekneftegaz (UzCNPC Petroleum) to explore five onshore exploration oil and gas blocks: Ustyurt, Buxoro, Amu Darya, Xiva, and Fargana.[95]

The two parties also agreed on a second project. On August 30, 2006, CNPC formed an international consortium comprising CNPC, Uzbekneftegaz, Lukoil, Petronas, and South Korean KNOC. The parties signed a 35-year production sharing agreement (PSA) with the Uzbek government for the exploration and development of the Uzbek section of the Aral Sea.[96] While from the Uzbek side, the joint venture would help meet the demand for oil and ease energy pressures in the country, for CNPC, the two projects involved potential oil and gas discoveries of a viable commercial scale and would likely increase CNPC's reserves,[97] although the size of the reserves in the fields remains unclear. Moreover, it would boost the development of the natural gas upstream business and energy supply in China. Lastly, it would boost the Central Asia–China natural gas pipeline project in which CNPC is involved. There is no evidence that CNPC paid more than market price. Thus, this agreement reflects economic interests.

State interests

Two years later, in June 2006, without any connection to political visits, Beijing granted an Eximbank loan of $397 million to the Uzbek government. It was a 20-year preferential credit loan with a five-year grace period and a 3 percent interest rate as export buyer's credit to be given for ten projects in Uzbekistan covering infrastructure and urban development.[98] According to President Karimov, the assistance and preferential loans to Uzbekistan will be "very important to Uzbek social and economic development."[99] Even if the Eximbank loan was not given in conjunction with a state visit, as the loan was provided at the same time that CNPC entered the joint venture with Uzbekneftegaz and the international consortium to explore two very promising oil and gas fields, the preceding loan was likely given to help CNPC win these acquisitions. As a further indication of the motives of the Chinese leadership, there were two important state visits prior to the acquisitions, one by President Hu Jintao to Tashkent in June 2004 and the other by President Karimov to Beijing in May 2005. Thus, even if indicators of economic interests are present, overall, the key decision examined here, CNPC's acquisitions in Uzbekistan in 2004–06, reflect state interests, as both the aid and visits functioned as bait to win the acquisitions.

How does the analysis here compare to the quantitative analysis? The quantitative analysis shows that economic interests dominated relative to state interests/concerns with domestic stability in 2004 (ratio of 5.0:1) and in 2005 (ratio of 3.7:1), only to lose out to state interests/domestic stability in 2006 (ratio of 0.5:1). As a result of the combination of the agreements, reciprocal visits by Presidents Hu and Karimov, and the donation of the loan, state interests dominated in 2006. As CNPC's agreements were only settled in 2006, here we consider 2006 the key year. Thus, in 2006, the quantitative analysis reveals a dominance of state interests, meaning that the results from the quantitative and qualitative analyses are consistent.

Key Decision 2: May 2005 Uzbekistan crackdown

Here, we focus on the link between instances involving ethnic separatists in Uzbekistan and their implications for Chinese domestic stability. Given the strong links between the Uighurs living in Xinjiang and the Uighurs in Uzbekistan, links are expected to be found between the events in Uzbekistan and Chinese domestic stability. The key decision in focus here is China's decision to meet with the Uzbek president subsequent to an Uzbek crackdown on a terrorist group, the Islamic Movement of Uzbekistan (IMU), in 2005.

State interests

On May 13, 2005, the Uzbek government suppressed an anti-government demonstration in Andijon that they attributed to the Islamic extremist group IMU. This incident is investigated here, as it is deemed to illuminate the hypothesis related to concerns with domestic stability. While there were other incidents involving extremist groups in Uzbekistan in the period from 2002, including the killing of 19 people and wounding of 26 in a series of IMU terrorist incidents in Tashkent and Bukhara in March/April 2004, as well as attacks by unnamed militants in Khanabad and bombings in Andijon in May 2009 (May 25–26),[100] we focus here on the 2005 incident, as the Uzbek response was particularly harsh and illustrates how the Uzbek government does not support extremist groups in its territory.

The Uzbek government itself estimated that 187 people died, including 94 terrorists and 60 civilians, and that 76 terrorists were injured as a result of the suppression of the demonstration on May 13, 2005, in Andijon.[101] Non-government sources estimate the casualties at 700 civilians killed and up to 2,000 wounded.[102] Subsequent to the crackdown, several Western countries, including the United States, called for an independent international investigation of the events. President Karimov rejected this as a violation of Uzbek sovereignty. Instead, he suggested that outside forces were at work "to create instability and undermine the region economically in order to impose their own development model."[103]

Only a week after the Andijon riots, President Karimov visited Beijing on May 25–27, 2005, where he met President Hu Jintao. A number of agreements were signed during the visit, including a $600 million oil and gas joint venture; a

$35 million loan was extended to the Uzbek government for oil and gas transport system improvements, and Beijing promised the implementation of projects worth $1.5 billion (unspecified, ed.). Moreover, a package of investment proposals to Chinese companies, including 50 projects in areas such as information technology, mechanical engineering, and manufactured construction materials, was made.[104] This also came immediately after CNPC had promised to invest in oilfields in Uzbekistan in a 50–50 joint venture with Uzbekneftegaz. Thus, the visit, aid, and agreements are linked together and function as bait to obtain the agreement.

The support from the Chinese leadership for the Uzbek government was linked to the color revolutions in other countries, such as Georgia and the Ukraine, and the fear that these revolutions would spread. Thus, when Hu Jintao met with President Karimov, rather than this being related to events in Uzbekistan, it was related to fear that similar occurrences would spread to China. At the time, there was a perception that the United States and other Western countries were behind these color revolutions. This would explain why the US military base on Uzbek territory would be seen by China as constituting a threat. Shortly after Karimov's visit to Beijing, the United States was asked to leave the Uzbek military base.[105] This, in turn, can be viewed as damaging US interests, as the Uzbek base had been important for American activities in Afghanistan, and thus the role of the other great power in the region.

While IMU is a terrorist group with links to al-Qaeda, no attacks have been launched from Uzbek territory on Chinese territory, nor have any Chinese nationals been killed in Uzbekistan in recent years as a result of attacks from extremist groups. Moreover, the Uzbek government has initiated attempts to uncover and prevent attacks.

There is no evidence of the Andijon riots in May 2005 receiving any domestic attention in terms of Chinese social media or the Chinese leadership taking action to mediate the situation.[106] Thus, there is not sufficient evidence to claim that events related to extremist activity in Uzbekistan have had implications for domestic stability in China. Rather, there is evidence of economic interests, as economic agreements during the state visit in 2005 were settled.

How does the analysis here compare to the quantitative analysis? The quantitative analysis reveals that economic interests dominated in 2005 relative to state interests/concerns with domestic stability (ratio of 3.7:1). Looking at the ratio of state interests to concerns with domestic stability, at the time of the 2005 riot in Uzbekistan, the data reflect a relative increase in the importance of state interests (ratio of 4.3:1) as compared to the previous year (ratio of 27:1). Still, overall, this case provides evidence of economic interests. This means that the quantitative and qualitative analyses confirm one another.

Key Decision 3: Uzbekistan-China pipeline, 2007

The third key decision considered here is the case of the China-Central Asia pipeline and its route. We look at the CNPC decision to build the pipeline through Uzbek territory rather than through Kazakh territory.

State interests

The Central Asia–China gas pipeline spans 1,833 km, transporting gas from Turkmenistan (the Amu Darya River) through Uzbekistan and southern Kazakhstan to Xinjiang, China, where it links up with China's 8,653 km Second West-East gas pipeline (see figure 8.3.6 for map). The whole pipeline cost $7.3 billion to build and was largely funded by China.

The pipeline has three sections: The first, through Turkmenistan (188 km); the second section, through Uzbekistan (530 km); and the third section, through Kazakhstan (1300 km). In January 2010, the pipeline began supplying gas to Urumqi, Xinjiang.[107] The Uzbekistan-China stretch cost a total of $2.98 billion, of which CNPC has invested $244.35 million.[108] PetroChina is the sole importer of gas from Turkmenistan and Uzbekistan via the Central Asia–China pipeline network.[109]

Up to the decision on the Uzbek stretch of the Central Asia–China pipeline in late 2007, China negotiated with Kazakhstan to find a viable solution for the pipeline route, either a Sino-Turkmen or Sino-Uzbek pipeline. Two routes were proposed: one through Uzbekistan and the other through Kazakhstan. The latter route would pass through Kazakhstan to join the already-existing Bukhara-Ural pipeline. The former route would pass through the Ferghana Valley of Uzbekistan, then Kyrgyzstan, before entering China.

In 2006, the Chinese authorities seemed to prefer the route through Kazakhstan instead of the Uzbek route. In turn, this would mean that Uzbekistan would lose an important transit duties market and be at least partially marginalized from new export routes. On April 30, 2007, however, during a visit between Uzbek President Islam Karimov and Ma Kai, the Chinese minister of NDRC, an agreement was reached pertaining to the construction of a 30 billion m³ capacity, 530 km pipeline

Figure 8.3.6 China–Central Asia Pipeline

through Uzbekistan.[110] The pipeline agreement was then signed on August 18, 2007, during a visit by Chinese President Hu Jintao to Astana.[111]

The result was fortunate for Uzbekistan. The building of the pipeline through Uzbek territory will allow Uzbekistan to increase its gas exports to Central Asia and China rather than being a mere transit country. Moreover, the long-term deals with the CNPC can solve the regular energy shortages in the country's south.

A motive for China in this decision, in turn, was that the opening of the pipeline would break Russia's long-standing dominance over natural gas exports from Central Asia, as the pipeline provides an alternative energy outlet to Russia for Central Asian energy producers, which would have geopolitical consequences. This would also increase the use of pipelines as an alternative to importing oil with tankers, thus reducing transportation costs. Moreover, it will increase the security of gas supply for China.

Conclusion, Key Decision 3

While it has great significance for Uzbekistan if the pipeline is built through Uzbekistan or Kazakh territory, it would appear to be of less significance for China, as the same amount of gas will eventually be imported to China. Rather, the significance of the pipeline is that the agreement can be used as bait in return for support in the security sphere. Thus, the pipeline agreement would appear to reflect state interests. At the same time, there was no evidence of aid given in 2007, and no visits or statements were made. While Wen Jiabao met with Uzbek President Karimov in November 2006, the meeting did not take place in Uzbekistan but rather in Kazakhstan. There is no evidence of the concerns with domestic stability (*weiwen*) here.

How does the analysis here compare to the quantitative analysis? Contrary to the analysis that indicates that the security implications of the pipeline would trump the economic interests, the quantitative analysis reveals that economic interests dominated in 2007 relative to state interests/concerns with domestic stability (ratio of 2.4:1). Thus, in this key decision, the results from the quantitative and qualitative analyses are not corroborated.

While there always will be inconsistencies between different types of evidence, there is evidence of strong economic interests in this instance, as the pipeline would allow for further export from CNPC's exploration sites in Uzbekistan. Still, as the pipeline will provide the Chinese regime with a reliable source of energy and thereby contribute to energy security, looking at the overall evidence, in this instance, the evidence of state interests is more credible.

Conclusion

The expectation in the case of Uzbekistan was that the companies would have little incentive to become involved because of the limited quantities of oil available. At the same time, the Chinese government attributes strategic importance to Uzbekistan. Consequently, we expect to find evidence here of state interests.

Here, the qualitative analysis shows that CNPC's acquisitions in Uzbekistan in the period from 2004–06 provide evidence of state interests (for 2006), the Chinese support of Uzbekistan following the crackdown in 2005 shows evidence of economic interests, and state interests dominated the 2007 decision to build the pipeline through Uzbekistan. The quantitative analysis corroborates these results, except in the case of the 2007 decision to build a pipeline through Uzbekistan. Still, looking more closely, the evidence for state interests is more credible.

Thus, the quantitative and qualitative analyses partially support the empirical expectation presented earlier.

Denmark

It is important to note that even though the Faroe Islands and Greenland are treated as independent nations in some contexts, I include them in the analysis of Denmark, as they both officially belong to the Kingdom of Denmark (see figure 8.4.1 for map).[112]

Figure 8.4.1 Map of Denmark

Figure 8.4.2 Map of Greenland

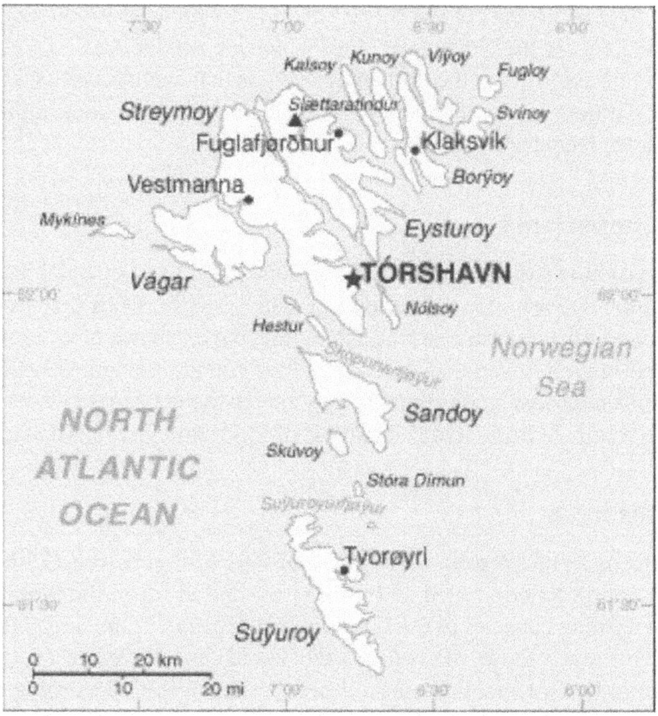

Figure 8.4.2a Map of Faroe Islands

Background

The state of China-Denmark relations

Denmark and China established diplomatic relations on May 11, 1950, Denmark being one of the first Western nations to do so. In 2008, the two countries established a comprehensive strategic partnership but had a diplomatic crisis when China suspended ties with Denmark after Danish Prime Minister Løkke Rasmussen met the Dalai Lama in May 2009. Six months later, relations were resumed and have developed since. Still, overall, visits between the leaders of the two countries have been relatively limited.

History of Chinese oil companies in Denmark

None of the Chinese oil companies are operating in Denmark (or Greenland): neither CNPC, Sinopec, or CNOOC have assets in Denmark. While some Chinese companies are involved in mining in Greenland, as this study does not include mining, we will not pursue this further here.

Oil production in Denmark is relatively limited.[113] Denmark has 15 oilfields, all situated in the Danish part of the North Sea (12 of which are producing).[114] There are four gas fields in the North Sea, all of which are producing.

Thus, in summary, given the limited oil and gas that Denmark possesses and the absence of Chinese oil company activity in Denmark, China does not import any oil or gas from Denmark.[115]

Strategic importance[116]

Denmark is of little strategic importance to China, as illustrated in table 8.4.1. This is seen in the relatively limited number of state visits between the two countries and the limited bilateral trade. At the same time, the existence of extremist groups in Denmark (but not linked to al-Qaeda) and the country being a US alliance partner renders Denmark of some strategic importance to the Chinese leadership. Still, overall, the results indicate that Denmark is of little strategic importance to China.

Oil and gas levels

In 2013, Denmark had proven oil reserves of 0.81 billion barrels (39th largest in the world) and production of 0.297 million oil bpd (37th in the world).[117] Denmark has a refining capacity of 0.17 million bpd (2012).[118] The Faroe Islands have no proven oil reserves (2014) (91st in the world) and therefore no oil production.[119] Similarly, Greenland has no oil production.[120] Still, according to the US Geological Survey (USGS) 2001 estimates, the waters off northeastern Greenland may contain up to 110 billion barrels of oil and actually hold the world's largest remaining oil reserves.[121]

Denmark has proven gas reserves of 43.04 billion m^3 (2014) (64th in the world) and production of 5.80 billion m^3 (2013) (50th in the world).[122] Greenland has no proven gas reserves.[123]

Thus, relatively speaking, Denmark has neither very rich oil or gas reserves nor high production.

The empirical expectation

The data compilation indicates that Denmark is a country with little oil and of limited strategic importance to China. It is therefore hypothesized that neither strategic importance nor economic interests are the dominant driving force in Denmark. Thus, based on the characteristics presented earlier and the history of the case, the

Table 8.4.1 Level of strategic importance: Denmark (for more detail, see the Appendix)

Country	*1. Level of political relations*	*2. Role for CCP regime stability*	*3. Salience of territory*	*4. Role for other great power*	*5. Bilateral trade*	*Total*
Denmark	1	0	0	1	0	0

empirical expectation is that, in Denmark, *the companies have little incentive to become involved because of the limited availability of oil. And as the Chinese government attributes little strategic importance to Denmark, the state will not seek to pursue its interests there. Neither state interests nor economic interests will dominate.*

Quantitative analysis

For Denmark, as presented earlier, the hypothesis is that we will not find evidence of either state or economic interests. The quantitative analysis of the Chinese state media shows that 87 percent of the articles have a preponderance of economic interests over the ten-year period under investigation. Thus, the activities are driven by commercial interests, and the preceding hypothesis is not supported. However, because the quantitative analysis of the Chinese state media for Denmark is based on a mere 78 articles, the quantitative findings for this case are rather unstable; however, this is a fact determined by the nature of the evidence.

The results from the quantitative analysis of the period 2002–12 illustrate that economic interests dominated the period relative to state interests/domestic stability. Economic interests were particularly strong relative to state interests/domestic stability in 2003 (ratio of 22.44:1) and 2009 (ratio of 21.77:1). State interests and concerns with domestic stability had more importance in 2004 (ratio of 2.25:1), as well as in the periods 2005–08 (ratios of 5.79:1–7:1) and 2010–12 (ratios of 4.88:1–10.15:1). Thus, there is a significant change over the course of this period of time, as illustrated in figure 8.4.2.

Zooming in and looking at particular ratios, such as the ratio of economic interests to state interests, it becomes apparent that, overall, economic interests dominated the decade. As illustrated in figure 8.4.3, economic interests peaked in 2003 (ratio of 23.3:1). Then, state interests were relatively stronger in the years 2004–08 (ratios of 2.8–8.7:1) and 2010 (ratio of 5.8:1).

Proceeding to the relationship between economic interests and concerns with domestic stability (*weiwen*), as figure 8.4.4 demonstrates, overall, economic interests dominated the period relative to concerns with domestic stability. Economic interests peaked in 2005 (ratio of 142:1) and 2009 (ratio of 141.5:1). Still, the concern with domestic stability was notable in the years 2003–04 (ratio of 11.3–28.9:1), 2008 (ratio of 19.8:1), and 2012 (ratio of 9.8:1).

Finally, comparing the ratio of state interests to concerns with domestic stability (*weiwen*), figure 8.4.5 shows that, overall, state interests dominated the period relative to concerns with domestic stability. State interests dominated most clearly in 2005 (ratio of 15.0:1) and 2010 (ratio of 13.8:1). Still, in 2003, concerns with domestic stability had more importance (ratio of 0.29:1), and, interestingly, state interests and concerns with domestic stability were equally important in 2012 (ratio of 1:1).

Overall, these results are rather surprising. They disprove the hypothesis presented here that neither state nor economic interests are expected to dominate. Instead, we find evidence that economic interests dominated. The remainder of this section explores the extent to which the results from the quantitative and qualitative analyses corroborate one another.

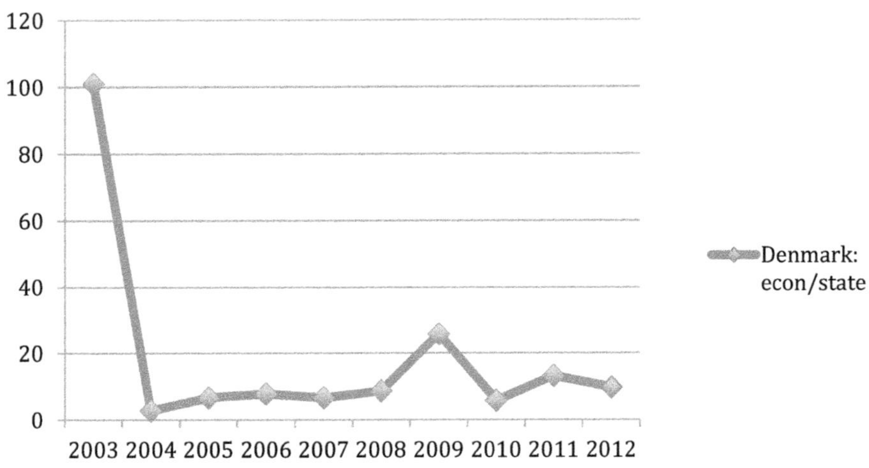

Figure 8.4.3 Ratio of economic interests to state interests

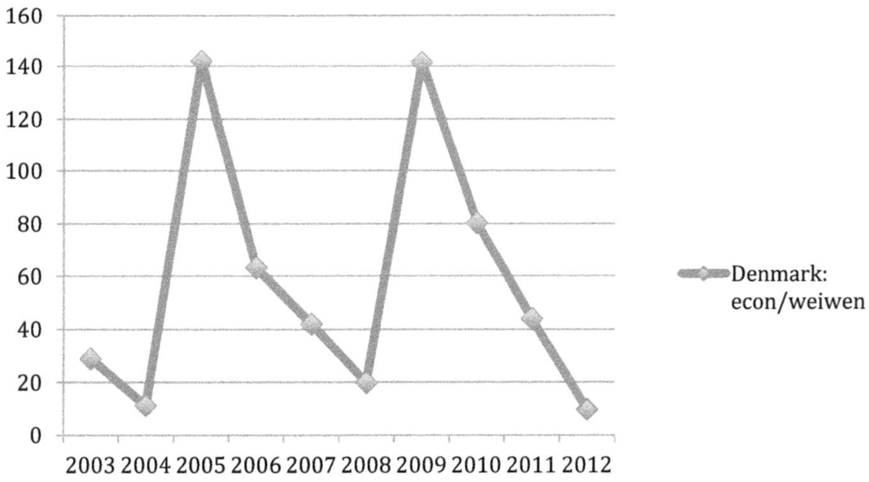

Figure 8.4.4 Ratio of economic interest to domestic stability

Qualitative analysis

The following focuses on two key decisions, the study of which is intended to illuminate important aspects of the activities of Chinese companies in Denmark and their possible impact on Chinese foreign policy. As there are no Chinese energy companies operating in Denmark, the material does not allow for analysis of a third key decision. While the lack of a third key decision creates a certain level of

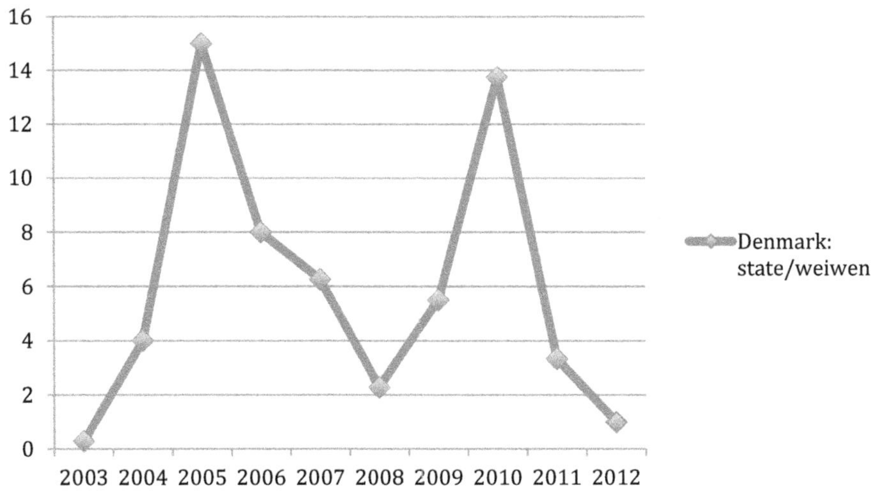

Figure 8.4.5 Ratio of state interests to domestic stability

asymmetry compared to the other mini-cases, it is hardly surprising in light of the fact that the mini-case about Denmark is selected on the grounds that there is little oil and little strategic importance attributed to Denmark. The key decisions are, first, the diplomatic crisis between Denmark and China in May 2009 and, second, China becoming a permanent observer of the Arctic Council in 2013. They have been selected to allow for analysis over time. One might also have focused on Husky Oil's acquisitions in 2007 or London Mining's Isua project in Greenland in 2012, but as Husky Oil is not a Chinese NOC and London Mining is not involved in the oil sector in Greenland, these were not selected for analysis here.[124] The two key decisions under discussion are the most significant and representative in terms of the activities of Chinese companies in Denmark over the last decade, the analysis of which will help us understand if Chinese foreign policy toward Denmark is dominated by state interests, economic interests, or concerns with domestic stability (*weiwen*).

Key Decision 1: May 2009 diplomatic crisis

In 2009, there was a diplomatic crisis after Danish PM Lars Løkke Rasmussen met with the Dalai Lama on May 29 of that year at the PM's official residence, Marienborg. This meeting triggered protests from China, meetings with Danish ministers were cancelled, and the Chinese leadership ultimately suspended relations with Denmark. Here, we examine the decision made by the Chinese leadership to sever relations with Denmark in 2009 and whether it reflects economic interests, state interests, or concerns with domestic stability (*weiwen*).

Meeting with Dalai Lama, 2009

On May 29, 2009, then PM Lars Løkke Rasmussen, met with the Dalai Lama at the PM's official residence, Marienborg. According to several accounts, the meeting resulted in a "freeze" in the relations between the two countries from May to December 2009.[125] What was the process leading up to this "freeze" of relations?

Prior to the Danish PM's meeting with the Dalai Lama in 2009, the Chinese leadership had issued numerous warnings to the Danish leadership. And the Danish leadership could see what had happened to other European leaders who had met with the Dalai Lama. For example, when French President Nicolas Sarkozy met with him in November 2008, China canceled the upcoming EU-China summit, resulting in a serious crisis in French-Chinese relations. Relations were first repaired on April 1, 2009, when the French "seriously kowtowed."[126]

Second, there were direct warnings in terms of various statements made by Chinese leaders prior to the Dalai Lama's visit; in May 2009, Chinese Foreign Minister Yang Jiechi issued an "open warning" to the Danish leadership not to meet with the Dalai Lama.[127] On May 15, the Chinese ambassador to Denmark stated that "[t]he Dalai Lama has separatist behavior. . . . Thus, for him to be received in a Danish official formal meeting shows contempt for the Chinese regime."[128]

PM Rasmussen then met the Dalai Lama on May 29. Rasmussen pointed out that it was not a "political meeting" but instead an "unofficial private meeting," as the two only met in a private capacity.[129] Even if the Danish PM met with the Dalai Lama, the Danish PM assured that Danish policy toward China remained unchanged: Denmark still recognized that Tibet is part of China.

How did the Chinese leadership subsequently respond to the meeting? Serious protests were issued from the Chinese mainland, which "brought the relationship between China and Denmark into a state of tension."[130] A Chinese academic article mentions how, despite having established a strategic partnership in 2008, China and Denmark have political problems because of "the problem with the Dalai Lama."[131]

In fact, China suspended ties with Denmark.[132] Relations were first resumed after the Danish government issued a *note verbale* (public statement) on December 12, 2009.[133] Moreover, China cancelled all of the meetings between ministers of the two parties in the period from May 29 until the *note verbale* was issued on December 12.

However, the meeting also had an economic face in the shape of a financial loss of DKK 1.5–2 billion in lost business contracts.[134] Moreover, a number of Danish companies, such as Carlsberg, experienced that the approval of their projects by Chinese authorities was delayed for months, resulting in further economic losses.[135] Thus, in addition to a political crisis, the meeting resulted in significant economic losses.

State interests

According to the *note verbale*, Denmark "opposes Tibetan independence."[136] It states that "Denmark reaffirms its One-China Policy and its unchanged position that

Tibet is an integral part of China."[137] By issuing this statement, the Danish government recognized the one-China policy, stated its opposition to Tibetan independence, and assured that it will not invite the Dalai Lama again before first asking for the views of the Chinese government. Subsequently, relations were normalized.[138]

The Dalai Lama is important to the Chinese leadership, as according to Chinese Foreign Ministry Spokeswoman Hua Chunying, the "Tibet issue involves China's core interests and national feelings. The Dalai Lama . . . has been engaged in splitting China and undermines China's national unity and international activities."[139] Thus, for other countries' state leaders to meet with the Dalai Lama is perceived as a way of interfering in China's domestic affairs, a way of "splitting China," which triggers domestic instability.

Conclusion, Key Decision 1

Here, we have seen how China's concern about outside interference in what its leadership considers their domestic affairs led the leadership to take concrete steps, which, in turn, affected China's relations with Denmark, even to the point of incurring economic losses. However, it can be observed that the economic loss was possibly felt more severely by the Danish side than the Chinese, as China was one of the only countries in the world to remain relatively unaffected by the financial crisis and, thus, was an attractive business partner.

This key decision thus provides evidence of state interests, as, despite financial losses, the Chinese state leaders decided to suspend ties with Denmark.

How does the analysis here compare to the quantitative analysis? The quantitative analysis shows that economic interests dominated in 2009 relative to state interests/concerns with domestic stability (ratio of 21.8:1). In fact, economic interests dominated much more strongly relatively in 2009 compared to 2008 (ratio of 6.1:1) and 2010 (ratio of 5.4:1). Thus, the results from the quantitative analysis are not consistent with those from the qualitative analysis.

Since there will always be some divergence between different types of evidence, the question becomes whether they are in *overall* agreement. Still, while there is evidence of economic interests here, since both countries are motivated by bilateral trade, this instance shows that when other state leaders meet with the Dalai Lama, the implications of such meetings for Chinese domestic stability are considered more significant to the Chinese leadership than short-term economic interests. Thus, examining the overall evidence, evidence of state interests is more credible.

Key Decision 2: the Arctic Council, 2013

Here, we study the key decision whereby China obtained permanent observer status in the Arctic Council in 2013. China first applied for such status in April 2007.

The Arctic Council is the most important regional governance regime with regard to the Arctic region.[140] Importantly, the Arctic Council is not an international organization with a firm legal charter but rather an international forum designed to foster cooperation and collaboration on Arctic issues.[141]

While China has been an *ad hoc* observer[142] at Arctic Council meetings since 2007, both at council meetings in April 2007 and 2009, China applied to become a *permanent* observer of the Arctic Council rather than merely an ad hoc observer. At both of these meetings, however, the decision to allow new permanent observers to the Arctic Council had been postponed.

State interests

Why was the Chinese leadership interested in becoming a permanent observer of the Arctic Council? Permanent observers are automatically invited to Arctic Council activities and meetings and can contribute to working groups. In contrast, *ad hoc* observers must wait for an invitation. Still, as neither permanent nor *ad hoc* observers have the right to vote, neither has any influence on the decision-making process in ministerial meetings. It is worth noting that Chinese decision-makers consider the council to be the most important forum for governance and cooperation in the Arctic region.[143] Even if observer status does not give the right to vote, the perspective is that being a permanent observer can guarantee Beijing's "legitimate rights and activities in the region."[144] Two former assistant foreign ministers, Hu Zhengyue and Liu Zhenmin, publicly declared China's interest in observer status in the Arctic Council in 2009 and 2010, respectively.[145]

For China, the UN Convention on the Law of the Sea (UNCLOS) provisions constitute the legal basis for China's activities in the Arctic as the only existing law regulating maritime activities in the Arctic.[146] The Chinese leadership acknowledges that, as China does not border the Arctic Ocean, it has no sovereign rights in the region. Thus, under international law, China's rights in the Arctic are limited. Still, to the objections that China is not an Arctic state and thus should not be included in a forum (the Arctic Council) that focuses on Arctic issues, Chinese decision-makers have stated that despite not being an Arctic state and having no territory in the Arctic region, it is, however, a "near-Arctic state" and an "Arctic stakeholder."[147]

Finally, some Chinese scholars have stressed that the melting Arctic icecap has global, rather than only regional, implications. The argument here is that because environmental changes in the Arctic have an impact on the environment in China, the country should have a right to participate in the Arctic Council and other fora devoted to Arctic governance.[148]

Because the Chinese leadership regards the Arctic Council as the most important forum for governance and cooperation in the Arctic region, it is important for China to be part of this forum.

The process

What did the application by the Chinese leadership to become a permanent observer of the Arctic Council involve? At the 2009 meeting in Tromsø, Norway, the question of whether to admit new observers was postponed until 2011. At the 2011 meeting in Nuuk, Greenland, the decision was once again postponed until the 2013 meeting.

Prior to the 2013 meeting in Kiruna, Sweden, China was more successful than had been the case in 2007, as a number of countries now supported the Chinese bid, including Iceland, Denmark, and Sweden. Referring to China, Danish Foreign Minister Villy Søvndal stated that "Our opinion is that the countries which have a legitimate interest in discussing Arctic issues must be accepted as observers in the Arctic Council."[149] In November 2011, Danish Ambassador to China Friis Arne Petersen said that the "Danish government wants China to become an official observer of the Arctic Council."[150] Denmark even lobbied for China to receive permanent observer status, which can possibly be interpreted as an attempt at patching up relations after the 2009 diplomatic crisis.

Thus, at the ministerial meeting in May 2013, China was approved as a permanent observer of the Arctic Council.

Visits

Several visits were conducted to ensure the support of the Arctic Council member states for the Chinese observership bid: in 2005, then Prime Minister of Greenland Hans Enoksen visited China; in February 2012, Premier Wen Jiabao met with Canadian PM Harper in Beijing; in April 2012, Wen visited both Sweden and Iceland; and in June 2012, Chinese President Hu Jintao paid an official state visit to Denmark. This was the first visit to Denmark by a Chinese head of state, during which he met with Queen Margrethe and PM Helle Thorning-Schmidt. During the visit, 17 government agreements were signed in addition to deals worth more than $18 billion.[151] According to a Chinese language news article, the motive from the Danish side was to mend relations after PM Rasmussen had met with the Dalai Lama in 2009.[152] While the Arctic was not officially on the agenda for the visit, the question of China's bid to become a permanent observer to the Arctic Council was brought to the discussion by the Chinese delegation.[153] In fact, during this visit to Denmark, Hu Jintao brought up the matter of China becoming a permanent observer on the Arctic Council.[154] Subsequently, the Danish government did considerable diplomatic work for China to achieve this end.[155] Thus, given that the bid for Arctic Council observership was supported by the visit by Hu Jintao to Denmark, this key decision reflects state interests.

Economic interests

With the melting icecap, the Arctic region is becoming increasingly ice-free, which in turn results in increasingly navigable polar shipping routes. At the same time, the higher temperatures in the Arctic Ocean open up new fishing grounds. While being a permanent observer of the Arctic Council does not in itself have an impact on questions pertaining to shipping, fisheries, or access to resources, the general take among both Chinese policy-makers and Chinese academics is that there is such a link.

Thus, it is worth noting the implicit existence of a link between Arctic Council observer status and shipping lane access among Chinese scholars.[156] Similarly, Li Zhenfu, a scholar at Dalian Maritime University, has stated that access to the Arctic shipping routes is of utmost importance, urging the Chinese government to do more to assert China's Arctic interests.[157] As China is the largest trade nation in the world, the opening of Arctic sea lanes could cut Chinese transport costs significantly.

With respect to fishing, the Arctic region is also of economic importance to China, as the melting icecap will open new waters for fishing. Even if there is no direct link between Arctic Council observership and having influence on fisheries regulations, Chinese academics advocate that China should make every effort to ensure that it will be included in decisions pertaining to Arctic governance, including Arctic Council observership, so as to strengthen China's ability as a non-Arctic state to access Arctic fishing waters.[158]

Lastly, improving relations with the permanent Arctic Council members was attractive to China in order to gain access to the advanced Arctic technology possessed by most of these countries.[159] Thus, becoming a permanent observer of the Arctic Council is a possible means to gaining access to advanced technology, which is then evidence of economic interests.

*Domestic stability (*weiwen*)*

There is no evidence of the concern with domestic stability (*weiwen*). Given that there are very few Chinese workers in Denmark, including Greenland, there is no evidence that the safety of Chinese workers has any effect domestically in China or for the bid to become a permanent observer of the Arctic Council.

Conclusion, Key Decision 2

This key decision is evidence of economic interests, as gaining permanent observer status on the Arctic Council is about gaining access to Arctic shipping routes, fishing, access to natural resources, and access to technology. It is a way for Chinese companies to earn profits. At the same time, there was evidence of state interests, as Hu Jintao travelled to Denmark and brought up the question of Arctic Council observer status, even if no credit lines were offered. Chinese decision-makers consider the Arctic Council to be the main venue when considering Arctic affairs. Given the current inadequate legal framework in the Arctic region, Arctic Council observer status would grant access to information about regional affairs to China. The forum is about prestige, and China wants to be part of a forum of the great Arctic powers, which includes both the United States and Russia, and to be recognized there as an equal. Still, even if the pursuit of permanent observer status provides evidence of some state interests, when considering the overall evidence, as it relates to access to profits related to access to resources, fishing, and shipping lanes, this key decision reflects economic interests.

How does the analysis here compare to the quantitative analysis? It is worth noting that the quantitative analysis is limited to the period 2002–12 and does not cover 2013. Nevertheless, when China was bidding for Arctic Council observer status in 2012, the results from the quantitative analysis reveal a dominance of economic interests relative to state interests and concerns with domestic stability (ratio of 4.9:1). The results from the quantitative and the qualitative analyses are therefore consistent.

Conclusion

The expectation in the case of Denmark was that Chinese companies have little incentive to become involved because of the limited amounts of available oil and, as the Chinese government attributes little strategic importance to Denmark, it will not seek to pursue its economic interests there. For this reason, the empirical expectation is that neither state nor economic interests will dominate in the case of Denmark.

Overall, the quantitative analysis provides evidence of economic interests. It should, however, be noted that the quantitative findings for Denmark are rather unstable, as they are based on a mere 78 media articles. But this is a fact determined by the nature of the evidence.

The qualitative analysis shows that the suspension of diplomatic ties between China and Denmark in 2009 provides evidence of state interests, and the decision to obtain permanent observer status in the Arctic Council in May 2013 is a case of economic interests.

The results from the quantitative and qualitative analyses are corroborated except in the case of the 2009 diplomatic crisis. Still, when considering the evidence, state interests appear more credible.

The empirical expectation is thus supported by the quantitative and qualitative analyses, as there is evidence of both state and economic interests.

Notes

1 These mini-cases have been shortened from the original version in my PhD dissertation. For the complete version of these mini-cases, see T. Kasandra Behrndt-Eriksen, "Chinese Energy Companies' Acquisitions Abroad" (PhD diss., University of Copenhagen, 2016).
2 Sebastian Peyrouse, "The Economic Aspects of Chinese – Central Asia Rapprochement," Silk Road Paper, September 2007, Central Asia Caucasus Institute, Silk Road Studies Program.
3 Peyrouse, "The Economic Aspects of Chinese – Central Asia Rapprochement."
4 Guangcheng Xing, "China and Central Asia," in *Central Asian Security: The New International Context*, eds. Ron Allison and Lena Jonson (London, UK and Washington, DC: Royal Institute of International Affairs and Brookings Institution Press, 2001), 152–72.
5 Li Xiangyang [李向阳]. 中国钢管进入俄罗斯泰纳线 ["Chinese Steel-pipeline Enters Russia's 'Taina Line'"], *中国石油报 (China Petroleum Report),* June 4, 2007).

For more, see *Xinhua News Agency*, "Kazakhstan Oil Piped into China," May 25, 2006.

6 Marlene Laruelle and Sebastian Peyrouse, *The Chinese Question in Central Asia: Domestic Order, Social Change and the Chinese Factor* (London: Hurst & Co, 2012), 69; Xing, "China and Central Asia," 156.

7 Set up in Hong Kong in 1979 by former vice president Rong Yiren as the government's main overseas investment arm, the Citic Group is one of China's biggest conglomerates.

8 *China National Petroleum Corporation Yearbook 2010* [中国石油天然气集团公司年鉴], Beijing: 石油工业出版社 (Petroleum Industry Press), 137; China National Petroleum Corporation (CNPC), "CNPC in Kazakhstan," accessed December 15, 2015, www.cnpc.com.cn/en/Kazakhstan/country_index.shtml, www.cnpc.com/cn/en/Kazakhstan/country_indix.html; *China National Petroleum Corporation Yearbook 2006* [中国石油天然气集团公司年鉴] (Beijing: 石油工业出版社 Petroleum Industry Press), 182; *GOV.cn*, "CITIC to acquire Kazakhstan oil assets from Canada's Nations Energy," October 27, 2006, accessed December 15, 2015, www.gov.cn/english/chinatoday/2006-10/27/content_425766.html.

9 *U.S. EIA*, "China."

10 *U.S. EIA*, "Kazakhstan," accessed December 15, 2015, www.eia.gov/countries/country-data.cfm?fips=KZ&trk=m.

11 For more on the level of strategic importance of Kazakhstan, see: Behrndt-Eriksen, "Chinese Energy Companies' Acquisitions Abroad."

12 *U.S. EIA*, "Kazakhstan."

13 *U.S. EIA*, "Kazakhstan."

14 Didar Kassymova, Zhanat Kundakbayeva and Ustina Markus, *Historical Dictionary of Kazakhstan* (Lanham, MD: Scarecrow, 2012), 4.

15 *U.S. EIA*, "Kazakhstan."

16 Ryan Kennedy, "In the 'New Great Game', Who Is Getting Played? Chinese Investment in Kazakhstan's Petroleum Sector," in *Caspian Energy Politics: Azerbaijan, Kazakhstan and Turkmenistan*, eds. Indra Overland, Heidi Kjaernet and Andrea Kendall-Taylor (London: Routledge, 2010), 116–35, 128.

17 Michael Lee, "Kazakhstan"; UOB Kay Hian, CNOOC Ltd., *U.S. EIA*, March 28, 2003, 4.

18 Kennedy, "In the 'New Great Game,'" 128.

19 C. Khoo and D. Yu, "China National Offshore Oil Corporation," *UBS Warburg Asia*, May 12, 2003, 1–3.

20 *Stratfor Global Intelligence*, "Failed Sinopec Bid Follows in CNOOC's Footsteps," May 16, 2003, accessed December 15, 2015, www.stratfor.com/analysis/failed-sinopec-bid-follows-cnoocs-footsteps.

21 *Asia Pacific Foundation of Canada*, "Canada – Canada Asia Commentary," August 30, 2003, 9, accessed December 15, 2015, www.asiapacific.ca/sites/default/files/cac30.pdf.

22 Kennedy, "In the 'New Great Game,'" 128. A. Pulsihpher and M. Kaiser, "Business Environment Still Seen as Risky in Kazakhstan," *Oil & Gas Journal*, July 17, 2006.

23 *Reuters*, "China Buys into Kazakh Oilfield for $5 Billion," September 8, 2013.

24 C. Khoo and D. Yu, "China National Offshore Oil Corporation," *UBS Warburg Asia*, May 12, 2003, 1–3, 1.

25 Michael Lee, CNOOC Ltd., UOB Kay Hian, March 28, 2003.

26 *China Daily*, "Hu's Visit Seals Energy Deals," June 3, 2003.

27 *China Mergers and Acquisitions Yearbook 2008* [中国企业并购年鉴], 北京交通大学中国企业兼并重组研究中心编 (Beijing: Jiaotong University Research Center on Mergers and Acquisitions of Chinese Enterprises), 401.

28 *Financial Times*, "China Takes a Great Leap forward into Its Neighbour's Oil Business," August 23, 2005.

29 *Reuters*, "Lukoil Hopes to Settle PetroKaz Row with Buyer CNPC," October 28, 2005.

30 *Kazakhstan International Business Magazine*, "PetroKazakhstan Oil Products: On the Modernisation Trail!" 4 (2008).
31 Li Xiangyang [李向阳], 中国钢管进入俄罗斯泰纳线 ["Chinese Steel-pipeline Enters Russia's "Taina Line"].
32 *China National Petroleum Corporation Yearbook 2010* [中国石油天然气集团公司年鉴], Beijing: 石油工业出版社 (Petroleum Industry Press), 138.
33 *China Mergers and Acquisitions Yearbook 2008* [中国企业并购年鉴], 北京交通大学中国企业兼并重组研究中心编 (Beijing Jiaotong University Research Center on Mergers and Acquisitions of Chinese Enterprises), 401.
34 Consulate General of the People's Republic of China in San Francisco, "Hu Jintao Holds Talks with Nazarbayev and Announces the Establishment of the Strategic Partnership between China and Kazakhstan," July 4, 2005, accessed December 15, 2015, www.chinaconsulatesf.org/eng/xw/t202534.html.
35 Bruce Pannier, "China/Kazakhstan: Forces Hold First-Ever Joint Terrorism Exercises," *The Uyghur American Association*, August 24, 2006.
36 *Guardian*, "Police Officers Fire on Protesters in the Oil Town of Zhanaozen on the 20th Anniversary of Kazakhstan's Independence," December 16, 2011.
37 *Voltaire Network*, "China Believes Unrest in Kazakhstan Supported by External Forces," December 21, 2011, accessed December 15, 2015, www.voltairenet.org/China-believes-unrest-in.
38 Paul M. Evans, *Engaging China: Myth, Aspiration, and Strategy in Canadian Policy from Trudeau to Harper* (Utp Insights) (Toronto, ON: University of Toronto Press, 2014); Huhua Cao, *The China Challenge: Sino-Canadian Relations in the 21st Century* (Ottawa, ON: University of Ottawa Press, 2011).
39 *China National Petroleum Corporation Yearbook 1997* [中国石油天然气集团公司年鉴], Beijing: 石油工业出版社 (Petroleum Industry Press), 249; *China National Petroleum Corporation Yearbook* [中国石油天然气集团公司年鉴], Beijing: 石油工业出版社 (Petroleum Industry Press), 2011, 138.
40 *U.S. EIA*, "China."
41 China Commerce Yearbook 2003–2011 [中国商务年鉴], 北京:中国商务出版社 (Beijing, China: China Commerce and Trade Press).
42 *U.S. EIA*, "Canada," accessed December 15, 2015, www.eia.gov/countries/cab.cfm?fips=ca.
43 *U.S. EIA*, "Canada."
44 *U.S. EIA*, "Canada."
45 *U.S. EIA*, "Canada."
46 *U.S. EIA*, "Canada."
47 *U.S. EIA*, "Canada."
48 *U.S. EIA*, "Canada."
49 An alternative to the failed Encana deal in 2010/2011 would have been to include Sinopec's acquisition of Syncrude. However, as the Syncrude acquisition, like the Nexen acquisition, is in oil sands, I include the Encana deal, because it offers an insight into shale gas.
50 *The Canadian Press*, "Clement Approves PetroChina Purchase of Athabasca Oil Sands Properties," December 30, 2009.
51 *China National Petroleum Corporation Yearbook 2011* [中国石油天然气集团公司年鉴], (Beijing: 石油工业出版社 Petroleum Industry Press), 158.
52 *Xinhua News Agency,* "Canada's Athabasca to Sell Oilsand Stake to PetroChina," September 1, 2009.
53 J. Dziuba and R. Ollenberger, "Athabasca Oil," *BMO Capital Markets*, September 3, 2012, 5.
54 Baizhen Chua, "PetroChina Wins Approval for $1.8 Billion Acquisition," *Bloomberg,* December 30, 2009, accessed December 15, 2015, https://wikileaks.org/gifiles/docs/16/1634819_-fwd-b3-china-canada-energy-petrochina-wins-approval-for-1-8.html.

55 James Mahony, "Athabasca Oil Sands Prepared for Government Review of PetroChina Deal," *The Daily Oil Bulletin*, September 1, 2009.
56 Mahony, "Athabasca Oil Sands Prepared for Government Review of PetroChina Deal."
57 Jeff Meunier, "Athabasca Oil Sands Corp. – Initiating Coverage," *TD Newcrest,* May 19, 2010, 1–5.
58 Mahony, "Athabasca Oil Sands Prepared for Government Review of PetroChina Deal."
59 *Shanghai Municipal Government* [中国上海], "PetroChina Wins Projects Nod," December 31, 2009, accessed December 15, 2015, www.shanghai.gov.cn/shanghai/node17256/node18151/userobject22ai35849.html.
60 *China National Petroleum Corporation Yearbook 2010* [中国石油天然气集团公司年鉴], Beijing: 石油工业出版社 (Petroleum Industry Press), 138.
61 In China, oil sands is referred to as "heavy oil" (API 11–200) (Kang Wu, "China's Energy Security: Oil and gas," *Energy Policy* 73 (2014): 4–11); Li Kai [厉凯], Wang Min [王敏], Ge Guangtao [葛广涛], and Liu Wenmei [刘文梅]. 油砂资源及其开采工艺技术 ["Oil Sands and Mining Technology"], *科技信息) (Science and Technology Information)*, September 15, 2007; Wang Haibo [王海波], Li Dongdong [李冬冬], Yang Cheng [杨成], and Wang Jiandong [王建东]. 沥青砂油页岩的开发技术与应用 ["Development Technology and Application of Oil Shale"], 内蒙古石油化工 *(The Petrochemical Industry of Inner Mongolia)*, August 30, 2010.
62 Lu Xiangyi, [路相宜], 中石油掘金加拿大油砂 ["CNPC Digs the Canadian Oil Sands"], 中国石油石化 *[China Petroleum and Petrochemical Industry],* July 15, 2007. For more on the attractiveness of SAGS methods, see Shang Yanli [尚艳丽] and Peng Zhengxin [彭正新], 加拿大油砂资源开发的机遇与风险 ("Risks and Hazards of Canada's Oil Sands Exploration"), 国际石油经济 (*The International Petroleum Economy*), March 20, 2006.
63 Guo Dongliang [郭栋梁], 油砂时代 ("Age of Oil Sands"), 中国海关 (*China Customs*), March 10, 2011. Liu Hong [刘洪], 国际石油巨头关注油砂资源开采 ["International Oil Magnates Focus on Oil Sands Exploitation"], *中国税务报 (China Taxation News)*, October 18, 2006.
64 Interview with Chinese informant, 2012.
65 Lu Xiangyi [路相宜], 中石油掘金加拿大油砂 ["CNPC Digs the Canadian Oil Sands"], *中国石油石化 [China Petroleum and Petrochemical Industry],* July 15, 2007.
66 *Platts Oilgram News*, "Canada Faces Political Test over PetroChina Oil Sands Bid," September 8, 2009.
67 Yang Liqiang, [杨立强], 用责任和创新攻克超稠油开发难题 ["Using Responsibility and Innovation to Solve Problems in Heavy Oil Development"], 石油政工研究 [*Oil Lands Research*], March 30, 2010.
68 Yang Liqiang, [杨立强], 用责任和创新攻克超稠油开发难题 ["Using Responsibility and Innovation to Solve Problems in Heavy Oil Development"], 石油政工研究 [*Oil Lands Research*], March 30, 2010.
69 Bernard Simon and Leslie Hook, "Shale Gas Deal Collapses," *Financial Times*, June 22, 2011.
70 *China National Petroleum Corporation (CNPC)*, "PetroChina to Acquire 50 Percent Interest in Encana's Cutbank Ridge Business Assets for C$5.4 Billion," February 10, 2011, accessed December 15, 2015, www.cnpc.com.cn/en/nr2011/201409/67a18d134 95a48e3a80b6faf1a7cd71d.html; *Reuters*, "UPDATE 4-Encana, PetroChina take $2.2 bln. Stab at Joint Venture," December 13, 2012.
71 Brian Dutton, J. Frew and C. Morris, "Encana Corp," April 13, 2010, *Credit Suisse*, April 13, 2010, 1–6; Thomas Driscoll, "Encana Corp," *Barclays,* April 14, 2010, 1–13.
72 *Ministry of Foreign Affairs of the People's Republic of China*, "Promote the All-round Development of the China–Canada Strategic Partnership," June 25, 2010,

accessed December 15, 2015, www.fmprc.gov.cn/mfa_eng/topics_665678/hjtfwjnd4thG20_665786/t712797.html.

73 *Shanghai Municipal Government* [中国上海], "PetroChina Wins Projects Nod," December 31, 2009, www.shanghai.gov.cn/shanghai/node17256/node18151/userobject22ai35849.html.

74 Bernard Simon and Leslie Hook, "Shale Gas Deal Collapses," *Financial Times*, June 22, 2011.

75 Simon and Hook, "PetroChina Shale Gas Deal Collapses."

76 *Stocks and Bonds*, [证券之星],中石油放弃加拿大54亿美元页岩气项目("CNPC Abandons the Canada $5.4 Billion Shale Gas Project"), June 2, 2011, accessed December 15, 2015, http://stock.stockstar.com/SN2011062300000216.shtml.

77 *U.S. EIA*, "Natural Gas," accessed December 15, 2015, www.eia.gov/dnav/ng/hist/rngwhhdd.html; *MIT Study on the Future of Natural Gas*, "Appendix2D: ShaleGas EconomicSensitivities," accessed December 15, 2015, https://mitei.mit.edu/system/files/NaturalGas_Appendix2D.pdf.

78 From June 25, 2010, until the following day on the stock exchange, the PetroChina share price increased by 2.60%, the Sinopec share price was the same, and the CNOOC share price increased by 2.52% (Behrndt-Eriksen, "Chinese Energy Companies' Acquisitions Abroad," 277).

79 *Standard Chartered*, "CNOOC – Nexen Acquisition Is Credit Negative," July 24, 2012, accessed December 15, 2015, https://research.standardchartered.com/configuration/ROW%20Documents/CNOOC_ – _Nexen_acquisition_is_credit_negative__24_07_12_06_43.pdf.

80 Stilkeman Elliot, "Investment Canada Act: SOE Guidelines and CNOOC/Nexen," December 17, 2012, accessed December 15, 2015, www.stikeman.com/cps/rde/xchg/se-fr/hs.xsl/17141.html.

81 *Standard Chartered*, "CNOOC-Nexen Acquisition."

82 Interview with Chinese informant, 2014.

83 Interview with Chinese informant, 2014.

84 Thomas Driscoll, I. Krasetva, and J. Feng, "Nexen Inc – Downgrading NXY Reflecting Limited Upside," *Barclays*, August 30, 2012, 1–7.

85 Zhang Yiming, [张一鸣], 中国三大石油公司瞄上加拿大 ("China's Three Major Oil Companies Took Aim at Canada), July 30, 2012.

86 Charlie Zhu and Bill Powell, "Special Report: The Education of China's oil Company," *Reuters*, October 6, 2013.

87 Elizabeth Wishnick, "Growing U.S. Security Interests in Central Asia," *The Strategic Studies Institute*, October 2002, accessed December 15, 2015, www.strategicstudiesinstitute.army.mil/pdffiles/PUB110.pdf.

88 BBC, "Uzbekistan to Supply 3bn cu.m. of Gas to Kazakh South Annually," November 28, 2012.

89 *U.S. EIA*, "Uzbekistan," accessed December 15, 2015, www.eia.gov/beta/international/analysis.cfm?iso=UZB.

90 *BBC*, "Experts Say Uzbekistan's Reliance on Oil Import to Increase," Oct. 22, 2009.

91 *U.S. EIA*, "Uzbekistan."

92 *U.S. EIA*, "Uzbekistan."

93 An anonymous reviewer argued that the analysis here seems to focus mostly on oil while the key importance of Uzbekistan lies in its gas reserves. Moreover, an additional advantage of building the pipeline across Uzbekistan is that CNPC's gas from that country can feed into the pipeline. While it is true that the analysis could place greater emphasis on Uzbekistan's gas reserves, for the simplicity of the argument, I keep it the way it is done.

94 During the 2004 visit, it was also announced that the SCO center, RATS, will be based in Tashkent (Laruelle and Peyrouse, *The Chinese Question in Central Asia*, 78; *BBC*, "Uzbekistan, China Sign Economic, Cultural, Partnership Accords," June 16, 2004.

95 *BBC*, “Chinese Energy Giant to Prospect for Oil in Uzbekistan,” June 26, 2006.
96 *Oil & Gas Journal*, “Uzbekistan, Oil Firms Ink PSA for Aral Sea Section,” December 2, 2007.
97 *Xinhua News Agency*, “CNPC to Tap Oil and Natural Gas in Uzbekistan,” September 3, 2006.
98 *Xinhua News Agency*, “China to Offer Uzbekistan $397 Million in Export Buyer’s Credit,” June 10, 2006.
99 *Xinhua News Agency*, “China, Uzbekistan Sign Documents to Cement Cooperation,” June 16, 2004.
100 Prior to 2002, there were two incidents: first, in 1997 unnamed militants were behind a series of killings of officials in the Fergana Valley of Uzbekistan. Second, on February 16, 1999, IMU was behind bombings in Tashkent with 19 people killed and more than 100 wounded. (Vyacheslav Belokrenitsky, “Islamic Radicalism in Central Asia: The Influence of Pakistan and Afghanistan,” in *Central Asia at the End of the Transition*, ed. Boris Rumer (Armonk, NY: M.E. Sharpe, 2005), 152–94, ft. 51).
101 On May 12, 2005, a group stormed a prison in the eastern town of Andijon, where those on trial were held, and released hundreds of inmates. Subsequently, these people joined others in storming government buildings. Uzbek troops fired on the demonstrators. The protestors had gathered to demand the end of a trial of local businessmen charged with belonging to an Islamic terrorist group (Jim Nichol, “Unrest in Uzbekistan: Context and Implications,” *CRS Report for Congress*, June 8, 2005, 2; Adeep Khalid, *Islam After Communism: Religion and Politics* [Berkeley, CA: University of California Press, 2007], 155).
102 According to human rights activists, up to 750 people were killed, and eyewitnesses said that Uzbek troops used weapons against the crowd in Andijon (*Moscow Times*, “Joining Forces in Central Asia,” May 26, 2005).
103 *AP*, “China, Russia-Led Alliance Wants Date for U.S. Pullout,” July 5, 2005.
104 *BBC*, “Uzbekistan to Obtain 35m-dollar Chinese Loan to Upgrade Gas Pipeline Network,” July 8, 2005; Martin C. Spechler, *The Political Economy of Reform in Central Asia: Uzbekistan under Authoritarianism* (London: Routledge, 2008), 115.
105 Shortly after Karimov’s visit to Beijing, at the Astana Summit in 2005, the objectives of the SCO were modified. It was agreed that “non-interference in the domestic affairs of sovereign countries” was a top priority for the SCO, and coordination against what was now qualified by the whole SCO as the “three evils” (separatism, extremism, and terrorism) was strengthened. This was an indirect message to the United States that its military base was unwelcome (*China Daily*, “Declaration of Heads of Member States of SCO,” July 6, 2005).
106 Chris Buckley, “China Opens Arms to Uzbek Chief, Beijing Endorses Bloody Crackdown,” *International Herald Tribune*, May 26, 2005.
107 *Platts Oilgram News*, “China Works on Receiving Point for Central Asia Gas,” July 29, 2008.
108 *BBC*, “Construction of Uzbek Segment of Gas Pipeline to China Enters ‘Active Phase,’” January 7, 2009.
109 *Platts Oilgram News*, “Favors Tight Gas over Shale,” March 25, 2013.
110 *Platts Oilgram News*, “Uzbekistan, China Sign Deal to Build Gas Pipeline,” May 3, 2007.
111 Peyrouse, “The Economic Aspects of Chinese – Central Asia Rapprochement.” *Petroleum Economist*, “Uzbekistan Targets Chinese Gas Market,” June 2011; China *National Petroleum Corporation Yearbook* [中国石油天然气集团公司年鉴] (Beijing: 石油工业出版社 Petroleum Industry Press, 2011), 166.
112 *Statsministeriet*, “Den grønlandske selvstyreordning,” accessed December 15, 2015, www.stm.dk/_a_2566.html; *Statsministeriet*, “Oversigt over sagsområder, der er overtaget af Grønlands hjemmestyre (I og II) henholdsvis Grønlands Selvstyre

(III)," accessed December 15, 2015, www.stm.dk/multimedia/Oversigt_sagsomr_der_241111.pdf.

113 Li Guoyu, *World Atlas of Oil and Gas Basins*: *Norway, Sweden, Finland, Denmark and Iceland* (Chichester, UK: John Wiley &Sons Ltd, 2011), 292–3.

114 *Danish Energy Agency*, "Oil and Gas Production in Denmark 2013 and Subsoil Use," June 2014, accessed December 15, 2015, www.ens.dk/sites/ens.dk/files/energistyrelsen/Nyheder/2014/oil_and_gas_production_in_denmark_2013_uk.pdf.

115 David R. Wilburn and K.A. Stanley, 2013, "Exploration Review Annual Review 2012," *Mining Engineering* 32 (65): 5.

116 It could be argued that the role played by Denmark in the Arctic region through its relationship to Greenland renders Denmark important to the Chinese leadership. Still, given the distance from Denmark to China and the fact that there are no ethnic ties between the countries, it is argued here that the "salience of territory" is relatively limited. Similarly, for the mini-case of Canada, the salience of the territory for China is limited, despite Canada's having territory in the Arctic.

117 *U.S. EIA*, "Denmark," accessed December 15, 2015, www.eia.gov/countries/country-data.cfm?fips=DA&trk=m.

118 *U.S. EIA*, "Denmark."

119 *U.S. EIA*, "Faroe Islands," accessed December 15, 2015, www.eia.gov/countries/country-data.cfm?fips=FO.

120 *U.S. EIA*, "Greenland," accessed December 15, 2015, www.eia.gov/countries/country-data.cfm?fips=GL&trk=m.

121 Slim Allagui, "Greenland Makes Oil Companies Melt," *Agence France-Presse*, July 16, 2006.

122 *U.S. EIA*, "Denmark."

123 *U.S. EIA*, "Greenland."

124 While Husky Oil, a private Hong Kong company, holds exploration rights in three licenses off the west coast of Disko Island, Greenland, Husky Oil is not an SOE, and there is no evidence that it has any links to the Chinese state (*Marketline*, "Husky Energy Inc – Strategy, SWOT and Corporate Finance Report Mergers & Acquisitions (M&A), Partnerships & Alliances and Investments," REFERENCE CODE: 31EFAD85-456A-48F7-967A-3BCBB8E5A025, August 2014, 21–2).

125 Clemens Stubbe Østergaard, "Danish-Chinese Relations: Continuity and Change 1949–2011," *Danish Foreign Policy Yearbook 2011*: 48–77, 67; *AFP*, "China, Denmark Sign Deals Worth Billions as Hu Ends Visit," June 16, 2012.

126 Østergaard, "Danish-Chinese Relations," 66–7; *Xinhua News Agency*, Full text: "Press Communique Between China and France," April 1, 2009, accessed December 15, 2015, www.china.org.cn/international/2009-04/01/content_17538757.html.

127 It is unclear on which day the warning was made (*Nanyang*, [南洋], 不理中国警告 丹麦首相盼5月会晤达赖 ["The Danish Prime Minister Ignores China's Warning and Hopes to Meet with the Dalai Lama in May"], March 20, 2009, accessed December 15, 2015, www.nanyang.com/node/165597?tid=459).

128 *Vision Times* [看中国], 中共驻丹麦大使恼极成羞, 首相要见达赖 ("The Chinese Ambassador in Denmark Is Angry that the Danish PM Will Meet with the Dalai Lama"), May 19, 2009, accessed December 15, 2015, http://m.secretchina.com/node/292773.

129 *Office of His Holiness the 14th Dalai Lama*, 丹麥首相拉斯穆森與達賴喇嘛尊者會面 ["Danish Prime Minister Anders Fogh Rasmussen met with the Dalai Lama"], May 30, 2009.

130 *Huanzhong* [还中网], 丹麥稱 政府官員不會與達賴喇嘛會面 ("Denmark Says that Danish Government Officials Will Not Meet with the Dalai Lama"), February 12, 2015, accessed December 15, 2015, www.huanzhongnet.com/article-13157-1.html.

131 Chen Zhimin [陈志敏] and Peng Zhongzhou [彭重周], 比较欧盟成员国与中国的关系发展:一项初步的尝试 ("Comparison of Different European Countries' Relations with China: A Preliminary Study), *欧洲研究 (European Research)* 20 (2), 2012: 7–29.

132 John Pomfret, "China's Strident Tone Raises Concerns among Western Governments, Analysts," *Washington Post,* January 31, 2010.

133 *Consulate General of People's Republic of China in Toronto*, 外交部发言人秦刚就丹麦政要会见达赖答记者问 ["Foreign Ministry Spokesman Qin Gang Answered Reporters' Questions concerning Danish Political Leaders' Meeting with Dalai Lama"], May 30, 2009, accessed December 15, 2015, http://toronto.china-consulate.org/chn//fyrthhz/fyrth/t565332.html.

134 Interview, Danish Foreign Ministry, 2015. This number is corroborated by looking at the numbers for the bilateral trade in that period. In 2008, bilateral trade was $8.17 bn. In 2009, it fell to $6.51 bn. In 2010, it increased to $7.83 bn, thus, a fall of $1.67 bn in 2009. (*National Bureau of Statistics of the People's Republic of China, China Statistical Yearbook*, Beijing: National Bureau of Statistics, 2003–2014).

135 Christina Boutrup, *Den røde løber: Kinas Fremmarch i Europa* [The red carpet: China's entry into Europe] (Copenhagen: Gyldendal, 2014), add page numbers.

136 Det Udenrigspolitiske Nævn 2009–10 UPN alm. del Bilag 24 [The Foreign Policy Committee 2009–10, doc. nr. 24]; Offentligt [Public], accessed December 15, 2015, www.ft.dk/samling/20091/almdel/upn/bilag/24/772818.pdf.

137 Interview, Danish Foreign Ministry, 2015. See also *Huanzhong* [还中网], 丹麥稱政府官員不會與達賴喇嘛會面 ("Denmark Says that Danish Government Officials Will Not Meet with the Dalai Lama"), February 12, 2015.

138 *Embassy of the Republic of China in the Kingdom of Denmark* [中华人民共和国驻丹麦王国大使馆], 中国驻丹麦大使谢杭生为旅丹华人举办新春招待会 ["The Chinese Ambassador to Denmark Xie Hangsheng held Chinese New Year's Reception at the Embassy for Chinese Citizens in Denmark"], February 11, 2010, accessed December 15, 2015, www.fmprc.gov.cn/ce/cedk/chn/lxdm/dtxx/t657643.html.

139 *FreeOz* [论坛], 不受丹麦领导人待见 达赖喇嘛自圆其说 ("Danish Leaders Will Not Meet with the Dalai Lama and Dalai Lama Justifies the Excuse"), February 13, 2015, accessed December 15, 2015, https://freeoz.org/ibbs/thread-1183402-1-1.html.

140 Established by the Declaration on the Establishment of the Arctic Council (Ottawa Declaration), September 19, 1996; inaugurated September 17, 1998.

141 Interview, Arctic Council, 2015.

142 These are also called "accredited observers." Here, I maintain the use of the term "permanent observer," as this term is used in most of the literature (as well as by the Chinese leadership).

143 Liu Zhenmin, Chinese Assistant Foreign Minister, "China's View on Arctic Cooperation," Speech, July 30, 2010, accessed December 15, 2015, www.fmprc.gov.cn/mfa_eng/wjb_663304/zzjg_663340/tyfls_665260/tfsxw_665262/t812046.html.

144 *Xinhua News Agency*, "Xinhua Insight: Arctic Council Observer Status Guarantees China's Legitimate Rights," May 16, 2013.

145 Ning Xiaoxiao [宁宵宵], '地球 未来的缩影 – 外交部部长助理谈北极研究之旅' ["A Microcosm of the World's Future – Assistant Foreign Minister talks about 'High North Study Tour'"], *Shijie Bolan* [世界博览] 19 (2009): 58; Liu Zhenmin, Chinese Assistant Foreign Minister, "China's View on Arctic Cooperation," Speech, Ministry of Foreign Affairs of the People's Republic of China, July 30, 2010, accessed December 15, 2015, www.fmprc.gov.cn/mfa_eng/wjb_663304/zzjg_663340/tyfls_665260/tfsxw_665262/t812046.html.

146 Importantly, the ultimate authority of UNCLOS is the UNSC, of which China is a member. It is the most comprehensive international legal framework for the governance of state activities on the world's oceans, including the Arctic Ocean (See Liu

Zhenmin, Chinese Assistant Foreign Minister, "China's View on Arctic Cooperation" speech).

147 Jin Shen [今参], 关于北极航道的开发前景 ["Perspectives on the Development of the Arctic Waterways"], *港口经济* (*Port Economy*), 12 (2011). Christoph Seidler, "The Resource Race: China Dips Toes in Arctic Waters," *Der Spiegel,* January 25, 2013.

148 Linda Jakobson and Jingchao Peng, "China's Arctic Aspirations," SIPRI Policy Paper, No. 34, November 2012; H. Liu, '中国可以在北极做什么' ["What Can China Do in the Arctic?], *Jingji Cankao Bao* [经济参考报], December 27, 2011. L. Jakobson and Syong-Hong Lee, "The North East Asian States' Interests in the Arctic and Possible Cooperation with the Kingdom of Denmark," Report prepared for the Ministry of Foreign Affairs of Denmark, April 2013, 4.

149 Alistair Macdonald and Ellen E. Jervell, "Arctic Body Weighs China's Bid," *Wall Street Journal,* May 14, 2013.

150 *Dushiwang* [都市网], 中评社 胡锦涛访丹麦 重视北欧地缘价值 ("Hu Jintao's Visit to Denmark Shows Northern Europe's Geopolitical Importance"), June 20, 2012.

151 *Xinhua News Agency [新华新闻],* "综述:中丹全面战略伙伴关系加速深化" ["Synopsis: China and Denmark's Comprehensive Strategic Partnership to Be Deepened"], September 18, 2012, accessed December 15, 2015, http://news.xinhuanet.com/world/2012-09/18/c_113119042.html.

152 *RFI* [世界之声], 胡锦涛将展开对丹麦的访问 ("Hu Jintao's Visit to Denmark to Begin"), December 6, 2012, accessed December 15, 2015, http://cn.rfi.fr/中国/20120612-胡锦涛将展开对丹麦的访问/.

153 Ming Ou Lü, *Sermitsiaq*, "Hu, Helle og Grønland var enige" [Hu, Helle, and Greenland agreed] *Sermitsiaq,* June 18, 2012; Interview, Danish Foreign Ministry, 2015.

154 Interview, Danish Foreign Ministry, 2015.

155 Interview, Danish Foreign Ministry, 2015.

156 Stephen Chen, "Landmark Decision Sees China Join Arctic Council as an Observer," *South China Morning Post*, May 19, 2013.

157 Li Zhenfu [李振福], 中国参与北极航线国际机制的障碍及对策 ["Obstacles to China's Participation in the International Arctic Route Mechanism and Countermeasures"], 中国航海 [*Zhongguo Hanghai]* 32 (2) (June 2009): 98–102.

158 *Research on Arctic Issues* [北极问题研究] (Beijing: Ocean Press [海洋出版社], June 1, 2011), 364.

159 Qu Jing [璩静] and Zhang Xudong [张旭东], '我国科考队踏上北极之旅 将首次穿越俄北方航道' ["Chinese Scientists Have Embarked on Another Arctic Expedition and Will Traverse the Northern Sea Route for the First Time in History"], *Xinhua News Agency*, July 2, 2012; Jakobson and Peng, "China's Arctic Aspirations," 10. Liu Jiaqi [刘嘉麒], 漫话地球两极 ["Conversation on the Two Poles"], *自然杂志 (Nature Magazine)* 2 (2006).

References

Agence France-Presse (*AFP*). "China, Denmark Sign Deals Worth Billions as Hu Ends Visit." June 16, 2012.

Allagui, Slim. "Greenland Makes Oil Companies Melt." *AFP*, July 16, 2006.

Asia Pacific Foundation of Canada. "Canada – Canada Asia Commentary." No. 30. August 2003. Accessed 12/15/2015. wwxw.asiapacific.ca/sites/default/files/cac30.pdf.

Associated Press. "China, Russia-Led Alliance Wants Date for U.S. Pullout." July 5, 2005.

BBC. "Chinese Energy Giant to Prospect for Oil in Uzbekistan." June 26, 2006.

BBC. "Construction of Uzbek Segment of Gas Pipeline to China Enters 'Active Phase'." January 7, 2009.

BBC. "Experts Say Uzbekistan's Reliance on Oil Import to Increase." October 22, 2009.

BBC. "Uzbekistan, China Sign Economic, Cultural, Partnership Accords." June 16, 2004.

BBC. "Uzbekistan to Obtain 35m-dollar Chinese Loan to Upgrade Gas Pipeline Network." July 8, 2005.

BBC. "Uzbekistan to Supply 3bn cu.m. of Gas to Kazakh South Annually." November 28, 2012.

Behrndt-Eriksen, T. Kasandra, "Chinese Energy Companies' Acquisitions Abroad. Implications for the Foreign Policy of an Authoritarian State." Ph.D. diss., University of Copenhagen, 2016.

Belokrenitsky, Vyacheslav. "Islamic Radicalism in Central Asia: The Influence of Pakistan and Afghanistan." In *Central Asia at the End of the Transition*, edited by Boris Rumer, 152–94. Armonk, NY: M.E. Sharpe, 2005.

Boutrup, Christina. *Den røde løber: Kinas Fremmarch i Europa [The red carpet: China's Entry into Europe]*. Copenhagen: Gyldendal, 2014.

Buckley, Chris. "China Opens Arms to Uzbek Chief; Beijing Endorses Bloody Crackdown." *International Herald Tribune*, May 26, 2005.

Cao, Huhua. *The China Challenge: Sino – Canadian Relations in the 21st Century*. Ottawa, CA: University of Ottawa Press, 2011.

The Canadian Press. "Clement approves PetroChina Purchase of Athabasca Oil Sands Properties." December 30, 2009.

Chen, Stephen. "Landmark Decision Sees China Join Arctic Council as an Observer." *South China Morning Post*, May 19, 2013.

Chen Zhimin [陈志敏] and Peng Zhongzhou [彭重周]. 比较欧盟成员国与中国的关系发展:一项初步的尝试 ("Comparison of different European Countries' Relations with China: A Preliminary Study"), *欧洲研究 (European Research)* 20 (2) (2012): 7–29.

China Commerce Yearbook [中国商务年鉴], 北京: 中国商务出版社 (Beijing: China Commerce and Trade Press, various years.

China Daily. "Declaration of Heads of Member States of SCO." July 6, 2005.

China Daily. "Hu's Visit Seals Energy Deals." June 3, 2003.

China Mergers and Acquisitions Yearbook [中国企业并购年鉴]. 北京交通大学中国企业兼并重组研究中心编 Beijing: Jiaotong University Research Center on Mergers and Acquisitions of Chinese Enterprises, various years.

China National Petroleum Corporation (CNPC). "CNPC in Kazakhstan." Accessed 12/15/2015. www.cnpc.com.cn/en/Kazakhstan/country_index.shtml.

China National Petroleum Corporation (CNPC). "PetroChina to Acquire 50 Percent Interest in Encana's Cutbank Ridge Business Assets for C$5.4 Billion." February 10, 2011. Accessed 12/15/2015. www.cnpc.com.cn/en/nr2011/201409/67a18d13495a48e3a80b6faf1a7cd71d.shtml.

China National Petroleum Corporation Yearbook [中国石油天然气集团公司年鉴]. Beijing: 石油工业出版社 Petroleum Industry Press, various years.

Chua, Baizhen. "PetroChina Wins Approval for $1.8 Billion Acquisition." *Bloomberg*, December 30, 2009. Accessed 12/15/2015. https://wikileaks.org/gifiles/docs/16/1634819_-fwd-b3-china-canada-energy-petrochina-wins-approval-for-1-8.html.

Consulate General of the People's Republic of China in San Francisco. "Hu Jintao Holds Talks with Nazarbayev and Announces the Establishment of Strategic Partnership Between China and Kazakhstan." July 4, 2005. Accessed 12/15/2015. www.chinaconsulatesf.org/eng/xw/t202534.html.

Consulate General of People's Republic of China in Toronto 外交部发言人秦刚就丹麦政要会见达赖答记者问 ("Foreign Ministry Spokesman Qin Gang Answered Reporters' Questions Concerning Danish Political Leaders' Meeting with Dalai Lama), May 30,

2009. Accessed 12/15/2015. http://toronto.china-consulate.org/chn//fyrthhz/fyrth/t565332.html.

Danish Energy Agency. "Oil and Gas Production in Denmark 2013 and Subsoil Use." June 2014. Accessed 12/15/2015. www.ens.dk/sites/ens.dk/files/energistyrelsen/Nyheder/2014/oil_and_gas_production_in_denmark_2013_uk.pdf.

Det Udenrigspolitiske Nævn 2009–10 UPN alm. del Bilag 24 [The Foreign Policy Committee 2009–10, doc. nr. 24]"; Offentligt [Public]. Accessed 12/15/2015. www.ft.dk/samling/20091/almdel/upn/bilag/24/772818.pdf.

Driscoll, Thomas. "Encana Corp." *Barclays*, April 14, 2010.

Driscoll, Thomas, I. Krasetva and J. Feng. "Nexen Inc. – Downgrading NXY Reflecting Limited Upside." *Barclays*, August 30, 2012.

Dushiwang [都市网]. 中评社 胡锦涛访丹麦 重视北欧地缘价值 ("Hu Jintao's Visit to Denmark Shows Northern Europe's Geopolitical Importance)), June 20 2012. Accessed 12/15/2015. www.dushi.ca/tor/news/bencandy.php/fid25/aid71548.

Dutton, Brian, J. Frew and C. Morris. "Encana Corp." *Credit Suisse*, April 13, 2010.

Dziuba, J. and R. Ollenberger. "Athabasca Oil." *BMO Capital Markets*, September 3, 2012.

Embassy of the Republic of China in the Kingdom of Denmark [中华人民共和国驻丹麦王国大使馆]. 中国驻丹麦大使谢杭生为旅丹华人举办新春招待会 ["The Chinese Ambassador to Denmark Xie Hangsheng Held Chinese New Year's Reception at the Embassy for Chinese Citizens in Denmark"). February 11, 2010. Accessed 12/15/2015. www.fmprc.gov.cn/ce/cedk/chn/lxdm/dtxx/t657643.html.

Evans, Peter M. *Engaging China: Myth, Aspiration, and Strategy in Canadian Policy from Trudeau to Harper* (Utp Insights). Toronto: University of Toronto Press, 2014.

Financial Times. "China Takes a Great Leap forward into Its Neighbour's Oil Business." August 23, 2005.

FreeOz [论坛]. 不受丹麦领导人待见 达赖喇嘛自圆其说 (Danish Leaders Will Not Meet with the Dalai Lama, and Dalai Lama Justifies the Excuse"). February 13, 2015. Accessed 12/15/2015. https://freeoz.org/ibbs/thread-1183402-1-1.html.

GOV.cn. "CITIC to Acquire Kazakhstan Oil Assets from Canada's Nations Energy." October 27, 2006. Accessed 12/15/2015. www.gov.cn/english/chinatoday/2006-10/27/content_425766.html.

The Guardian. "Police Officers Fire on Protesters in the Oil Town of Zhanaozen on the 20th Anniversary of Kazakhstan's Independence." December 16, 2011.

Guo Dongliang [郭栋梁]. 油砂时代 ("Oil Sands Age"). *中国海关 (The China Seas)*, March 10, 2011.

Huanzhong [还中网]. 丹麥稱 政府官員不會與達賴喇嘛會面 ("Denmark Says that Danish Government Officials Will Not Meet with the Dalai Lama). February 12, 2015. Accessed 12/15/2015. www.huanzhongnet.com/article-13157-1.html.

Jakobson, Linda and Syong-Hong Lee. "The North East Asian States' Interests in the Arctic and Possible Cooperation with the Kingdom of Denmark." Report prepared for the Ministry of Foreign Affairs of Denmark, April 2013.

Jakobson, Linda and Jingchao Peng. "China's Arctic Aspirations." Stockholm International Peace Research Institute (SIPRI) Policy Paper No. 34, November 2012.

Jin Shen [今参]. 关于北极航道的开发前景 ["Perspectives on the Development of the Arctic Waterways"]. *港口经济 (Port Economy)* (12) (2011).

Kassymova, Didar, Zhanat Kundakbayeva and Ustina Markus. *Historical Dictionary of Kazakhstan*. Lanham, MD: Scarecrow, 2012.

Kazakhstan International Business Magazine. "PetroKazakhstan Oil Products: On the Modernisation Trail!" (4) (2008).

Kennedy, Ryan. “In the ‘New Great Game’, Who Is Getting Played? Chinese Investment in Kazakhstan’s Petroleum Sector.” In *Caspian Energy Politics: Azerbaijan, Kazakhstan and Turkmenistan*, edited by Indra Overland, Heidi Kjaernet and Andrea Kendall-Taylor, 116–35. London: Routledge, 2010.

Khalid, Adeep. *Islam After Communism: Religion and Politics*. Berkeley, CA: University of California Press, 2007.

Khoo, C. and D. Yu. “China National Offshore Oil Corporation.” *UBS Warburg Asia*, May 12, 2003.

Laruelle, Marlene and Sebastian Peyrouse. *The Chinese Question in Central Asia: Domestic Order, Social Change and the Chinese Factor*. London: Hurst & Co, 2012.

Lee, Michael. “CNOOC Ltd.” *UOB Kay Hian*, March 28, 2003.

Li Guoyu. *World Atlas of Oil and Gas Basins: Norway, Sweden, Finland, Denmark and Iceland*. Chichester, UK: John Wiley & Sons, 2011.

Li Kai [厉凯], Wang Min [王敏], Ge Guangtao [葛广涛] and Liu Wenmei [刘文梅]. 油砂资源及其开采工艺技术 [“Oil Sands and Mining Technology”], *科技信息) (Science and Technology Information)*, September 15, 2007.

Li Xiangyang [李向阳]. 中国钢管进入俄罗斯泰纳线 [“Chinese Steel-pipeline Enters Russia’s ‘Taina line’”], *中国石油报 (China Petroleum Report)*, June 4, 2007.

Li, Zhenfu [李振福]. 中国参与北极航线国际机制的障碍及对策 [“Obstacles to China’s Participation in the International Arctic Route Mechanism and Countermeasures”], 中国航海 *[Zhongguo Hanghai]* 32 (2) (June 2009): 98–102.

Liu Hong. “中国可以在北极做什么” [“What can China do in the Arctic?”], Jingji Cankao Bao [经济参考报], December 27, 2011.

Liu Hong [刘洪]. 国际石油巨头关注油砂资源开采 [“International Oil Magnates Focus on Oil Sands Exploitation”], *中国税务报 (China Taxation News*), October 18, 2006.

Liu Jiaqi [刘嘉麒]. 漫话地球两极 [“Conversation on the Two Poles”]. *自然杂志 (Nature Magazine*) 2 (2006).

Liu Zhenmin. “China’s View on Arctic Cooperation.” Chinese Assistant Foreign Minister’s Speech, July 30, 2010. Ministry of Foreign Affairs of the People’s Republic of China. Accessed 12/15/2015. www.fmprc.gov.cn/mfa_eng/wjb_663304/zzjg_663340/tyfls_665260/tfsxw_665262/t812046.shtml.

Lü, Ming Ou. “Hu, Helle og Grønland var enige. [Hu, Helle and Greenland agreed].” *Sermitsiaq*, June 18, 2012. Accessed 12/15/2015, http://sermitsiaq.ag/node/129012.

Lu Xiangyi [路相宜]. 中石油掘金加拿大油砂 [“CNPC Digs the Canadian Oil Sands”]. 中国石油石化 *[China Petroleum and Petrochemical Industry]*, July 15 2007.

Macdonald, Alistair and Ellen E. Jervell. *The Wall Street Journal*. “Arctic Body Weighs China’s Bid.” *The Wall Street Journal*, May 14, 2013.

Mahony, James. “Athabasca Oil Sands Prepared For Government Review of PetroChina Deal.” *Daily Oil Bulletin*, September 1, 2009.

Marketline. “Husky Energy Inc – Mergers & Acquisitions (M&A), Partnerships & Alliances and Investments.” Reference Code: 31EFAD85-456A-48F7-967A-3BCBB8E5A025, August 2014.

Meunier, Jeff. “Athabasca Oil Sands Corp. – initiating Coverage.” *TD Newcrest*, May 19, 2010.

Ministry of Foreign Affairs of the People’s Republic of China. “Promote the All-round Development of the China – Canada Strategic Partnership.” June 25, 2010. Accessed 12/15/2015. www.fmprc.gov.cn/mfa_eng/topics_665678/hjtfwjnd4thG20_665786/t712797.shtml.

MIT Study on the Future of Natural Gas. “Appendix2D: Shale Gas Economic Sensitivities.” 2011. Accessed 12/15/2015. https://mitei.mit.edu/system/files/NaturalGas_Appendix2D.pdf.

Moscow Times. "Joining Forces in Central Asia." May 26, 2005.

Nanyang [南洋]. 不理中国警告 丹麦首相盼5月会晤达赖 ("The Danish Prime Minister Ignores China's Warning and Hopes to Meet with the Dalai Lama in May"). March 20, 2009. Accessed 12/15/2015. www.nanyang.com/node/165597?tid=459.

National Bureau of Statistics of the People's Republic of China. *China Statistical Yearbook*. Beijing: National Bureau of Statistics, various years.

Nichol, Jim. "Unrest in Uzbekistan: Context and Implications." CRS Report for Congress, June 8, 2005.

Ning, Xiaoxiao [宁宵宵]. 地球未来的缩影 – 外交部部长助理谈北极研究之旅 ["A Microcosm of the World's Future – Assistant Minister of Foreign Affairs talks about 'High North Study Tour'"], *Shijie Bolan* [[世界博览] 19 (2009).

Office of His Holiness the 14th Dalai Lama. 丹麥首相拉斯穆森與達賴喇嘛尊者會面 ("The Danish Prime Minister Anders Fogh Rasmussen Met with the Dalai Lama.") May 30, 2009. Accessed 12/15/2015. www.dalailamaworld.com/topic.php?t=434&sid=4b6c4728896cf48cfbf3aa34a2b01c44.

Oil & Gas Journal. "Uzbekistan, Oil Firms Ink PSA for Aral Sea Section." December 2, 2007.

Østergaard, Clemens S. "Danish – Chinese Relations: Continuity and Change 1949–2011." *Danish Foreign Policy Yearbook*, Dansk Institut for Internationale Studies (DIIS), 2011.

Pannier, Bruce. "China/Kazakhstan: Forces Hold First-Ever Joint Terrorism Exercises." The Uyghur American Association, August 24, 2006.

Peyrouse, Sebastian. "The Economic Aspects of Chinese – Central Asia Rapprochement." Silk Road Paper, September 2007, Central Asia Caucasus Institute, Silk Road Studies Program.

Platts Oilgram News. "Canada Faces Political Test over PetroChina Oil Sands Bid." September 8, 2009.

Platts Oilgram News. "China Works on Receiving Point for Central Asia Gas." July 29, 2008.

Platts Oilgram News. "PetroChina Favors Tight Gas Over Shale." March 25, 2013.

Platts Oilgram News. "Uzbekistan, China Sign Deal to Build Gas Pipeline." May 3, 2007.

Petroleum Economist. "Uzbekistan Targets Chinese Gas Market." June 2011.

Pomfret, John. "China's Strident Tone Raises Concerns Among Western Governments, Analysts." *The Washington Post*, January 31, 2010.

Pulsihpher, A. and M. Kaiser. "Business Environment Still Seen as Risky in Kazakhstan." *Oil & Gas Journal*, July 17, 2006.

Qu, Jing [璩静] and Zhang Xudong [张旭东.'我国科考队踏上北极之旅 将首次穿越俄北方航道' ["Chinese scientists Have Embarked on Another Arctic Expedition and Will Traverse the Northern Sea Route for the First Time in History."], *Xinhua*, July 2, 2012.

Research on Arctic Issues [北极问题研究]. Beijing: Ocean Press [海洋出版社], June 1, 2011.

Reuters. "China Buys into Kazakh Oilfield for $5 billion." September 8, 2013.

Reuters. "Lukoil Hopes to Settle PetroKaz Row with Buyer CNPC." October 28, 2005.

Reuters. "UPDATE 4-Encana, PetroChina take $2.2 bln Stab at Joint Venture." December 13, 2012.

RFI [世界之声], 胡锦涛将展开对丹麦的访问. ("Hu Jintao's Visit to Denmark to Begin"), December 6, 2012. Accessed 12/15/2015. http://cn.rfi.fr/中国/20120612-胡锦涛将展开对丹麦的访问/

Seidler, Christoph. "The Resource Race: China Dips Toes in Arctic Waters." *Der Spiegel*, January 25, 2013.

Shang Yanli [尚艳丽] and Peng Zhengxin [彭正新]. 加拿大油砂资源开发的机遇与风险 ("Risks and Hazards of Canada's Oil Sands Exploration"), *国际石油经济 (The International Petroleum Economy)*, March 20, 2006.

Shanghai Municipal Government [中国上海]. "PetroChina Wins Projects Nod." December 31, 2009. Accessed 12/15/2015. www.shanghai.gov.cn/shanghai/node17256/node18151/userobject22ai35849.html.

Simon, Bernard and Leslie Hook. "PetroChina Shale Gas Deal Collapses." *Financial Times*, June 22, 2011.

Spechler, Martin C. *The Political Economy of Reform in Central Asia: Uzbekistan under Authoritarianism*. London: Routledge, 2008.

Standard Chartered. "CNOOC- Nexen Acquisition Is Credit Negative." July 24, 2012. Accessed 12/15/2015. https://research.standardchartered.com/configuration/ROW%20Documents/CNOOC_–_Nexen_acquisition_is_credit_negative__24_07_12_06_43.pdf.

Statsministeriet [Prime Minister's Office]. "Den grønlandske selvstyreordning [Greenland's self-government agreement]." June 21, 2009. Accessed 12/15/2015. www.stm.dk/_a_2566.html.

Statsministeriet [Prime Minister's Office]. "Oversigt over sagsområder, der er overtaget af Grønlands hjemmestyre (I og II) henholdsvis Grønlands Selvstyre (III) [Areas governed by Greenland's home rule (I and II) and Greenland's government (III)]." Accessed 12/15/2015. www.stm.dk/multimedia/Oversigt_sagsomr_der_241111.pdf.

Stilkeman Elliot. "Investment Canada Act: SOE Guidelines and CNOOC/Nexen." December 17, 2012. Accessed 12/15/2015. www.stikeman.com/cps/rde/xchg/se-fr/hs.xsl/17141.html.

Stocks and Bonds [证券之星]. 中石油放弃加拿大54亿美元页岩气项目 ("CNPC Abandons the Canada $5.4 billion Shale Gas Project"). June 2, 2011. Accessed 12/15/2015. http://stock.stockstar.com/SN2011062300000216.shtml.

Stratfor Global Intelligence. "Failed Sinopec Bid Follows in CNOOC's Footsteps." May 16, 2003. Accessed 12/15/2015. www.stratfor.com/analysis/failed-sinopec-bid-follows-cnoocs-footsteps.

U.S. Energy Information Administration (EIA). "Canada." Accessed 12/15/2015. www.eia.gov/countries/cab.cfm?fips=ca.

U.S. EIA. "China." Accessed 12/15/2015. www.eia.gov/beta/international/analysis.cfm?iso=CHN.

U.S. EIA. "Denmark." Accessed 12/15/2015. www.eia.gov/countries/country-data.cfm?fips=DA&trk=m.

U.S. EIA. "Faroe Islands." Accessed 12/15/2015. www.eia.gov/countries/country-data.cfm?fips=FO.

U.S. EIA. "Greenland." Accessed 12/15/2015. www.eia.gov/countries/country-data.cfm?fips=GL&trk=m.

U.S. EIA. "Kazakhstan." Accessed 12/15/2015. www.eia.gov/countries/country-data.cfm?fips=KZ&trk=m.

U.S. EIA. "Natural Gas." Accessed 12/15/2015. www.eia.gov/dnav/ng/hist/rngwhhdd.html.

U.S. EIA. "Uzbekistan." Accessed 12/15/2015. www.eia.gov/beta/international/analysis.cfm?iso=UZB.

Vision Times [看中国]. 中共驻丹麦大使恼极成羞，首相要见达赖 ("The Chinese Ambassador in Denmark is Angry that the Danish PM will Meet with the Dalai Lama"), May 19, 2009. Accessed 12/15/2015. http://m.secretchina.com/node/292773.

Voltaire Network. "China Believes Unrest in Kazakhstan Supported by External Forces." December 21, 2011. Accessed 12/15/2015. www.voltairenet.org/China-believes-unrest-in.

Wang Haibo [王海波], Li Dongdong [李冬冬], Yang Cheng [杨成] and Wang Jiandong [王建东]. 沥青砂油页岩的开发技术与应用 ["Development Technology and Application of Oil Shale"]. *内蒙古石油化工* (The Petrochemical Industry of Inner Mongolia), August 30, 2010.

Wilburn, David R. and K.A. Stanley. "Exploration Review, Annual Review 2012." *Mining Engineering* 32 (2013) (65).

Wishnick, Elizabeth. "Growing U.S. Security Interests in Central Asia." *The Strategic Studies Institute*, October 2002. Accessed 12/15/2015. www.strategicstudiesinstitute.army.mil/pdffiles/PUB110.pdf.

Wu, Kang. "China's Energy Security: Oil and Gas." *Energy Policy* 73 (2014): 4–11.

Xing, Guangcheng. "China and Central Asia." In *Central Asian Security: The New International Context*, edited by Ron Allison and Lena Jonson, 152–72. London, UK and Washington, DC: Royal Institute of International Affairs and Brookings Institution Press, 2001.

Xinhua News Agency. "Canada's Athabasca to Sell Oils and Stake to PetroChina." September 1, 2009.

Xinhua News Agency. "CNPC to Tap Oil and Natural Gas in Uzbekistan." September 3, 2006.

Xinhua News Agency. "China to Offer Uzbekistan $397 Million in Export Buyer's Credit." June 10, 2006.

Xinhua News Agency. "China, Uzbekistan Sign Documents to Cement Cooperation." June 16, 2004.

Xinhua News Agency. "Full Text: Press Communique Between China and France." April 1, 2009. Accessed 12/15/2015. www.china.org.cn/international/2009-04/01/content_17538757.html.

Xinhua News Agency. "Kazakhstan Oil Piped into China." May 25, 2006.

Xinhua News Agency. "Xinhua Insight: Arctic Council Observer Status Guarantees China's Legitimate Rights." May 16, 2013.

Xinhua News Agency [新华新闻]. "综述:中丹全面战略伙伴关系加速深化" ["Synopsis: China and Denmark's Comprehensive Strategic Partnership to be Deepened"]. September 18, 2012. Accessed 12/15/2015. http://news.xinhuanet.com/world/2012-09/18/c_113119042.html.

Yang Liqiang [杨立强]. 用责任和创新攻克超稠油开发难题 [Using Responsibility and Innovation to solve Problems in Heavy Oil Development], 石油政工研究 [*Oil Lands Research*], March 30, 2010.

Zhang, Yiming. [张一鸣]. 中国三大石油公司瞄上加拿大 ("China's Three Major Oil Companies Took Aim at Canada"). July 30, 2012.

Zhu, Charlie and Bill Powell. "Special Report: The Education of China's Oil Company." *Reuters*, October 6, 2013.

9 Conclusion

This book is an effort to define, analyze, and test for the effects of domestic interest groups on Chinese foreign policy. It has sought to unpack the foreign policy of the authoritarian state. Little research has been done that goes into depth on the role of the NOCs and, in particular, their role in foreign policy. Little effort has been made to examine closely the role of NOCs in a manner that is falsifiable and from which researchers can make significant predictions about the effects of these domestic groups on foreign policy. While a claim has been made concerning the emergence of domestic interest groups and how this matters, it has never been tested. With the rise of China on the global scene and as the importance of the Chinese NOCs challenges existing explanations of state behavior, it is important to further explore the role of NOCs in foreign policy.

The claim here is that this increasing role for NOCs is a particular characteristic of the foreign policy of the authoritarian state. As noted, there have been few previous contributions regarding the characteristics of the foreign policy of authoritarian states. The study of authoritarian foreign policy is underdeveloped, the only theoretical work being that relating to audience cost. By contrast, my work adds to this limited body of literature by unpacking the foreign policy of the authoritarian state and examining how non-state actors possibly matter.

My research for this undertaking involved designing and executing a rigorous test of the importance of interest groups (SOEs) in foreign policy. The test focuses on the NOCs as a subgroup of SOEs. To carry out the test, I established a framework in which, depending on the oil reserves and the level of strategic importance to China of the country in question, I would expect SOEs to have an impact on foreign policy in relation to some countries but not others.

The general idea is that the relations between the government and companies in particular countries or regions are related to the amount of oil available and the level of strategic importance of the country (or region) to China. The central claim is that the country's oil reserves and the country's level of strategic importance to China explain whether economic interests, state interests, or concerns with domestic stability (*weiwen*) drive the corporate activities. Specifically, I examined whether the activities of Chinese companies in a number of countries reflect state interests, economic interests, or concerns with domestic stability.

Three hypotheses are presented: one speaks to state interests dominating, one speaks to SOE interests dominating, and the third speaks to the concern with domestic stability dominating. The hypothesis about state interests follows from the structural realist assumption about the relationship between companies and the state. The hypothesis is that even when SOEs interests are very strong, security interests dominate foreign policy. The hypothesis about economic interests is based on a perspective of companies as rational, profit-maximizing entities that pursue action after carrying out a means-ends calculus. The hypothesis is that even when security interests are strong, economic interests will dominate. The hypothesis about the concern with domestic stability (*weiwen*) is based on the perspective that the activities in the actual country are related to the CCP's concern with maintaining power. Here, it is important to consider the salience of the concern with domestic stability for the Chinese leadership.

I develop a framework according to which, depending on different values for the independent variable, that is, their level of oil and level of strategic importance, the SOEs in some countries have an impact on foreign policy while the SOEs in other countries do not. Thus, this project presents an explanatory model according to which the level of strategic importance and the level of the oil in the country condition which of the three hypotheses have an effect in the individual case. This project draws on these different explanatory dynamics.

I place particular emphasis on the argument that the separation of economic and state interests makes sense also in the Chinese case. For that reason, Chapter 3 provides the background for illustrating why companies can be thought of as entities that are separate from the political system in China. The chapter tells the story of the (flawed) reform process and the respective levers of control available to the companies and government. While it thus provides the reader with some context for understanding the domestic context of the activities of the Chinese NOCs abroad, at the same time, the tests of the hypotheses executed in this study already do that. I have assumed that the companies are independent, and, as I find variation across the cases, the results presented here in themselves speak to how it makes sense to operate with a separation of economic and state interests.

This book presents two central claims. First, the SOEs play a growing role in foreign policy. Second, this increasing role is a characteristic of the foreign policy of the authoritarian state.

The main cases

This study investigates the activities of Chinese energy companies in Africa. Four countries were selected – Nigeria, Angola, Sudan, and Tunisia – which vary maximally in terms of the two key independent variables: strategic importance and oil reserves. The findings suggest the following:

First, in Nigeria, the Chinese companies were expected to have an incentive to become involved because of the large quantities of available oil. At the same time, the Chinese government attributes strategic importance to Nigeria. In the case of Nigeria, we therefore expect both state and economic interests to be in play. This empirical expectation is supported by the qualitative results, as there is evidence of equal amounts of state and economic interests. In the case of the oil-for-infrastructure deal in 2006–07, state and economic interests coincided; in Sinopec's acquisition of Addax in 2009, economic interests dominated; and in the case of the 2012 killing of Chinese workers, economic interests dominated rather than as expected concerns with domestic stability. In contrast, the quantitative analysis reveals a dominance of economic interests over the course of the decade. Looking more closely at the case of the large oil-for-infrastructure agreement in 2006–07, given that there is evidence of strong economic interests in addition to evidence of strong state interests, the evidence that state and economic interests coincide is more credible. This means that the qualitative and quantitative analyses are in overall agreement. As the quantitative and qualitative analyses both produce evidence of state and economic interests, the preceding empirical expectation is supported.

Second, with respect to Angola, the Chinese companies were expected to have an incentive to become involved because of the large quantities of oil. As the Chinese government attributes little strategic importance to Angola, however, the state will not seek to pursue its interests there, and the companies will be in the driver's seat. In this case, we therefore expect economic interests to dominate. The qualitative analysis does not entirely confirm this empirical expectation: in the case of an Eximbank loan to Angola in 2004, state and economic interests coincided; in the case of the failed refinery deal in 2006–07, economic interests dominated; and in the failed attempt of Sinopec and CNOOC in 2009–10, state interests dominated. The quantitative analysis corroborates the results, except in the case of the Eximbank loan in 2004. Here, it is argued that the evidence that state and economic interests coincided is more credible, as there is also evidence of state interests in addition to economic interests. In summary, then, the two methods were corroborated in two of the three key decisions. Thus, the empirical expectation presented here is only partially supported, as the quantitative and qualitative analyses show evidence of both economic and state interests.

Third, in Sudan, Chinese companies were expected to have little incentive to become involved because of the limited quantities of available oil. At the same time, the Chinese government attributes strategic importance to Sudan. Therefore, the empirical expectation is that evidence of state interests will be found in this case. The qualitative analysis produced evidence of state interests and concerns with domestic stability, as well as economic interests, but with variation over time. The analysis shows that in the case of the 2006–08 foreign policy change, state interests dominated. In the case of the killed Chinese nationals in 2008, concerns with domestic stability dominated. Finally, in the case of the oil shutdown in 2012, economic interests dominated. Interestingly, I find particular evidence of the concern with domestic stability in 2008, which is a novel finding. The quantitative analysis corroborates these results in two of the key decisions but not in the case of the killed oil workers in 2008. Still, it is argued that the evidence of concerns with domestic stability is more credible in this instance. Summing up, generally speaking, the two methods were corroborated. The quantitative and qualitative analyses only partially support the empirical expectation, as the results show evidence of both economic interests and state interests/domestic stability (*weiwen*).

Fourth, in Tunisia, state and economic interests were expected to balance against one another. The quantitative analysis shows that, overall, economic interests dominated the decade. The qualitative analysis shows that economic interests dominated the Sinochem acquisition in 2003. In the CNPC acquisition in 2004, state and economic interests coincided, and economic interests dominated in the Tunisian Revolution in 2011. Comparing the results from the two methods, looking at the 2004 CNPC acquisition, the evidence of state and economic interests as coinciding is more credible. As the qualitative and quantitative analyses produce evidence of both state and economic interests, the empirical expectation is supported.

Overall, these results suggest that the respective empirical expectations regarding expected behavior are supported to some extent. The specific empirical expectations find support in the cases of Nigeria and Tunisia, whereas they are only partly supported in the cases of Angola and Sudan.

The African cases reveal variation in the activities found and confirm the general idea that government-business relations are related to the amount of oil available and the level of strategic importance. In countries of strategic importance to China – Sudan and Nigeria – the state is involved for state interests, that is, to ensure its security. Conversely, in countries of little strategic importance – Angola and Tunisia – the companies are freer to pursue their interests and go about their business irrespective of state interference. The results generally show that where there is a lot of oil – Nigeria and Angola – the companies are very interested in becoming involved, as there are large profits to be made.

The mini-cases

In addition to the main cases, this study included a number of mini-cases – Kazakhstan, Canada, Uzbekistan, and Denmark. The purpose of including these was to examine the extent to which the results found for Africa can travel across regions – that is, whether the conclusions are generalizable. The findings that appear suggest the following:

In Kazakhstan, the companies were expected to have an incentive to become involved because of the availability of large quantities of oil and the potential to make large profits. At the same time, the Chinese government attributes strategic importance to Kazakhstan. In the case of Kazakhstan, the empirical expectation is that evidence of both state and economic interests would be found. The quantitative analysis showed that economic interests dominated most years. The qualitative analysis here shows that the failure of CNOOC and Sinopec to acquire a stake in the Agip KCO international consortium provides evidence of economic interests. CNPC's acquisition of Petrokazakhstan in 2005 provides evidence of state interests. Finally, rather than the instances of ethnic separatism in Kazakhstan in 2011 being evidence of concerns with domestic stability, they provide evidence of economic interests. The results from the quantitative analysis corroborate the results from the qualitative analysis except in the cases of the failure of CNOOC and Sinopec to acquire a stake in the Agip KCO consortium and in the Petrokazakhstan acquisition.

Still, it is argued that, overall, the evidence for economic interests is more credible in the case of the Agip KCO consortium, and the evidence of state interests is more credible in the case of the Petrokazakhstan acquisition. The empirical expectation finds support, as the quantitative and qualitative analyses show evidence of both economic and state interests.

Second, in Canada, the companies were expected to have an incentive to become involved because of the large quantities of available oil. At the same time, the Chinese government attributes limited strategic importance to Canada. For this reason, economic interests were expected to dominate in the Canadian case. The qualitative analysis here reveals that economic interests dominated the PetroChina acquisition of AOSC, the case of the failed attempt to acquire Encana in 2010–11, and the case of the CNOOC acquisition of Nexen in 2012. The quantitative analysis also reveals a dominance of economic interests over the course of the period. Thus, the quantitative and qualitative analyses corroborate one another, and the empirical expectation finds support.

Third, in Uzbekistan, the companies were expected to have little incentive to become involved because of the limited quantities of available oil. At the same time, the government attributes strategic importance to the country. The empirical expectation is therefore that evidence of state interests will be found in the case of Uzbekistan. The qualitative analysis shows that CNPC's acquisitions in Uzbekistan in the period 2004–06 produce evidence of state interests (for 2006), the Chinese support of Uzbekistan following the crackdown in 2005 shows evidence of economic interests, and state interests dominated the 2007 decision to build a pipeline through Uzbekistan. The quantitative analysis corroborates these results except in the case of the Uzbekistan pipeline decision. Still, looking more closely, the evidence for state interests is more credible in this instance. Thus, the quantitative and qualitative analyses partially support the empirical expectation presented earlier.

Fourth, in Denmark, the Chinese companies were expected to have little incentive to become involved because of the limited amounts of available oil. And as the Chinese government attributes little strategic importance to Denmark, the state will not seek to pursue its economic interests there. The empirical expectation is therefore that, in the case of Denmark, we will expect neither state nor economic interests to dominate. Generally speaking, the quantitative analysis provides evidence of economic interests. It is worth noting that the quantitative findings for Denmark are rather unstable, as they are based on a mere 78 media articles. But this is a fact determined by the nature of the evidence. The qualitative analysis shows how the suspension of diplomatic ties between China and Denmark in 2009 provides evidence of state interests, and the decision to obtain permanent observer status in the Arctic Council in May 2013 was a case of economic interests. The results from the quantitative and qualitative analysis are corroborated, except in the case of the 2009 diplomatic crisis. Still, when considering the evidence, the evidence of state interests is more credible. The empirical expectation is supported by the quantitative and qualitative analyses, as they both produce evidence of state and economic interests.

The following table, table 9.1, shows the results for the eight case countries.

Table 9.1 Results for the eight case countries

	Empirical expectation	*Key Dec. 1*	*Key Dec. 2*	*Key Dec. 3*	*Results*
Nigeria	Both state and econ. int.	Quan.: econ. int. Qual.: state and econ. int. Overall: state and econ. int.	Quan.: econ. int. Qual.: econ. int. Overall: econ. int.	Quan.: econ. int. Qual.: econ. int. Overall: econ. int.	Supported
Angola	Econ. int.	Quan.: econ. int. Qual.: state and econ. int. Overall: state and econ. int.	Quan.: econ. int. Qual.: econ. int. Overall: econ. int.	Quan.: state int. Qual.: state int. Overall: state int.	Partially supported
Sudan	State int./ concerns with domestic stability	Quan.: state int. Qual.: state int. Overall: state int.	Quan.: state int. Qual.: concerns with domestic stability Overall: concerns with domestic stability	Quan.: econ. int. Qual.: econ. int. Overall: econ. int.	Partially supported
Tunisia	Neither state nor econ. int.	Quan.: econ. int. Qual.: econ. int. Overall: econ. int.	Quan.: econ. int. Qual.: state and econ. int. Overall: state and econ. int.	Quan.: econ. int. Qual.: econ. int. Overall: econ. int.	Supported
Kazakhstan	Both state and econ. int.	Quan.: state int. Qual.: econ. int. Overall: econ. int.	Quan.: econ. int. Qual.: state int. Overall: state int.	Quan.: econ. int. Qual.: econ. int. Overall: econ. int.	Supported
Canada	Econ. int.	Quan.: econ. int. Qual.: econ. int. Overall: econ. int.	Quan.: econ. int. Qual.: econ. int. Overall: econ. int.	Quan.: econ. int. Qual.: econ. int. Overall: econ. int.	Supported

(*Continued*)

Table 9.1 (Continued)

	Empirical expectation	*Key Dec. 1*	*Key Dec. 2*	*Key Dec. 3*	*Results*
Uzbekistan	State int.	Quan.: state int. Qual.: state int. Overall: state int.	Quan.: econ. int. Qual.: econ. int. Overall: econ. int.	Quan.: econ. int. Qual.: state int. Overall: state int.	Partially supported
Denmark	Neither state nor econ. int.	Quan.: econ. int. Qual.: state int. Overall: state int.	Quan.: econ. int. Qual.: econ. int. Overall: econ. int.	-	Supported

The results for the mini-cases generally supported the results from the main cases, as table 9.2 shows:

Table 9.2 Results from mini-cases versus main cases

	High oil	*Low oil*
High strategic importance	Nigeria (Kazakhstan)	Sudan (Uzbekistan)
Low strategic importance	Angola (Canada)	Tunisia (Denmark)

Here, with the countries of high strategic importance – Kazakhstan and Uzbekistan – the state has a strong interest in becoming involved in order to protect national security interests. In states of little strategic importance, such as Canada and Denmark, the state interest is less visible: the companies are more clearly involved to pursue commercial interests and profit alone. Overall, the results from the mini-cases suggest that the data generally supports the empirical expectations presented. These expectations find support in the cases of Kazakhstan, Canada, and Denmark, whereas they are only partially supported in the case of Uzbekistan.

The mini-case results thus indicate that the results from the main cases are, in fact, generalizable. They would generally appear to find even stronger evidence of state interests, as in the case of Kazakhstan, which is much more strategically important to China than a country like Nigeria. Similarly, Uzbekistan was a much more clear-cut case of high strategic importance/low oil than Sudan. Lastly, Canada was more of a clear-cut case of low strategic importance/high oil than Angola. Finally, the results from Tunisia/Denmark, for the model here, are of less relevance: they clearly show that when there is little oil/low strategic importance, the Chinese government has little incentive to become involved.

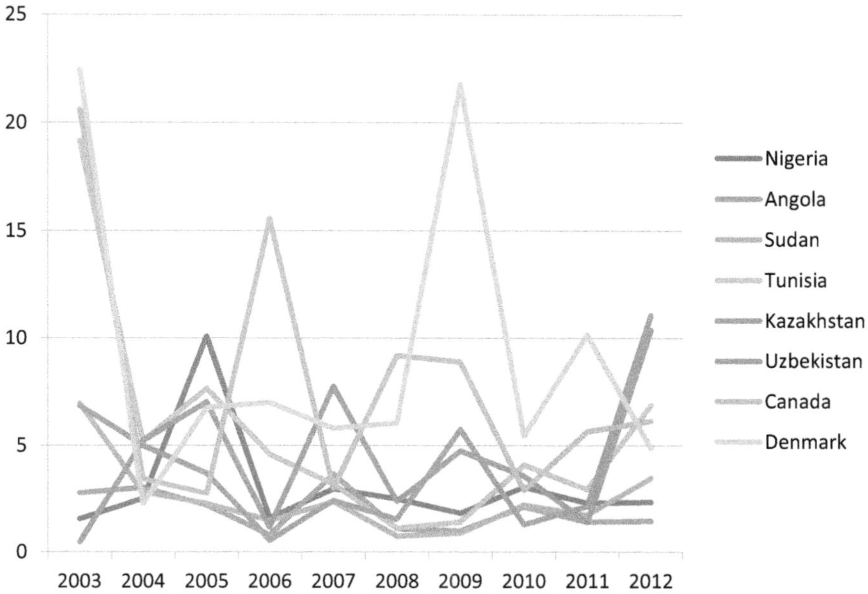

Figure 9.1 Results from the quantitative analyses for the eight case countries[1]

The purpose of the mini-cases was to see whether the results that I found for Africa were valid for other regions. When including the mini-cases, the conclusions that I find are true for China's energy policy across regions – that is, they can say something about Chinese foreign policy in general. As this is a cross-national study examining the activities of Chinese NOCs in different countries, it provides a strong basis for the claims about the similarities and differences between the roles of Chinese SOEs in different contexts.

The project has combined qualitative and quantitative analyses for empirical leverage while testing the extent of the explanations.

The graph in figure 9.1 illustrates the results from the quantitative analyses for the four African and four non-African countries.

The role of NOCs in foreign policy

What are the findings in this study regarding the role of NOCs in foreign policy? In terms of theoretical implications, this analysis has documented that, following the Chinese companies' increasing activities abroad, SOEs have become stronger and more profitable over the course of the ten-year period under investigation. The analysis has provided evidence that following the rise of SOEs, there has been a key change in the actors involved in foreign policy and in "Going Out" (走出去/*zouchuqu*) policy, and the SOEs now have an impact on Chinese foreign policy. There is evidence that the NOCs play an independent role in foreign policy in the following cases.

In the case of Angola and the failed refinery deal, there is evidence of the Chinese leadership being interested in the Lobito refinery, as it represented a way of guaranteeing Chinese oil imports, an avenue for oil security. A total of 80 percent of the oil refined at Lobito was to be exported to the Chinese market, which would be to the benefit of China rather than to the local Angolan market.[2] Important visits took place – including Wen Jiabao's 2006 visit to Angola – to pave the way for the refinery, accompanied by statements made by Wen Jiabao that stressed the importance of building the refinery. In contrast, from Sinopec's side, the refinery was high risk; it was unlikely that the company would ever turn a profit from this venture. Sinopec abandoned the project, as it was not considered commercially viable. The withdrawal from the Sonaref refinery did not favor the state, as Chinese companies, CNOOC and Sinopec, subsequently lost important bids for promising stakes that would otherwise have granted them access to important technology and increased the two companies' reserves. The Sinopec–CNOOC joint bid for Block 32 was later blocked. Importantly, this had negative consequences for China's aid-for-oil strategy. In this sense, this is a case where the company acted independently, pursuing its own commercial interests, which later proved to have consequences for foreign policy. In other words, this case demonstrates the increased significance played by NOCs with respect to Chinese foreign policy.

In the case of Sudan, in the period prior to the Darfur crisis, the companies had largely been left on their own. This changed with the international criticism of China's role (or lack thereof) in relation to Darfur leading up to the 2008 Beijing Olympics. In 2006–07, we see that the Chinese government made an important foreign policy shift, which can be interpreted as strong state interests trumping the commercial interests of Chinese companies. It was the independent activities of NOCs and the profitable business in Sudan at the time of the Olympics that came to have negative ramifications for Chinese foreign policy. This would be consistent with the role played by NOCs in foreign policy. After 2006, however, there was more control with the NOCs. In the case of the 2012 oil shutdown in Sudan, the CNPC was then left on its own (which expresses a profit logic). This demonstrates how it was only when national security and the pride of the nation as embodied by the Olympics were at stake that Beijing would intervene. But the Chinese government would not intervene at the risk of economic losses. Despite a major crisis (the oil shutdown), the Chinese leadership decided to merely stand on the sidelines. Thus, the non-interference principle once again came to characterize Chinese foreign policy toward the two Sudans, and commercial interests again came to dominate. This is consistent with NOC interests, which again could be consistent with a greater role played by the NOCs.

Finally, in the case of the proposed Encana deal in Canada in 2010–11, there is evidence that the political leadership in Beijing wanted the Encana deal to go through, as the political leadership prioritizes gas and high technology. Moreover, the June 2010 visit by Hu Jintao to Canada when the MoU on the agreement was signed was a very strong indication of the intentions of the Chinese leadership. Later, when PetroChina pulled out of the Encana deal, it was out of concern that the acquisition would not be profitable. This case points out how PetroChina withdrew out of concerns for commercial viability and, more to the point, did so without coordinating the decision with the political leadership. This would indicate that PetroChina pursued its own interests in this instance, even when they contrasted with the policy line from Beijing, thereby further demonstrating the greater role played by the NOCs.

The study shows that, overall, economic interests dominated the activities of the Chinese NOCs abroad during the period under study. This is a contribution to the literature on international relations and political economy, as in much of the secondary literature, Chinese NOCs are not expected to be driven by commercial interests but rather by security imperatives. Here, the activities of the Chinese NOCs are deemed to be part of an expansionist strategy on the part of the Chinese regime to lock up oil and gas, constituting a threat to other states in the international system. The findings here speak to the China-rise literature, as it illuminates how, contrary to the standard take in much of the secondary literature, the rise of China will be peaceful.

It should be noted that what is presented here is a quantitative text analysis, which reveals the state-controlled discourse. It is a story about what matters on the discursive level and tells the story of what the Chinese state media considers to be the main interests at stake. The study then supplements with case studies of certain key decisions, including particular acquisitions.

Contributions

What, then, is the implication of these findings regarding the role played by SOEs in the foreign policy of the authoritarian state? Do they affect our understanding of Chinese foreign policy and our understanding of the role played by SOEs in foreign policy in the international relations literature?

My findings and the framework I have developed for explaining the individual cases are important for empirical and theoretical reasons. Empirically, I find that in the ten-year period under investigation, there is variation in the autonomy of SOEs in China. The study finds that commercial actors have an impact on Chinese foreign policy and has presented clear evidence that these non-state actors play a role in foreign policy and sometimes go against the policy line from Beijing.

The study presents variation in the dominance of state interests *vis-à-vis* economic interests and the concern with domestic stability (*weiwen*) over time. For example, in the case of Sudan up until the years 2006–08, economic interests dominated the activities of the NOCs in the country. Then, state interests and concerns with domestic stability came to dominate in the years from 2006–08. In subsequent years, economic interests again dominated as the main motive guiding the Chinese NOCs in Sudan.

Another significant finding is how the study reveals that state interests and concerns with domestic stability have increased in relative terms over the last ten years. For example, in the case of Sudan, at the time of the 2008 Beijing Olympics, state interests and the concerns with domestic stability came to have great importance. Chinese companies are now facing increased constraints from the leadership. Still, overall, economic interests dominate the activities of the Chinese NOCs abroad during this period.

Theoretically, this study illuminates the increasing role played by NOCs in foreign policy and contributes with a first step toward quantifying the foreign policy of the authoritarian state and the role herein played by non-state actors. The study here concludes that an important characteristic of the foreign policy of the authoritarian state is the role played by NOCs. A particular model was conceptualized, according to which the fragmented character of the state can account for the role that NOCs play in foreign policy. This study thus seeks to fill a hole in the literature concerning the foreign policy of the authoritarian state and takes a first step toward establishing the more general elements for describing the foreign policy of an authoritarian state.

Moreover, this research contributes to the debate on whether structural factors, characteristics of the Chinese authoritarian state, or concerns with legitimacy can explain the change we see in key actors in China's foreign policy over the last ten years. This study suggests that regime type plays a greater role for Chinese foreign policy than do structural factors. A second level variable can add great insight to an analysis. If we consider only structural factors, we cannot explain the greater role that non-state actors play in Chinese foreign policy.

This study provides a test that shows that domestic interest groups, that is, non-state actors, play an important and growing role in the foreign policy of the authoritarian state. The study argues that the ability of non-state actors to influence foreign policy is a particular characteristic of the foreign policy of the authoritarian state. I focus on one authoritarian state – China – and argue that the ability of non-state actors to influence the country's foreign policy is a particular characteristic of this (one) authoritarian state.

One could argue that it is difficult to conclude firmly that the NOCs play a foreign policy role and that the empirical chapters of this book fail to answer the question of the role of non-state actors in the foreign policy of the authoritarian state or that they do not fully depict the role of non-state actors in foreign policy. One could also argue that it is unclear how the study of the specific question about China and the case studies enable us to understand the role of non-state actors in authoritarian states. At the same time, the argument here is that if economic interests were found to dominate, then this could be seen as evidence that the NOCs have a role in foreign policy. Moreover, there has been evidence in the case analyses of the role played by the NOCs in foreign policy decision-making.

In terms of the foreign policy of the authoritarian state, it is unclear how the study of the specific question about China and the case studies enable us to understand the role of non-state actors in foreign policy. Here, the claim is that if economic interests dominate, it is evidence of a role played by NOCs. At the same time, every causal argument has some degree of uncertainty. One can never prove in an absolute sense that a change in the independent variable leads to a change in the dependent variable. One can show that there is no other plausible variable capable of explaining the change in the dependent variable, either logically or empirically. Still, it is always going to be possible that one has missed a factor or variable or that the evidence of causality is not as crisp as one might like. Nevertheless, I argue that the analysis has shown that among the range of plausible explanations, the dominance of economic interests is most likely a function of the power of NOCs.

China as an authoritarian state

Why is it particularly in the authoritarian state that NOCs are playing an increasing role? As pointed to in Chapter 2, the Chinese state has become more fractured in recent years as a result of the reform processes. A hypothesis was established here about the characteristics of the foreign policy of the authoritarian state in which the rise of SOEs was a significant characteristic. Specifically, the hypothesis was that the fragmentation of the political and administrative systems has led to a pluralized policy process, which in turn has reduced the capacity of the state. The pluralization of the policy process and weakened leadership allowed SOEs to obtain greater influence over economic decision-making, thus enabling them to play a greater role in foreign policy. Consequently, there was a role to be played by non-state actors.

This study presents a model that works particularly for an authoritarian state. Whether it works for non-authoritarian states is a question that cannot be answered here. Given that the study merely focuses on one authoritarian state, it lies outside the conclusions here whether the role played by NOCs in authoritarian states is similar to the role they play in democratic states and whether the fact that they are authoritarian means that one can assume a different state-company constellation than in democratic states. Here, I merely seek to fill a void in the literature on the authoritarian state. The conclusions found are valid for this one state, China. At the same time, they might also be valid for other states (authoritarian or not).

The framework of the foreign policy of the authoritarian state presented here illustrates the growing role of SOEs. While this framework might be able to work across states and find variation in types of authoritarianisms, this study only considers the case of China as an example of the argument. It uses the Chinese case as a plausibility probe. As I only focus on one state, this analysis therefore does not allow for cross-national variation. At the same time, because this framework is something few people have considered, I deem that the preceding problem is counterbalanced by the novelty of this approach.

*Concerns with domestic stability (*weiwen*)*

In a novel step, this study presents a hypothesis that is related to the concern with domestic stability in China (维稳/*weiwen*). It examines the role and significance of domestic stability in Chinese foreign policy and presents a link between the activities of Chinese energy companies abroad and domestic stability in China. The argument here is that the national oil companies play a particular role in terms of ensuring the energy resources necessary for the Chinese state to maintain economic growth and thus stability – and therefore for the CCP to be able to maintain its rule. It speaks to interests other than security interests occasionally holding great importance for the state. It shows how the companies are tasked with an important job in getting the resources for the CCP regime to sustain its rule. While there could be more evidence of this component working, the argument here is that it still provides useful insights.

The project casts light on the connection between CCP rule and concerns with domestic stability (*weiwen*), which is a novel aspect. Within the Chinese politics literature on domestic legitimacy, it is unclear *specifically* how the concern with domestic legitimacy affects Chinese foreign policy and in particular how these concerns impact the role played by SOEs in foreign policy. While I tested this third hypothesis across the cases, I did not find evidence in all of them. At the same time, the hypothesis was productive, finding evidence in some cases. In the case of Sudan, for example, the investigation focused on the killing of Chinese workers in October 2008, with particular emphasis on the domestic impact of this incident in China. We saw how in response to incidents where the domestic audience was aware (e.g., on 微博/*Weibo*) that the lives of Chinese workers were at risk, the Chinese government sent a high-level delegation to Sudan to put pressure on the Sudanese government. Thus, evidence of this variable was found in the case of Sudan.

In other cases, however, no such evidence was found. In Nigeria, for example, when Chinese workers were killed in 2012, as well as with the attacks on and kidnappings of 30 Chinese nationals over a span of 11 years, this had no consequences for China's foreign policy or for the investment decisions of Chinese companies in Nigeria. The Chinese government did not send a high-level delegation to Nigeria to put pressure on the government. Nor is there evidence that the domestic audience was aware of the incidents – no references are found to these incidents on微博 *(Weibo)*, for example. Even so, Chinese companies have taken steps to handle security on the ground in Nigeria in their own ways; for example, Chinese oil companies have hired security companies to protect Chinese oil installations. But this is not evidence of this variable as it is conceptualized here. Similarly, there was no evidence of this variable in the cases of Angola, Canada, and Denmark. It is hardly surprising that no evidence of this variable is found in these countries or, for that matter, in Tunisia, as these countries are characterized by being of little strategic importance to the Chinese leadership.

Other conceptualizations of this variable were also attempted. In the Tunisian case, for example, the investigation focused on whether evidence could be found of links between the Tunisian Revolution and concerns with domestic stability in China. The results show that Chinese investments (such as Sinochem and CNPC) were unaffected. The Tunisian Revolution did not result in any financial losses for Chinese commercial interests in Tunisia. Thus, no evidence was found of this variable here. The Chinese leadership maintained its policy of non-interference in the wake of the Arab Uprisings, not only with regard to its stance toward Tunisia but also in its stance toward countries such as Libya and Syria.

In Kazakhstan, we examine an incident in December 2011, when oil workers were killed (none of whom were Chinese, but there were Chinese oil workers in the country) and the impact this had on Chinese domestic stability. Here, oil workers at state-run KazMunaiGas Exploration Production (RDGZ) in Zhanaozen rioted after disputes over wages and the firing of almost 1,000 workers. While there was a link, namely that the riots in Kazakhstan were related to a KMG subsidiary, a Chinese oil company operating in Kazakhstan, there is no evidence that the December 2011 riots had any impact on domestic stability in China. However, given the strong links between Uyghurs living in Xinjiang, China, and the Uyghurs in Kazakhstan, by implication, there is a potential link between the events in Kazakhstan and Chinese domestic stability – even if no Chinese oil workers were killed. Even so, the way it was conceptualized here was not useful, as there is no evidence that the riots in Kazakhstan had an impact on domestic stability in China.

In the case of Uzbekistan, the investigation focused on the Chinese support for Uzbekistan in the face of international condemnation in 2005 after a crackdown by Uzbek security forces on its own population. Subsequently, the Chinese government decided to support the Uzbek government and receive President Karimov on a state visit in Beijing immediately after the incident, ultimately because the Chinese leadership was concerned that similar "public riots" could spread to China. Thus, Beijing was motivated by its concerns for domestic stability when receiving President Karimov. It is worth noting that shortly after the visit, a declaration by the SCO was made concerning foreign states' military interference in the region, and the Uzbek government asked the US government to shut down its military base in the country. While one can argue that it would be in China's interest for a US military base here to be closed down, as the variable is conceptualized, there is no direct link between the concern with domestic stability in China and the closure of a military base.

Thus, the results were not strong with regard to the hypothesis concerning domestic stability in most of the cases. This might be because this third hypothesis should be modified and improved, as its current conceptualization does not capture the concepts at stake (i.e., how the killing of foreigners abroad is linked to domestic stability in China). One could also argue that this factor is very peripheral and that it will likely only have an effect in exceptional instances. Finally, it could be argued that since the drivers for the third and first hypotheses are similar, they should be put together. Nevertheless, I maintain that it is useful to retain and present this third hypothesis. It is theoretically sound to speculate whether the activities of NOCs abroad have an impact on domestic stability, as it is based on a solid theoretical position in the Chinese politics literature. In other words, even if the results do not find strong support, it does not necessarily make the endeavor wrong.

Finally, generally speaking, the countries in Africa are not as strategically important to China as those in Central Asia. Thus, when we see an effect for the hypothesis regarding the concerns with domestic stability, even in the case of Sudan, one would expect an even stronger effect in a Central Asian country, such as Kazakhstan. This could also point to how to further develop the indicators of this hypothesis, as this hypothesis would be expected to find evidence in cases in the near region, such as Kazakhstan and Uzbekistan.

In fact, the third hypothesis regarding concerns with domestic stability (*weiwen*) adds to our understanding of foreign policy. Thus, the test here represents a first step toward conceptualizing the significance and role of domestic stability in Chinese foreign policy and also, more generally, in the authoritarian state and its foreign policy. For these reasons, rather than remove this third hypothesis, I keep it here. In future work, the conceptualization of this variable could be fine-tuned.

A few methodological points are worth particular mention. First, this study distinguishes between commercial and state interests. It could be argued that China is special, as in the case of an authoritarian state, where the state might be assumed to be all-controlling, it makes no sense to draw such a distinction. It could be argued that there are incidents in which the state can carry economic interests in addition to security interests, for which reason the separation does not make sense. Overall, however, I find that the distinction is relevant. This study has shown how companies can be thought of as relatively autonomous and how at times they make independent decisions that are contrary to the policy of the political leadership. This study has shown that China is not a special case, and it makes sense to operate with this distinction.

Second, operating with the distinction between state interests and economic interests has helped illuminate the trade-offs that states must make between state interests, economic interests, and concerns with domestic stability. It shows in detail when states are protecting state interests at the expense of economic interests and how the state might be motivated by concerns with domestic stability (*weiwen*) in contrast to the pursuit of economic interests. In this way, the study illuminates how concerns with domestic stability (*weiwen*) have an impact on foreign policy and, in particular, how the implications of the activities of NOCs abroad affect foreign policy.

Finally, within the international relations tradition, the aim is often to generalize across states. Accordingly, one would seek to extrapolate from the Chinese case. In contrast, within the China studies tradition, one would look at China *sui generis*, because China is argued to constitute a rich and complex case in itself, and, given access to Chinese language sources, a rich study of China is sufficient unto itself and there is no need to generalize broader than that. Moreover, the argument would be that the results would be true for one state, China, and cannot be generalized to account for authoritarian states (in general). Thus, the question is the tension between whether the aim is to generalize versus looking at China as a particular case. Here, similar to the first position, the aim is to generalize. China is seen as an example of an authoritarian state, and the conclusions are generalized to account for the foreign policy of authoritarian states in general.

Implications for international relations theory

In addition to offering a first step toward a theory of the foreign policy of the authoritarian state, this study holds several implications for the study of international relations more broadly. It makes intellectual contributions to several distinct debates about the foreign policy of the authoritarian state.

First, this study of Chinese foreign policy adds to our knowledge in the field of international relations by examining whether China, given its growing capabilities both economically and militarily relative to other powers, behaves as other growing powers have done in the past. According to this study, companies are expected to play an even larger role in relation to foreign policy. In fact, at times, the companies can be seen as relatively independent, (i.e., as acting outside of the control of the state). Here, foreign policy can be expected to be more economically oriented. Along these lines, a rising China will not be expansionist; rather, it will pursue its economic interests in ensuring sufficient supplies to fuel the economy. This is thus an implication that stands in stark contrast to much of the literature on Chinese foreign policy. The view, in general, in the literature is that the Chinese state uses the oil companies to lock up oil around the world as part of an expansionist strategy of the Chinese state. At the same time, this study casts light on when the two interests – economic and state interests – collapse. In the case of Sudan up to the Olympics, for example, when the NOCs had been free to pursue their interests irrespective of state interests, the companies incurred financial losses when the state ultimately interfered. Then, after the Olympics, economic interests again came to dominate. This shows how the two interests collide, providing insights as to the role that the NOCs play in foreign policy and also showing incidents when they are acting outside of the control of the leadership in Beijing. This means that we cannot *a priori* assume that a "rising" China will necessarily be expansionist. Rather, we can expect a "rising" China to be increasingly motivated by economic interests.

Second, this study adds to our knowledge in the field of international relations by examining the role of non-state actors in foreign policy. According to most forms of realism, companies are seen as an extension of the state, and the motives of the company and the state are understood to be aligned. To be sure, the results of this study show that there are instances in which it would appear as though the companies are best seen as an extension of the state, for example, in the case of Sudan up to the Beijing Olympics, when the companies came under stronger state control despite financial losses. Also, in the case of Uzbekistan, evidence of independent companies is difficult to find, and the motives of the company and state are best seen as aligned. Yet the results show that while there is occasionally alignment between the companies and political leadership, this is not always the case. In the cases of Angola, Sudan, and Canada, for example, the companies have pursued their interests independently, thereby offering evidence that non-state actors play a role in foreign policy and an affirmation of liberal theories. At the same time, liberal theories will have difficulty explaining all of the cases, as the evidence here also illuminates how, on occasion, there is alignment between the political leadership and NOCs abroad. This points to what is really interesting: the interplay between the two; in fact, it is the trade-off between them that is of greatest interest.

In this way, this study contributes more generally to a larger body of literature on the impact of first-level variables as related to structural variables. The framework here considers the effect of two types of domestic variables – both non-state actors (NOCs) and concerns with domestic stability (*weiwen*) – in their interplay with structural variables. Along the lines of structural realism, one would not usually open the black box of the state; one would not include unit-level variables. In contrast, theories that give primacy to unit-level variables usually do not include structural variables. Thus, the model presented here is novel in the sense that it includes both levels and then tests their respective effects on a number of cases. It shows that important insights can be gained from including first-level variables in an analysis that are not captured when considering structural variables alone. It can illuminate why it is important to consider the role of non-state actors, as these, at times, can have an individual role for foreign policy.

In the international relations literature, some scholars have noted the role that a unit-level variable can play. For Christensen, it is "national political power."[3] For Zakaria, it is "state strength."[4] In the literature, however, this unit-level variable has not previously been conceptualized as "domestic interest groups," as is the case in this study. Moreover, this study can show particular instances where the non-state actors have a role and instances where they do not. In the international relations literature, this is a contribution in the sense that there is a lack in the literature that can explain how non-state actors can influence foreign policy as well as how this changes over time.

Finally, this study contributes to what the character of the state means for foreign policy, that is, whether a given state is authoritarian or not. The argument is that a characteristic of the authoritarian state is that because of the fragmented character of the state, NOCs can have a role. While this argument might be applicable to other authoritarian states, here, the argument is that it is limited to the particular case of China. In the international relations literature, there is a lack of theories that can explain what the "authoritarian-ness" means for foreign policy. One scholar who has looked at the characteristics of the foreign policy of the authoritarian state is Jessica Weeks. She unpacks the authoritarian states, analyzes the differences in audience costs between different regime types, and finds variations in the types of authoritarianism.[5] However, here, the purpose of this study is not to look at audience costs. Other attempts to unpack the characteristics of the foreign policy of the authoritarian state would be to assess variations in authoritarianisms – that is, to focus on the institutions within the state that matter in different types of regimes, for example, one where the military plays a role and one where it does not, and how this relates to foreign policy, as for example Barbara Geddes has done.[6] One could also focus on the characteristics of a personalist dictatorship in contrast to other types of authoritarian regimes, as do Mark Peceny et al.[7] However, because the purpose here is not to assess the variation in authoritarian regimes and their impact on foreign policy and as China is a one-party state rather than a personalist regime, these attempts were unhelpful.

Within the strain of international relations theory referred to as structural realism, domestic factors, including regime type, are not included in the analysis, and the state is generally treated as a "black box." Some realist scholars have studied the regime type and its impact on foreign policy.[8] However, they do not venture into a systematic analysis of what the "authoritarian-ness" is and how these characteristics influence foreign policy. Within the liberal school of international relations theory, attempts have been made to examine the role of regime type with respect to foreign policy outcome. However, these liberal theories do not systematically examine the mechanisms of the foreign policy of the authoritarian state, other than a general notion of non-peacefulness; nor do they address whether the role of non-state actors in influencing foreign policy is a particular characteristic of the authoritarian state. Thus, to understand the workings of an authoritarian state and how variations in authoritarianism affect foreign policy, neither realist nor liberal theories are helpful.

Rather, this study has attempted to fill this gap by constructing a theoretical framework that explains the workings of the foreign policy of the authoritarian state. It builds a framework that includes both realist and liberal theories as well as theories of Chinese politics into a comprehensive whole. Through very detailed case studies, it is able to explain under what conditions each of these theories have explanatory power and in which combinations. Moreover, it can explain how there is variation over time in terms of which theory has explanatory power. In the argument presented here, the claim is that one characteristic of the foreign policy of the authoritarian state is the rise of state-owned enterprises (SOEs) and their impact on foreign policy. Even if what is presented here is merely a first step, it is still a contribution to the international relations literature, as this has never been done before.

Third, this study contributes to the international relations literature with regard to the role of legitimacy and domestic stability in foreign policy. There have been few previous contributions to this. As a result of China's regime insecurity, some studies have focused on how Chinese foreign policy can be expected to be expansionist.[9] Similarly, this study shows that concerns with domestic stability do affect Chinese foreign policy, as they cause China to pursue its security interests. In the international relations literature, the question of how concerns with domestic legitimacy relate to foreign policy is an unexplored one. The general logic in the literature is that in order to shore up legitimacy, authoritarian leaders will resort to nationalism or be challenged by threats from nationalist movements, which will in turn lead to a conflictual foreign policy. At the same time, importantly, while this literature sheds light on how concerns with domestic legitimacy impact foreign policy, the exact mechanism under which concerns with domestic legitimacy are translated into the foreign policy of the authoritarian state remains unclear. This study contributes with insight as to the role played here by NOCs. The study has shown how the more the regime is concerned with social stability, the less independent the energy companies will be. In this way, this study makes a contribution to the literature by explaining how concerns with domestic legitimacy influence the foreign policy of the authoritarian state, which is a novel thing. It illuminates the link between the concerns with ensuring energy supplies and the CCP regime stability, which is a particular characteristic of the authoritarian state. This is a contribution to both the international relations literature and the literature on Chinese politics.

Finally, the project also contributes insight into the role and significance of energy in the foreign policy of the state. It casts light on the steps that a state will take to ensure a sufficient energy supply, in other words energy security. There is a lack of theories in the international relations literature that are capable of explaining what the role of energy means for foreign policy. For example, within structural realism, while we can deduce from the theory that energy would implicitly be considered important for the foreign policy of the state, it can be criticized for a lacking explication of the role of energy in foreign policy as well as its ability to function as a theory of the foreign policy of the state, as it does not sufficiently account for the relationship between the different components of power (i.e., how the military component of state power is related to the other components of power, such as energy.[10]

Similarly, within classical realism, the role of energy in the foreign policy of states is understudied. Attempts have been made to address the role of energy in foreign policy, through the lens of the relationship between energy security and foreign policy,[11] the analysis of resources as important for state power as in power transition theory,[12] the role of resource endowment for the foreign policy of the state,[13] and the importance of raw materials and resources to the economy and thus for the state.[14] However, all of these accounts suffer from a lack of clarification of the role of energy in the foreign policy of the state, and, in general, they share the assumption that, in guiding foreign policy, resources are considered less important than other dimensions, such as the military.

Other attempts to address the role of energy in the foreign policy of the state include looking at how the energy companies are used as part of an "economic technique" for achieving foreign policy goals as part of a *grand strategy*, as, for example, Henrik Spruyt[15] has done, or as *economic techniques of statecraft*, as David Baldwin has done.[16] Still, the link here between the economic techniques and foreign policy is not very explicit. Thus, the literature lacks sufficient clarity regarding *how* the state would be able to *use* the companies to pursue foreign policy objectives.

This study can contribute to international relations theory in the following manner; it can illuminate the importance of access to sufficient natural resources for a state and the role played by NOCs in this regard. The NOCs are tasked with the important job of obtaining energy resources. This study can show how the companies go abroad in order to ensure the necessary resources to supply the economy. In that way, considering the companies is the missing link in realist theory for explaining how and if energy is ensured domestically for the economy to grow. Thus, the state depends on the activities of NOCs for survival. In fact, the study here shows how the energy sphere is the conundrum linking realist theories, liberal theories, and theories that focus on domestic stability together, as it provides the link between the three. In realist theory, sufficient energy supplies are taken as a given. In liberal theories, energy is not taken as a given, the focus instead being on independent companies that pursue their activities. In theories relating to domestic (Chinese) politics, energy has the role of being a contributing factor to domestic stability and, thus, for the Chinese state to survive.

Notes

1 It shows the ratio of economic interests to state interests / domestic stability (*weiwen*) for all the case countries.
2 Interviews, Luanda, Angola, 2014.
3 Thomas Christensen, *Useful Adversaries: Grand Strategy, Domestic Mobilization, and Sino-American Conflict, 1947–1958* (Princeton, NJ: Princeton University Press, 1996), 11.
4 Fareed Zakaria, *From Wealth to Power. The Unusual Origins of America's World Role* (Princeton, NJ: Princeton University Press, 1998).
5 Jessica L. Weeks, "Audience Costs: Regime Type and Signaling Resolve," *International Organization* 62 (1) (Winter 2008): 35–64.
6 Barbara Geddes, "Authoritarian Breakdown," UCLA (Jan. 2004), downloaded from website on January 20, 2013, www.international.ucla.edu/cms/files/authn_breakdown.pdf.
7 Mark Peceny and Caroline C. Beer, "Dictatorial Peace?" *American Political Science Review* 96 (1) (March 2002): 15–26; Mark Peceny and Christopher K. Butler, "The Conflict Behavior of Authoritarian Regimes," *International Politics* 41 (4) (2004): 565–81.
8 Robert Ross, *Chinese Security Policy: Structure, Power and Politics* (London: Routledge, 2009).
9 See, for example, Susan Shirk, *Fragile Superpower: How China's Internal Politics Could Derail Its Peaceful Rise* (Oxford: Oxford University Press, 2007).
10 Kasandra Behrndt-Eriksen, "China's Engagement in Africa. A Strategy to Secure Survival," paper presented at the third China Goes Global Conference, Harvard University, October 2, 2009.
11 Robert Ross, "China's Naval Nationalism. Sources, Prospects and the U.S. Response," *International Security* 34 (2) (Fall 2009): 46–81.
12 Abramo F.K. Organski, *World Politics* (New York, NY: Alfred A. Knopf, 1965); Abramo F.K. Organski and Jack Kugler, *The War Ledger* (Chicago: University of Chicago Press, 1980).
13 Hans J. Morgenthau, *Politics Among Nations* (New York, NY: Alfred Knopf, 1948).
14 Stephen Krasner, *Defending the National Interest: Raw Materials, Investment and U.S. Foreign Policy* (Princeton, NJ: Princeton University Press, 1978), 38.
15 David A. Baldwin, *Economic Statecraft* (Princeton, NJ: Princeton University Press, 1985).
16 Baldwin, *Economic Statecraft.*

References

Baldwin, David A. *Economic Statecraft*. Princeton, NJ: Princeton University Press, 1985.

Behrndt-Eriksen, Kasandra. "China's Engagement in Africa. A Strategy to Secure Survival." Paper presented at the 3rd China Goes Global Conference, Harvard University, October 2, 2009.

Christensen, Thomas. *Useful Adversaries: Grand Strategy, Domestic Mobilization, and Sino – American Conflict, 1947–1958*. Princeton, NJ: Princeton University Press, 1996.

Geddes, Barbara. "Authoritarian Breakdown." University of California Los Angeles (January 2004). Accessed January 20, 2013. www.international.ucla.edu/cms/files/authn_breakdown.pdf.

Krasner, Stephen. *Defending the National Interest: Raw Materials, Investment and U.S. Foreign Policy*. Princeton, NJ: Princeton University Press, 1978.

Morgenthau, Hans J. *Politics Among Nations*. New York, NY: Alfred Knopf, 1948.

Organski, Abramo F.K. *World Politics*. New York, NY: Alfred A. Knopf, 1965.

Organski, Abramo F.K. and Jack Kugler. *The War Ledger*. Chicago, IL: University of Chicago Press, 1980.

Peceny, Mark and Caroline C. Beer (2002) "Dictatorial Peace?" *American Political Science Review* 96 (1) (March 2002): 15–26.

Peceny, Mark and Christopher K. Butler. "The Conflict Behavior of Authoritarian Regimes." *International Politics* 41 (4) (2004): 565–81.

Ross, Robert. "China's Naval Nationalism. Sources, Prospects and the U.S. Response." *International Security* 34 (2) (Fall 2009): 46–81.

Ross, Robert. *Chinese Security Policy: Structure, Power and Politics*. London, UK: Routledge, 2009.

Shirk, Susan L. *Fragile Superpower: How China's Internal Politics Could Derail Its Peaceful Rise*. Oxford, UK: Oxford University Press, 2007.

Weeks, Jessica L. "Audience Costs: Regime Type and Signaling Resolve." *International Organization* 62 (1) (Winter 2008): 35–64.

Zakaria, Fareed. *From Wealth to Power. The Unusual Origins of America's World Role*. Princeton, NJ: Princeton University Press, 1998.

Appendices

2 Foreign policy of the authoritarian state

THE QUANTITATIVE CONTENT ANALYSIS

For the quantitative content analysis, material was downloaded from the database CNKI (中国知网/*zhongguo zhiwang*), the largest Chinese language database in China. The CNKI material was downloaded in the following way: searches on CNKI were made using key words, years, sources, authors, and so on. Searches were made in terms of "country" (e.g., Sudan) and "oil" over a ten-year period (2002–12). For Sudan, there were 560 articles; for Angola, 226 articles; for Nigeria, 517 articles; and so forth. For each case country, all of the articles were downloaded. In a second turn, 100 articles for each case were selected based on random selection.

The coding list used for the quantitative analysis conceptualizes the categories corresponding to the dependent variable in this study – that is, *state interests*, *economic interests*, and *concern with domestic stability* (维稳/*weiwen*). It is a list of words most likely to be used as *references for* "state interests" and "economic interests" (企业利益/*qiye liyi*) and "concern with domestic stability" (维稳/*weiwen*). The categories for economic interests, state interests, and concerns with domestic stability (*weiwen*) are conceptualized so that they are clearly separate. Robustness tests ensure that the results are significant.

The coding list aims to present four-syllable words, that is, definite terms used in Chinese to designate either state interests, economic interests, or concerns with domestic stability. The list combines words to form terms used as standard references in the Chinese media to talk about either of these three. It will not include two-syllable words such as "important" (重要/*zhongyao*), "influence" (影响/*yingxiang*), and "contribution" (贡献/*gongxian*) as distinct terms, as they can be combined in many ways, such as "important company" (重要企业/*zhongyao qiye*). Even so, given the problems when trying to pick up words using Chinese segmenters, certain important two-syllable words are included, such as the words for "strategy" (战略/*zhanlue*) and "cooperation" [合作/*hezuo*], as a robustness test; for example, the term (合作/*hezuo*) shows that it is predominantly used for state interests. Words related to aid "subsidy" (资助/*zizhu*) or "disaster relief"

(救灾/*jiuzai*) are not included, as robustness tests show that including either does not alter the results.

In terms of the coding list for *state interests*, words that relate to the energy field, such as "rights" (权益/*quanyi*) and "equity oil" (份额石油/*fen'e shiyou*) and words denoting "diversification," (多样化/*duoyanghua*) and (多元化/*duoyuanhua*), are not included. It does not include words for peace, such as "peace" (和平/*heping*) and "harmony" (和谐/*hexie*), as they are too general. In terms of conditional statements, it is worth noting that the word for "reporting" (汇报/*huibao*) is included when used together with verbs that give it the connotation of control. Secondly, the word for "inspect" (考察/*kaocha*) is included in conjunction with leadership visits.

In terms of the coding list for *economic interests*, the term for "compete/competitive" [竞争 (力)/*jingzhengli*] is included, as robustness tests show that it is predominantly used to denote economic interest. When "企"(*qi*) stands alone, it is not included. The word for "company" (公司/*gongsi*) is included even if it refers to a specific company, as it is less likely to show up in articles about state interests.

It is worth noting that including "company" (公司/*gongsi*) might be problematic, as the word often appears as part of particular company names, e.g. CNPC (中国石油天然气集团公司/*zhongguo shiyou tianranqi jituan gongsi*) without carrying the connotation of a general company. Moreover, the count for (公司/*gongsi*) is relatively high, thus having a high influence on the results. To control for this, two counts of all of the articles are made: one that includes (公司/*gongsi*) and another that does not.[1] The coding list excludes the words "profit" (利益/*liyi*) and "profit" (收益/*shouyi*) as standalones, as they could refer to political benefits and interests as well – that is, references to state interests. In fact, doing a concordance using *Yoshikoder* shows that the word for "interest" (利益/*liyi*) is used to refer both to economic and state interests. The coding list for economic interests excludes the word for "economic behavior," such as "compete" (竞标/*Jingbiao*), as well as more general words to denote "something economic," such as "service" (服务/*fuwu*), "science" (科学性/*kexuexing*), "costs" (成本/*chengben*), "goods" (产品/*chanpin*), "target" (目标/*mubiao*), and "management" (管理/*guanli*). It does not include the word for "trade" (商务/*shangwu*), as it is too general, or the terms "trade" (贸易/*maoyi*), "foreign trade" (对外经贸/*duiwai jingmao*), or "go on the market" (上市/*shangshi*) and the term for "opportunity" (机遇/*jiyu*).

In terms of the coding list for the term for concern with domestic stability (*weiwen*), it uses the word for "national security" (国家安全/*guojia anquan*) rather than just "security" (安全/*anquan*), as that might also have connotations to economic risk. It will not include terms for "crisis" (危机/*weiji*) or the verb to "threaten" (威胁/*weixie*), as they are too general. It includes the term for "risk" (风险/*fengxian*), as this is related to concern with Chinese workers and therefore also with concerns for the stability of the country – even if it could be said to have an impact both on economic and state interests as well. At the same time, robustness tests show that even if "risk" (风险/*fengxian*) is placed as part of economic interest, the results are unchanged; thus, this particular term is of less significance for the results here. The word for "political stability" (政治稳

定/*zhengzhi wending*) is included when it is used as a threat to China. As words for "terrorism" (恐怖/*kongbu*), it includes the following: "terrorist attack" (恐怖袭击/*kongbuxiji*), "arms/military" (武装/*wuzhuang*), and "terrorism" (恐怖主义/*kongbuzhuyi*). These are included when they refer to China.

In terms of *other methodological concerns*, the word for "oil" (石油/*shiyou*) is not counted, as the coding results are unrelated to the number of counts of "oil" (石油/*shiyou*). The coding list excludes the *chengyu* (成语) and allegories as references to state interests, such as "domino theory" (多米诺骨牌/*duominuogupai*), as their use is infrequent and their inclusion thus has little impact.[2] The coding list will not include "stand-alone words," such as the word for "winning" (赢/*ying*), as the computer program is unable to pick up such words. Words longer than five characters, such as "mutual oil cooperation" (双边石油合作/*shuanbian shiyou hezuo*) that might be thought of as economic interest are not included, as doing so would make the coding list too extensive. The words for "country" (国家/*guojia*) and (中国/*Zhongguo*) are terms that are included in names, such as company names, for example "Sudapet" (苏丹国家石油公司/*Sudan guojia shiyou gongsi*) and therefore have a disproportionately high count. Thus, these are not included. Finally, words that are not clearly related to the three terms, for example "diversification" (多样化/*duoyanghua*), are not included here.

The coding list

State interest

Zhanlue zhongyaoxing [**战略重要性**]: strategic importance
Zhanlue [战略]: strategy/strategic
Zhanlue huoban[战略伙伴]: strategic partner
Zhimin [殖民]: colonize
Guanxi [关系]: relation to/relationship
Shuangbian guanxi [双边关系]: bilateral relations
Gongying [共赢]: mutually profitable, "win-win"
Shuangying [双赢]: "win-win," mutually beneficial
Xingxiang [形象]: image
Shiyou hezuo [石油合作]: oil cooperation
Huli hezuo [互利合作]: mutually beneficial cooperation
Hezuohuoban [合作伙伴]: cooperation partner
Hezuo guanxi [合作关系]: cooperation relationship
Hezuo gongying [合作共赢]: "win-win" cooperation
Hezuo [合作]: cooperate/cooperation
Zuguo [祖国]: motherland
Waijiao [外交]: foreign policy
Yiyu [意图]: intent/intention
Zhengzhi [政治]: politics/political
Youyi [友谊]: friendship
Pengyou [朋友]: friend

Huibao [汇报]: report
Kaocha [考察]: inspect
Names of political leaders, e.g. 周永康 [Zhou Yongkang], 胡锦涛 [Hu Jintao]
Zouchuqu [走出去]: the "going out" strategy

Economic interest

Qiye liyi [企业利益]: company interest
Qiye [企业]: company
Gongsi [公司]: company
Lirun [利润]: profit
Shouru [收入]: revenue, earnings
Yingye [营业]: to do business, to trade
Jingzheng (li) [竞争(力)]: to compete, competitive strength
Youshi [优势]: superiority, advantage
Jingji shili [经济实力]: economic strength
Huibao (lu) [回报(率]: rate of return
Jishu [技术]: technology/skill
Chenggong [成功]: succeed, success
Chengji [成绩]: achievement
Yeji [业绩]: performance, growth
Xiaoyi [效益]: effectiveness, benefit, efficiency
Xiaolu [效率]: efficiency
Shichang [市场]: market
Shili [实力]: strength
Jingying [经营]: to manage, to operate, to engage in
Jingli [经理]: manager, director
Maoyihuoban [贸易伙伴]: economic partner, trade partner
Touzi [投资]: investment, to invest

Concern with domestic stability (*weiwen*) [维稳]

Shuxue [输血]: "to transfuse blood," to give aid and support
Daqing jingshen [大庆精神]: Daqing spirit
Tieren jingshen [铁人精神]: Ironman spirit
Shehui zeren [社会责任]: social responsibility
Fenzi [分子]: member of [political] group, word denoting "political"
Dang [党]: party, word denoting the "political"
Guojiaanquan [国家安全]: national security
Kongbu [恐怖]: terrorism, terror, terrorist
Zhengzhi wending [政治稳定]: political stability
Fengxian [风险]: risk
Kongbuxiji [恐怖袭击]: terrorist attack
Wuzhuang [武装/]: arms, military
Kongbuzhuyi [恐怖主义/]: terrorism

3 The Chinese energy sector

Table A.1 The three large NOCs in China

China National Petroleum Corporation (CNPC) CNPC was created on September 17, 1988, when the Ministry of Petroleum Industry was dissolved and the upstream (exploration and production) assets of the MPI were transferred to this company. CNPC is the largest oil producer in China. It was the fourth largest corporation in the world in 2014 and the second largest in China. CNPC's 2014 revenues were $432.0 billion,[1] amounting to total profits of $18.5 billion.[2] CNPC has 1.7 million employees. CNPC is the parent company of public-listed PetroChina, a company created in 1999 as part of the restructuring of CNPC.
China Petroleum and Chemical Corporation (Sinopec) Sinopec was established on July 12, 1983, from the downstream (refining and marketing) assets of the MPI and the Ministry of Chemical Industry. In 2000, Sinopec Corp. was established and listed in the Hong Kong, New York, and London stock exchanges. Sinopec is China's (and Asia's) largest petroleum refiner, supplying 80% of China's fuel. It was the largest corporation in China and the third largest in the world in 2014, with total revenue of $457.2 billion and total profits of $8.9 billion in 2014.[3] It had 1.02 million employees in 2011.
China National Offshore Oil Corporation (CNOOC) CNOOC was founded on February 15, 1982, and was established as a cooperation under MPI to form joint ventures with foreign firms to operate domestically in China. It is mainly focused on China's offshore oil industry. CNOOC is China's largest offshore oil and gas producer. CNOOC ranked as the 79th largest corporation in the world in 2014. Its 2014 revenues amounted to $96.0 billion with total profits of $7.7 billion.[4] It has 98,750 employees (2011).

1 Unless stated otherwise, all monetary amounts are in U.S. dollars.
2 *Fortune*, "Global 500 2014, China National Petroleum Corporation," http://fortune.com/global500/china-national-petroleum-4/
3 *Fortune*, "Global 500 2014, Sinopec Group," http://fortune.com/global500/sinopec-group-3/
4 *Fortune*, "Global 500 2014, China National Offshore Oil," http://fortune.com/global500/china-national-offshore-oil-79/

4 Nigeria

Table A.2 Nigeria's level of strategic importance

Country	*1. Level of political relations*[1]	*a. Level of partnership*	*b. Number of state visits of senior leaders*[2, 3]
Nigeria	1	1	1 (14) – from China: 7 – to China: 7

(*Continued*)

Table A.2 (Continued)

	2. Role for CCP regime stability	*a. Whether an extremist group has established a branch*	*b. Level of fatalities from militant activities (on Chinese nationals)*	*c. Relations with Taiwan*	*3. Salience of territory*	*a. Ethnic ties*	*b. Strategic location*
Nigeria	2	Yes	2	No	1	No	1

	4. Role for other great power	*a. U.S. alliance partner*	*b. UN sanction*	*5. Bilateral trade*[4]	*Total*
Nigeria	2	No	No	2	2

1 This is measured in the following way: if there are established relations between the two sides, it is measured as "0"; if there is a strategic partnership, it is measured as "1"; if there is a comprehensive strategic partnership, it is measured as "2."

2 If there are from 0–10 visits, it is measured as "0"; if there are from 11–20 visits, it is measured as "1"; if there are more than 20 visits, it is measured as "2."

3 For detailed data on senior visits from China to Nigeria and from Nigeria to China in the period from 2000–14, look here: Behrndt-Eriksen, Chinese *Energy Companies' Acquisitions Abroad.*

4 This is measured in the following way: if bilateral trade is from $0–10 billion, it is measured as "0"; if bilateral trade is from $10–20 billion, it is measured as "1"; if bilateral trade is more than $20 billion, it is measured as "2."

5 Angola

Table A.3 Angola's level of strategic importance

Country	*1. Level of political relations*	*a. Level of partnership*	*b. Number of state visits of senior leaders*[1]
Angola	1	1	1 (11) – from China: 3 – to China: 8

	2. Role for CCP regime stability[2]	*a. Whether an extremist group has established a branch*	*b. Level of fatalities from militant activities*	*c. Relations with Taiwan*	*3. Salience of territory*	*a. Ethnic ties*	*b. Strategic location*
Angola	0	No	0	No	1	No	1

	4. Role for other great power	*a. U.S. alliance partner*	*b. UN sanction*	*5. Bilateral trade*	*Total*
Angola	1	No	No	2	1

1 For detailed data on senior visits from China to Angola and from Angola to China in the period from 2000–14, look here: Behrndt-Eriksen, *Chinese Energy Companies' Acquisitions Abroad.*

2 This is measured in the following way: if no branch has been established, it is measured as "0"; if there is a branch, it is measured as "1"; if there have been fatalities of Chinese nationals, it is measured as "2."

6 Sudan

Table A.4 Sudan's level of strategic importance

Country	*1. Level of political relations*	*a. Level of partnership*	*b. Number of state visits of senior leaders*[1]
Sudan	0	0	0 (9) – from China: 3 – to China: 6

	2. Role for CCP regime stability	*a. Whether an extremist has set up a branch*	*b. Level of fatalities from militant activities*	*c. Relations with Taiwan*	*3. Salience of territory*	*a. Ethnic ties*	*b. Strategic location*
Sudan	2	Yes	2	No	2	No	2

	4. Role for other great power	*a. U.S. alliance partner*	*b. UN sanction*	*5. Bilateral trade*	*Total*
Sudan	2	No	Yes	1 (in 2011)	2

1 For detailed data on senior visits from China to Sudan and South Sudan and from Sudan and South Sudan to China in the period from 2000–14, look here: Behrndt-Eriksen, *Chinese Energy Companies' Acquisitions Abroad.*

7 Tunisia

Table A.5 Tunisia's level of strategic importance

Country	*1. Level of political relations*	*a. Level of partnership*	*b. Number of state visits of senior leaders*[1]
Tunisia	0	0	0 (5) – from China: 4 – to China: 1

(*Continued*)

Table A.5 (Continued)

	2. Role for CCP regime stability	*a. Whether an extremist has set up a branch in the country*	*b. Level of fatalities from militant activities*	*c. Relations with Taiwan*	*3. Salience of territory*	*a. Ethnic ties*	*b. Strategic location*
Tunisia	1	Yes	No	No	0	No	0

	4. Role for other great power	*a. U.S. alliance partner*	*b. UN sanction*	*5. Bilateral trade*	*Total*
Tunisia	1	No	No	0	0

1 For detailed data on senior visits from China to Tunisia and from Tunisia to China in the period from 2000–14, look here: Behrndt-Eriksen, *Chinese Energy Companies' Acquisitions Abroad.*

8 Kazakhstan, Canada, Uzbekistan, and Denmark

Kazakhstan

Table A.6 Kazakhstan's level of strategic importance

Country	*1. Level of political relations*	*a. Level of partnership*	*b. Number of state visits of senior leaders*[1]
Kazakhstan	2	2	2 (38) – from China: 18 – to China: 20

	2. Role for CCP regime stability	*a. Whether an extremist group has established a branch*	*b. Level of fatalities from militant activities*	*c. Relations with Taiwan*	*3. Salience of territory*	*a. Ethnic ties*	*b. Strategic location*
Kazakhstan	2	Yes	0	No	2	Yes	2

	4. Role for other great power	*a. U.S. alliance partner*	*b. UN sanction*	*5. Bilateral trade*	*Total*
Kazakhstan	1	No	No	2	2

1 For detailed data on senior visits from China to Kazakhstan and from Kazakhstan to China in the period from 2000–14, look here: Behrndt-Eriksen, *Chinese Energy Companies' Acquisitions Abroad.*

Canada

Table A.7 Canada's level of strategic importance

Country	*1. Level of political relations*	*a. Level of partnership*	*b. Number of state visits of senior leaders*[1]
Canada	0	1	0 (10) – from China: 3 – to China: 7

	2. Role for CCP regime stability	*a. Whether an extremist has established a branch*	*b. Level of fatalities from militant activities*	*c. Relations with Taiwan*	*3. Salience of territory*	*a. Ethnic ties*	*b. Strategic location*
Canada	0	No	0	No	0	No	1

	4. Role for other great power	*a. U.S. alliance partner*	*b. UN sanctions*	*5. Bilateral trade*	*Total*
Canada	1	Yes	No	2	0

1 For detailed data on senior visits from China to Canada and from Canada to China in the period from 2000–14, look here: Behrndt-Eriksen, *Chinese Energy Companies' Acquisitions Abroad*.

Uzbekistan

Table A.8 Uzbekistan's level of strategic importance

Country	*1. Level of political relations*	*a. Level of partnership*	*b. Number of state visits of senior leaders*[1]
Uzbekistan	1	1	1 (16) – from China: 6 – to China: 10

	2. Role for CCP regime stability	*a. Whether an extremist group has established a branch*	*b. Level of fatalities from militant activities*	*c. Relations with Taiwan*	*3. Salience of territory*	*a. Ethnic ties*	*b. Strategic location*
Uzbekistan	2	Yes	0	No	2	Yes	2

(*Continued*)

Table A.8 (Continued)

	4. Role for other great power	*b. U.S. alliance partner*	*c. UN sanction*	*5. Bilateral trade*	*Total*
Uzbekistan	2	No	No	0	2

[1] For detailed data on senior visits from China to Uzbekistan and from Uzbekistan to China in the period from 2000–14, look here: Behrndt-Eriksen, *Chinese Energy Companies' Acquisitions Abroad.*

Denmark

Table A.9 Denmark's level of strategic importance

Country	*1. Level of political relations*	*a. Level of partnership*	*b. Number of state visits of senior leaders*[1]
Denmark	1	2	1 (18) – from China: 8 – to China: 10

	2. Role for CCP regime stability	*a. Whether an extremist has established a branch*	*b. Level of fatalities from militant activities*	*c. Relations with Taiwan*	*3. Salience of territory*	*a. Ethnic ties*	*b. Strategic location*
Denmark	0	Yes	0	No	0	No	1

	4. Role for other great power	*a. U.S. alliance partner*	*b. UN sanction*	*5. Bilateral trade*	*Total*
Denmark	1	Yes	No	0	0

1 For detailed data on senior visits from China to Denmark and from Denmark to China in the period from 2000–14, look at Behrndt-Eriksen, *Chinese Energy Companies' Acquisitions Abroad.*

Notes

1 In fact, when including 公司, nine of the articles that otherwise would be coded as belonging to state interests are allocated to the economic interests category.
2 For example, see Hu Wenbo [胡文博]. 南苏丹独立：石油财富悬疑 [Independence of South Sudan: Suspense of Oil Riches], *中国石化报* (*China Petrochemical News*), July 29, 2011.

Index

acquisitions 1–3, 26, 48, 50, 54n1; in Angola 97, 99–100, 105–8, 109, 238; in Canada 187, 191–8, 223n49, 240; in Denmark 215; in Kazakhstan 175, 177, 180, 183–4; in Nigeria 61, 69, 73–6, 80, 238; in Sudan 120, 129; in Tunisia 155, 161–7, 169, 239; in Uzbekistan 203–5, 209, 240
Addax Petroleum Corporation 69, 73–6, **74**, 80, 238
Afghanistan 122, 156, 206, *207*
Africa 1–2, 5, 31, 237–9, 243; al-Qaeda in 28, 63, 65, 91, 122, 136, 155, 156; Chinese relations with 71, 104, 250; strategic importance of **31**; *see also* Angola; Nigeria; Sudan; Tunisia
AFRICOM (US Africa Command) 123
Agip KCO 120, **181**, 185, 239, 240
AktobeMunaiGaz 176
Algeria 28, 94
Al-Ingaz regime (Sudan) 118
al-Qaeda **136**, 212; in Africa 28, 63, 65, 77, 91, 122, 136, 155, 156; in Central Asia 177, 200, 206; *see also* extremist groups
Alves, Ana C. 89
AMIS (African Union Mission in Sudan) 129
Amum, Pagan 141
Andrews-Speed, Philip 23
Angola 8, 31, 65, 87–117, *88*, *92*, 237–9, 251; Angola model in 87, 89, 98–9; bureaucracy of 88, 89; Chinese relations with 87, 90, 93, 262; Civil War in 89, 97; Eximbank loan to (key decision 1) 97–101, **99**, 109, 238; failed acquisition attempt in (key decision 3) 97, 105, **106**, 107–9, 238; history of NOCs in 90; literature on 87–90; vs. Nigeria 91, 93, 94, 100; oil and gas levels in 93–4, 238; qualitative analyses of 97–108, 109, 238, 241, **241**; quantitative analysis of 94–7, *95*, 108, 109, 238, **241**, 243, *243*; Sonaref refinery in (key decision 2) 97, 101–5, *102*, 109, 244; strategic importance of **29**, **30**, **31**, 90–3, *93*, **93**, 94, 109, 238, **242**, 248, **262–3**; vs. Sudan 124, 125
Annan, Kofi 129–30
AOSC (Athabasca Oil Sands Corporation) **191**, 192–4, 198, 240
A.P. Møller-Mærsk *51*, **52**, **53**
AQIM (al-Qaeda in the Islamic Maghreb) 155
Arab uprisings 153–4, 156, 167, 168, 169, 249
Arctic Council 215, 217–20, 240
Atlantis Holding Norway AS 161–4, **162**
AU (African Union) 129–35, 140
authoritarianism 12, 13, 26, 247, 252, 253
authoritarian states: audience costs in 11–12, 236, 252; China as 34n29, 247; domestic stability in 250; foreign policy of 4–5, 7, 11–42, 236–55; hypotheses on foreign policy of 16–19, 21–2, 236–7, 247; literature on 12–14; non-state actors in 7, 13, 245–7; personalist dictatorship type of 12, 252, 253; types of 12, 13, 246, 247, 252–3
AU-UN Mission in Darfur (UNAMID) 129–35
Ayoob, Mohammed 13
Azar, Edward 13

Baldwin, David 16, 254
Bashir, Omar al- 2, 129–34, 140, 141
Beijing Olympics (2008) 126–7, 134, 135, 139, 142, 244, 246, 251; and international opinion 131–2
Ben Ali, Zine El Abidine 153, 156, 163

Bernardo, João Manuel 99
Biden, Joseph 132
Bi Jianhai 16
bin Laden, Osama 122, 124
Boko Haram 63, 77, **78**, 79
Boras, Alan 195
Bouazizi, Mohammed 167
Bourguiba regime (Tunisia) 155
BP (British Petroleum) *51*, **52**, **53**, 62, 74, 100, 120
British Gas (BG Group) **181**

Campo, Indira 89
Canada 8, 31, 32, 186–98, *186*, 240–3, 251; Chinese relations with 186–7, 265; CNOOC's acquisition in (key decision 3) 191, 196–8, 223n49, 240; CNPC acquisitions in (key decision 1) **191**, 192–4, 240; failed Encana deal in (key decision 2) **194**, 195–6, **197**, 240, 244, 245; history of NOCs in 187; oil and gas levels in 187–8, 198, 240; qualitative analysis of 191–6, 198, 240, 241, **241**; quantitative analysis of 188–91, *189*, *190*, 193–4, 196, 198, 240, **241**, *243*; strategic importance of **29**, **30**, **32**, **187**, 188, 198, 240, **242**, 248, **265**
capabilities: economic vs. military 15, 251; technological 163; *see also* military power
CDB (China Development Bank) 48; and Angola 107, 108; and Canada 192, 193, 194, 196, 198
Central Asia 2, **32**, 197, 200, 250; pipeline through 49, 203, 204, 206, *207*, 208, 209, 239, 240; *see also* Kazakhstan; Uzbekistan
Chang Hexi 103
Chen Deming 197
Chen Xiaodong 141
Chevron *51*, **52**, **53**, 62, 74, 120
China Construction Bank 98
China International Fund (CIF) 98, 111n41
China National Offshore Oil Corporation *see* CNOOC
China National Petroleum Corporation *see* CNPC
China Petoleum & Chemical Corp. *see* Sinochem
China Petrochemical Corporation *see* Sinopec
China Sonangol (oil company) 106, 107, 108, 113n88, 113n96
Chinese Communist Party (CCP): and Angola 91, 93; and Arab uprisings 153, 168; and Canada 187, 193; Central Committee of 49, 56n19, 193; and Chinese state 4, 9n10, 36n54; and Denmark 211; and domestic stability 3, 4, 7, 19, **28**, **30**, 63, 65, **66**, 91, **93**, 122, **125**, 134, 138, 155, **157**, **177**, **187**, **200**, **212**, 237, 248, 254, 262, **264**, **265**; and economic development 14–15, 18, 21; and energy 18, 27, 43–8, 254; and Kazakhstan 177; legitimacy of 5, 14–15, 19–21, 138, 248, 253–4; and Nigeria 63, 65, 66; and NOCs 47–8, 49, 54, 56n19; Organization Department of 48; Politburo of 18, 28, 48, 142, 166; and strategic importance 25, **28**, 30; and Sudan 122, 125, 134, 138; and technology acquisition 193; and Tunisia 153, 155, 157, 168; and Uzbekistan 200
Chinese nationals: in Angola 91, 97, 98, 100, 101, 262, **262**; attacks on **30**, 63, 65, 67–70, 72, 76–80, **78**, 122, 125, 127, 129, 135, **136**, 137–9, 143, 248, **262**, **263**, **264**, **265**, **266**; in Canada **265**; in Denmark 219–20, **266**; and domestic stability 3, 20–1, 37n66, 76, 79, 80, 135–9, 143, 248; in Kazakhstan 184, **264**; in Nigeria 61, 63, 65, 67–70, 72, 76–80, **78**, 238, **262**; and social media 26–7, 76, 80; and strategic importance 28, 30; in Sudan 122, 125, 127, 129, 135, **136**, 137–9, 142, 143, 238, **263**; in Tunisia 156, 161, 167, 168, **264**; in Uzbekistan 206, 265
Chinese politics theory 4, 14, 249, 253, 254, 255
Chrétien, Jean 189
Christensen, Thomas 16, 20, 252
CITIC 176, 222n7
classical realism 12, 254
Clinton, Bill 124
Clinton, Hilary 91
CNOOC (China National Offshore Oil Corporation) 17, 43–4, **261**; in Angola 97, 105–8, 109, 238, 244; in Canada 187, 191, 196, **197**, 198, 223n49, 240; in Denmark 211; in Kazakhstan 176, **181**, 182–3, 184, 185, 239; in Nigeria 62, 69, 71, 72, 79; profitability of *51*, **52**, **53**, 54; share prices of 75, 163, 195, 197; size of 50; state control of 22, 54; subsidiaries

of 48, 49, 50, 196; in Sudan 120; in Tunisia 155; in Uzbekistan 199
CNPC (China National Petroleum Corporation) 17, 19, 43–4, **261**; in Canada 187, **191**, 192–3, **194**, 198, 240; in Denmark 211; in Kazakhstan 175, 176, 180–2, **183**, 184, 239; in Nigeria 62, 69–73, 75, 79, 82n36; profitability of *51*, 52–4; quasi-governmental status of 49; share prices of 75, 107, 197; size of 50; state control of 22, 54; subsidiaries of 48, 49, 50, 165, 191; in Sudan 118, 120, 122, 123, 129, 130, 132, 134, 136–42, 244; in Tunisia 155, 161, 164–7, 168, 169, 239; in Uzbekistan 199, 203–9, 240
CNPCI (China National Petroleum Corporation International) 165
Cold War 91
color revolutions 36n48, 206
Comprehensive Peace Agreement (CPA; Sudan) 140
Conoco 120
Cuba 91

Dalai Lama 187, 211, 215–17, 219
Darfur conflict (Sudan) 129–35, 137, 139, 141, 145n45
democracies 11, 23, 247
democratic peace theory 13
Deng Xiaoping 18, 87
Denmark 8, 31, 32, 209–21, *209*, *210*; and Arctic Council (key decision 2) 215, 217–20, 240; Chinese relations with 211, 266; diplomatic crisis with (key decision 1) 215–17, 220, 221, 240; history of NOCs in 211; oil and gas levels in 212, 213, 221, 240; qualitative analysis of 214–21, 240, **242**; quantitative analysis of 213, *214*, 216–17, 220, 221, 240, **242**, *243*; strategic importance of **29**, **30**, **32**, **212**, 212, 215, 221, 240, **242**, 248, **266**
developmental state theory 46
diplomatic (political) relations **28**, **29**; with Angola 87, 90, **93**, **262**; with Canada 186, **187**, **265**; with Denmark **212**, **266**; with Kazakhstan 175, **177**, **264**; with Nigeria 63, **66**, **261**; and NOCs 50, *51*; and strategic importance 27–8, 29, 30; with Sudan 118, 122, **125**, **263**; with Tunisia 153, 155, **157**, **263**; with Uzbekistan 199, **200**, **265**
domestic stability (*weiwen*) **24**, **241**; and Angola 90, 91, 93, 94, *95*, *96*, 97, 100, 101, 104–6, 108, 248, **262**; in authoritarian states 245, 250; and Canada **187**, 188–91, *189*, *190*, 193–6, 198, **265**; and CCP 3, 4, 7, 19, 27, 28, 30, 63, 65, 66, 91, 93, 122, 125, 134, 138, 155, 157, 177, 187, 200, 213, 237, 248, 254, 262; coding for 257–60; and Denmark **212**, 213, *214*, *215*, 216–17, 220, **266**; as dependent variable 26–7; and economic development 5, 20–1, 248; and economic interests *6*, 250; and energy security 24–5, 255; and foreign policy 7, 14–15, 245, 247–50, 253; hypotheses on 21, 24, 33, 236–7, 241; and Kazakhstan **177**, 178, *179*, *180*, 181, 182, 184–5, 239, **264**; and legitimacy 19–21; and Nigeria 62, 63, 65, **66**, *67*, *68*, *69*, 71–3, 76, 79, 80, 238, 248, **262**; and NOCs 2, 19–21, 247–50, 252, 253; and safety of Chinese workers 3, 20–1, 37n66, 76, 79, 80, 135–9, 143; and social media 26–7, 248; and SOEs 7, 19–21, 247–50, 252; and state interests *6*, 21, 25, 37n66, 139, 250; and strategic importance 24–5, 28; and Sudan 120, 122, **125**, *126*, 127, *128*, 129, 133–9, 142, 143, 238, 246, 248, **263**; and Tunisia 153–4, 155, **157**, 158, *159*, *160*, 161, 164–9, **264**; and Uzbekistan **200**, *201*, *202*, *203*, 205, 206, 208, **265**
dos Santos, José 87, 95, 102, 104, 107

economic development: in Angola 89, 90; and CCP 14–15, 18, 21; and China–US rivalry 14; and domestic stability 5, 20–1, 248; and energy 15–16, 21; and foreign policy 1–3, 251; and good governance norms 62, 87, 89, 120; in Nigeria 61–2; and strengthening of SOEs 3–4, 17; in Sudan 118–19, 120; and technology acquisition 193; in Uzbekistan 204; Western model of 89
economic interests **24**, **241–2**; in Angola 90, 94, *95*, *96*, 97, 99–100, 101, 103, 105–7, 108, 109, 238, 251; and authoritarian states 245–7; in Canada 188, *189*, *190*, 191–8, 240, 251; and Chinese state 7, 14; coding for 257–60; in Denmark 213, *214*, 216–17, 219–20, 240; as dependent variable 26–7; and domestic stability

6, 250; and energy administration 43; and foreign policy 4, 245–7; hypotheses on 21, 24, 33, 236–7, 241–2; in Kazakhstan 177, *179*, *180*, 181–6, 239, 240; in Nigeria 62, 66, *67*, *68*, 69, 71–6, 80–1, 237–8; and NOCs 3, 7, 46, 245, 246–7; of SOEs 5, 18; and state interests 3–4, *6*, 23, 54, 245, 251; and strategic importance 24, 27–9; in Sudan 119, 120, *126*, *127*, 128, 129, 132, 134, 135, 139, 143, 238, 245–6, 251; in Tunisia 158, *159*, *160*, 161–9, 239; in Uzbekistan 200, *201*, *202*, 203–6, 208, 209, 240, 251; *see also* trade, bilateral

Egypt 28, 90, 122, 155, 167, 168

elites: in Angola 88–9; in authoritarian states 11; in China 18–19; in Nigeria 61, 71, 72; in Sudan 119

Encana Corporation 191, **194**, 195–6, 198, 223n49, 240, 244, 245

energy: and CCP 18, 27, 43–8, 254; consumption of 1, 15–16, 47, 54n1; crises in 49; imports of 1–2, 44, 45; laws on 50; vs. military power 15, 16; policy on 18, 23–4, 25, 46–7, 48–9, 54; state control of 18, 47–9; and state interests 15, 16, 24, 43; *see also* oil and gas levels

energy administration 18, 43–8; decentralization of 45, 46, 47, 54; and economic interests 43; Energy Bureau (NDRC) 45, 49; local actors in 46–7; Ministry of Energy 43–5, 54; NEA (National Energy Administration) 50; NEC (National Energy Commission) 45; NELG (National Energy Leading Small Group) 45; reforms to 23, 43, 44–5, 47, 54; structure of 43–4

energy security 16, 18, 24–5, 89, 119, 208, 254–5

Eni S.P.A. *51*, **52**, **53**, 62

En Nadha 156

Enoksen, Hans 219

ETAP (Entreprise Tunisienne d'Activites Petrolieres) 165, 166

ethnicity: and Angola 91, 262, **262**; and Canada 265, **265**; and Denmark 266, **266**; and Kazakhstan 264; and Nigeria 63, 262, **262**; and strategic importance 29, **30**, 37n74; and Sudan 122, 263, **263**; and Tunisia 156, 264, **264**; and Uzbekistan 265, **265**

Eximbank (Export-Import Bank of China) 48, 204; and Angola 89, 97–101, 107, 108, 109, 238; and Nigeria 70, 71, 72, 75; and South Sudan 148n112

extremist groups: in Angola 91, 262, **262**; in Canada **265**; in Denmark 212, **266**; in Kazakhstan 177, 181, **264**; in Nigeria 28, 63, 65, 76, 91, **262**; and strategic importance 28, **30**; in Sudan 122, 124, 125, 263, **263**; in Tunisia 155–6, **264**; in Uzbekistan 199–200, 205–6, 226n100, 226n105, **265**; *see also* al-Qaeda

Exxon Mobil *51*, **52**, **53**, 62, 74, 107

Faroe Islands 209, 212

Farrow, Mia 132

Fidelity Investments 132

Flaherty, Jim 193

FNLA (Frente Nacional para Libertação de Angola) 87, 91

foreign aid: to Angola 89, 97, 99, 107, 244; appreciation of 71, 99, 104, 133, 137, 166, 193; to Nigeria 61, 62, 70, 72, 73; and state control of NOCs 3, 26, 48; to Sudan 118, 129, 133, 135, 138, 139, 142; to Tunisia 156, 161, 164, 168, 169; to Uzbekistan 204, 206, 208; *see also* loans

foreign direct investment (FDI) 56n22, 65

foreign policy: actors in 13–14, 22, 26; on Africa 104; on Angola 87, 89, 97, 100, 101, 105; of authoritarian states 4–5, 7, 11–42, 236–7, 245–7, 250; on Canada 191; on Denmark 215; and economic development 1–3, 251; and economic interests 4, 245–7; and energy requirements 15–16; expansionist strategy in 61, 62, 89, 120, 245, 251, 253; factors in 21–2, 251, 254; of "Going Out" (*zouchuqu*) 2, 11, 37n71, 48, 136, 243; hypotheses on 16–19, 21–6, 32–3, 236–7, 243; and international opinion 131–2, 134–5; on Kazakhstan 181; literature on 12–14, 89, 118; on Nigeria 59, 61, 69, 76; and NOCs 4, 7, 15–16, 61, 104, 164, 196, 236–7, 243–7, 251–2, 253; of non-interference 131, 133, 134, 141, 142, 143, 161, 167–9, 244, 249; and non-state actors 4, 13–14, 236, 245–7, 251, 253; and safety of Chinese workers 76, 80, 139; shifts in 129–35, 238, 244, 246, 251; and SOEs 2–3, 7,

11, 12, 14, 16–19, 24–6, 236–7, 243, 253; structural variables in 26, 252; on Sudan 2–3, 19, 119, 127, 129–35, 238, 246, 251; and Taiwan 19, 20, 28, 30; on Uzbekistan 203
France 156, 170n13, 215
Fu Chengyu 74

Gallacher, Bill 192
Gandur, Jean Claude 73
garbage can model 22
Gazprom **52**, **53**
Geddes, Barbara 12, 252
geographic factors (salience of territory) 37nn74–5; and Angola 91, 93, **93**, 262, **262**; and Canada 187, **187**, 227n116, 265, **265**; and Denmark 212, **212**, 227n116, 266, **266**; and Kazakhstan 177, **177**, 264, **264**; and Nigeria 63, 66, **66**, 262, **262**; and strategic importance 27, **28**, 29, **30**, 31; and Sudan 122–3, **125**, **263**; and Tunisia 156, **157**, **264**; and Uzbekistan **200**, **265**
Georgia 19, 36n48, 206
Germany 1
Ghannouchi, Mohamed 166
globalist theory 87, 89, 90, 118, 120
Global Times 138, 168
GNPOC (Greater Nile Petroleum Operating Company) 136
"Going Out" (*zouchuqu*) policy 2, 11, 37n71, 48, 136, 243
Greenland 209, 211, 212, 215, 219, 227n116; *see also* Denmark

Han Gensheng 163
Harper, Stephen 186–7, 188, 194, 197, 198, 219
Hartley, Peter 50
Hensel, Paul R. 37nn74–5
Hong Lei 79, 141
Houser, Trevor 46
Hua Chunying 216
Hu Jintao 18, 36n48, 48; and Canada 188–9, 194, 196, 198, 245; and Denmark 219, 220, 221; on "harmonious world" 147n76; and Kazakhstan 178, 182, 184; and Nigeria 59, 67, 69, 70, 71, 72, 73, 82n34; and Sudan 122, 129–35, 145n45; and Uzbekistan 201, 204, 205, 206, 208
Husky Oil 215, 227n124
Hu Zhengyue 218

Iceland 219
IMF (International Monetary Fund) 89, 97
IMU (Islamic Movement of Uzbekistan) 205–6, 226n100
infrastructure 29, 48, 54n1; in Angola 89, 91, *92*, 97, 98, 100, 104, 105, 108; in Canada 187; in China 47; in Kazakhstan 177, 183; in Nigeria 59, 61, 63, *64*, 66, 69, 70–3, 75, 80, 238; oil for 61, 70–3, 75, 80, 238; in South Sudan 148n112; in Sudan 118, 120, *123*, 125, 129, 133, 140, 142; in Tunisia 153, 156, 165; in Uzbekistan 204
International Criminal Court (ICC) 141
international oil companies (IOCs): in Angola 102, 107; in Canada 192; in Kazakhstan 182, 183; in Nigeria 59, 62, 74, 76–7; profitability of 50–4; in Sudan 120; in Tunisia 155; in Western states 23
international relations: and authoritarian states 245, 250, 251–5; balance of power in 15–16; vs. domestic issues 20; economic 1, 23; and foreign policy 131–2, 134–5; literature of 4, 8, 12–15, 245, 250, 251–5; *see also* diplomatic (political) relations
investments 47, 48, 49, 54; *see also* acquisitions
Iran 176
Iraq 74, 156

Japan 1, 20, 36n51
JEM (Justice and Equality Movement; Sudan) **136**, 137
Jiang Yu 132
Jiang Zemin 18, 59, 163, 164
Job, Brian 13
Jonathan, Goodluck Ebele 59
Jordan 167

Karimov, Islam 201–8, 249
Katzer, J. 23, 47
Kazakhstan 8, 31, 32, 175–86, *176*, 180, 239–43, 250; Chinese relations with 175, 177, 264; CNOOC and Sinopec failure in (key decision 1) **181**, 182–3, 184, 239; CNPC's acquisition in (key decision 2) 176, 180, **183**, 184; ethnic separatists in (key decision 3) 181, 184–5, 239, 249, 264; history of NOCs in 175–7; oil and gas levels in 177–8, 185, 239; qualitative analysis of

181–5, 186, 239, 240, **241**; quantitative analysis of 178, *179*, *180*, 181, 182, 184, 185–6, 239, 240, **241**, *243*; strategic importance of **29**, **30**, **32**, **177**, 177, 185, 239, **242**, **264**; vs. Sudan 183; and Uzbekistan 199, 200; and Uzbekistan-China pipeline 206, *207*, 208, 239
KazMunaiGas Exploration Production (RDGZ) 184, 185, 249
Kiir, Mayardit Salva 122, 140, 142, 148n112
KNOC (South Korea) 204
Kong, Bo 46
Korea, Democratic People's Republic of (DPRK; North Korea) 19
KPC (Kuwait Petroleum Corp) 165
KUFPEC (Kuwait Foreign Petroleum Exploration Company) 165
Kurdistan 74
Kyrgyzstan 19, 36n48, 199, 207

Latin America 2
leadership 18–19, 21; of NOCs 54, 56n19; of SOEs 48; types of 18
leadership visits 28, **29**; with Angola 87, 90, 94, 97, 99, 101, 102, 104, 105, 107, 108, 244, **262**; with Canada 187, 188–9, 193, 194, 196, 197, 198, 245, **265**; with Denmark 212, 219, **266**; with Kazakhstan 175, 177, 178, 182, **264**; with Nigeria 59, 63, 65, 67, 69, 70, 71, 72, 73, **261**; with Sudan 118, 122, 123, 125, 129, 130, 133, 135, 141, 142, 248, **263**; with Tunisia 153, 155, 161, 163, 164, 166, 167, **263**; with Uzbekistan 199, 201, 203, 204, 205, 206, 208, 249, **265**
legitimacy: of CCP 5, 14–15, 19–21, 138, 248, 253–4; of Chinese state 5, 14–15, 19–21, 138, 246, 248, 253–4; and domestic stability 19–21
liberal theory 3, 4, 13, 24, 251, 253, 255; on Angola 87; on Nigeria 59; on Sudan 118
Libya 77, 163, 167, 169, 249
Li Chengwen 137
Li Keqiang 193
Li Peng 175, 176
Liu Guijin 131, 132, 133, 137, 142
Liu Weimin 141
Liu Zhenmin 218
Li Yizhong 56n19
Li Zhenfu 220
loans: to Angola 87, 89, 97–101, 104, 105, 107–8, 109, 238; to Canada 192, 193, 196, 198; to Kazakhstan 184; to Nigeria 69, 70, 71, 72, 75; to NOCs 47, 48, 61; to South Sudan 148n112; to Sudan 133, 142; to Uzbekistan 204, 205, 206
Lobito refinery *see* Sonaref refinery
London Mining 215
Loro (branch of Boko Haram) 63
Lukoil (Russia) 183, 204
Lundin (Sweden) 163
Luo Xiaoguang 140, 141

Ma Fucai 56n19
Ma Kai 207
Mali 91
Mao Zedong 18
Mao Zefeng 195
Marathon Oil 106, 107
Martin, Paul 188–9
mass incidents 19, 36n46
Ma Yingjiu 28
Medlock, Kenneth 50
MEND (Movement for the Emancipation of the Niger Delta) 77, **78**
military factors 27–9, 63, 91, 123, 156, 206, 249
military power 1; and domestic stability 19, 20, 138; vs. energy 15, 16, 254; and types of authoritarian states 12, 252
Ministry of Commerce (China) 45
Ministry of Energy (China) 43–5, 54
Ministry of Foreign Affairs (MFA; China) 17, 27, 45
Ministry of Land and Resources (China) 45
Ministry of Petroleum Industry (MPI; China) 43–4, 45
Ministry of Trade (China) 98
Mitchell, Sara M. 37nn74–5
Moran, Theodore 61
Morocco 77
MPLA (Moviemento Popular de Libertação de Angola) 87
Mubarak, Hosni 167

National Energy Leading Small Group (NELG) 45
nationalism 19, 20, 36n51, 134, 253
nationalist economic theory 24
Nazarbayev, Nursultan 178
NCP (National Congress Party; Sudan) 118, 119

NDRC (National Development and Reform Commission; China) 18, 45, 48, 49, 50, 77, 130
NEA (National Energy Administration; China) 45, 50
NEC (National Energy Commission; China) 45
neo-classical realism 12
Nexen 191, 196, **197**, 198, 223n49, 240
NIF (National Islamic Front) 118
Niger 77
Nigeria 8, 28, 31, 59–86, *60*, 239, 241–3; vs. Angola 91, 93, 94, 100; attacks on Chinese workers in (key decision 3) 63, 65, 67–70, 72, 76, *77*, 78–80, 238, 248; Chinese relations with 59, 63, 261; history of NOCs in 62–3; literature on 59–62; oil and gas levels in 66, 237; oil for infrastructure in (key decision 1) 70–3; qualitative analysis of 69–80, 238, **241**; quantitative analysis of 66, *67*, *68*, *69*, 238, **241**, *243*; Sinopec acquisition in (key decision 2) 73–6, 80, 238; strategic importance of **29**, **30**, **31**, 63–5, **66**, 237, **242**, **261**–**2**; vs. Sudan 125
Nomenklatura system 47, 48, 54
non-state actors 3–4, 17, 23; in authoritarian states 7, 13, 245–7; and foreign policy 4, 13–14, 236, 245–7, 251–3; *see also* oil companies, national; state-owned enterprises

Obasanjo, Olusegun 59, 70, 71, 72, 82n34, 83n48
oil and gas levels 37n70; in Angola 93–4, 238; and bilateral trade 29–30; in Canada 187–8, 198, 240; in Denmark 212, 213, 221, 240; and hypotheses *6*, 27, 30–2, 236, 237, 239, 242; in Kazakhstan 177–8, 185, 239; in Nigeria 66, 237; and strategic importance 5, 24–5; in Sudan 125, 238; in Tunisia 157–8, 169; in Uzbekistan 200, 208, 240
oil companies, national (NOCs) 43–58, **261**; in Angola 87–117; in Canada 186–98; and CCP 47–8, 49, 54, 56n19; and China–US rivalry 14; in Denmark 209–21; dividends from 47, 55n17; and domestic stability 2, 19–21, 247–50, 252, 253; and economic interests 3, 7, 46, 245, 246–7, 254; and foreign policy 4, 7, 15–16, 61, 104, 164, 196, 236–7, 243–7, 251–2, 253; independence of 18, 20, 21, 46, 49–54, 89, 94, 105, 110n11, 119–20, 134, 135, 182, 196, 237, 244, 250, 251, 253, 255; international stock exchange listings of 2, 17, 23, 44, 45, 49, 50, 53, 54; investments by 47, 48, 54; in Kazakhstan 175–86; leadership of 54, 56n19; loans to 47, 48, 61; in Nigeria 59–86; professionalization of 49, 50; profitability of 26, 37n68, 43, 49, 50–1, **52**, 53–4; as profit-maximizing entities 22, 43, 46, 50, *51*, 53, 54, 237; protests against 56n19; quasi-governmental status of 49; regulation of 47, 48; size of 49–50, 54; state control of 17, 18, 22, 33, 46–9, 54, 90; and state interests 2, 3–4, 5, 7, 254–5; subsidiaries of 17, 44, 48, 49–50, 106, 194; in Sudan 118–52, *121*; in Tunisia 153–74; in Uzbekistan 199–209; *see also* CNOOC; CNPC; Sinopec
Oliver, Joe 197
Olympics *see* Beijing Olympics
Oman 161, 162
One-China policy 63, 153, 215, 216
ONGC (Oil and Natural Gas Corporation; India) 99, 102, 106, 183

Peceny, Mark 12, 252
People's Daily 138, 139
Petersen, Friis Arne 219
Petrobras 106
PetroChina (PetroChina International Investment Company) 44, 50–1, **52**, **53**, 132, 240; in Canada **191**, 192–6, 198, 245; share prices of 163, 195; and Uzbekistan-China pipeline 207
PetroKazakhstan 181, **183**, 184, 185, 239, 240
Petróleo Brasileiro *51*, **52**, **53**
Petroleum Geo-Service (PGS; Norway) 161, **162**
Petronas 204
Philips oil company 62
political economy literature 4, 34n30; on Angola 87, 88–9; on Nigeria 59, 61; on Sudan 118–19; on Tunisia 153
Pollack, Jonathan 153
power: Chinese 1; national political 252; *see also* Chinese Communist Party, legitimacy of; military power
Power, Marcus 89

power transition theory 16, 254
principal-agent literature 46

Rasmussen, Lars Løkke 211, 216, 219
realist theory 1, 13, 16, 251, 253, 254–5; on Angola 87; on Nigeria 59, 61; on Sudan 118
reform 19, 237, 247; economic 8, 17, 46, 47; of energy sector 18, 23, 43, 44–5, 54
Rong Yiren 222n7
Ross, Robert 13
Royal Dutch Shell *51*, **52**, 53, **53**, **99**; in Angola 99; in Nigeria 62, 63, 74; in Sudan 120
Russia 199, 200, 208, 220; *see also* Soviet Union

Sabir, Mohammed 140
salience of territory *see* geographic factors
SASAC (State Asset Supervision and Administration Commission) 22, 47
Saudi Arabia 122
Schweller, Randall 13
SCO (Shanghai Cooperation Organization) 175, 226n105, 249
Serbia 19, 36n48
Shirk, Susan 18, 19, 20
Sinochem (China Petoleum & Chemical Corp.) 44, **52**, **53**, 169, 170n8; in Tunisia 155, 161–4, 169
Sinohydro 138
Sinopec (China Petrochemical Corporation) 17, 19, 43–4, **99**, **261**; in Angola 97, **99**, 100, 101–8, 109, 238, 244; in Canada 187; and Denmark 211; in Kazakhstan 176, **181**, 182–3, 184, 185, 239; in Nigeria 62, 69, 73–6, 80, 238; profitability of *51*, 52–4; quasi-governmental status of 49; share prices of 75, 76, 163, 195, 197; size of 50; state control of 22, 54; subsidiaries of 48, 49, 50, 73, 113n96; in Sudan 120, 142; in Tunisia 155, 162; in Uzbekistan 199
SIPC (Sinopec International Petroleum Exploration and Production Company) 73, **74**, 75–6
SLA (Sudan Liberation Army) **136**
social media: and Angola 97, 101, 106; and attacks on Chinese workers 26–7, 70, 76, 79, 80, 135, 138, 139, 248; and Kazakhstan 185; and Nigeria 70, 73, 76, 79; and Sudan 129, 133–4, 135, 138, 139; and Tunisia 161, 167, 168; and Uzbekistan 206; *see also Weibo*
Sonangol (Sociedade Nacional de Combustiveis de Angola) 88, 99, 102–3, 104, 105, 106; *see also* China Sonangol
Sonaref refinery (Lobito, Angola) 101, **102**, 103–5, 107, 109, 244
South Africa 65, 87, 90, 103; vs. Angola 91; strategic importance of 29, 30; vs. Sudan 122, 124; vs. Tunisia 155
South Sudan 121–2, 124, 138, 148n112; independence of 118; oil production shutdown by 125, 129, 139–43
Soviet Union (USSR) 14, 15, 16, 91; *see also* Russia
Søvndal, Villy 219
SPLA-North (Sudan People's Liberation Army) 138
SPLM (Sudan Peope's Liberation Movement) **136**, 141
Spruyt, Hendrik 16, 254
SRF (Sudan Revolutionary Front) 138
SSI (Sinangol Sinopec International) 97, 99, 101, 102, 104, 113n96
state, Chinese: as authoritarian state 34n29, 247; bureaucracy of 17–18, 43–5, 48, 54; and CCP 4, 9n10, 36n54; control of NOCs by 17, 18, 22, 33, 46–9, 54, 90; as creditor 47, 48; decentralization in 17, 45, 46, 47, 54; and economic interests 7, 14; fragility of 19, 20; fragmentation of 3, 4, 14, 17–18, 19, 21, 54, 246, 247; legitimacy of 5, 14–15, 19–21, 138, 246, 248, 253–4; and non-state actors 3–4; as regulator 47, 48; "rise" of 1, 7, 14–15, 18, 21; and SOEs 18, 22–4, 47, 247; *see also* Chinese Communist Party; diplomatic (political) relations; energy administration; foreign policy; reform
State Council 48
statecraft, techniques of 16, 254
State Development Planning Commission (SDPC) 44
State Economic and Trade Commission (SETC) 44, 45
State Energy Office (SEO) 45
state interests **24**, **241–2**; in Angola 90, 94–109, *95*, *96*, 238, 251; and attacks on Chinese workers 67–8, 70, 76, 80, 135, 139, 143; in Canada 188, *189*, *190*, 191, 193–4, 196, 197–8, 240, 251; coding for 257–60; in Denmark 213, *214*, *215*, 215–18, 220, 221, 240; as

dependent variable 26–7; and domestic stability *6*, 21, 25, 37n66, 139, 250; and economic interests 3–4, *6*, 23, 54, 245, 251; and energy 15, 16, 24, 43; hypotheses on 24, 33, 236–7, 241–2; in Kazakhstan 177, *179*, *180*, 181–6, 239, 240; and multinational companies 23; in Nigeria 62, 66, *67*, *68*, *69*, 70–3, 75, 76, 80–1, 237–8; and NOCs 2, 3–4, 5, 7, 254–5; in Sudan 120, *126*, *127*, *128*, 129–30, 133, 134, 135, 139, 140–1, 143, 238, 246, 251; in Tunisia 158, *159*, *160*, 161, 163–4, 166–7, 169, 239; in Uzbekistan 200, *201*, *202*, *203*, 204–9, 240, 251
state-owned enterprises (SOEs): and Chinese state 18, 22–4, 47, 247; and domestic stability 7, 19–21, 247–50, 252; economic interests of 5, 18; and foreign policy 2–3, 7, 11, 12, 14, 16–19, 24–6, 236–7, 243, 253; and hypotheses 243; independence of 20, 21, 26, 245; leadership of 48; as non-state actors 4, 7; as profit-maximizing entities 22; strengthening of 3–4, 17; *see also* oil companies, national
Steinfeld, Edward 22, 23
strategic importance **31**, **32**, **261**–**6**; of Angola **29**, **30**, 90–3, **93**, 94, 109, 238, **242**, 262–3; of Canada **29**, **30**, 187, **187**, 188, 198, 240, 248, 265; and case selection 30–2; and CCP 25, **28**, **30**; of Central Asia 250; of Denmark **29**, **30**, 212, **212**, 213, 215, 221, 240, 248, 266; and diplomatic relations 27, **28**, **29**, **30**; and domestic stability **24**, 25, **28**, 248; and economic interests **24**, 27–9; and ethnicity **29**, **30**, 37n74; factors in **24**, 25, 27–31; hypotheses on 5–7, 236, 237, 239, 242; of Kazakhstan **29**, **30**, 177, **177**, 185, 239, 264; of Nigeria **29**, **30**, 63–6, **66**, 237, **261**–**2**; of Sudan **29**, **30**, 122–4, **125**, 126, 143, 238, 263; of Tunisia **29**, **30**, 155–6, **157**, 158, 161, 169, 263–4; of Uzbekistan **29**, **30**, 199, **200**, 208, 240, 250, 265–6
strategic partnerships 27–8, **29**; with Angola 90, 106, 107, 108, **262**; with Canada 187, 194, **265**; with Denmark 211, 216, **266**; with Kazakhstan 177, 184, **264**; with Nigeria 59, 63, 65, 70, 71, 72, 82n34, **261**; with Sudan 118, 122, 141, **263**; with Tunisia 155, **263**; with Uzbekistan 199, 203, **265**
structural realism 5, 12, 13, 15–16, 237, 252–4
Sudan 8, 19, 28, 31, 118–52, *119*, 237–9, 241–6; vs. Angola 91, 124, 125; and Beijing Olympics 126–7, 131–2, 134, 135, 139, 142, 244, 246, 251; change in foreign policy towards (key decision 1) 129–35, 238, 244, 246, 251; Chinese relations with 118, 122, 125, 263; civil wars in 118, 125; Darfur conflict in 2–3, 129–35, 137, 139, 141, 145n45, 244; division of 118, 125, 139, 140; vs. Egypt 122; history of NOCs in 120, *121*, 122; vs. Kazakhstan 183; kidnapping of Chinese workers in (key decision 2) 129, 135–9, 238, 248; literature on 118–20; vs. Nigeria 125; oil and gas levels in 125, 238; oil production shutdown in (key decision 3) 125, 129, 139–43, 238, 244; qualitative analysis of 128–43, 238, 241; quantitative analysis of 126–8, *126*, *127*, *128*, 238, 241, **241**, 243, *243*; vs. South Africa 122, 124; strategic importance of **29**, **30**, **31**, 122–4, **125**, 126, 143, 238, **242**, 250, **263**
Su Shulin 19
Sweden 219
Syncrude 191, 223n49
Syria 19, 28, 169, 249

Taha, Ali Uthman Muhammad 131
Taiwan **30**; and Angola 90, **262**; and Canada **265**; and Chinese nationalism 36n51; and Denmark **266**; and foreign policy 19, 20, 28, 30; and Kazakhstan **264**; and Nigeria 59, 63, **262**; and Sudan 118, 122, **263**; and Tunisia 155, **264**; and Uzbekistan **265**
Tajikistan 199, *207*
Talisman (firm) 191
technology acquisition 26; in Angola 99–100, 101, 107, 108, 244; in Canada 192, 193, 195, 196, 197, 198, 244; in Denmark 220, 221; in Kazakhstan 182, 183–4; in Nigeria 70, 73, 74, 75; in Tunisia 163, 165–6
Texaco oil company 62
Thorning-Schmidt, Helle 219
Tiananmen Incident (1989) 19, 36n48
Tibet 215

Total S.A. *51*, **52**, 53, **53**, 62, 74, 106, 107
trade, bilateral 2, 29–30; with Angola 65, 87, 91, *93*, **93**, 102, 244, **263**; with Canada **187**, 194, **265**; with Denmark **212**, 217, 228n134, **266**; with Kazakhstan 175, **177**, **264**; with Nigeria 62–3, *65*, **66**, **262**; and strategic importance **30**; with Sudan 121–2, 124, *124*, **125**, **263**; with Tunisia 156, *157*, **157**, **264**; with Uzbekistan 199, **200**, **266**
Tunisia 8, 31, 153–74, *154*, 237, 241–3; Chinese non-interference in (key decision 3) 153, 161, 167–9, 239, 248–9; Chinese relations with 153, 155, 157, 263; CNPC acquisition in (key decision 2) 161, 164–7, 169, 239; vs. Egypt 155; history of NOCs in 155; literature on 153–5; oil and gas levels in 157–8, 169; qualitative analysis of 161–9, 239, **241**; quantitative analysis of 158, *159*, *160*, 164, 166, 169, **241**, *243*; Sinochem acquisition in (key decision 1) 161–4, 169, 239; strategic importance of **29**, **30**, **31**, 155–6, **157**, 158, 161, 169, **242**, **263–4**
Tunisian (Jasmine) Revolution (2011) 153, 161, 167–9, 239, 248–9
Turkmenistan 200, 207

UAE (United Arab Emirates) 161, 162
Uyghurs 184, 199, 205, 249
Ukraine 19, 36n48, 206
UNITA (União Nacional para a Indêpendencia Total de Angola) 87, 91
United Kingdom 23, 62; *see also* BP; British Gas
United Nations (UN) 29, 30; and Angola 91, **263**; and Canada **265**; Convention on the Law of the Sea (UNCLOS) of 218, 228n146; and Denmark **266**; and Kazakhstan **264**; and Nigeria 63, 65, **262**; and strategic importance **30**; and Sudan 2, 118, 122, 124, 125, 129–35, 145n30, **263**; and Tunisia 156, **264**; and Uzbekistan **266**
United States (US): and Angola 91, **93**, **263**; and Canada **187**, **265**; Chinese relations with 14, 15, 16, 20, 36n51; and Denmark **212**, 220, **266**; and Kazakhstan **177**, **264**; and multinational companies 23; and Nigeria 62, 63, 65, **66**, **262**; and strategic importance **28**, 29, **30**; and Sudan 123–4, **125**, 129, **263**; and Tunisia 156, **157**, 163, 164, **264**; and Uzbekistan **200**, 205, 226n105, 249, **266**
Uzbekistan 8, 31, 32, 199–209, *199*, 208, 251; Chinese relations with 199, 265; CNPC's acquisitions in (key decision 1) 203–5, 209, 240; crackdown on IMU in (key decision 2) 203, 205–6, 209, 240, 249; history of NOCs in 199; oil and gas levels in 200, 208, 225n93, 240; qualitative analysis of 203–8, 240, **242**; quantitative analysis of *201*, *202*, *203*, 205, 206, 208, 209, 240, **242**, *243*; strategic importance of **29**, **30**, **32**, 199, **200**, 208, 240, **242**, 250, **265–6**; and Uzbekistan-China pipeline (key decision 3) 203, 206, *207*, 208, 209, 239, 240; violent incidents in 226nn100–1, 226n102
Uzbekneftegaz 204, 206

Veritas (firm) 161, 162
Vernon, Raymond 23, 50
Vicente, Manuel 102, 103
Vines, Alex 89

Waltz, Kenneth 15
Wang Dongjin 137
Wang Guangya 130
Wang Wei 132
Weber, Robert Philip 32
Weeks, Jessica 11–12, 252
Weibo (website) 27, 37n69, 79, 80, 138, 185, 248; *see also* social media
Wei Liucheng 56n19
Wen Jiabao 45, 208, 219; and Angola 95, 99, 101, 104, 105, 244
Western management practices 50, 107, 182, 192, 197
World Bank (WB) 89
WTO (World Trade Organization) 23, 45, 48

Xie Hangsheng 138
Xi Jinping 90, 107, 108
Xinjiang 175, 184, 205, 207, 249
Xu Chunming 193

Yang Jiechi 141, 142, 215
Yar'Adua 59, 71, 75, 83n48

Zakaria, Fareed 252
Zeng Peiyan 102, 104

Zeng Qinghong 166, 167
Zeng Xingqiu 163
Zhai Jun 130, 131, 133
Zhang Dong 130
Zhang Hanhuy 185
Zhang Yesui 137
Zhong Jianhua 142
Zhou Enlai 153, 155
Zhou Wenzhong 130
Zhou Yongkang 19, 193
Zhu Feng 135
Zhuhai Zhenrong 44
Zhu Rongji 48
Zweig, David 16

For Product Safety Concerns and Information please contact our EU representative GPSR@taylorandfrancis.com
Taylor & Francis Verlag GmbH, Kaufingerstraße 24, 80331 München, Germany

www.ingramcontent.com/pod-product-compliance
Ingram Content Group UK Ltd.
Pitfield, Milton Keynes, MK11 3LW, UK
UKHW022015180926
475701UK00003B/373
9780367542344